James Colston

Trinity College and Trinity Hospital

A Historical Sketch: Vol. I

James Colston

Trinity College and Trinity Hospital
A Historical Sketch: Vol. I

ISBN/EAN: 9783337020699

Printed in Europe, USA, Canada, Australia, Japan

Cover: Foto ©ninafisch / pixelio.de

More available books at **www.hansebooks.com**

TRINITY COLLEGE
AND
TRINITY HOSPITAL

A Historical Sketch

BY

JAMES COLSTON

AUTHOR OF "THE GUILDRY OF EDINBURGH: IS IT AN INCORPORATION?"
"THE EDINBURGH AND DISTRICT WATER SUPPLY, A HISTORICAL SKETCH";
"HISTORY OF THE INCORPORATED TRADES OF EDINBURGH";
"THE TOWN AND PORT OF LEITH, ITS HISTORICAL CONNECTION WITH EDINBURGH";
"HISTORY OF THE SCOTT MONUMENT," ETC., ETC.

VOL I

Edinburgh

PRINTED FOR THE MAGISTRATES AND TOWN COUNCIL

MDCCCXCVI

Excerpt from the Minutes of the Town Council of Edinburgh, of date 3rd September 1895.

After the Magistrates and Council, as Governors and Administrators of the Trinity Hospital, had disposed of the report of their Committee recommending the election of Pensioners, the Lord Provost indicated that it would be very desirable that the Governors should have some authentic record of the History of the Charity, and on his Lordship's motion, the Magistrates and Council unanimously asked Councillor Colston, the present Convener of the Committee, to undertake the compilation of such a History.

TRINITY COLLEGE

AND

TRINITY HOSPITAL

[To face Dedication.]

UNTO

THE RIGHT HONOURABLE ANDREW M^cDONALD,
LORD PROVOST,

AND

THE HONOURABLE THE MAGISTRATES AND COUNCILLORS
OF THE CITY OF EDINBURGH,

THE GOVERNORS AND ADMINISTRATORS OF TRINITY
HOSPITAL CHARITY,

This Volume

IS MOST RESPECTFULLY DEDICATED

BY

THE AUTHOR.

IMPRESSION

FOUR HUNDRED COPIES.

PREFACE.

WHEN requested a year ago—by the Lord Provost, Magistrates, and Town Council of the City—to draw up a Historical Sketch of that now most important Charity, known as "Trinity Hospital," I deferred complying with their desires, until I had made sufficient inquiry as to the resources available for the somewhat arduous work. After a few weeks' consideration and consultation, I had the satisfaction of communicating to the Town Clerk that I saw my way to fall in with the wishes of my Colleagues.

I found that in the course of the work, I would require to deal with three distinct epochs of the history of the Charity.

Firstly—I had to examine the Charter of Foundation as contained in several Bulls of the Pope and other relative documents, as well as the Rules laid down for the management of the pious gift of Queen Mary of Gueldres, so long as the affairs of the College and Hospital were conducted during the pre-reformation period, when the staff of the Institution consisted of a Provost as Principal, several Prebendaries or Priests, as well as Choiristers or Clerks, and thirteen Beidmen. There were also to be inquired into the sources of income or emolument attached to the several officials. Some of the Bulls or Charters had first seen the light of day about half a century ago, having been printed at the instance of the *Bannatyne Club.* My chief source of information was derived, however, from a volume containing all the documents fully printed in mediæval Latin, with an English translation at the foot of each page, prepared for and issued by the Town Council, when Sir James D. Marwick, LL.D., was Town Clerk of Edinburgh.

Secondly—I had to make special reference to the relative Charters and Grants from the Crown, as well as to minutes of the Town Council of the period, when the Church and Hospital came directly under the municipal control after the Reformation. The rules laid down for the new system of government had also to be quoted. The appropriation of the revenues of the College which were chiefly devoted to the higher education, viz., to the University and Schools, required also to be dealt with, as well as the means taken to uphold the fabric of the Hospital and to support the inmates, by pious donations from fellow-citizens at a time particularly when—the regal Court and the Scottish nobility having been transferred to London—the ancient capital was deprived of much of the wealth which prior to that period circulated so freely among its inhabitants.

The first fifty years of last century told very severely upon the monetary condition of Edinburgh, and the Charity of Trinity Hospital was no exception to the rule.

Thirdly—The removal of the Church and Hospital for the purpose of accommodating the North British Railway is the next distinct epoch, and dates back nearly half-a-century ago. It was requisite to relate the bitter feud which so long prevailed in the Town Council Chambers and the Law Courts as to the re-building of the edifices and the appropriation of the money received from the Railway Company. I have thought it right, lest there should arise misapprehension or misconstruction of the views of parties, to give the decisions of the Law Courts, and the opinions of both appellate Courts *in extenso;* and I have endeavoured to explain the peculiar social, political, and religious position of the various contending parties at the time.

As helping to the result eventually attained, it is proper to mention the name of Mr James Gifford,—the respected father of the late Lord Gifford,—a former Treasurer of Trinity Hospital, who, in a series of letters in the *Witness* newspaper, a bi-weekly of the period, strongly advocated the views ultimately given forth by the House of Lords. Mr Gifford wrote anonymously, under the name of "Justitia," but it was well-known at the time that these letters came from his pen.

It is a singular fact that while these pages are passing through the press, the author has seen a small volume recently issued, entitled "John Gifford—Memories and Letters—edited by his sister, Mary Raleigh," in which the following passage occurs:—"In his (Mr James Gifford) thoughts, he was often in advance of his time. . . . When the North British Railway Company was empowered to buy Trinity College Hospital, which stood in the valley beneath the North Bridge, James Gifford startled his friends by saying that all his influence would be used to prevent its ever being rebuilt. His long experience of such institutions taught him that it was very undesirable to place under one roof old people who had little or no occupation, and whose long acquired tastes and habits unfitted them to live together in peace. The change he desired was made in Trinity Hospital. Gillespie's Hospital followed suit after a time."

The last thirty years of the Hospital's affairs has been a period of remarkable progress. The revenues derived from the sale or feuing of ground at the estate of Quarryholes on the Easter Road will be found fully referred to in Chapter XV. During the last few weeks, the Governors have received from the Caledonian Railway Company a sum of upwards of £20,000, for the sale of six acres of land for railway purposes. This has enabled them to add a few more pensioners to the roll at the two last half-yearly elections.

I have endeavoured in this volume to give a succinct view of the Charity during these successive stages of its history. For a considerable period of time, there were no records available to me. The reader, however, must always be the best judge of the manner in which any author discharges his duty. I have done what I could, while I must add in the language of the bankers "*erroribus exceptis.*"

I have to express my obligations to Mr Robert Adam, F.S.A. Scot., our former much respected City Chamberlain, who for a period of thirty-three years was connected officially with the Charity, first as City Accountant for ten years, and latterly as the Treasurer of Trinity Hospital for twenty-three years. Mr Adam took great care and trouble in revising the proof sheets, and made useful suggestions to me. It is right to say that the Chapter regarding the Hospital Revenues is almost entirely the work of Mr Adam. I have also to thank Mr David M'Laren, D.L., of Rydal House, Putney—a former Governor of the Hospital, and a zealous supporter of the late Professor Dick in the action taken by the latter on behalf of the beneficiaries of the Charity. Mr M'Laren rendered aid to me in the same manner as Mr Adam has so freely done.

I likewise acknowledge my obligations to the eminent publishing firm of Messrs Cassells & Company Limited, for granting me the privilege of reproducing several wood engravings of theirs which were prepared for that interesting work, "Grant's Old and New Edinburgh."

Mr Thomas Lauder Sawers is deserving of high recognition for the artistic share he has had in the Work, especially for his reproduction of the diptych in Holyrood wherein the portrait of the illustrious Foundress of the Hospital and other Members of the

Royal Family, as well as the portrait of Sir Edward Boncle, the first Provost of the College, appear. I also take occasion to refer to the kind consideration of the Master and Assistants of the Merchant Company of Edinburgh, in permitting Mr Sawers access to Drawings of the Old Trinity Hospital which are now in their possession.

The second volume will contain a full narrative of the manner in which the Charity is administered under the new scheme of the Court of Session, as well as a historical list of the various benefactions to the Hospital as these are set forth in the voluminous Report to the Court of Session by Ex-Professor Norman Macpherson, as well as other important documents relative thereto.

J. C.

23 Regent Terrace,
October 1, 1896.

CONTENTS.

CHAPTER I.

CHAPTER II.

CHAPTER III.

CHAPTER IV.

PAGES

CHAPTER V.

CHAPTER VI.

CHAPTER VII.

CHAPTER VIII.

CHAPTER IX.

CHAPTER X.

CHAPTER XI.

CHAPTER XII.

CHAPTER XIII.

CHAPTER XIV.

CHAPTER XV.

CHAPTER XVI.

CHAPTER XVII.

CHAPTER XVIII.

CHAPTER XIX.

CHAPTER XX.

CHAPTER XXI.

CHAPTER XXII.

CHAPTER XXIII.

LIST OF ILLUSTRATIONS.

A variety of Wood Engravings at the end of each of the Chapters serve to show Specimens of the Carvings which appeared on the gurgoyles and corbels of the old Trinity College Church.

TRINITY COLLEGE AND TRINITY HOSPITAL.

CHAPTER I.

ORIGIN AND FOUNDATION.

THE first historical reference that is made to the foundation of Trinity College and Trinity Hospital in the Burgh of Edinburgh, is contained in a Bull, by Pope Pius II., dated at Rome, the 10th day before the Calends of November (*i.e.*, the 23d day of October) 1460.

The object of the Pope's Bull was to declare the erection of the Hospital of Soltray at an end, and that the same should be suppressed by desire of the illustrious Mary (of Gueldres), the widowed Queen of King James II. of Scotland. The Hospital of Soltray had been created for the poor of the Diocese of St Andrews, by Pope Nicholas V., a predecessor of Pope Pius II., already referred to; and, of apostolic authority, he had, with the consent of Alan

Cant, rector of the said hospital, attached to the institution the dignity termed "The Chancellorship of the Church and Diocese of St Andrews," and had constituted the said Alan Cant the Chancellor. The office of Chancellor, which was in the "laic patronage" of the King of Scotland, became vacant through the death of Cant, who to the end of his life peaceably possessed the said distinguished position.

At the time of Cant's death, which occurred "outwith the Roman Court," James, King of Scotland, presented John of Tyry, clerk of the Diocese of St Andrews, bachelor in law, to the vacant Chancellorship; and the Bishop of St Andrews, as in duty bound, inducted the new incumbent into his office. But Queen Mary of Gueldres did not permit this arrangement long to continue.

Queen Mary very soon indicated her desire, and that of her son, King James III., that the Hospital of Soltray * should be united and annexed to the Church and Hospital of the Holy Trinity in Edinburgh, requiring at the same time, that the Bishop of Glasgow—after due

* Soltray, "Soltre" or "Soutra," is an ancient parish in Haddingtonshire. It possessed in an early period of Scotland's history a Church and Hospital, which were built near to the top of Soutra hill. The latter is said to have been founded by King Malcolm IV. (The Maiden), about the middle of the twelfth century. Some historians have given the precise date as 1164, one year before his death. It was established for pilgrims, travellers, and poor people, and was dedicated to the Holy Trinity. After its annexation to the Trinity College, near Edinburgh, as related above, divine service was still maintained, and a smaller institution was kept up. At the time of the Reformation, it ceased to exist as a distinct parochial charge. The buildings fell into a ruinous condition, and about forty-five years ago (1850), with the exception of a small aisle, which had been secured as a burial vault by the Pringles of Beatman's Acre, all the walls and foundations were dug up and carted away. Soutra hill is the most westerly ridge of the Lammermuirs. It stands about 1209 feet above the level of the sea, and commands a fine panoramic view of the Lothians and the Firth of Forth, as well as the fertile fields of Fife. The parish of Soutra has been annexed, since 1589, to the adjacent parish of Fala, in Mid-Lothian—See—"*Registrum Domus de Soltre*," by the late David Laing, LL.D (*Bannatyne Club*, 1861).

enquiry, and on his obtaining the consent of the parties interested —should suppress the said Chancellorship. Having thus reduced the Hospital of Soltray to its primitive condition, the result was to unite and incorporate the same with the Church and Hospital of the Holy Trinity near the Burgh of Edinburgh.

John of Tyry, the successor of Cant in the Chancellorship, offered no resistance to the change, but willingly and freely resigned his office. The annual emoluments of the position did not exceed the sum of sixty pounds sterling per annum. The dignified office of Chancellor was therefore suppressed. The Bishop of St Andrews, and other ecclesiastical dignitaries, were called in, according to use and wont, to see the matter properly arranged; so that the future Rector of the new Hospital of the Holy Trinity should, by himself, or others on his authority, take and retain "corporal possession of the Hospital of Soltray, and its rights and pertinents aforesaid, and to receive its fruits, rents, and proceeds, to be applied for the maintenance of the poor and the infirm, and otherwise for the use of the said hospitals, according to the form of constitution of Pope Clement V. of pious memory, and predecessor." Provision was further made that the foresaid Hospital of Soltray should not be defrauded of its due services, but that its accustomed burdens should be duly supported.

This Bull, of which the preceding narrative is an abstract, was subscribed at St Peter's, at Rome; and it was given forth, within the Church of St Michael in the Burgh of Linlithgow, in the presence of Sirs Thomas of Kirkpatrick, Patrick Brown, John Pettigrew, priests; and James Stewart, John Neilson, Andrew Greenlaw, and George Clark, witnesses to the premises. It was also, in accordance with the custom of the time, attested by a Notary Public in the presence of the Lord Bishop of Glasgow, as a public instrument, with the notary's name and seal attached thereto, as well as the name and seal of the

Lord Judge and Bishop. The name of the notary subscribing was Richard Roberts, priest of the Diocese of St Andrews, by imperial authority. The document was made public, or promulgated, on the 6th day of March 1461-2.

The next historical reference that is made is by a Confirmation Charter by James Kennedy, Archbishop of St Andrews, as to the foundation of the Collegiate Church and Hospital of the Holy Trinity, St Andrews, dated 1st April 1462. That Charter ordains that there should be founded and endowed within the City of Edinburgh, a College, or Collegiate Church, with an Hospital, under the name and designation of "The College and Hospital of the Holy Trinity." This College, or Collegiate Church, was to be provided with a provost,—eight prebendaries, priests, or chaplains,—two boys, otherwise designated choiristers or clerks,—and thirteen poor persons, commonly called "beidmen," who were all to be maintained in the Hospital. These beidmen were clad, like the pensioners of royalty in more recent times, in blue gowns, which they had themselves to provide, and they were bound to pray for the soul of the royal foundress. For the maintenance of the College and Hospital, various lands and revenues were given over. Among these were the estates and income of the Hospital and Church of the Holy Trinity of Soltray (already referred to), the lands of Ballerno, the Hospital of Athrogle (or Utherogall),* the Rectory of Wemyss, the lands of the town of Hangandshaw, with their pertinents, and the Church of Lempetlaw, with all the fruits thereto belonging; but it was conditioned that for the two churches assigned to him, the

* Utherogall, in Monimail, was previously a leper hospital, and with the lands of Hospital-Milne, in the adjoining parish of Cults, was (as the Statistical Account of Scotland says) given by Mary of Gueldres to the Trinity Hospital, and after the suppression, it went eventually to the Earls of Leven. According to Sir Robert Sibbald, the parish church of Easter Wemyss, in Fife, also belonged "to the *Collegiata Sancta Trinitis de Edinburgh.*"

Provost should bear the Episcopal and Archidiaconal dues of the said churches according to former usage.

It was provided that the Provostry, or Provost, should be set over the others in pre-eminence, honour, and dignity in the College, as regards the regulation of the choir, and in divine worship, and that sufficient maintenance should be provided for him and those serving under him. He was required to pay the pension to the Vicar of the Church of Soltray, and to sustain three poor persons living there, as well as to keep the building in proper repair.

It was ordained that the first Prebendary, after the Provost, should be called "The Master of the Holy Trinity near Edinburgh." He was to have for his prebend and suitable maintenance, one fourth part of the revenues of the Rectorial Church of Strathmartin, in the Diocese of St Andrews, two pounds land in the town of Fawlahill within Heriot Moor, two merks of annual rent from the house of the late William Clunes in Leith, twenty shillings in the town of Risolton, five shillings of annual rent from the houses of John Allanson and John Lawson in Leith, twenty shillings yearly from * * * Waulket in Edinburgh, five shillings from the house of the Lord Thomas, Bishop of Dunkeld, six shillings and eight pence from the town of Lauder, a like sum from the town of Strathmiglo, ten shillings from a town near Linlithgow, besides certain other revenues to be afterwards specified. All these the Master of the Hospital had full power to dispense for the good of the poor persons under his care, "so that he may providently and prudently make provision for all and each, in all necessaries, according to God and a good conscience, and the capabilities of the fruits." He was required at least twice a-year to render an account of his stewardship to the Provost and Chapter.

The second Prebendary after the Provost was termed "The Sacristan." To him was committed the full disposal of all the fruits pertaining to the Community and Chapter, to be collected and disposed of for the daily necessaries of the Collegiate Church. He had to render an account to the Provost and Prebendaries, four times in the year, "on the four Saturdays of the four Seasons." He could not, however, settle any important business without the advice of the Provost and Chapter. He had laid upon him the duty of keeping the church in all propriety. He had the custody of the ornaments, jewels, and sacred vessels; he supplied the wine, bread, and wax candles, and he was further enjoined to exercise all the other functions which "according to laudable and observed usage in other churches, are known to belong to the office of Sacristan." He received as his prebend, or emoluments, five merks of lands in the town of Hill, within the Lordship of Ballerno, five merks of the lands of Browderstanes and Gileston, of the Lordship of Soltray, and a fourth part of the profits of the Rectory of Strathmartin.

The third Prebendary was styled "The Prebendary of Browderstanes." He had for his prebend five merks of the lands of Browderstanes and Gileston, and another fourth of the fruits of the Rectory of Strathmartin, already referred to.

The fourth Prebendary was named "The Prebendary of Strathmartin." His prebend consisted of five merks of the lands of Browderstanes and Gileston, and the last fourth of the fruits of the Rectory of Strathmartin.

All these previously-mentioned Prebendaries were bound to undertake all the dues which of right used to be paid to the Bishop, Archdeacon, and others, with the repair and upholding of the church from the first fruits of the Rectory of Strathmartin, equally divided among the foresaid Prebendaries. The other four Prebendaries had likewise their emoluments and duties assigned to them.

The fifth Prebendary was called "The Prebendary of Gileston." He had assigned to him five merks of the lands of Browderstanes and

Gileston, and the first fourth-part of the fruits of the Rectory of Ormiston, in the Diocese of St Andrews.

The sixth Prebendary was styled "The Prebendary of Ormiston," and his prebend was similar to the former, having five merks of the one and the second fourth-part of the other.

The seventh Prebendary was named "The Prebendary of Hill," and he had assigned to him five merks of the lands within the Lordship of Ballerno, and the third fourth-part of the fruits of the Rectory of Ormiston.

The eighth Prebendary was called "The Prebendary of Newlands," and he had given to him five merks of the lands of Newlands, in the Lordship of Soltray, along with the last fourth-part of Ormiston, already referred to.

It was ordained that these four last-mentioned Prebendaries should bear the dues to the Bishop and Archdeacon, with the repair and upholding of the Church of Ormiston from the first fruits of the same, with the other burdens wont to be discharged, according to law and custom.

The Charter further provides for the two clerks or choiristers that they shall have for their maintenance, ten pounds of the lands of Ballerno, to be equally divided between them, and that they should be removable at the pleasure of the Provost and College. It also provides for the maintenance of the thirteen beidmen; and, for this purpose, it sets aside and ordains the Hospital of Utherogall and the Rectory of Wemyss, in the Diocese of St Andrews, and ten pounds of the annual rents of the town of Edinburgh, from the common good of the same,*

* In the Appendix to one of the Vols. of Records of the Burgh of Edinburgh, printed for the Scottish Burgh Records Society, for the period A.D. 1528—1557, appears a sample of the Town's Accounts of the period (1552-3), in which there is the following entry (page 271):—

"Item, to the beidmen of the Trinetie College for thair annuall, . . . x^{li}."

besides ten pounds from certain lands and tenements, with certain acres and annual rents in the town of Leith. For the repair of the Collegiate Church, and for the supply of necessaries in the same, forty-six pounds, nine shillings of the profits of the Rectory of Kirkurd, in the Diocese of Glasgow, are set aside, along with the remainder of the lands of Ballerno. The Sacristan is ordained to bear the burdens of the dues in wont to be paid to the Bishop, Archdeacon, and others, along with the repair and upholding of the Church of Kirkurd; and he shall, as before stated, have the receivings of all the goods.

The duty of the Provost was to be present at matins, mass, and vespers on festival days. He was bound to make personal residence; and, if he happened to be absent for fifteen consecutive days, the Chapter of the College had the power to enforce his residence by an appeal to the Patron to compel him. In the event of his not returning to reside, with the intention of remaining at his post, the Provostship would be considered, *ipso facto*, to be rendered vacant, even without any formal deliverance of the Judge. If within fifteen days after such vacancy, the Patron should not have presented a new Provost, then the Chapter had the right to present another Provost to the Ordinary. It was also provided that when the office of Provost was vacant, the new Provost required to be presented to the Ordinary by the King of Scotland and his successors in office.

The general duty of all the Prebendaries was, on every day of the year to sing matins, high mass, vespers, and compline, with notes. They were required also to make personal residence, and to discharge all duties laid upon them, by themselves personally, and "not by others, one or more."

None of the Prebendaries or the clerks could absent himself without first having obtained leave of the Provost; while he, on the other hand, had the power to grant leave of absence restricted to fifteen days, unless

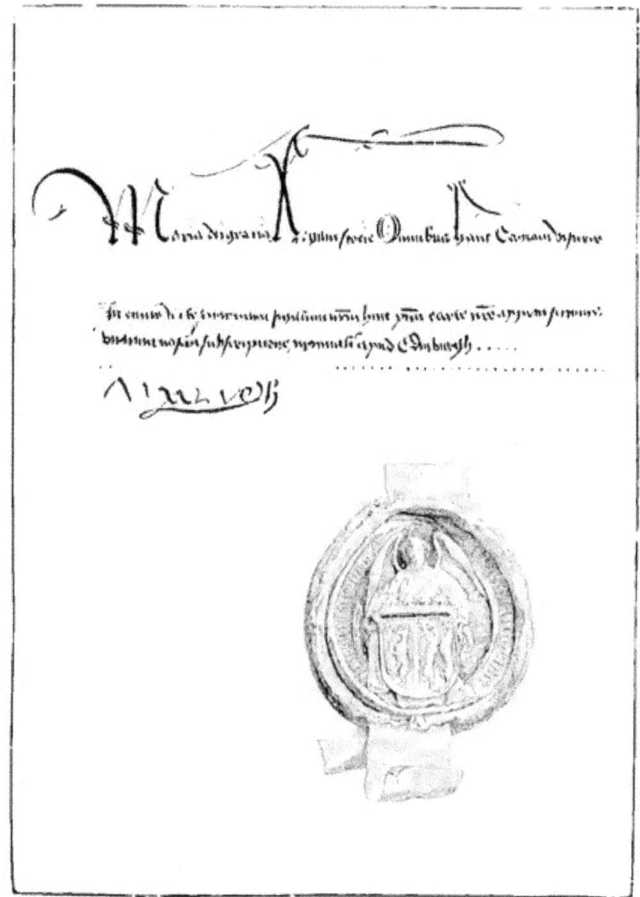

SEAL AND HANDWRITING OF QUEEN MARY OF GUELDRES.

[To face p. [illegible]]

for great and pressing reasons. Even the latter licence could only be granted with consent of the Chapter required and obtained. Anyone disobeying, lost, *ipso facto*, his right of prebend, his position in the College was rendered vacant, and was at the free disposal of the Provost and Chapter, and the provision of the Ordinary. It was likewise ordained, that "if any of the Prebendaries shall keep a concubine or chamberwoman, and shall not dismiss her on being thrice admonished by the Provost, his prebend shall be held to be, and shall be vacant, and at the collation of the Ordinary in manner aforesaid."

Regarding the qualifications of the various officials of the College and Hospital, and their various duties, the Charter practically goes on to state:—The extra-collegiate Vicars of the Churches foresaid, and the Prebendaries of the said College, shall be presented by the Provost and his Chapter to the Ordinary, from whom they shall receive canonical institution; and no Prebendary shall be appointed "unless he shall be capable of reading and singing in plain chant and descant." The boys, moreover, shall be capable of learning these. It was also ordained that each of the Prebendaries, when he shall be disposed, should have the power to celebrate mass, and afterwards, robed in his sacerdotal habiliments, should go with hyssop to the tomb of the foundress, and there devoutly read the *De Profundis*, with the prayer of the faithful and an exhortation of the people to devotion. It was likewise provided that between the terms of Whitsunday and Michaelmas, matins should commence at the fifth hour of the morning; while, on the other hand, between Michaelmas and Whitsunday the hour should be six o'clock; and on matins being concluded, at the altar of the blessed Virgin, that the weekly mass should be celebrated for travellers; and that a weekly mass should also be performed in the Chapel of the Hospital, at the ninth hour, for the poor and infirm living there.

Provision was also made that, during the lifetime of Queen Mary of Gueldres, an anniversary service should be devoutly held for the late most illustrious prince, James King of Scots, "our most tender husband; and after our decease, on the respective days of his and our decease, they shall sing and celebrate his and our anniversaries, for us and our children, our ancestors and successors, as also for the foresaid reverend Father in Christ, James, the present Bishop of St Andrews, after his decease in all time to come."

This second Charter, like the former, was duly ratified and subscribed by the requisite authorities at St Andrews, with the seal duly affixed.

This, then, practically gives the origin, foundation and constitution of the original Trinity College and Trinity Hospital of Edinburgh, as it was designed to be erected by Queen Mary of Gueldres, with the advice and sanction of her clerical advisers at the time.

CHAPTER II.

THE FOUNDRESS—POPE'S BULLS—THE SITE.

QUEEN MARY OF GUELDRES, the Foundress of Trinity College and Trinity Hospital, was the daughter of Arnold, Duke of Gueldres, who was allied to the Royal Family of France—her mother having been daughter of John, Duke of Burgundy. She became the Queen Dowager of King James II. of Scotland.

According to Drummond, the Historian, she was "young, beautiful, and of a masculine constitution." She arrived in Scotland, from the Netherlands, accompanied by a great concourse of princes, prelates, and nobility, who were all witnesses of the marriage, which took place in the Abbey of Holyrood House, where she was crowned.

When she arrived in Leith, on the 18th day of June 1449, she proceeded on horseback, immediately behind the Count de Campvere, the Arch-Duke of Austria, and the Duke of Brittany—all of them being brothers-in-law to the King of Scotland—together with the Dukes of Savoy and of Burgundy, who formed a grand convoy, to her apartments in the Convent of the Greyfriars, in Edinburgh, which had been specially assigned to her as a temporary residence, until she became the wife of the King. She was also escorted by a body guard of 300 men-at-arms, all *cap-à-pie*, with the citizens also in their armour, under Patrick Cockburn of Newbigging, Provost of Edinburgh and Governor of the Castle; and she was warmly welcomed by her future husband. She was visited in the Convent, by the mother of her royal lover, on the day after her arrival. The historian Tytler informs us that "from the moment of the arrival of the Princess of Gueldres, till the solemnization of her marriage and coronation, the time was occupied with feastings, masks, revelry and tournaments." * Contemporary historians relate that her nuptials were celebrated, during the following month of July with the utmost pomp and solemnity, and that there were great rejoicings on the occasion. Eleven years thereafter, viz., in 1460, her royal husband was killed, at the siege of Roxburghe Castle, which, at the time referred to, was in the possession of "our auld inimies of England," and had been held by them after the battle of Durham. It was situate on an eminence, near the junction of the Tweed and the Teviot, and its walls were as strong as the engineers and the builders of the time could raise. The occasion of the King's death was the bursting of a famous cannon, called "The Lyon."

This event occurred on the 3d day of August, in the twenty-ninth year of the King's age, and the twenty-fourth year of his reign. He is stated to have been brought up, from the days of his youth in a knowledge of all profitable sciences. He bore either adversity or prosperity with great calmness of mind and moderation of temper. He manifested great bravery amongst his soldiers, and showed sufficient fortitude against his adversaries; in a word, he was much beloved by his

* History of Scotland, Vol. IV. page 67.

people; and great and unfeigned regret was expressed at his only too sudden demise.

The Queen's firmness of character, on that occasion, as well as during the few remaining years of her life, proves her to have been a princess of no ordinary strength of mind. She took a most active part in the government of the Kingdom, when her son (King James III.) was a mere child. Indeed, it has been stated, by Hector Boece as well as by Drummond of Hawthornden, and other chroniclers of the period, that, at the time of her husband's death, lest the soldiers present should have felt discouraged by the event, after they had covered his body, she with her eldest son, came on that very day into the camp, and with most unexampled courage, continued the siege, and took the castle, and razed it to the ground. It is right, however, to state that this circumstance, which has been recorded by these Scottish historians, is, by others, as stoutly denied; and the general opinion now prevails that the latter are correct.

Queen Mary of Gueldres died on the 16th day of November 1463,—three years, three months, and thirteen days, after her royal husband—and her remains were interred under the north aisle of what was afterwards known as "the Old Trinity College Church." This was in the centre of what was termed the "Lady Chapel," or "the sacristy" of old, latterly denominated "the vestry." At the time when the ancient edifice was taken down, for the purposes of the North British Railway in 1848, her mortal remains were lifted, and reverently placed in a new coffin, covered with purple cloth, whence they were conveyed to the Abbey of Holyrood, to which a more specific reference will be made at a future stage.

Prior to the death of the Queen, another Charter (the third) regarding the foundation of the Hospital falls to be referred to. It was a Bull by Pope Pius II., addressed to Her Majesty, confirming the annexation of the Hospital of Soltray to the Collegiate Church and Hospital of the Holy Trinity. It is dated on the 14th Calend of July (viz., 18th June 1462). This Charter records the singular decision of "our most beloved daughter in Christ, Mary, the illustrious Queen of Scots, and of her great devotion toward us, and the Church of Rome." It goes on to state, that, if it is desirable that such devotion deserves that we should add the confirmation of our "apostolical muniment to the arrangements that have been made by pious ordinance, for the praise and glory of the Divine name, as well as for the advantage of the poor and the necessitous, and the weal of souls, so that they may be enriched by continual additions, and remain for ever unimpaired." It then refers to the previous Bull of Pope Nicholas, already quoted from, and to the steps taken for the removal of the Chancellorship, an office of high dignity in the Diocese of St Andrews. It then goes on to relate as follows:—"It being subjoined that thou, of the goods bestowed on thee by God, hadst anew founded, and in splendid manner hadst caused to be constructed and erected, to the praise of Almighty God, a Collegiate Church, with an Hospital for the poor, near the Burgh of Edinburgh, on the north side, in the said Diocese, for the furthering of Divine worship, for the reception of Christ's poor and other miserable persons." It then refers to the foundation of the Hospital of Soltray, for the use of Christ's poor, and to King James, the illustrious King of Scots, whose forefathers had furnished the said Hospital; to the erection of the said Chancellorship already referred to, and to the desire of the Queen that the same should be merged in, or incorporated with, the newly-erected (created) Hospital of the Holy Trinity for ever.

It further narrates that the said John (Tyry) proposed of his own will and freely to resign the Chancellorship which he held, in favour of such union, and also, "in order that the said Chancellorship should be reconverted into the Hospital of Soltray as it had been formerly." It then goes on to state, that Pope Pius II. being favourably disposed to the change had commissioned the Bishop of Glasgow, that, having summoned all those who had any interest in the matter, he might be diligently informed concerning all and sundry the things aforesaid, and their attendant circumstances; and, in the event of his deeming it advisable, he should receive and accept the said resignation, if it were freely and properly offered. In the event of this having been accomplished, he was enjoined to take over the said Chancellorship, which should become vacant, unless anyone had a special right in it; but declaring that the express consent of the King should be added. By this Bull, the Chancellorship was entirely suppressed, the Hospital of Soltray was reduced to its pristine condition, and was united, annexed, and incorporated with the New Hospital and College of the Holy Trinity in Edinburgh; its rents, profits, and fruits were reserved for the sustentation of the poor and the infirm; and otherwise for the use of the said Hospitals, according to the form and constitution of our predecessor Pope Clement V. of pious memory, promulgated regarding the matter in the Council of Vienne, the permission of the Diocesan of the place not being required. The Charter then refers to the fact that "our venerable brother Thomas, present Bishop of Dunkeld," and not the foresaid Alan (Cant) procured the Chancellorship to be created, and at the time of the date of the same letters, the foresaid Church had not as yet been wholly collegiated, nor completed in splendid structure, and that the fore-mentioned John made the said resignation in the hands of the foresaid Bishop of St Andrews, and thereafter in those of the same Bishop of Glasgow, on account of which doubts might perchance be entertained regarding the validity of the said letters, " We, being favourably disposed towards thy supplications in that regard, and desiring to guard against the possibility of the said letters being on that account branded as surreptitious, will, and by Apostolic authority have decreed, that our foresaid letters, and the proceedings had in respect thereof, and whatsoever has followed thereon, may from the date of these presents have force, and may obtain the full force, and validity, in all and through all, as if in them it had been expressly set forth, that Thomas and not Alan, had procured the said erection to be made, and that the foresaid John had made the said resignation to this effect, first in the hands of the foresaid Bishop of St Andrews, the Ordinary of the See, and afterwards in those of the Bishop of Glasgow, and that at the time of our said letters, no mention had been made that the said Church was wholly complete, and had been erected into a Collegiate Church. The premises, and all those things in the said letters which we wish not to stand in the way, and everything else to a contrary purpose notwithstanding. Let no one, therefore (dare) to infringe (the tenor) of our will and constitution. But if anyone, etc. (*sic*). Given at Viterbo, in the year, etc., M.CCCC.LXII. the fourteenth Calend of July, of our pontificate the fourth year."

The fourth or last Charter during the lifetime of the Foundress in regard to the constitution of the Hospital, etc., was contained in another Bull by the Pope, reciting the foundation of the Collegiate Church and Hospital of the Holy Trinity, and confirming the annexation thereto of the Hospital of Soltray, and the Chapel of Utherogall in Fife. It is dated on the sixth of the Ides of July (10th July) 1462, and is recorded "for future memory of the fact."

It is somewhat similar in terms to what has been previously narrated, in so far as the historical matter is concerned. It, however, winds up with the following:—"We, therefore, who with our whole mind desire the increase of Divine worship, and the advantage of poor

ENTRANCE TO HOLYROOD PALACE—THE OLD GATEWAY

(*After an Etching by James Skene of Rubislaw.*)

To face page 16.]

and miserable persons, listening favourably to these supplications, of Apostolic authority, by the tenor of these presents, approve and confirm the foundation, endowment, union, and annexation aforesaid, holding them, and whatsoever has followed thereupon, fixed and approved, supplying all defects, if any perchance shall be found in the same, and nevertheless for the purpose of greater security, erecting of new the said Church into a Collegiate Church, with Collegiate insignia. Decreeing, moreover, that whatever offerings of the faithful shall from time to time fall to the said Church shall be applied upon its fabric and the repair thereof; and we, by the authority of these presents, grant full and free power and authority to the Master of the New Hospital, or to the Rector for the time, to administer all and each of the sacraments of the Church, to all the faithful of both sexes, dwelling therein for a time, and those dying there, as well as to others serving therein, notwithstanding any Apostolic constitution, ordinances, and others contrary whatsoever. For we, from this time forth, declare whatever may be attempted to the contrary in these matters, by any one, on any authority, knowingly or ignorantly, null and void. Let no one, therefore, etc., dare to infringe the tenor of our confirmation, approbation, restoration, erection, constitution, and will. If any one, moreover, etc. Given in the Abbey of St Salvator, in the Diocese of Clusium, the year, etc., M.CCCC.LXII. sixth of the Ides of July. Of our pontificate the fourth year."

It is proper to state that all the Charters relating to the foundation were composed and written in Mediæval Latin—that being, at the time, the language of the Church and the learned. In fact all important documents of the period were so composed and written.

Sir Edward Boncle was appointed the first Provost, and the plans of the buildings, with the various architectural designs, were prepared by Mr John Halkerstone,* who was designated "Master of the fabric." The original design, it is understood, embraced a choir, nave, transepts, chantry chapel, muniment room, in addition to the house for the Provost and the Prebendaries, and the Hospital for the thirteen beidmen.

During the lifetime of the Dowager Queen, the work proceeded with very great energy. But her premature death, so soon after the date of the Charter of foundation, seems to have had a somewhat depressing influence on those engaged in the work. In all probability it was the means of preventing the original design of the Church being fully carried out, and the buildings completed. The Church, as finished, consisted only of the choir and transepts, with the central tower partially built. The Collegiate buildings were erected to the south of the Church, and the Hospital for the beidmen stood opposite to the foot of Leith Wynd, while on the other side of the road stood the building of Saint Paul's Work, which at one time was an institution of a somewhat similar kind to the Hospital. It is to be afterwards referred to, and was situated near to where Macdowall Street recently stood. Leith Wynd was at that time the chief access from the Royalty of Edinburgh to the Port of Leith, by way of St Ninian's Row and Greenside. In the row, there was in those days, an ancient chapel dedicated to St Ninian. It is recorded that the crypt and other remains of St Ninian's Chapel were removed in the year 1814, for the purpose of clearing the site for the Regent Bridge, which now spans the valley beneath. The chapel of St Ninian must have had some connection with the parish of the same name in Stirling;

* It would be interesting to know whether Halkerstone's Wynd, which still leads from the High Street to the site of the Physic Gardens, was built or designed by the John Halkerstone above referred to, and was for that reason named after him.

THE PHYSIC GARDENS—THE ORPHAN HOSPITAL TO THE LEFT—LADY GLENORCHY'S CHAPEL IN THE CENTRE—TRINITY COLLEGE CHURCH TO THE RIGHT.

To face page [illegible]]

because up till very recently several houses in the district were assessed for poor-rates by the Stirling authorities. As in Stirling, so in Edinburgh, the colloquial phrase, being no doubt a corruption of the word, was not St Ninian's, but "St Ringan's." St Ninian's Row in later days had the more common appellation of "The Beggar's Raw."

The situation of the College and Hospital, according to the opinion of the late Sir Daniel Wilson, was not by any means a favourable one. It was placed in a low lying locality, and in a very poor district of the city. It was situated in what has recently been termed "the Low Calton," not very far from the precipitous rock on which the Edinburgh Jail stands. That rock used to bear the designation of the "Dhu Craig." In the *Diurnal of Occurrents*, under date 1571, it is so styled, wherein it is recorded that a battery was erected on "the Dow Craig, abone Trinity College, to ding and siege the north-east quarter of the burgh."

The Hospital, as the writer can remember it, was an exceedingly plain and most unpretentious edifice—the architectural features of the buildings connected with the foundation having been no doubt reserved for the Church. The district was regarded, in more modern times, as essentially a poor one. The adjoining buildings consisted of the "old Orphan Hospital," now transferred to the Dean, "Lady Glenorchy's Church"* (a very plain structure), now transferred to

* Lady Glenorchy's Church, or "Chapel" as it used to be called, was founded by Her Ladyship, who was a Member of the Breadalbane family, in 1772. It was intended to be a Chapel of Ease—a relief church to the other city charges. The building was finished in 1774, and the city ministers used at first each to take turn in conducting the services. In course of time, Lady Glenorchy sent a communication to the Presbytery of Edinburgh, expressing her desire to present a Mr Grove,—who was at that time preacher to a dissenting Congregation in England—as pastor of her chapel. To this, the Presbytery gave a civil reply, to the effect that "although they approved of her piety, they could not give countenance to the appoint-

Roxburgh Place, and the houses, warehouses, and other business premises, which found a local habitation in what was then known as "The Old Physic Gardens," which were in the occupation of the late Professor Hope of the Edinburgh University, who afterwards transferred his Botanic Gardens to some fields of his own property in Leith Walk. Eventually the Gardens were removed to a more suitable place in Inverleith Row, where they are now well known as the Royal Botanic Gardens.

Critics, antiquarians, and historians have, as a rule, condemned the Church site. Nevertheless, there is something to be said on the other side of the question. One must bear in mind the date of the foundation, and the surroundings of the period, when taken in contrast with the much more recent development. In those days there were not breweries, foundries, manufactories, or business premises in the district. The situation was outside of the Royal Burgh, and beyond the city

ment of a minister who was no member of the clerical order of the Church of Scotland." Her Ladyship then intimated her intention to present the Rev. Mr Balfour, minister at Lecropt. The Presbytery again intimated to her, that while they heartily approved of her choice, they could not consent to install him, unless there was a regular call from the Congregation and a legal security for the minister's stipend. Lady Glenorchy, however, was far from complying with these conditions. She wrote to them "That the Chapel was her private property, and had never been intended to be put on the footing of the establishment, nor connected with it, but as a Chapel of Ease in the City of Edinburgh. That having built the Church at her own expense, she was entitled to name the minister. By a majority the Presbytery agreed, in the circumstances to induct the minister. This resolution was appealed to the Synod, and afterwards to the Assembly. Suitable arrangements were, however, eventually come to. At the beginning of the present century the late Rev. Dr Jones was the Pastor of the Congregation, and the late Rev. Dr James Begg, afterwards well known in the city of Edinburgh, was his assistant in 1827. Dr Begg received a call to Paisley, which he accepted. He was afterwards translated to the Parish Church of Liberton. He was one of the leaders of the movement which terminated in the formation of the Free Church in 1843, commonly called "the Disruption." He was instrumental in founding, and was for many years minister of, the Newington Free Church, in South Clerk Street.

walls. To the east of it was the Court end of the old Capital, with the mansion-houses of the nobility and gentry, and the beautiful gardens which at that time surrounded these handsome residences. The existence of the Physic Gardens which were, for so long a period, occupied for the use of the students of botany in the University of Edinburgh, would indicate that the site was, even in later times, looked upon as garden ground. Canongate was not then, as it is now, a hive of industry; but it was the place of fashion and courtly leisure. To the west of the buildings of the Collegiate Church and Hospital, were the North Loch and the grassy sward and braes of the Bearford Parks on which part of the New Town has been built. The North Bridge and the New Town were conceptions of the Corporation upwards of three hundred years afterwards. No doubt, the Trinity College buildings were placed in a valley, or, as it may be averred, hidden in a valley; but does not the same remark apply to Melrose, Dryburgh, and many of the other abbeys in the Kingdom, not forgetting even the Abbey of Holyroodhouse? It was not the practice of the monks of old to live in castellated palaces. They seemed to prefer situations where the rude winds would not blow so fiercely upon them, as they unquestionably would have done on the higher altitudes. Before condemning the site of Trinity Hospital and the Collegiate Church, one would require to understand the surroundings of the period, and not be so rash as to judge of the situation about four centuries after the selection of the site.

CHAPTER III.

RELIGIOUS HOUSES—INDULGENCES—DUNNOTTAR, ETC.

THE foundation of Trinity College and Trinity Hospital must always be regarded as the outcome of a desire on the part of those who, having had means at their disposal, considered it to be their duty in Catholic times to establish religious and charitable houses in various localities throughout Scotland.

The late Rev. Mr Stothert, who himself was well known in this city as a most devoted Catholic Priest, in his Lectures on the Religious Antiquities of Edinburgh, read to the Holy Gild of St Joseph (Vol. II. page 168), thus refers to these houses:—"The foundation of monasteries was followed by the establishment of smaller houses, called hospitals, once very numerous throughout Christendom. The contracted form of the word Spital, is found in several places in Scotland, and always marks the ancient site of one of these lesser religious houses. They were sometimes called 'Maisons Dieu,' or houses of God. Their uses were very various; either as the home of the sick, or of pilgrims, or orphan children, or of the aged and infirm poor. In their internal arrangements, they very nearly resembled a house of monks. They were governed by a Master, and the hours of prayer and of reading, and refection, and sleep, followed in the same order as in the larger religious houses."

The Poet Spencer, in his "Fairie Queene" thus describes one of those religious houses:—

> "Eftsoones unto an holy hospitall,
> That was foreby the way, she did him bring;
> In which seven beidmen, that had vowed all
> Their life to service of high heaven's King,
> Did spend their daies in doing goodly thing;
> Their gates to all were open evermore,
> That by the wearie way were travelling;
> And one sat wayting ever them before,
> To call in commers-by, that needy were and poore."

It is right to mention that in none of the Charters regarding Trinity Hospital is anything stated as to the duties to be performed by the beidmen, or as to the qualifications or conditions under which they were to be received as inmates.

There can be no doubt—what differences soever may have existed, or do still exist, in regard to religious polity, or Christian doctrine—that all will be agreed as to the moving principle which actuated those who, whether rightly or wrongly, gave of their means and substance for what they conceived to be the temporal and spiritual benefits of their fellow-creatures. Their intentions and actions, as they were undoubtedly beneficent, could not fail to be regarded as a boon and a blessing to humanity. Christ's own earthly life was unquestionably one of pure and undefiled charity. They were, therefore, only following, according to their own light, in the footsteps of their blessed Redeemer and Master.

Trinity Hospital, and the Collegiate Church attached thereto, formed one of those religious houses which existed in Edinburgh, as well as in other districts of Scotland, prior to the Reformation, for the worship of God and the good of souls, according to the wisdom and custom of the times and of the Church.

Pope Pius II. was not unmindful of the Queen's benefaction. On the 27th day of August 1463, about three months prior to her death, he issued another Bull, to all the faithful in Christ, granting a plenary indulgence to all those who, in a devout spirit of contrition, did visit the Church of Trinity College, in the course of five years, during the Feast of its Dedication, on the 10th of July, or its Octaves, etc.

The Pope, in his charter, refers to the great gift which had been given by Her most Gracious Majesty, as a blessing to her Christian people, for the purpose of—and out of an opportune piety—compassionately washing away the stains (or sins) of souls; and for the purpose of procuring happiness in Heaven, more especially when the House of God is increased, and more help is afforded to those who may be justly designated as "Christ's Poor."

The Bull went on to say, that the Almighty God Himself does repay the faithful, with greater gifts than they deserve; but yet, for their confirmation, and for the purpose of stimulating them, the Church of Christ has, in its great clemency, been accustomed to open to them its benignant bosom, and that of its most pious Mother. It then goes on to relate, as a matter of fact, that a famous Collegiate Church, or Chapel, or Hospital of the Poor of the Holy Trinity, outwith the royal town of Edinburgh, in the diocese of St Andrews, had been founded by our "dearest daughter in Christ," Mary, widow of King James II., and the same has been erected and carried on, by magnificent and expensive workmanship, to serve the Most High, by the various officials who were

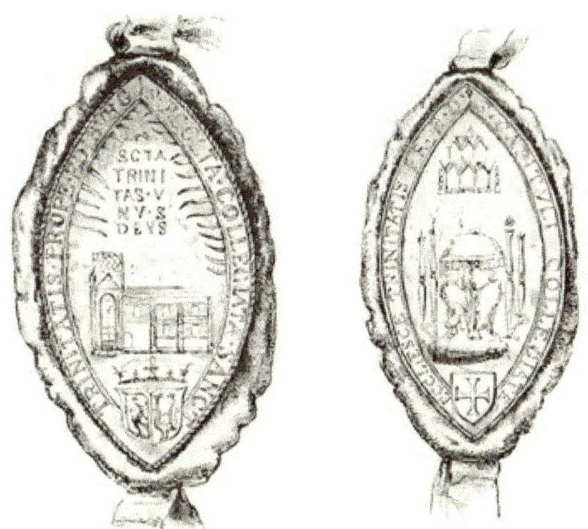

THE OLD COLLEGIATE SEALS OF TRINITY COLLEGE.

To face page 74.]

appointed to attend to the same; and which work, our dearly beloved son in Christ, King James III., son of the foresaid Queen, intends to complete:—WE, in consideration of both of them, and that the faithful may be more readily induced and incited to similar devotion, do, by these presents, Grant and Bestow, on all the faithful in Christ, of both sexes, from what place soever they may come, after they have declared themselves as truly penitent, and have made confession of their sins or their transgressions—who, "on the tenth day of the month of July, which is the day of dedication of the said Church, and on the Octave of the same, from the first vespers to the second vespers inclusive, shall, within the appointed five years have visited the said Church, Chapel, or Hospital, contrite in heart, and confessing with the mouth, and shall have stretched out helping hands to this pious work, according to their abilities, and by advice of their confessor"—plenary absolution and indulgence of all their sins, crimes, and excesses, even in cases reserved to the Holy See. The same indulgence and absolution were likewise granted to the "poor faithful in Christ" who were resident in the Church or Hospital for the time; as also to those who may have died there, and who, at the moment of death, and at other times were contrite in heart, and confessed with the mouth their sins, according to the best of their remembrance. The date when this indulgence was to come into effect was fixed as the day of the said dedication in the ensuing year, and to continue in force on its successive recurrence every fifth year for the space of fifty years only. For those taking advantage of the same, and that they might more easily obtain the salvation of their souls and the divine compassion, Pope Pius II. granted, by these presents, to suitable confessors, seculars or regulars of whatsoever order, to be deputed, as shall seem expedient by the

D

Provost of the said Church, and the Collector of the Apostolic Chamber for the time being, on the said quinquennial day of the said dedication, four days before and four days after, and on their Octaves—to hear confessions, and with full power to grant absolution from sins and to enjoin salutary penance.

There was provision made in the Bull, that all the moneys paid for such indulgences, as well as for future remission of sins, should be faithfully and religiously kept in a box. This box was to be locked with two keys. Of these keys, it was ordained that one of them should be in the possession of the Provost and two Seniors of the College for the time being, while the Collector of the said Chamber in the Kingdom of Scotland should hold the other key. It was provided that one-third part of "all moneys and effects arising from such offerings and alms, without any fraud," should be reserved to the same Apostolic Chamber, and be immediately handed over by the said Collector for the defence and furtherance of the Catholic faith, "against the most impious and fierce enemies of the name of Christ." To the Provost and the two Seniors of the College, the remaining two-thirds of the money was granted. They were enjoined to devote this revenue towards the completion of the building, the supply of ornaments, the upkeep and repair of the fabric, and "for the poor and the said place only, and not in any other way." Failing their doing so, and using these alms for other purposes, they were assured that they would incur the Divine wrath, besides that of the Apostles Peter and Paul.

The Bull aforesaid closes with these words:—"Let no one, therefore, dare to infringe the tenor of our concession, grant, and will, etc. But if anyone shall presume to attempt this, let him know that he will incur the indignation of Almighty God Himself, and of the Apostles Peter and Paul aforesaid. Given at Tibur, the year, etc., M.CCCC.LXIII. the sixth of the Calends of September, of our pontificate the fifth year."

It is proper here to state that in consequence of the unsettled state of the country, Sir Edward Bonele, the first Provost, was soon obliged to apply to the Scottish Parliament for assistance in the realisation of payment of his rents in Teviotdale.

In June 1526, and for many years thereafter, the Provost of the Trinity College had a seat in the Scottish Parliament.

Nearly forty years had elapsed since the Bull of Pope Pius II. had been issued (1463), and although the buildings of the College were not completed, the College seems to have been, in the opinion of its ecclesiastical superiors, so successful that, on the 14th day of November 1502, James, Archbishop of St Andrews, granted a charter, to annex the Church of Dunnottar to the Trinity College, for the support of two additional prebendaries. These two additional officials were to be respectively styled "The Dean" and "The Prebendary of Dunnottar"—thus making in all ten prebendaries. At this time Master John Brady was Provost of the Collegiate Church of the Holy Trinity at Edinburgh. The Archbishop of St Andrews was a near relative of the royal family. He was Primate of the whole Kingdom of Scotland, and Legate of the Apostolic See, Duke of Ross, and perpetual Commendator of the Monastery of Dunfermline, etc.

The grant made of the revenues of the Church of Donnottar, was done on the request of Brady, in which he set forth that, if the number of prebendaries were increased in the Collegiate Church of the Holy Trinity in Edinburgh, it would tend to the great advancement of Divine worship, and to the honour and profit of the Collegiate Church itself. It was required that Master Walter Stratoun, the Rector of the Parish Church of Dunnottar, should resign, and demit it to others; and that the said two new prebendaries of Trinity

Church "should take corporal, real and actual possession of the said Parish Church, and of the rights and pertinents of the same, by their proper authority, and to convert and for ever retain the same for the use and profit of the said prebendaries themselves, and of a Vicar to be appointed by us (the Archbishop of St Andrews), the licence of any other superior being nowise required for that effect."

The function of the Dean consisted in this,—that, when the Provost of the College was absent, he became, for the time being, "Principal and President in the choir and chapter of the said Church;" but when the Provost was present, the Dean's jurisdiction and power ceased. One half of all the fruits, oblations, and teinds, parsonage and vicarage of Dunnottar fell to him; while the other half of these fell to his Colleague, the prebendary of Dunnottar. It was required of the latter, that he should be "expert and well-learned in organs, and that he shall play upon them on the proper feasts," and he is enjoined to celebrate mass for James, present Archbishop of St Andrews, brother-german of the King of Scotland, when he shall be appointed, at the eleventh hour before noon. Both of these prebendaries, like the others, required to be priests, and learned and expert in reading and understanding plain chant, and responding. They were also required to give personal residence, and be obedient to the Provost.

It was expressly laid down that the Parish Church of Dunnottar should not, by reason of the change, be deprived of due services, or that the cure of souls should be neglected. The two new Prebendaries of Trinity College were charged with a yearly payment of twenty merks of the current money of Scotland to a vicar pensioner, for his maintenance. Half of the amount had to be paid by the Dean at the feast of Whitsunday, and the other half by the Prebendary of Dunnottar at the feast of Martinmas. While the election of the Vicar was reserved by the Archbishop of St Andrews, for himself and successors in office, there was a right of veto on the part of the Provost and the Prebendaries of the said Collegiate Church, for the time being, so that they might decline and refuse any one as unworthy, whom they, after his nomination, deemed "not qualified and learned according to the tenor of the old foundation" of the College. The Archbishop further reserved to himself and his successors the episcopal, archidiaconal, and other rights as these had existed according to law or custom, prior to the present erection, union, and incorporation. The deed was duly signed and attested by a Notary Public—all in the presence of witnesses, whose names and avocations are duly set forth in regular form.

There seems to have been no increase of the establishment after the Dunnottar benefaction, with its two prebendaries. The last important increase of its property during Catholic times was a royal grant in 1502 of the lands of Powis de Erth, and of Cummystoun or Maxwell-Riggs, which were granted to the prebendaries and chaplains of the Collegiate Church.

Twenty-nine years had passed away since the additional two prebendaries had been added. King James III. had been killed at an early age (1489), and he had been succeeded by his son King James IV. when the latter was only fifteen years of age. He, who was much beloved by his people, fell in the battle of Flodden, on the 9th of September 1513, in the fortieth year of his age, and twenty-fifth year of his reign. He was succeeded by his son, James V., an infant at that time, only two years old. A considerable period of Regency and of very great complications was the result. Meantime the buildings of the Trinity Hospital and Trinity College were still progressing slowly. When the King arrived at the age of twenty, he seems to have shown a great amount of interest in the religious house founded by his great-grandmother. From Stirling Castle, where he was resident at the time, he addressed a letter, dated the 22nd March 1531, to His Holiness Pope Clement VII., beseeching of him that he would grant indulgences to those who should visit the Trinity College, and should aid in the completion of the building. The letter is couched in the following terms, viz. :—

To OUR MOST HOLY LORD, THE POPE.

MOST BLESSED FATHER,—After the most humble prostration at your most holy feet—there is a somewhat famous College, near to our town of Edinburgh, founded by the most Serene Princess, Mary, formerly Queen of Scotland, our great-grandmother, the Provost of which is John Dingwall, a prudent and good man, prothonotary of the Roman See, who has purposed with himself to make the rest of the church conformable to the magnificently-constructed choir, having thus undertaken a work not to be completed without great expense, which, that he may the more easily accomplish, and that he may be assisted by the help of the public, he desires that by the beneficence of your Holiness, gracious indulgences may be granted, for the lifetime only of the Provost himself, to all who shall visit the College, on this feast of the Holy Trinity, and during the Octaves, for the purpose of devotion, being truly penitent, contrite, and making confession, and who shall put forth helping hands to the building of the same, and that he may be empowered to hear the confessions of those who shall assemble for the sake of obtaining such indulgences, and to absolve them either personally, or by suitable presbyters. Wherefore, we crave your Holiness kindly to assent to these so pious wishes, and to grant indulgences as plenary as possible, and all other things, which the Provost himself may with justice humbly crave. Most Blessed Father, may God Almighty very long preserve your Holiness in felicity! From our Castle at Stirling, on the twenty-second day of the month of March, in the year one thousand five hundred and thirty-one from our Lord's incarnation. Your most Holiness'

Devoted Son, The King of Scots,

JAMES, R.

No reply seems to have been received in answer to this communication, as otherwise it would have appeared in the charters connected with the Collegiate Church and Hospital. It may be, however, explained, that about this time there were very serious disputations in several countries of Europe, as well as in England and Scotland, which may have been the cause of the Pope's neglecting the request contained in the royal message.

Before passing on to the next chapter, it is proper that some allusion should be made to John Dingwall, the Provost of the Trinity College, at the time when King James V. sent to the Pope the communication already referred to. Sir John Dingwall was a man of some consequence in his day. He was Archdeacon of Caithness, Rector of Strabrok in Linlithgowshire, and one of the spiritual Lords of the College of Justice in Scotland. He is stated to have been the son of a Priest who gave him a good education, and was instrumental in most materially helping him to ecclesiastical preferment. He was held in good esteem for his natural talents and his acquired gifts. He was employed at the Court of Rome, and it has been alleged that, in his day, he became possessed of very considerable means, a portion of which he bequeathed to help on the buildings of the Trinity College Church and Hospital. He built a house on the grounds of Trinity Hospital, and in close proximity thereto. This house used to be known as "Dingwall Castle." The ruins of it appear in Gordon's View of the City as a square keep, with round towers at three of the angles; and a ruinous building, in all probability the chapel, on the east side. All these edifices were eventually cleared away for the building of the Orphan Hospital, which afterwards occupied the ground.

CHAPTER IV.

THE REFORMATION—GIFT TO THE TOWN COUNCIL.

THE Reformation, which may be justly designated as the historical name for the great religious movement of the sixteenth century, had far-reaching effects not only in Scotland and England, but over a considerable part of the Continent of Europe. In Germany, Switzerland, Holland, and France, it unquestionably exercised a most powerful influence for the good of these communities. With the time of the Reformation, the period called "the Middle Ages" might be said to have terminated, and a new era in regard to Europe, and its general culture, had begun. The movement tended, in a great measure, to foster a very strong spirit of civil and religious liberty among the people at large. The invention of the art of printing, which has undoubtedly conferred so much good on society, as well as the circulation of good and wholesome literature as a necessary concomitant,—could not fail to serve as most powerful aids in the great struggle for freedom. Prior to the Reformation, it is stated in Chambers' Encyclopædia (Vol. VIII. p. 611), "The power

TRINITY COLLEGE CHURCH, AND PART OF TRINITY HOSPITAL TO THE RIGHT.
(*After a Drawing by Clerk of Eldin*, 1780.)

To face page [illegible]

of the Church underlay all human relations. It was the consecration of the Church that constituted the family; the Church defined the relations of rulers and their subjects; and the Church was the final court of appeal on the ultimate questions of human life and destiny. In the nature of things, such a power could never be realised as it was ideally conceived. Yet during the eleventh and twelfth centuries, the period when the power of the Popes was most adequate to their claims, they went far to make the idea a reality. But the energies of the human spirit were bound sooner or later to issue in developments with which mediæval conceptions were fundamentally irreconcilable. By the thirteenth century, along every line of man's activity, there were already protests, conscious and unconscious, against the system typified in the Pope at Rome."

In 1532, England had shaken itself free of the papal control. In Scotland, the movement was twenty-eight years later. In 1559, John Knox had returned to Edinburgh, after a long sojourn abroad. His strong personality, combined with commendable zeal and untiring energy, did much to advance the movement for reform. In 1560, the Protestant faith became the religion of the country.

It is not the purpose of the writer to refer more specifically to the causes or the controversies which led up to this state of matters, or the various complications attendant thereon. But, considering the effect produced upon the affairs and arrangements of the Collegiate Church and Hospital of the Holy Trinity near Edinburgh, it is requisite that some passing allusion should be made to the altered system of Church polity which had brought about so great a change.

Immediately after the Reformation, the Magistrates and Town Council of the City of Edinburgh, took steps to obtain grants of the church revenues and lands which had then fallen to the Crown, or part thereof, that the same might be applied for the maintenance of the reformed clergy, and for the establishment and support of schools, colleges, and hospitals for the poor. The Minute of the Town Council of 23d April 1561, is to the following effect:—It is deemed desirable that the rents, annual proceeds, and other emoluments, which used formerly to be paid for lands and tenements within this Burgh, to papists, priests, friars, monks, and nuns, and others of that wicked sort, for the maintenance of idolatry and vain superstition, seeing that it has pleased the Almighty to open the eyes of the public, and to give them knowledge regarding such vain abuses;—therefore that the said rents and emoluments be applied to more profitable and godly uses, such as the sustenance of the true ministers of God's Word, the building of hospitals for the poor, and colleges for the upbringing of the youth, and other such godly works.* Following out this resolution, a special application was made by the Town Council to Queen Mary on the 27th August 1561, praying for a grant of the site of the Blackfriars Monastery, together with the yards attached thereto, for the purpose of building a hospital upon it for the poor people who are to wear an uniform, and that we may have the place, church, chambers, and offices of the Kirk of Field—offering a reasonable price therefor, for the purpose of building a school: Also, that your Grace would give and dispone to us for the maintenance of the foresaid hospital and school the annual proceeds

* The words of the original minute are as follow:—"It is thocht gude that the renttis, annuellis, and utheris emolumentis, quilkis of before war payit furth of landis and tenementis within yis Bur^{t.} to papestis, priestis, frieries, monkis, and nonnis, and utheris of yat wicket sort, for mainteinying of idolatrie and vaine superstitioun, seeing it has plesit ye Almichtie to oppin ye eis of all pepile, and to gif yame ye knowledge of sic vaine abusis—Thairfore yat the saidis renttis and emolumentis be applyit to mair profitable and godlie uses, sic as for sustenying of the trew ministereis of Goddis Word, and biging of hospitalis for the pure, and colleges for lernying and upbringing of ze youth, and sic other godlie warkis."

which used to go to the chaplains and friars, and which are presently in your Grace's hands, and whatsoever more remains of the same and which pertains to your Grace; because our town contains a large number of inhabitants, and many of them are poor.*

In answer to these applications, Queen Mary granted the kirk-livings to the Provost, Bailies, Council and Community of the Burgh of Edinburgh. The Charter is dated 13th March 1566-7.

In that Charter the Queen goes on to relate that, considering how dishonestly a great number of the prebendaries, chaplains, and friars have, since the change of religion, disponed, alienated, and given away into the hands of certain persons, the lands, annual rents, and emoluments previously mortified to their chaplainries, prebends, and other places respectively; and also, that very many of our lieges have claimed for themselves, by brieves of our chancery, the right to certain lands, tenements, and annual rents, mortified by their predecessors, or otherwise have obtained sasine as heirs of their predecessors, who previously gifted the same to the Church, which has happened partly by the officers of our said Burgh, and partly by the collusion of the said prebendaries, chaplains, and friars: WHEREFORE we by these presents, rescind and annul all and sundry such alienations, dispositions and sasines, by which the first will and purpose of the founders is infringed, altered and changed by perverting the same to individual (or private) uses, to the effect that the same be converted to proper and legitimate uses.

The Charter by the Queen (which is addressed to all good men

* The words of the original minute are as follow:—"Ye situation quhar ye black friers war, togidder with zair yards, to beig ane hospitale upoun for ye pouir, and als cause some dress be made, yat we may have ye place, kirk, chalmeris, and houses of ye Kirk of Field, to beig ane scule for said, ye annuellis of chaplanries and freris, being presentlie in your Grace's handis, and ye remanent of the samin quhen yai sall pertene to zoure Grace, and beaus owre said town is populous, and the multitude yairof greit."

of her own land, clerics and laics) goes on to state that, reflecting upon her duty towards the service of God, and of the ardent zeal which she had for the civil polity, and for preserving good order among her subjects, but chiefly within the Burgh of Edinburgh; and also that she was bound by her office to be careful of her duty towards her God, by whose good providence she was called upon to reign over her kingdom; and considering, further, that it was her duty, by all honest means, to provide for the ministers of God's Word, and that hospitals for poor mutilated and miserable persons, orphans and children deprived of their parents, may be maintained within her said Burgh, did, on attaining her majority, with the advice of the Lords of the Privy Council, give, grant and dispone, for her and her successors in office, for ever, to her well beloved, the Provost, Bailies, Councillors, and Community of the said Burgh of Edinburgh, and their successors for ever—"All and Singular the lands, tenements, houses, buildings, churches, chapels, yards, orchards, crofts, annual rents, fruits, duties, profits, emoluments, rents, alms, daill-silver, obits and anniversaries whatsoever, which anywise belonged, or are known to belong to any chaplainries, altarages, and prebends, founded in any church, chapel or college, within the liberty of our said Burgh, by whatsoever patron, in possession whereof the chaplains and prebendaries of the same formerly were," wheresoever the same are to be found or where their respective emoluments were formerly lifted, together with "the manor places, orchards, lands, annual rents, emoluments and duties whatsoever which formerly belonged to the Dominican or Preaching Friars, and to the Minorites or Franciscans of our said Burgh of Edinburgh."

The Charter likewise provided that the Provost, Magistrates, and Town Council, as acting on behalf of the Community, should possess all the lands, houses, and tenements, within the same Burgh and the liberties thereof, and the annual proceeds of the same, as had been previously given, founded, and granted for religious purposes. They were required to HOLD and to HAVE the same, and all the proceeds already enumerated; and to have free ish and entry; with all the rights pertaining thereto, under-ground as well as above-ground, and which may be said to justly belong to them in any manner of way. They were enjoined to hold the same "freely, quietly, fully, wholly, honourably, well, and in peace, for the time to come, without revocation or challenge whatsoever."

Provision was also made that the Town Council, on behalf of the Community and their successors, could by themselves or their collectors collect and receive the rents, fruits, duties, profits, etc.; as well as to remove any lands or tenements, build and repair ruinous places, and restore and apply the same for purposes of hospitality as to them, with the advice of the ministers and elders of the Burgh, seemed expedient—in a word all such powers as seemed to be possessed by the Provost, prebendaries, chaplains, and friars formerly mentioned. They were also taken bound, as well as their successors, to support the ministers, readers, and any other ecclesiastical charges out of the aforesaid revenues, and to repair those buildings which were devoted to purposes of hospitality. A direction was further given to "our comptrollers, present and future, and their collectors, factors, and others, whom it concerns in general as well as in special, that none of them presume to receive or levy the said fruits particularly above described, for any time whatsoever, past or future, or offer any obstruction or impediment to the foresaid Provost, Bailies, Councillors, and Community, and their successors, in the peaceable possession of the same." The deed goes on further to relate:—"Requiring and ordaining also our Lords of Session that they direct letters, in all the four forms, at the instance of the said Provost, Bailies, Councillors, Community, and their successors to the effect above written" . . . "Also commanding all intromitters with the said fruits, that they give prompt attention, (and that they) obey, and make willing and ready payment of the same." The great seal is affixed to the document. The witnesses duly verified the same. The Deed is subscribed at Edinburgh, the thirteenth day of the month of March, in the year of our Lord, one thousand, five hundred and sixty-six, and the twenty-fifth of our reign.

It has already been explained, in the Charter quoted from, that Queen Mary of Scots had just reason to complain of the dishonesty of some of the prebendaries, chaplains, and friars of the period. This is not to be wondered at. Too sudden conversion is always questionable.

The next Charter to which reference requires to be made is what is designated "Letters of Remission by King James VI.," in which he agrees to dispense with the erection of an Hospital on the Blackfriars Yards, and grants the site and buildings, etc., of the Trinity College to the Provost, Bailies, Council, and Community of Edinburgh for the purposes of an Hospital. It is dated on the 3d day of January 1567-8. The year should be 1568.

This Charter is to the following effect:—That his said mother (Queen Mary of Scots) having under her Great Seal, granted and disponed the place and yards of the Blackfriars, "commonly called Friars Preachers," burgesses of our Burgh of Edinburgh, with the cemeteries and other pertinents of the same, to erect an Hospital for the poor, by the present Provost, Magistrates, Councillors, and Community of the same, and their successors: And because it was promised that they should begin the same within one year after the date of the said infeftment, and should finish the same within ten years thereafter: And because it has been clearly shown to us, and the Archbishop of St Andrews, that the friars' place before mentioned is not so suitable or convenient for the building or construction of the said Hospital as the site of the College of the Holy Trinity, and the yards, houses, and buildings of the same, by reason of the great crowd and concourse, both of the strangers and of the lieges of our Kingdom, who daily approach or pass through and frequent the same, by whom some profit and aid may daily accrue to the said Hospital, and may thereby be of benefit to the indigent persons resident within the same; and which [Hospital] the said Provost, Bailies, Councillors, and Community have promptly commenced to build and repair, and this all the more willingly, because of the profit and advantage of that particular site, or of its bounds and continuity with the friars' place, may be expended and laid out on the said Hospital of the fore-mentioned College: THEREFORE, and for divers other good or pious reasons and considerations, moving us and our Regent aforesaid, by the tenor of these presents, we have dispensed and do dispense, in favour of the said Provost, Bailies, Councillors, and Community of our said Burgh of Edinburgh, with that part and clause of the said infeftment relating to the commencement, completion, and building of the foresaid Hospital upon the place and bounds of the fore-mentioned friars within the time before written, and with all loss, injury and prejudice which can accrue to and fall on them from their infeftment above mentioned, for the non-completion or implementing of the same.

The Charter then goes on to state that the said infeftment was to abide in full force, to them and their successors, and also that they were to have full power to lease, use, and dispone upon the foresaid place, yard, gardens, houses, cemetery, and such pertinents, in feu-farm or yearly rent, as shall be deemed by them to be most expedient. It was likewise provided, that the annual profit, rents, and duties of the same should be applied to the sustentation of the said Hospital of the College of the Holy Trinity, and of the poor residing in the same, and of no others. The Charter was granted "under the testimony of our great seal, at Edinburgh, the third day of the month of January, in the year of our Lord, one thousand five hundred and sixty-seven, and the first of our reign."

The Town Council, as representing the Community at large, were thus relieved of their promise to the Crown to devote the ground and revenues of the Blackfriars to the purposes originally intended. The reason for this step being taken, was that their energies might be concentrated upon the building up, and better control of, as well as extending the usefulness and increasing the benefits of the Trinity Hospital.

It may be here remarked in passing, that in the Accounts of the Gude Toun, printed as an Appendix to the Burgh Records, Vol. III. page 289, there is the following entry :—

> Item, the compter is to be dischargit of xj^s x^d for the bringing of ten geistis fra the schip to the Bray Heid of Leith, and for the closing of ane hoill aboun the yet of the well of the Trinete College; summa, xj^s x^d.

This was in 1553-4, more than fifteen years before the Hospital began to be managed by the Town Council.

VIEW OF TRINITY HOSPITAL AND PART OF TRINITY COLLEGE CHURCH.

To face page 41.]

CHAPTER V.

GIFT OF THE BUILDINGS AND SITE, ETC.

DOWN to the year 1567, the Collegiate Church and Hospital of the Holy Trinity remained in the hands of the Crown, as yet undisposed of. Neither the buildings, nor the revenues belonging thereto, were included in any grant that had been previously made. The Magistrates and Town Council were, however, desirous to erect an Hospital for the maintenance and support of the poor within their burgh. Queen Mary, as we have already seen, by a letter or writing, dated 17th August 1562, in answer to their application had promised that, whenever proper provision was made for the building of "ye Hospitale and schule within written," her Grace would provide "ane rowme (room) convenient yairfore." On the tenth day of November 1567, Sir Simon Preston,* of that Ilk and Craigmillar,

* The following are the terms of the Minutes of the Town Council as to this matter (as contained in the Burgh Records—Scottish Burgh Records Society, 1875):—*10th November* 1567.—[The bailies, council and deacons of crafts] being convenit in the counsalhous of this burgh, comperit Sir Symon Prestoun of Craigmillar, Knycht, prouest of this burgh, and schew

Knight, at that time Provost of the City of Edinburgh, informed the Magistrates and Town Council, that he had obtained from the then Lord Regent Murray's hands, the gift of the Trinity College Kirk, houses, biggings, and yards adjacent thereto, and lying contiguous to the same, to be "ane Hospital to the puir, and to be biggit and uphaldane (built and upheld) by the good town, and the elimosinaries to be placed thereinto, by the Provost, Bailies, and Council for the time being;" and he thereby transferred and made over the same to the Magistrates and Town Council of the Burgh, for behoof of the Community.

Accordingly, on the 12th day of November of the same year (1567), a Charter was expede of King James VI. of Scotland, with consent of the Regent and the Lords of the Privy Council, in favour of the Civic Corporation and Community of the City, of the Collegiate Church and Hospital of the Holy Trinity. This Charter proceeds upon the narrative, that, moved by "a fervent and zealous purpose, to assist the poverty, penury, and want of many and divers honest, aged, and impotent persons, who, in their old age, have lost their means and substance, by accident and bad fortune, so that they may not utterly perish and die, through extreme hunger, penury, and want of their

and declarit to the saidis baillies counsall and dekynnis that he had obtenit and impetrat at my Lord regentis handis the gift of the Trinite College, kirk, houssis, bigginis, and yairdis adiacent thairto, and lyand contegue to the samyn, to be ane hospitall to the pure, and to be biggit and vphaldin be the gude toun, and the elimosinaris to be placit thairinto be the prouest, baillies and counsall, present and being for the tyme, and nochtwithstanding that he hes lauborit the samyn it wes nocht his mynde to laubour it to his awyn behuif, bot to the gude tounis as said is, and thairfore presently gaif the gift thairof to the gude toun, and transferrit all rycht and titill that he had or mycht haif thairto in the gude toun fra him and his airis for euir *ad perpetuam remanentiam*.

The prowest baillies and counsall foirsaid namit and constitute Adam Fullartoun, baillie, maister of wark to the hospitale to be founded in the Trinitie Colledge, with power to him to cheis his officiaris and warkmen as he sall think gude.

requisite sustenance; we, therefore, being moved by piety and a good conscience, to afford them such relief and assistance as their indigence and necessity require; as also, understanding that the aforesaid purpose cannot in all respects be conveniently begun and commenced nor conveniently perfected and accomplished, without our supplement, aid, and authority; and understanding that Sir Simon Prestoun, of that Ilk, Knight, intends—with deliberate, firm, and set purpose—to build, erect, and with all care and diligence, endow an Hospital, with reasonable support, for such honest, poor, and impotent persons, aged and advanced in years, or sick, being indwellers and inhabitants within our Burgh of Edinburgh; and also for such other old, indigent, and impotent people, as shall be found fit for receiving such benefits and charity in the said Hospital so to be founded: THEREFORE, we, and our foresaid Regent, perceiving that the foresaid purpose and work will be in every respect, not only good and Divine, but being also willing to give occasion to others, our subjects; and for the purpose of inclining the minds of certain others of our lieges and subjects, to accept such a Divine call to a similar purpose and work, with the advice and consent of the Lords of our Privy Council, have deemed it expedient and necessary, to gratify the said Sir Simon, Provost of our said Burgh of Edinburgh, with the gift and donation of such a place now vacant in our hands, and belonging and pertaining to our gift, as shall be most fit and convenient for constructing and building, repairing and perfecting the said Hospital, with the houses, buildings, and yards thereof, which the greatest multitude and concourse of people,* as well strangers as others our lieges of this our town, are seen to frequent and near which

* It would appear from the above, that King James VI. regarded the site of the Hospital as a most suitable one, in respect of the traffic which daily passed bye, and the pecuniary benefit which the Hospital was likely to receive from being continually before the eye of the public.

they chiefly have access to, and egress from the town, whereby the daily alms and contributions to the said Hospital are increased and will increase."

This, therefore, must always be regarded as the first Charter, by which the Town Council of the City of Edinburgh, on behalf of the public, became the Governors and Custodiers of what has for so many generations been known and acknowledged, as the great charity of the Trinity Hospital. The objects of the same and the persons for whose benefit the royal benefaction was so freely given are made sufficiently plain by the context.

The Charter goes on to state that, in consequence of the good, faithful, and gratuitous services which had been rendered from time to time by Sir Simon, towards ourself, our foresaid Regent, and the said Lords of our Privy Council, as well as for other causes moving us in favour of the Provost, Bailies, Councillors, and Community of our said Burgh of Edinburgh, we have GIVEN, GRANTED, and DISPONED, and by the tenor of this Charter, do GIVE, GRANT, and DISPONE, in their favour and that of their successors, All and Whole the Church called the Collegiate Church of the Trinity, with the churchyard, houses, buildings, ruinous and built, orchards, yards, crofts, dovecot, and pertinents thereof whatsoever, formerly occupied and inhabited by the Provost and Prebendaries of the said Collegiate Church, with all the buildings and yards of the said Hospital, lying contiguous to the said Church, with the yard lying on the west side thereof, at the foot or end of our street or vennel called Leith Wynd.

It then relates that the Crown having become the undoubted patron of the same, agreeably to the tenor of the Acts and Statutes passed and ordained shortly after the time of the Reformation of religion, and that the Hospital buildings should be used for the sustentation of the poor and the sick, and for no other use whatever,—it was expedient to transfer these to the Town Council and Community, "in free blench farm for ever." The consideration to be granted by them to the Crown was "a silver penny."

Provision was, however, made that this gift or grant should in no way be prejudicial to the Provost and Prebendaries of the said Collegiate Church, in regard to their infeftments, rights, and donations to so many of the poor, commonly called beidmen, "now resident in the Hospital, called the Trinity Hospital foresaid, after the tenor of the erection made thereupon." The Charter is duly attested, signed, and sealed in November 1567, being the first year of the reign of King James VI.

It may be proper to mention in passing, that an Act was passed by the First Parliament of King James VI., held at Edinburgh, on the 15th day of December 1567, by James, Earl of Murray, etc., Regent to this Realm and Lieges.* That Act referred to the Abolition of the Pope, by our Sovereign Lord, with advice of his dearest Regent, and the three Estates of Parliament, by the Statute "maid in the Parliament haldin at Edinburgh, the 24 day of August, the zeir of God, 1560 zeiris." The former Act was passed to confirm the latter, and to ordain it to be perpetual law. It states that the jurisdiction and authority of the Bishop of Rome, called "the Pope," has been not only "contumelious to the eternall God, but also very hurtfull and prejudiciall to our Soveraines authoritie, and common weil of this Realme." It then goes on to ordain that the Pope should in future have no jurisdiction or authority in this country; and that if any of our Sovereign's subjects desired title or right from the said Bishop of Rome, or his sect, each

* "The Lavvs and Actes of Parliament, maid be King James the First and his Svccessovrs Kinges of Scotland." *Imprented at Edinburgh, be Robert Waldegrave, prenter to the Kinges Majestie, 15 Martii. Anno Dom.* 1597.

such one would be subjected to the "paines of Barratrie, that is to say, proscription, banischment, and never to bruke honour, office, nor dignitie within this Realme." The "contraveneres" of this order were to be called before the justice or his deputes, or before the Lords of the Session (instituted by King James V. on the 17th day of May 1537) and punished therefor, conform to the laws of the country. Anyone who furnished money to such persons, or the purchasers of their title, or who acted as maintainers or defenders of them were to receive a like punishment. It was also statute and ordained, that no Bishop, or other prelate of the realm should use any jurisdiction in all time coming, by the authority of the Bishop of Rome, under similar penalties.

The other clauses of the Act refer to previous Statutes of the Scottish Parliament, and specially those made during the Reigns of King James the First, Second, Third, Fourth, and Fifth, in which it is alleged that they do not agree "with God's Holy Word, and be them divers persones tuke occasion to maintaine Idolatrie and superstition within the Kirk of God, and repressing of sik persones as were professours of the said Word, quhair throw divers innocents did suffer." All these Acts are declared annulled, and their provisions are to have no force, strength, or effect in all time coming, as being contrary and repugnant to the Word of God, and the Confession of Faith according to the said Word, ratified and approved by the Estates in this present Parliament.

The Act of Parliament goes on to narrate "The Confession of the Faith and Doctrine beleeved and professed be the Protestantes of Scotland, exhibited to the Estatis of the same in Parliament, and be their publick votis authorised, as a doctrine grounded upon the infallible Word of God."

The clauses referring to the same, and the subjects therein treated, number twenty-six,* and form quite a "Body of Divinity." There are upwards of 360 Scripture references on the margin which gives the Print more the appearance of what is known as a Reference Bible of the present day, than the rubric of an Act of Parliament. The document ends with the following words:—"*Arise* (*O Lord*) and let thy *enimies be confounded, let them flee from thy presence that hate thy godlie Name. Giue thy seruands strenth to speake thy word in bauldnesse, and let all Natiouns cleaue to thy trew knawledge.* AMEN."

"Thir Acts and Artickles ar red [*sic*] in the face of Parliament,
& ratifyed be the thre Estatis, At Edinburgh, the 17. day
of August, the zeir of God, 1560. zeiris."

There were other clauses, which followed thereafter "anent the trew and holy Kirk," also regarding the "King's aith at his Coronation," and as to judges of the Court of Session, etc., to which it does not seem requisite specifically to refer.

Maitland, in his "History of Edinburgh" (1753), page 210, says, "The Reformation of Religion being far advanced in Scotland, the Provost and Canons of this (Trinity) Church judged it their interest to embrace the same; and, to show they were in earnest, made the

* The following are the titles of the subjects dealt with, *verbatim et literatim*: viz.—1. Of God. 2. Of the Creatioun of Man. 3. Of Original Sinne. 4. Of the Revelatioun of the Promise. 5. The Continuance, Increase, and Preservatioun of the Kirk. 6. Of the Incarnation of Christ Iesus. 7. Why it behooued the Mediator to be very God and very Man. 8. Electioun. 9. Christ's Death, Passion, and Buriall. 10. Resurrectioun. 11. Ascension. 12. Faith in the Holy Ghost. 13. (Awanting.) 14. The Cause of Gude Warkes. 15. What Warkes ar reputed gude befoir God. 16. The Perfectioun of the Law, and the Imperfectioun of Man. 17. Of the Kirk. 18. The Immortalitie of the Saules. 19. Of the Notes, be the quhilk the trewe Kirk is decerned, fra the false, and quha sall be Iudge of the Doctrine. 20. The Authoritie of the Scriptures. 21. Of generall Councels,—of their power, Authoritie, and Cause of their Convention. 22. Of the Sacramentes. 23. Of the richt Administration of the Sacramentes. 24. To whome Sacramentes appertaine. 25. Of the Civile Magistrate. 26. The guiftes freelie giuen to the Kirk.—*Waldegrave ut antea*, 1597.

following Declaration or Order :—The Provost and Canons of this College, pursuant to the Reformation of Religion, or change of principles, make the following Articles for the regulation of their Beidmen. . . . The Statutes and Ordinances maid and renewitt be the Provost and Prebendaries be gadderit, to be observit and keipit be the Beidmen and Hospitularis now present and to cum, conform to yair Foundation, Actis and Constitutiones maid yair upoun, Day, Zeir and place foresaid." *

* The following are the Regulations referred to :—

Imprimis, The Hospitularis now present and to cum, sal be sworne to observe, keip, and fulfill the Statutes and Ordinances following, under the Panes contenit in the samyn ; and thai quha are now presentit alreddie, sal leir and have perfitlie the Ten Commandimentis of God, the Lordis prayer, and the Articles of the Belief ; and to yat Effect ane certane Day in the Owk to be set be the Maister Hospitaler for instructing of the ignorant ; and thai quha sal happin to be presentit and ressavit heirefter to be expert heirinto, or ellis not to be ressavit.

Item, It is ordanit, yat the Beidmen sall not be absent fra the Prayeris or Preiching, quhen it sal happin the samyn to be publict in the said College-kirk or Beid-house yairof, without sum leisum Caus and Licence askit and given be the said Maister Hospitaler to yat Effect, the Contempnar heirof to pay ilk Falt Thrie Pennies, or one Half-penny.

Item, It is ordanit, yat the saidis Beidmen sal prepair and mak ilk ane of yame on yair awin Expenses, ane Blew-gown, conform to the first Foundation, betwixt the Dait of this Presentis, and the first of *Junii, anno* 1576, nixt to cum, under the Pane of Depreivatioun of him yat sall happin to contempt yis Ordinance, quhais Beidship sal be gevin to ane uther fund qualifiit yairfore.

Item, Yat the Maister Hospitaler sal have the Cair of the Beidmen, and ressaive yair Dewties arissand yame thairof, as he will answer to God, and the Provost and Prebendaries ; and yat their Land or Teinds be set in Few or large Takis be yame and their said Maister Hospitaler, with Consent and Assent of the Provost and Prebendaries ; and yat the Interests and Gersome Silver yat sal happin to be obtenit yairfor, to be tane up and distributed be the Maister Hospitaler amang the said Beidmen equalie, at leist (gif Neid beis) the samyn to be applyit to the repairing and mending of the Hospitale, sa oft as the samyn sall have Neid thairof, as Use is ; and Compt yairof to be maid to the Provost and Chaptoure, sa oft as he sal require it.

Item, It is ordanit, gif ony of the Beidmen be drunkinsum, Twilziours, Bannaris, Severars, or outragius, to yair said Maister Hospitaler, to any of the Prebendaries, or to any of the Beidmen yair Brethring, being first reprovit be the Maister Hopitaler, and will not forbeir

TRINITY COLLEGE CHURCH.

To face page [illegible].]

The buildings of the Hospital at the period when the Town Council got possession of them seem to have been in a somewhat neglected if not a ruinous condition. They had suffered seriously from the invasion of the Duke of Hertford in 1544, when landing at Wardie, he and his army successively seized Newhaven and Leith, and marched on

the next Falt yairefter, the Offender to pay yairfore Sex Pennies, with Satisfactioun of the Party offendit; and the second Falt, Twall Pennies; the third Falt, the Offender to be put to the Stokkis for the Space of six Howeris and langer, induring the Maister Hospitaler's will.

Item, And gif it sal happin yis Offender to fail or offend any Man the theird time, it beand knewin and provin before the Maister Hospitaler, he sal be yairfore removit fra his Beadmanship, and all appertenand yairto, and ane uther qualifiit Persoun placit yairin be the Provost and Prebendaries; quilkis Faltis and Unlawers sal be tane up be the Maister Hospitaler, and Compt maid to the Chaptoure, sa aft as he sal be requirit, and the samyn to be applyit for beitting and mending of the Hospitale, and keipit to that Effect.

Item, It is ordanit be the Provost and Chaptoure foresaid, yat how sone it sall pleis God, the said Hospitale be repairit and mendit, yat all the said Beidmen sal have and use yairin Nicht and Day, without Leif askit and given be the said Maister Hospitaler; ilk Nicht yat thai ar absent, to pay Thrie Pennies the Man; and yat na Wyfe nor Barnis sal be halden to resort yairin Day nor Nicht, and especiallie in the Nicht, for molesting of the seik, under the Pane of Sex Pennies, to be payit be the Beidmen yat sall happin to have yat Wyfe or Barnis; and yat nane of the said Beidmen yat are desolate of Wyffis at this present or to cum, sal marie without the Maister Hospitaler's Leif, under the Pane of Depreivatioun, at the leist satisfying of the said Maister Hospitaler.

Item, It is ordanit, yat the Hospitulares present, and to cum, sal abyde and underly the Correctioun and Executioun of yir Premises of the Maister Hospitaler, and yat thai sal purchas na Lordshippis agains yir Ordinances above written, or to mak plant of yair said Maister, bot to the Provost and Chaptoure; and gif thai doe the contrair, being knawin, yair Places to waike, and utheris qualifyt to be placit yairin be the Provost and Chaptoure, and ressavit be the Maister Hospitaler, gevin his Ratificatioun of being ressavit yairin to the Persoun presentit, in Write and Possessioun in dew Form, as Use is; And yis to be done sa oft as ony sal happin to waike, provyding yat the Persoun presentit be examinat be the Maister Hospitaler; and yat it sall be lesum to the said Maister Hospitaler to agment heirto sic Ordinancis as sal be found relevant, and adapted to the Weill of the said Beidmen; ordinand him to put yame and yir present Ordinancis in dew Executioun, without Favour, as he sal anser to God, and to the Provost and Chaptoure. Subscrivit be the said Provost and Chaptoure, as follows:—Day, Zeir, and Place above written.

G

to Edinburgh. Of course the Trinity College and Hospital buildings were in the chief route at that time to the city on the west, and Holyrood Palace, Abbey and Chapel on the east. But all these buildings possibly suffered more at the time of the Reformation. The following extracts from *Wilson's Memorials of Edinburgh* may help to emphasise what is here stated and to explain the cause. It was at a time when religious feeling greatly excited all parts of the country. He says: (page 63) "The reforming party now proceeded to those acts of violence, which led to the destruction of nearly all the finest ecclesiastical buildings throughout Scotland. The Queen Regent (Mary of Guise), on learning of their proceedings at Perth, and elsewhere, wrote to the Provost and Magistrates of Edinburgh, requiring them to defend the town, and not suffer the Earl of Argyle and the Congregation to enter; offering the aid of her French troops for their defence. But this the Magistrates declined, declaring that the entire populace were prepared to favour that party, and could not be restrained by them. Upon receiving this reply, the Regent thereupon withdrew with her French guard from Holyrood Abbey, and retreated towards Dunbar. The Magistrates, though unable to resist this popular movement, exerted themselves to the utmost to restrain its violence. They sent a deputation to the leaders of the reforming party, entreating them to spare both their churches and religious houses,—the former to be continued in use, as places of Protestant worship, and the latter as seminaries of learning. They also placed a guard of sixty men for the protection of St Giles' Church, and as a further security removed the carved stalls of the choir, within the safer shelter of the Tolbooth; and such was the zeal they displayed, that the Regent afterwards wrote them a letter of thanks for their services. Upon the first rumour of the approach of the Earl of Argyle, the populace attacked both the monasteries of the Black and Grey-Friars, destroying everything they contained, and leaving nothing but the bare walls standing. When the Earl of Argyle entered the town with his followers, they immediately proceeded to the work of purification, as it was styled. Trinity College Church and the prebendal buildings attached to it were assailed, and some parts of them utterly destroyed; and both St Giles' Church, and St Mary's, or the Kirk of Field, were visited, their altars thrown down, and the images destroyed and burnt. They visited Holyrood Abbey, overthrowing the altars, and otherwise defacing the church, and they removed also from thence the coining irons of the mint, compelling the treasurer to deliver up to them a considerable sum of money in his hands."

It is not surprising, therefore, to find the following Minutes of the Town Council:—14th November 1567.—"The prouest, baillies, and counsall ordanis Adam Foulertoun, maister of wark of the Trinite College, to caus, with all deligence possibill, conforme to the devise takin be thame, enter to the bigging of the hospitall in the said college, and to transport and intromet with the townis tymmer (wood) lyand in the freris yardis, and to apply the samyn to the werk of the said hospitall, and siclike to mak money of the lime and stane in the saidis freir yardis to be warit vpoun the saidis hospitall as said is. . . . 20*th November* 1567.—The Counsall disponit to certaine persouns in feu farm, the lands sumtyne pertenin to the Blak freris and now to the toun of Edinburgh, for the interes ryluca and yeirlie annual vnderwrittin, to be payit to thair hospitale and sustening of the pure thairof."

In addition to the miserable condition of the fabrics, the arrangements for carrying on the Hospital did not appear to the Town Council to be of a satisfactory nature. It is not surprising, therefore, that they were compelled to apply to the Parliament for further powers to repair and increase the buildings, having in view the benevolent and charitable purposes to which in future these were to be devoted.* The Charter, moreover, which conveyed the buildings, did not convey the revenues of the original College of the Holy Trinity, or of the said Collegiate Church and Hospital. The Provost and Prebendaries, in the meantime, had retained possession of their endowments. These became subjects of after negotiation. The Town Council had to look to other sources for obtaining the requisite funds, whereby the inmates of the Hospital might be maintained.

* The words of the Act of Parliament [1587, c. 14] contain "The Kingis Maiesties general Revocatioun," and are in these words :— . . . "ITEM, we revoik all infeftmentis, giftis and dispositionis quhatsumeuer sett, gevin and grantit be ws in our minoritie to quhatsumeuer persoun or personis in fie feu ferme or lyfrent of quhatsumeuir hospittalis, maisondewis, landis, or rentis appertening thairto in hurt and preiudice of our conscience, to the end that the saidis hospitallis may be reduceit to thair first institution for vphalding of the puir: Prouiding alwayes that the rentis of the hospitall of the Triuitie College beside the burgh of Edinburgh, quhilk is now decayit, assignit and gevin to the new hospitall erectit to [by] the Prouest, Baillies, and Counsall of the burgh of Edinburgh be nawayes comprehendit vnder this present reuocatioun."

CHAPTER VI.

OTHER CHARTERS—THE GOLDEN CHARTER.

AS already mentioned, the Charter of 1567 did not convey any of the revenues or endowments of the Old Trinity College Church and Hospital, but merely the buildings and the grounds adjoining. This was, however, in course of time, rectified. By a Charter by King James VI., confirming Queen Mary's former one (of 13th March 1566), His Majesty conveyed of new the Kirk-livings to the Provost, Bailies, Council, and Community of the Burgh of Edinburgh. This Charter was executed at Stirling, on the 14th day of April 1582. As these Kirk-livings and two subsequent Charters will be more specifically referred to at a future time, when larger grants were obtained from the Crown, it seems undesirable at the present stage to give this deed more than a passing notice.

In 1585, the Magistrates and Town Council purchased from Mr Robert Pont,* the last Provost of the Trinity College, his benefice of the

* Pont was a Judge of the Court of Session, an eminent churchman, and a miscellaneous writer. He was the son of John de Pont, an illustrious Venetian, who came to Scotland in the train of Mary of Guise.

provostry, with all the estates, teinds, patronages, and other privileges and emoluments belonging thereto, which the said Robert Pont forthwith resigned into the King's hands for their behoof. This Contract between the Town Council and Mr Pont is dated at Edinburgh, the 26th April 1585. In it he states that he is moved to grant the same, by great zeal, good conscience, and an earnest desire to advance the Hospitals and Colleges of the said Burgh to be founded by the Town Council and their successors; as well as out of a regard for the poor, sick, aged, decrepid, fatherless and orphans; and for instruction of the youth in letters and virtue, whereby charity may increase, to the glory of God and for the sake of true religion within the realm. The sum which was agreed by the Provost, Bailies and Town Council to pay to Pont during all the days of his natural lifetime, was "ane hundreth threescoir pundis money foirsaid at twa termes in the yeir, Whitsounday and Martymes in winter be equale proportiones, begynnand the first termes payment at the feast of Martymes nixttocum." It was made a matter of paction that for the sure payment of the same, the Magistrates and Council bound and obliged themselves, for them and their successors, to infeft the said Mr Robert, or any other one he pleased to act for him, in an annual rent of the said amount, "furth of thair commoun mylnis, pertening to thair said Toun of Edinburgh, sufficientlie be charter and sesing, or at the leist be ane sufficient sesing to be given thairupon." The Contract bears the signatures of "M. ROBERT PONT, Prouest off the Trinitie College," and "ALEXANDER BORTHWICK of Nethirlany."

It is proper to state that, notwithstanding the great zeal and interest which Pont professed to take in polite learning and the cause of the poor, the Magistrates and Council had very great difficulty in dealing with him, and bringing him to terms. This we shall have occasion to see in a future chapter.

The Magistrates and Town Council having thus by the transaction with Sir Simon Preston in 1567, and by their subsequent contract with Robert Pont, acquired full right to the benefice of the Trinity College, with all its pertinents and appurtenances, they forthwith applied for and obtained a new Charter from King James. By this deed, which is dated at Dunfermline, the 23d day of June 1585 (about two months after the Town Council's contract with Pont), His Majesty made a new grant of the benefice, etc., to them. The subjects so made over were those assigned by the Foundation Charter of the Collegiate Church of 1462, for the support of the Provost and Prebendaries of the same. This Charter also authorises the Magistrates and Council to rebuild the Hospital which was then in a ruinous condition, in a more convenient situation at or near the College. The Magistrates and Council by this Charter—the details of which it is not requisite to relate,—came to be vested in the whole subjects, including the Church and Hospital buildings, for the objects specified in the writs referred to, viz., for the support of the sick and decrepid poor within the Hospital, and of poor scholars in the College and Schools.

Prior to this time, the old Hospital buildings were on the east side of Leith Wynd. The old buildings were then taken down, and part of the College buildings was fitted up and converted into a new Hospital. The buildings, so appropriated, were to the south of the College Church, immediately adjoining thereto, and on the same side of the Leith Wynd. These buildings were ever afterwards, until their removal in 1848 for railway purposes, used and employed to the purposes to which they were to be devoted—that is to say, the Hospital was used for hospital purposes, while the Church was appropriated by the Magistrates and Council to the use of the inhabitants of the quarter of the town in which it was situated. According to Maitland, the area of the parish belonging to this Church was as follows:—viz.— "The southern side of the Nordloch, from Warriston's Close eastwards;

all Halkerstone's Wynd, and from Gray's Close, eastwards; all the northern part of the High Street to the Netherbow Port, with all the closes, etc., therein; together with the western side of Leith Wynd, St Mary's Wynd, and the head of the Canongate." At the time Maitland wrote, there were in the parish six hundred and seventy-seven families; and of "examinable persons too thousand four hundred and sixty-seven." It is very questionable if the district contains at the present day one-third of the number of inhabitants, which it did then, viz., in 1753.

In 1587, the King granted another Charter, dated at Holyroodhouse, on the 26th day of May, in which he confirmed his previous Charter of 1585, and of new granted the Trinity College, and the whole endowments and property thereof, to the Provost, Bailies, Council, and Community of the Burgh of Edinburgh. That Charter proceeds upon a narrative of the faithful services of the Town, and of their zeal towards sustentation of the true gospel, etc. It sets forth as objects of the grant, that the study of humane letters might flourish and increase within the City, and that the indigent and diseased poor might be comforted by means of an hospital. It subsumes that the fruits, profits and emoluments of the Trinity College had been transferred for the use of the ministers, the professors of letters, and the support of the poor. It states that these are given and conceded to the Town Council on behalf of the Community, and to their successors in perpetuity, in order that the fruits, profits, and emoluments of the subjects so disponed may be applied to the sustentation of the ministers of the true religion, for the poor, and the cultivation of learning, by means of College and Grammar Schools. There is a clause specially declaring that the Magistrates and Council should have the full right of property in the subjects in all time coming. Power is also given to them to maintain as many poor persons in the Trinity Hospital, recently repaired by them, as its funds would admit of; and they were authorised to dispose of the old buildings, if they saw fit. The lands adjoining known as "Dingwall Castle" they were permitted to sell. This is the site on which the old Orphan Hospital used to stand in later times.

During the same year, His Majesty granted another Charter to the Town Council, proceeding on the narrative of his having attained majority, and of the general annexation of Church lands to the Crown; with the exception of what had been given over for the benefit of hospitals, schools and colleges;—of the zeal and liberality of the Magistrates and Town Council in providing for their ministers, for building of an hospital and sustaining of the poor, the erection of the College, and the want of a sufficient provision for the said ministers, hospitals, and schools. His Majesty, then, referring to the previous grants by Queen Mary and by himself—all of which had been excepted from the general revocation of the Crown grants—ratifies and approves of the whole preceding royal Charters, excepting that of 1582 (the Foundation Charter of the College or University of the City of Edinburgh). The Charter then contains a clause of *novodamus* making over to the Magistrates and Town Council the whole of the subjects which were contained in the Charters so confirmed, including the Trinity College Church and the Trinity Hospital. All these subjects were so made over to, and the grant was accepted by, the Magistrates and Town Council, under an express provision in the Charter as to the purposes for which they were to be applied—viz., for the maintenance and support of the clergy, and the poor, and for the support of educational establishments created and erected by the Corporation,* or their successors on behalf of the Community of Edinburgh.

* The terms of the Charter are as follow:—Pro ministrorum et pauperum sustentatione ac pro intertenuimento dictii collegij per ipsos nuper erecti . . . . . . quod dict prepositus ballivi et communitas et eorum successores tenebunter sustentari ministros apud suas ecclesias pro presenti ibid servien, et cetera, et cetera.

On the 5th day of June 1592, being the twelfth Parliament of King James VI., an Act was passed by the Scottish Legislature, ratifying the whole grants and mortifications by Queen Mary and her son, of the lands, benefices and rents devoted for sustentation of the ministers within the burgh, and their successors, in favour of their ministry and hospital, the subjects contained in the said grants to remain with the Provost, Bailies, Council, and Community of the said burgh, and their successors in time coming, for sustentation of their said ministry and Hospital. It also provided for half of the Vicarage of Currie, and the whole of the Vicarage of the Parish of Dumbarney being vested in the Town Council, for the purposes of Trinity College. It is also, by the said Act, enacted and declared, that the Magistrates and Council shall have full right of property and superiority of the said subjects. The lands, annual rents, houses, yards and buildings of the Trinity College are specially mentioned, as forming parts of the subjects annexed.* A subsequent Act to the same effect was passed during the following year, viz., on the 21st day of July 1593.

* The words of the Act of Parliament are to the following effect:—

The landes, annual rentes, houses, zairdes, and Biggings of the *Trinitie* College, situate within the said Burgh of *Edinburgh*, alsweil perteining to the Provest as to the Prebendars thereof, and commoun landes, and annual rentes of the same. Quhilk annexation his Hienesse with advise of his saidis Estaites in Parliament, ratifies and apprievis: As als His Majestie with advise of his saidis Estaites, of new annexis the vther halfe of the Vicarage of *Curry*, to the quhilk na person is provided: And the haill Vicarage of the said Kirk of *Dumbarny*, quhilk alswa vakis be deprivation of N. N., last possessour of the same: To remaine with the Provost, Baillies, Councell, and Communitie of the said Burgh, and their successoures in time cumming, for sustentation of their said ministerie and hospitall. And our Soueraine Lord, and Estaites foresaids, decernis and declaris, that nane of thir particulars before written, disponed of before, and newlie annexed, for sustentation of the said Ministerie and hospitall, were, ar, or salbe ever comprehended in the generall Annexation of the Ecclesiasticall lands and rentes to the Croun; Bot wer, ar, and salbe excepted therefra: Likeas his Majestie and Estaites foresaidis, of new exceptis the samin, not in onely fra the said annexation: bot fra his Hienesse reuocation, maid in time by-past, or maid in this present Parliament; And

In 1603, the Magistrates and Town Council obtained from King James VI. the chief Charter that he granted them during his reign. That deed, because of its great importance has been denominated, and is now well known as, "The Golden Charter." It was granted at Holyrood on the 15th day of March. The King had just completed the twenty-fifth year of his reign. The object of this Charter was to consolidate and ratify a large number of royal grants given to the City of Edinburgh, as well as to confirm several previous Charters, infeftments, precepts, instruments of sasine, and other documents relating to the burgh. It contains special confirmation of many of the Charters already referred to, particularly of those granted in 1566, 1567, 1582, 1585, and 1587, and of the whole properties or subjects belonging to the town. It contains a new grant of the whole, with a clause uniting the various subjects. It was granted by His Majesty in consequence of his ancestors, of most happy memory, having advanced Edinburgh into the dignity and eminence of a Royal City, and through the care, industry, and indefatigable labours of the citizens sailing to foreign regions and exercising trade, the revenue of our royal patrimony has been increased, the kingdom enriched, and our subjects by their example led to a more refined way of living; and that the said City, in bearing public burdens, in paying taxes and tributes, and in furnishing exactions and imposts, is subject to and sustains the greatest burden when compared with other cities, and that it is not only now, but for ages past has been, the first and most distinguished city of the whole kingdom, and most

declaris alswa, that the saidis Provest, Baillies, Councell and Communitie, and their successoures, in all time cumming, hes, and sall haue sik full richt of propertie and superioritie of the foresaidis landes, annuall rentes and revenues, tennentes and tennendries, and service of free-tennentes thereof: as had the Bishoppes, Abbotes, Priors, Friers, Monkes, Nunnes, Chaplanes, and Prebendares, to quhom the saidis landes and annuall-rentes, perteined of before: Notwithstanding, ony acte or constitution, preceding the dait hereof.—*Waldegrave, ut antea*, 1597.

fitted to show forth the dignity and increase the fame of our country; as being the place best fitted for holding public assemblies, where we, our nobles, counsellors, and courtiers most frequently reside, and the stated general conventions are usually held; which also the Supreme Court, constituted for the trial of civil suits, from its institution, and the supreme judge of capital or criminal causes, have chosen as their fixed quarters and seat: Moreover, calling to account most notable services rendered by the City to us and our illustrious predecessors, in time of peace and war, not only against foreign enemies, but also against rebels at home, in internal commotions as well as intestine wars, directed against the royal Crown, sometimes when the Princes were infants, with cruel effusion of blood, and plundering of their goods, as well as the burning of our buildings and property: Understanding that the Magistrates and Citizens of Edinburgh, have undertaken to renovate and extend their pier and port of Leith, to construct a market-place, as well as a proper area with a wooden fence, for the purpose of receiving and selling wool, logs, and timber of all sorts; for the erection of buildings, the repairing of streets, the building of more kirks and churches, and the planting of the same, with a sufficient number of ministers, liberal stipends out of the public funds being given to them, the erecting and founding of colleges for the study of letters, the building of hospitals and houses for orphans, and the supplying of them with sufficient revenues, and other great and distinguished public works, for the glory of the Divine name, the increase of religion and piety, and the advantage of our whole Kingdom—promoted by them at that time, with great diligence, and that they are daily contriving to do (or confer) still greater benefits: In the completion of which, and the prosecution of other affairs of still greater importance to our Majesty, by the payment of large sums of money, the Common Good and Revenues of the City are being expended, and the patrimonies of private citizens are being diminished and their means impaired: And WE, being neither in anywise like our predecessors, nor even inferior to them in our munificence or liberality, and the exhibition of our gratitude towards all our subjects, who by their industry, virtues, and magnanimity, can at all deserve well of us, HAVE RESOLVED TO LEAVE to this our city and its citizens,—for their sincere love and fidelity toward us, and services and deeds most worthy of commendation—a perpetual monument to posterity, and a testimony of our royal gratitude and favour, which shall endure to generations yet unborn, not only by a ratification of their original immunities and privileges, confirming their infeftments in public lands, revenues, and royal gifts or grants, but also by the enlargement or augmentation of new, greater, and more worthy [rights and privileges] beyond and above the other cities and towns of our Kingdom. For these and very many other just causes and reasons, moving and impelling us, after our perfect age, and long after our foresaid revocations, of our own proper motion and certain knowledge, and with the advice and consent of the Lords of our Privy Council, as well as with the expressed advice, consent, and assent of our most trusty and well-beloved councillors, Sir George Home of Spott, knight, our treasurer; and Sir David Murray of Gosperdy, knight, our comptroller, and Master John Preston of Fentonbarns, our collector-general and treasurer of our new augmentations of the Church lands of this our Kingdom to the Crown, we have ratified, approved, and for us and our successors confirmed for ever.

The "Golden Charter" then goes on to relate the Charter granted by Mary Queen of Scots "our late dearest mother," in 1556; it then narrates the Charter of Confirmation granted by King James himself in 1582. The details of both of these Charters are all recapitulated. Reference is then made to the Charter of 1567, and to the various rights, privileges, and grants or gifts therein conveyed. It then goes on to convey, and in feu-farm heritably demit, and by this our present Charter confirm, to our foresaid well-beloved servants, the Provost, Bailies, Councillors, Burgesses, and Community of our said Burgh of Edinburgh, and their successors for ever, ALL and WHOLE the foresaid Burgh of Edinburgh, with walls, bulwarks, ditches, gates, ways, streets, causeways, lands, territories, and community of the same, mills, mill-lands, multures, dams, banks, haughs, parts and pertinents, creating and erecting the foresaid Burgh into a free Royal Burgh, with all the sundry liberties, privileges, immunities, and jurisdictions which by the laws and custom of our Kingdom have pertained, do pertain, or can justly belong to a free Royal Burgh. This privilege was granted "in and through all the bounds as far as the sheriffdom principal of Edinburgh extends, or may be extended, both in length and breadth." A special reference is made thus:—"From the brae commonly called 'Edge Buklingbray' on the east to the water called 'Almound Watter' on the west, and as far as the foresaid sheriffdom extends towards the south, and to 'the myd watter of Forth' to the north."

Special allusion is then made to the provostry and prebends of Trinity College and Hospital, with the annual revenues pertaining to the same, to the Archdeaconry of Lothian, with the parsonage and vicarage of Curry,—all which the Provost, Bailies, Dean of Guild, Treasurer, Councillors, and Community of our said Burgh of Edinburgh, and their successors in all time coming, are freely and peaceably to enjoy and possess for the purposes already stated.

One other quotation cannot fail at the present time to be referred to. It is as follows:—"And we, considering the said Provost, Bailies, Councillors and Community of our said Burgh, to be a Corporation and Community which in its own nature endures, having no particular successor, ... therefore we decern and ordain that the foresaid sasine once taken, by virtue of this our present new infeftment, by the Provost or by one of the Bailies of our said Burgh, in name of all the Burgesses and Community of the same and their successors, by delivery of earth and stone for the foresaid Burgh lands, mills, and other accessories and dependencies of the same, and by the delivery of a golden penny for the rents, duties, customs, and others their accessories and dependencies, and by the delivery of a baton for the offices and jurisdictions foresaid, and for the superiority of the foresaid town of Leith, and others their accessories and dependencies, and for the delivery of a psalm book for the foresaid benefices, churches, teinds, rents, and others the accessories and dependencies of the same, shall stand and be for ever sufficient without any renovation, retaking, or obtaining of a new sasine hereafter," etc., etc.

The payment which the Town Council was required to make to the Crown for all the privileges, rights, and revenues conferred upon them by "the Golden Charter" was fifty-two merks sterling, at the terms of Whitsunday and Martinmas, by equal portions in name of feu-farm.

CHAPTER VII.

ST GILES—SCIENNES—PAUL'S WORK, ETC.

IN addition to those which have been already alluded to and specially to the "Golden Charter," there are two additional deeds which were subsequently granted. These are, first, a Charter granted by King James the Sixth, under his Great Seal, confirming previous grants of the Kirk-livings, and of new granting the same to the Provost, Bailies, Council, and Community of the Burgh of Edinburgh. This Charter was granted at Beauvoir Castle, on the 7th day of August 1612. The other is a Charter granted by King Charles the First, under his Great Seal, to the foresaid authorities, and it is signed at Newmarket, on the 23d day of October 1636. There are also several Acts of Parliament bearing on the same subject. It may be expedient, therefore, to allude to these in their chronological order.

The first, as already stated, is by King James VI., and it was the last of the charters he granted to Edinburgh. It recapitulates the grant made by "our dearest mother Mary and others and most noble progenitors of worthy memory, by virtue of divers infeftments, mortifications, annexations, gifts, and dispositions," granted by them to the Town Council of Edinburgh on behalf of the Community, towards the increase of policy within the Burgh, the proper support of the clergy, and the masters, regents, and other professors of liberal sciences within the College of the said Burgh; as well as for the support and entertainment of the Hospital's poor, mutilated and indigent persons, and for orphans and infants destitute of parents. It then goes on to enumerate all those grants which had been previously made in favour of chaplainries, altarages, and prebends, in any church, chapel, or college within the liberty of our said Burgh of Edinburgh, along with the emoluments and duties, which formerly belonged to and were uplifted by the Friars Dominican, Preachers, and Minorites or Franciscans of our said Burgh; together with all the proceeds which were annually given to, and collected ("given and doted") on behalf of "whatsoever chaplainries, altarages, churches, burials or anniversaries, wheresoever the same lie within our Kingdom of Scotland." It next narrated the benefice of the provostry of the Trinity College, situated near the Burgh, with all and sundry churches, teind sheaves, and other teinds, etc., with the rights of patronage of prebendaries, and chaplainries, and presentations of poor orators, in Scots called beidmen or bedlyaris, and other officers of Trinity College, belonging to, and incumbents of the same. It then referred to the parish churches of Soltray and Lempitlaw, and other churches and teinds annexed thereto, which had been given over to the provostry, together with the orchard and yard called "Dingwall Castle." This was, as has been already noticed, part of the Old Trinity Hospital ground. All these revenues, as have been specified, were anew granted to the civic authorities of Edinburgh, for the purposes already stated.

The Charter then proceeded to state, that "we had formerly annexed to the College of our said Burgh, the acres of land, place and tenements of the Church of the Fields, or Kirk of Field, situated within the liberty of our said Burgh," together with the parsonage and vicarage of the Church of Currie, and all the teinds, Church lands, pertinents, and privileges of the same, for the support of the masters, regents, and other professors serving the cure within the said College, to be intromitted with, uplifted, used, and disponed upon by the said Corporation of Edinburgh, as acting on behalf of the Community; and the same were ordained to be granted for the use of the said masters, regents, and other professors specified.

Provision is then made, with the advice of the Estates of our Kingdom of Scotland, which was convened in the Parliament held at Edinburgh, on the 5th day of June 1592, that all the "donations and mortifications made by our late dearest mother, of the lands, benefices, and rents founded and mortified for the sustentation of the ministers of the Burgh, and for the Hospitals, should be ratified, and of new annexed to the Community of the said Burgh, and their successors," as well as all lands and annual rents lying [outwith the freedom] of the said Burgh, annexed to any benefice, prebend, or religious place situated within the freedom of the said Burgh, with all "profits, emoluments, feu-fermes, maills, and duties thereof." The Provost, Bailies, Councillors, and Community of the Town were further surrogated in the full possession, right, and title of all the lands and their emoluments within the Burgh which had previously pertained to any bishop, abbot, commendator, prior, or other ecclesiastical superior within Scotland. A new infeftment was directed to be expede thereupon for security, if such a course should be deemed advisable.

The Church of Dumbarnie is then dealt with, along with the

churches of Potic and Moncrieff, lying within the Sheriffdom of Perth, as well as the vicarage of Currie, formerly referred to, together with all the buildings and yards of Trinity College, with the rights, possessions and revenues of the same which are duly handed over to the Town Council, as acting for the Community of Edinburgh, to be devoted in all time coming to the sustentation of their said ministry and hospital. Power was given to them to possess full right of property and superiority of the "said lands, annual rents and revenues, tenants, tendandries, and service of free tenants of the same, as had the bishops, abbots, priors, friars, monks, sisters, nuns, chaplains, and prebendaries to whom the said lands and annual rents formerly belonged, notwithstanding any Act or Constitution preceding the said Act of our Parliament, as in the same is more fully contained."

The Charter goes on to relate, that His Majesty being of lawful and perfect age, and having the advice and consent of the Lords of Privy Council, hereby ratifies, approves, and confirms all that had been done previously by himself, and by "our said late dearest mother, and others our most noble progenitors," in favour of the said Provost, Bailies, and Councillors of our said Burgh of Edinburgh, the College, Schools, and Hospitals of the same, for the entertainment of the ministry "serving the cure at the churches of the said Burgh," of the masters, regents, and other professors serving the cure within the foresaid College and Schools of poor scholars and other poor, aged, decrepit, indigent persons, orphans and infants destitute of parents within the said Burgh.

The Charter refers in detail to all that has been conveyed to the Town Council, which it is unnecessary here to repeat.

His Majesty then goes on to add to his gifts "All and whole the provostry of the church of St Giles, situated within our said Burgh, with all and sundry churches, prebends, and chaplainries belonging and pertaining thereto. There is likewise included all and whole the nuns' place of Scheynis, commonly called the Nunrie (Nunnery) of the Scheynis* (Sciennes, as it is now called,) lying within the freedom and territory of our said Burgh, with the place and yards of the same, and all the lands, houses, buildings, churches, chaplainries, prebends, teind sheaves, and other teinds, fruits, rents, emoluments, casualties, rights, profits, tenants, tenandries and service of free tenants, and their just pertinents whatsoever, pertaining and belonging to the same, wherever the same are or lie within our said Kingdom of Scotland.

There is also conveyed by the same deed to the Town Council, "All and whole the Hospital of the Work of St Paul, commonly called Sanct Paullis Work, lying at the foot of the vennel called Leyth Wynd," near our said Burgh of Edinburgh on the east side of

* About the year 1512, some pious ladies and others were engaged in founding a new Convent in Edinburgh, of the order of Dominican Nuns, under the invocation of St Katharine of Sienna. When the buildings were nearly completed, they applied for the sanction of the Holy See; and a copy of the Bull which Pope Leo X. sent them is understood to be preserved to the present day. It is styled "The Bull of Erection of the Convent of Sisters of St Katharine, of Senis, near Edinburgh." The Ladye Seytoun whose name occurs in the Bull, was a daughter of Patrick, first Earl of Bothwell. Her maiden name was Ladye Jane Hepburn. She was married to George, third Earl of Seytoun, and became the mother of three sons and a daughter. Her husband was killed at the battle of Flodden, and he was "earthed (buried) in the queir of Seytoun church (near Tranent, in East Lothian) beside his father." The Chronicle of Seytoun says,—After whose decease his lady remained a widow for forty-five years. She was a noble, wise, and generous widow. "Sche gydit (guided) her sonnis leving quhill he was cumit of age." She thereafter resided in the place of "Senis," on the Borough-muir, beside Edinburgh, during the remainder of her lifetime. "Quhilk place sche helpit to fund and big as maist principale. Sche did mony gude actis."

She lived to a good old age. She died in 1558, in the Convent of the Sciennes, and was buried in the choir of Seytoun beside her husband. She also devoted her means, according to her death-bed settlement, many sums of money to her friends, as well as to "religious places and Kirks."—*History or Chronicle of the House of Seytoun*, pages 37-41.

the same vennel. The Hospital of St Paul stood almost immediately opposite to the Trinity Hospital, on the south-east side of the road.

This charity foundation seems to have been given to the Town Council, by a Charter granted by Thomas Spence, Bishop of Aberdeen. The Hospital was dedicated to the Virgin Mary, and was called "The Hospital of our Lady in Leith Wynd." It was founded by consent of William, Archbishop of St Andrews, whose name was 'William Schevez,' who came to that See in the year 1478; and Bishop Spence, the founder, dying in the year 1482, it must therefore have been founded in 1479. The object of the benefaction was to entertain twelve poor men, or beidmen. It has been thought requisite to refer specially to Paul's Work,* as the funds are now

* The regulations made by the Town Council in 1582, in respect of the Master of Paul's Work (Council Register, Vol. VI. folio 190), were to the following effect:—

1. It is requisite that (the Master) in his outward Life and Manners, that he be of an gud Name, and honest Conversation, grave and digest in his Behaviour, not given to ony common or notabill Vice as ane Blasphemer of Goddis Name, and Swerer of execrable Aithes, ane Drunkard, Dyssyer, Cairter, contentious, or leading ane vagebund or idle life, but exerceing himself in sum honest Industrie.

2. That he can perfectlie reid and wryte, that he be of indifferent Knowledge, Witt, and Judgement, to behave himself circumspectlie, and in favour of all gud Men; diligent and expert to govern his Brethren, according to the Rewles given to them, and be cairfull thairinto.

3. In Religioun, that he be ane opin and zelous Professour of the trew Religioun, at present publicklie preichit within this Realme, and dilligentlie Keiper of the Preicheing and Prayers, habill and qualifiet to instruct his Brethren in the principal Grounds of Religioun, and na less cairfull to do the same, instructing and examining thame thairunto.

4. That he convene with his Brethren ilk day, at ten Houris before None, and thrie Houris after None, in the New Hospitale, in the Trinitie College, where he sall baith distinctlie and devoutlie reid to thame, and the Puir of the said Hospital, the Common Prayers; to be conversant togidder ane Hour or mair, in serving God, and praying for Increase of the Evangill, the Prosperitie of the King's Grace and haill Realme, and for the common Weill of this Town thair Patronis.

annually merged in Trinity Hospital, and as its revenues were at one time demanded to be handed over to the City Parochial Board, to which a future reference will be made.

It was originally endowed to the extent of £119, 15s. per annum, Scots money. But by the benefactions of other friends, chiefly through the influence and exertions of the Members of the Corporation, this was in 1573 increased to £137, 19s. 7d. of the same money. In 1582, the Lord Provost, Magistrates, and Councillors appointed a Master for the Paul's Work Hospital, and they at the

---

5. That he gif Attendance, that nane of his Brethren be absent from the said Prayers and execute upon theme (that are) the Paines conteith in the Rewles gevin to them, that he sie they keip lykwayes the Prayers and Preiching in the Town.

6. Anent the comon Rent of the said Hospitale, that he dilligentlie and cairfullie collect and in-bring the same upon his own Expensis, and distribute it faithfullie amongis his Brether, conforme to the principall Foundatioun, and sall mak Compt. thereof zeirlie, at the making of the Townis Comptis to the gud Town, their Patron.

7. That he do all Things appointit to him in the principall Foundatioun, according to the Mynd of the Foundator, and haif ane Copie in *Scottes*, gif he understand not the *Latin*, nor astricting him alwayes, nor his Brether, to ony thing contenit thairin, repugnant to the trew Religioun; nor zit astricting thame to that, quhilk, in respect to the present Estaite of the said Hospitale, is not possible to be keipit, quhil it be aither repairit, the Rent augmentit, or sic uther gud Order tane thairwith.

8. That he mention and reid to his Brether now present, and to everie ane that sall be admittet hereafter, at the Tyme of ressaving the Rewles in the said Foundatioun, togidder with thir present Articles and Laws gevin, alsweill to him as thame, that thay pretend na Excuse of Ignorance.

9. That he find sufficient responsall Suretie to the Patrons for doing his Office in the observing of the said Foundatioun and their present Rewles, and to be answerable for his Intromission with the comon Rent of the said Hospitale.

Fynallie, that he sall underly all further Order that shall be injoinit to him be his said Patrones or be the Kirk of this Burgh with their Avise.

Gif he failzie in ony Pointis heir mentionate or be found in Neglect and cairless of his Dewtie, or zit obstinate, wilfull, or disobedient, he sall be depryvit for ever fra the said office, and otherwayes punisit at the Discratioun of the said Patrones.

same time drew up a series of Orders which had to be observed by the Master, as well as by the Brethren and Beidmen.*

The Town Council of Edinburgh, in 1619, having taken into their most serious consideration, that the extension of woollen manufactures would not only be of great advantage to the nation at large, but to the City of Edinburgh in particular, by the employment of a system of government which it was likely to give to many poor persons; for this benevolent purpose, they entered into correspondence with a Mr William Dickson, of the City of Delft, in the province of Holland, to come to Edinburgh, for the express object of conferring with them regarding their proposed measures. Dickson duly arrived; and the Town Council of the day having, to their minds, sufficiently attested his work, entered into a contract with him to instruct the people in manufacturing woollen stuffs, such as grograms, says, bays, etc. Dickson was to engage and bring over from Delft four men who were expert in the art, with the necessary instruments or

* *Anent the Beidmen and Brether of the said Hospitale.*—Council Records, 1582, Vol. VI. folio 191.

1. In thair outword Lyfe and Manners, that thay be not defilit with Blame of any notable Vice, bot of gud Fame and Conversatioun, na Blasphemer or Swerer, Drunkard, Cairter, Dysser, Theffes, or Pykers, contentious, idill, or vagabund Persones, na oppin nor sturdie Beggars, bot exerceing thamselves in sum honest and lawfull Trade or Schift, gif Seikness, Aige, or Impotence may suffer thame.

2. That thay be obedient to their Maister, sua that he haif na Caus to complene; for the Persons, obstinate, willfull and disobedient, sall be extremelie punisit and depryvit.

3. In Religioun that they be na Papistes, bot of the trew Religioun, knawand the chief Groundes thairof, specially the Lordis Prayer, Belief, and Commandis, Keip the Preiching and Prayeris, and Examinatioun in the Town, and be cirnest and willing to seik God, and to leirne when they are ignorant.

4. That thay convene to the Prayeris with thair Maister ilk day in the new Hospitale, at nine Houris before None, and thrie Houris after None, ther to remayne in calling upon God for Incres of the Religioun, Prosperitie of the Town and Realme, and for the common Weill of the Town thair Patronis; and utherwayes serving God zealouslie an devoutlie an Hour or mair.

tools of manufacture, and to take and instruct such poor boys or girls as the Town Council should think proper. The terms were adjusted, and the work proceeded. An appeal was made to the public to help forward the work, especially as considerable buildings required to be erected. David Trotter and David Makcall, both merchants in Edinburgh, contributed one thousand merks each; David Jenkin gave five hundred merks for the same object. The former, on account of their liberality, obtained the right to present two boys to the Work, while the latter presented one.

Maitland remarks (page 471), "At what time, or on what occasion the name of the aforesaid Hospital was changed from that of *Our Lady* to that of *Paul's Work*, I cannot learn*; however, by converting the said Hospital into a Work house, though with a charitable view, cannot be justified; for by defeating the founder's intentions

5. The Persounes absent without Licence, and haill in Bodie, sall tyne ilk Tyme Twa Penies of his Leving, to be distribute among the Persounes present; and gif he continues in long Absence, sall be punisit as ane Contemner, and be depryvit for ever.

6. Anent thair Rent (allowance) thoch it be small, zit thay sall not drink, waist, nor dilapidate the same at anes, bot bestowe if faythfullie to their necessarie Sustentatioun; an Pairt in Meit and Drink, ane either in claithing, and quha sall be honest, and best Stewart theirof, sall haif his Portioun helpit best, as the comon Rent thairof may spair, or with sic Casualtie as the Patrounes of the Kirk sall bestowe upon thame.

7. That thay do all Things concerning thame as is contenit in the principall Foundatioun, according to the Mynde of the Foundator, sua far as is possible to be done, and as repugns not to the trew Religioun.

8. That thay sall, underly ony forther Order that sall be gevin thame be the said Patrounes, or be the Kirk with thair Avyse; and gif ony failzie or contravene ony Point of thir Premises, he sall be depryvit and punist at the Will of the Patrounes according to the Weight of his Fault.—*Maitland*, 1753, pp. 468-9.

* Arnot, who wrote at a later date (about 1780) says, that the Town Council, A.D. 1619, converted this hospital into a workhouse, bestowing upon it the name of *Paul's Work*, which it still retains.

and preventing the Constitution of this Hospital, men inclined to this kind of charity will be greatly discouraged and prevented from bestowing their money in that way, considering the little regard shown to the laudable foundation of Bishop Spence, by spurning at his will, and as it were despising his benefaction."

No doubt the Town Council of the day were actuated by a desire to make what they thought to be a better and more profitable use of the benefaction, in the much altered circumstances of the times. But the new project did not turn out a success. It had to be abandoned. The premises afterwards became, and for many years were continued, as the printing-house of the Messrs Ballantyne, from whose presses the Waverley Novels of Sir Walter Scott, Bart., were produced, at the time when the author was called "The Great Unknown." Paul's Work buildings have ceased to exist, the North British Railway having acquired the grounds. The revenues of Paul's Work now go to Trinity Hospital Fund—therefore it may now be written, "All's well that ends well."

The revenues, as we have already seen, belonging to the Paul's Work foundation, as well as those belonging to the Church of the Kirk of Field, with the Archdeaconry of Lothian and Church of Currie were likewise conveyed to the Town Council, to be intromitted with, uplifted, used and disponed as the members of the Corporation saw fit for the purposes foresaid.

It was likewise provided by the said Charter, that all the foresaid properties, lands, emoluments, revenues, etc., as these were most fully detailed, should be called now, and in all time coming, "OUR FOUNDATION OF THE MINISTRY AND HOSPITALITY OF EDINBURGH;" and we will and grant, and for us and our noble successors ordain, that the Sasine, now once taken by the Provost and Bailies, or any of them, at the Tolbooth of the Burgh, shall stand and be sufficient Sasine for ever in all time coming, for all those properties, rights and possessions already so fully enumerated; and we ordain them "TO HAVE AND TO HOLD all and sundry the foresaids," etc., which formerly belonged to the said Friars, Dominican Preachers, and Minorites or Franciscans of the said Burgh of Edinburgh.

The details of this Grant are so abundant, and so specifically detailed that it seems desirable that these should be fully given. They include "all the lands, tenements, annual rents, houses, buildings, yards, teind scheaves and other teinds, fruits, rents, profits, provents, emoluments, rights, casualties and duties, tenants, tenandries, services of free tenants, and just pertinents whatsoever . . . by all their just ancient marches and divisions, as they lie in length and breadth, in houses, buildings, woods, plains, moors, marshes, ways, paths, waters, ponds, streams, meadows, pastures and pasturages, mills, multures and their sequels, hawkings, huntings, fishings, peats, turfs, coals, coal pits, rabbits, warrens, doves, dove cots, forges, malt kilns, breweries, and heaths, woods, groves, thickets, wood, timber, stone quarries, stone and lime, with courts and their issues, herezelds, bludewites, marchets of women, with free ish and entry, and with all and sundry other liberties, commodities, profits, and easements, and their just pertinents whatsoever, as well named as not named, as well below the earth as above the earth, far or near, belonging or could justly belong in any manner of way in future, to our foresaid foundation and others the premises, with the pertinents, freely, quietly, fully, wholly, honourably, well and in peace, without any revocation, contradiction, or obstacle whatsoever."

All these properties, rights, and privileges are granted to the Town Council on behalf of the Community, that they and their successors shall offer devout and humble daily prayers to God Almighty for the preservation of us and our successors, and that they shall maintain the poor of the said Hospital, support the ministers, masters, and regents of the College and Schools, and their successors, and for "sustaining of the ministers serving the cure at the said churches respectively, and their successors, or paying for their sustentation the third part of the fruits and duties of the churches and benefices above mentioned, at the option of the said Provost, Bailies, Councillors, and Community, and their successors only."

The Charter was duly witnessed and attested by the Marquis of Hamilton, the Earls of Arran, Marshall, and Dunfermline, and other important personages of the period, and "our Great Seal" was affixed to the same.

CHAPTER VIII.

CHARTER OF NOVODAMUS BY CHARLES I.

THE last Royal Charter to the Provost, Bailies, Councillors, and Community of the City of Edinburgh, was in reality a Charter of Novodamus, with certain changes, and it was granted by King Charles I., the son and successor of King James VI. It is dated at Newmarket, on the 23d day of October 1636,—the twelfth year of His Majesty's reign.

It goes on to relate that, calling to mind and perfectly understanding the many good, notable, and thankful services rendered and performed by the Corporation and inhabitants of Edinburgh, which is the principal and capital City and Burgh of our ancient Kingdom of Scotland, not only to us from the time of our happy succession to the Kingdom, but also " to our dearest father of eternal memory," and to others, our most noble progenitors, Kings of Scotland, of which particular and notable expressions are contained in ancient infeftments granted to them by our predecessors of eternal memory. These remain to posterity as memorials of their fidelity, and of the great and remarkable services rendered and performed by them to the advantage and honour of the realm: Considering, also, that a certain question has been instituted in our said City of Edinburgh regarding the effect and the extent of a new infeftment, which was granted to them by King James VI. on March 15, 1603,—and that all difficulty should be averted as to the same, which might tend to the detriment of the common weal and the Kingdom in general, they voluntarily, and of their own free will, appeared in presence of the Lords of our Privy Council, on the 28th day of January 1630. At a meeting there was produced, in presence of the Corporation, as representing the Community of Edinburgh, a certain Act made by the Provost, Bailies, and Councillors, under the subscription of their common clerk, dated the said 28th day of January aforesaid, by virtue of which Act, they ratified the offer made by Sir John Hay, clerk of our register, concerning the restriction of the office of Sheriff and Coroner, contained in the said infeftment, granted in the year of our Lord 1603 as aforesaid, with jurisdiction of the same: As also, the holding of their Gild Courts, according to the bounds as after set forth, contained in an offer by our said City, to the nobles and gentry of West Lothian, which comprehends the lands following, viz.:—" Our burgh of Edinburgh, its common mills, common muir, common marsh or myre; our loch, walls and fosses of the same; the towns of Leith and Newhaven; our ports, stations of ships, bulwarks, piers, schoires, raides, links eister and wester of the same; the lands commonly called the commoun clossetts, burssis, hoilf hallis, and other lands properly belonging to our said Burgh, ways, paths, streets, places, and passages leading to our said Burgh, and from the same to Leith and Newhaven, or from the same respectively, through their common muir and marsh, and which have been either constructed or repaired by them, in so far as the said muir and march extend, with the ways and places leading to their common mills upon the Water of Leith, and from the same in so far as the said mills, with the mill lands which do properly belong to our said Burgh, do there extend." The Charter then goes on to relate, that as respects the renunciation on the part of the Crown of all rights of regality which were granted to them or their predecessors—if such ever did exist—with all other rights of escheats of criminals condemned before the Magistrates to death; as well as the escheats of those inhabitants of the Burgh as are put to the horn for civil causes, with all extraordinary liberties, if such exist and are contained in the foresaid infeftment, which have not hitherto been regarded as not competent, as not having been granted to sheriffs, coroners, or free burghs. It also provided that, in respect of the renunciation of all right which the Community had or did exercise, in regard to the south or north banks of our Castle of Edinburgh, without prejudice to anyone establishing before a competent Court of Law a higher and more legal claim, all and any right which the citizens or burgesses have to these banks beyond the memory of man. As also, that the said document contains a humble petition that the Crown would ratify the said Charter, and all the old infeftments therein contained, with free liberty, and the sole and exclusive trade within the bounds of West Lothian which pertained to a free royal Burgh, together with the said offices of Sheriff and Coroner within the bounds of our said Burgh of Edinburgh, the said towns of Leith and Newhaven, and others before and after referred to; together with all customs, petty customs, etc., of the said Burgh, as well as all liberties, and other privileges as these were contained in the said infeftment, according to the tenor thereof.

The said Charter goes on to state that, as the Town Council and Magistrates had made and subscribed a full renunciation and resignation of the premises in our favour, and that of our successors,

WE, out of our gracious respect and favour towards the City of Edinburgh, and as an incitement to them to continue in their good service to us and our successors, have been pleased to accept the said renunciation, and to ratify their said infeftments, with all liberties and privileges therein contained; THEREFORE, after our lawful and perfect age of twenty-five years complete, and after all our revocations, with the advice and consent of our beloved cousin and councillor, John, Earl of Traquair, Lord Lintoun and Caverstoun, etc., our High Treasurer, our comptroller and collector of our new augmentations of our Kingdom of Scotland, together with the advice and consent of the rest of the lords of our Exchequer of our said Kingdom of Scotland, our commissioners, have ratified, approved and confirmed,—as we now do, for ourselves and our successors for ever confirm, in favour of the Provost, Bailies, Councillors, and Community of our said City of Edinburgh, and their successors, the particular and several charters and infeftments, gifts and others underwritten. Reference is then specifically made to the following—viz. :—

1. A Charter made and granted by the former King Robert Bruce, King of Scotland.

2. A Charter made and granted by our said late dearest grandmother of the lands which belonged to the Friars Dominican and Franciscan, commonly called the Blackfriars and Grayfriars, with all the rights and privileges thereto pertaining, and which was dated on the 13th March 1566.

3. A Charter granted by our dearest father, under his great seal, dated at Stirling, on the 14th April 1582, by which he confirms the said former Charter, granted by his said late dearest mother regarding the foresaid lands, and by which he ratifies and approves the demission and renunciation made by John Gib, in favour of the Burgh of Edinburgh of his right to the provostry of the Kirk of Field, and the whole

houses, lands, etc.; and which were granted and disponed to the Corporation of the said Burgh, and their successors, with permission and liberty to erect a college, to construct and repair suitable houses for the reception of professors of humanity, letters and languages, philosophy, theology, medicine, laws, and all other liberal sciences; and to elect competent professors to teach the same.

4. A Charter made and granted by our said late dearest father, under his great seal, of date the 4th April 1584, by which, in consideration of the great charges and expenses incurred by the Corporation, in the erection of the said College and other requisite buildings, and for the support of the Rector and Regents, he conveyed to them All and Whole the archdeaconry of Lothian, with the parsonage of Currie, and all the globe lands, teinds, etc., pertaining to the same.

5. A Charter made and granted by our said dearest father, under his great seal, on the 26th May 1587, in which, in consideration of the great charges and expenses incurred by the Corporation, on behalf of the Community, in the erection of an Hospital, in sustaining their Ministers, and College foresaid;—he gave, granted, and disponed to the Provost, Bailies, Councillors, and Community of the Burgh of Edinburgh, and their successors, All and Whole the provostry of Trinity College, with all the lands, churches, rights, rents, emoluments, etc., belonging thereto.

6. A Charter made and granted by our said late dearest father, under his great seal, dated 29th July 1587, ratifying the infeftments granted by the late Queen Mary, his mother, of the church lands of Trinity College, provostry of Kirk of Field, and archdeaconry of Lothian: As also, containing a new gift of the said church lands, provostry, Trinity College, and archdeaconry of Lothian, with all their lands and teinds, for the use of the ministers, college, and poor.

7. A Charter made and granted by our said late dearest father,

under his great seal, dated at Beauvoir Castle, the 7th August 1612, ratifying the said previous grants, and the purposes for which these were destined,—with a new gift of the whole of them for the foresaid uses; provided such ratification shall in no wise comprehend any right of regality, nor shall be extended to the heritable offices of Sheriff and Coroner, and jurisdiction of the same, nor to the holding of Courts of Gild, but only within the bounds of our said Burgh, ... and within the towns of Leith and Newhaven, etc. And said ratification shall in no wise infer impediment nor prejudice to us in our right and royal prerogative to erect burghs of regality, or burghs of barony, in any other part of West Lothian beyond the bounds of the said Sheriffship and Coronership, to which the same is restricted in manner foresaid. The Castle Banks, north and south, were also excluded from the Burgh's jurisdiction. Power was also given to the Corporation to have the right, title, and privilege of nominating and presenting of the ministers to serve within the cure of the Burgh of Edinburgh.

. . . .

The Charter then concludes:—"Therefore, for the many good services rendered to us in times past by our said City of Edinburgh, and for inciting them to continue in the same in all time to come, we, of our own knowledge and free will, with advice and consent foresaid, of new have given, granted, disponed, and by this our present Charter confirmed, and by the tenor of the same of new give, grant and dispone, and for us and our successors for ever confirm, to the foresaid Provost, Bailies, Councillors, and Community of our said City of Edinburgh and their successors, All and Whole, our said City of Edinburgh, walls, ditches, ports, streets, etc., ... and we have united, erected, and incorporated, and by the tenor of our present Charter, unite, erect, and incorporate the said whole lands, ports, havens, customs, bulwarks, and others foresaid to our said City of Edinburgh, and have erected the same into a royal city, with all the liberties, privileges, and immunities belonging to a City or Burgh of Regality . . . . Paying therefor, yearly, the said Provost, Bailies, Councillors and Community of our said Burgh of Edinburgh, and their successors, to us and our successors, for our said City of Edinburgh, port and havens of Leith and Newhaven, with the whole privileges, liberties, jurisdictions, offices, and others above specified, annexed to our said City, the sum of fifty-two merks money of Sterling, as for the ancient burgh maill contained in the said infeftment of the said Burgh, granted to the said City by King Robert Bruce, at two terms of the year, to wit, Whitsunday and Martinmas in winter, by equal portions; and also the administration of justice in the said offices of Sheriff and Coroner and Justice of the Peace, with the services of burgh used and wont; and for the said ten acres of the lands of Hierigs (High Rigs); and for the said presentation and nomination of ministers to serve the cure within all the churches built or to be built in our said City, united and annexed to the same, as said is, two pennies in name of blanch farm, if asked only."

The Charter is duly sealed and witnessed, by the Archbishop of St Andrews, the Marquis of Hamilton, the Earl of Arran and Cambridge, Lord Aven and Innerdaill, the Earl of Haddington, Lord Binning and Byres (Keeper of our privy seal), the Earl of Stirling, the Viscount of Canada, Lord Tulliebodie (our secretary); together with our familiar councillors, Sir John Hay of Barro, clerk of our rolls, register and council; Sir John Hamilton, of Orbieston, our justice-clerk; and Sir John Scott, of Scottistarvet, director of our chancery—Knights.

There are several Acts of Parliament and other documents, which bear on the Trinity College and Trinity Hospital which it seems proper to refer to. These are:—

1. Act in fauoris of the Hospitall of Edinburgh. [1579, c. 51.]

2. Act regarding the Annexatioun of the temporalities of benefices to the Crown. [1587, c. 8.]

3. Act regarding the Kingis Maiesties general Revocatiouns. [1587, c. 14.]

4. Act regarding the Revocatioun of the landis and annuellis mortifiet to the Ministerie and Hospitall of Edinburgh. [1592, c. 82.]

5. Act regarding the Confirmatioun to the Burgh of Edinburgh of thair annuillis. [1593, c. 41.]

6. Act in fauoris of the Burgh of Edinburgh. [1606, c. 31.]

7. Warrant for an Act of Parliament superscribed by King James the Sixth, ratifying all previous Grants of Kirk Livings to the Burgh of Edinburgh. [22. October, 1612.]

8. Act regarding Ratificatioun of diuers infeftmentis grantit to the toun of Edinburgh, for sustentatioun of College, Ministeris, and Hospitallis. [1621, c. 79.]

9. Act regarding Ratification of His Majesties new Charter of Confirmation in favors of the Burgh of Edinburgh. [1661, c. 123.]

While these various documents are brought under notice, in passing, it does not seem requisite here to make any quotations from them, as their provisions are in accordance with those of the various Royal Charters which have been already somewhat fully set forth in these pages.

CHAPTER IX.

TOWN COUNCIL CONTROL.

THE Royal Charters are now done. The charter-chest has been closed. The olden days have passed away, and a new era has begun to dawn upon the Hospital. The Town Council is in undisputed possession. Provosts, prebendaries or priests, choiristers or clerks, as well as beidmen who formerly held the sway, notwithstanding of their professed attachment to the faith and tenets of the new or Protestant religion—all of them have to disappear under the new control. The last of these beneficiaries —the *ultimi Romanorum*—to leave the Hospital were of course the beidmen. When the Magistrates and Town Council got possession of the premises, there were thirteen beidmen on the benefaction, and provision was made for twelve more.

The Town Council began a new and separate building in 1567. But it does not appear to have been completed until 1578, when it is recorded that for the beginning of order in the Hospital in the Trinity College of this burgh the Council resolved, after having taken the advice of the ministers, to furnish twelve beds, and that there should be put therein twelve aged persons, who were infirm and unable to work, and that those so admitted should be sustained by donations put into the charity box of the said Hospital.*

Again in the Minutes of 28th April and 15th October 1568, it would appear that ten years earlier there were not only beidmen in the house, but also *hospitallers*. There were practically, therefore, two sets of beneficiaries. In all probability, the hospitallers were sick poor, who were resident for a time; whereas the beidmen had a *locus standi* under the old constitution, and could not well be deprived of their privileges, without their being reckoned with.

As tending to favour this view, it may be mentioned, that in the Town Council Minutes of the period, there is an entry to the following effect:—As to "translating of ye auld hospitall up to ye new hospitall," only one beidman has been traced as having been transferred. On the 10th day of December 1595, he is said to have "demittet and renounceit his plaice of beidmanschip in the awld hospitall in favouris of ye toun," and he was given "a plaice in ye toun's new hospitall amang yair awin puir." Prior to this it is

* The terms of the minute are to the following effect:—

21. *June* 1578.—(The provost, bailies, and council), efter avysement with the ministeris and kirk (Session) for begyning of ordour in the Hospitall in the Trinatie College of this burgh, they have concludit that thair salbe preparit and maid rady ane dosoun of furneist beds for the pure, and that thair salbe placit thairintill dosoun aigit pepill seiklie and vnabill to laubour for thair leving, quhilkis pepill salbe sustenit vpoun the commoun box in the said hospitall in all necessaries sa lang as thay are seiklie quhill farther ordour be taikin, and gif ony of thame convalescis or becumis haill, thay to be removit and vtheris sic personis callit bedrelis input in thair place at the discretioun of the provest, baillies and counsall, with avyse of the ministeris, quha sall present the saidis bedrelis to thame that salbe placit be the maisteris of the hospitall for the tyme, &c. Followis the names of the bedrellis enterit this day:—Walter Broun and his wyfe; Dauid Forester, blind man; Margaret Carnyis, in Sclateris Clois; Issobell Biset, in Vtterburnis Clois; Jhonne Brome, his wyfe, Cristiane Smyth; Nyniane Aitkene, and Jhonne Thomeson.

recorded on 1st August 1593, that four beidmen renounced their right of beidmanship in consideration of being granted yearly a pension of £16 each. On the 22d March 1593, another beidman is previously reported to have vacated his place on similar terms. The other beidmen gradually died out. No one of the same description was appointed in their place. Before 1600, all the old beidmen of pre-Reformation times, as well as those under the last Provost (Pont), had disappeared from the Hospital.

The Provost was not easily got rid of. He had to be settled with, and it was a very difficult matter to bring him to terms. The following extracts from the Town Council's Minutes of the day, will make this sufficiently plain.

"4. *February* 1579.—The provest, baillies, and counsell ordanis Johne Johnestoun and maister Johne Prestoun, with awyse of maister James Lowsoun, minister, to entir in ressonying with maister Robert Pount, provest of the Trinitie College, in the materis betuix the towne and him concernyng the hospitall thair, and to repoirt thair ansuir the nixt counsall day.

"25. *February* 1579.—The prouest, bailleis, and counsell ordanis Alexander Clerk, Williame Litle, and Johne Johnestoun to convene vpone Setterday eftirnone nixt with maister Robert Pont, and entir in forther ressonyng with him tuiching the erectioun and fundatioun of the uniuerseteis in the Trinitie College, and repoirt thair ansuer the nixt counsall day."

The matter then seems to have gone asleep for several years, until the following Minute was passed :—

"27. *November* 1584.—Gevis commissioun to Henrie Nesbet, bailyie, William Fairlie, Alexander Owsteane, to confer and intreatt of new with maister Robert Pont for his rycht of the Provestrie of the Trinitie College, and to sie quhow resonablie thai can agrie with him for ane yeirlie dewtie to be payet to him be the guid toun to thair thesaureris, swa suir as he can devyse, and to report agane Wednisday.

"17. *March* 1585.—Ordanis Thomas Aikinhead and Alexander Owsteane to pas, intreatt and confer with maister Robert Pont anent the title of his benefice of the

Trinitie College and dismissioun thairof in favouris of the toun, and to report his ansuer thairupoun.

"25. *March* 1585.—The baillies [council and deacons of crafts] vpon the declaratioun of the persouns quha wes direct to confer with maister Robert Pont, anent his rycht of the Provestrie of the Trinitie College, fynds it maist expedient to appoynt and agrie with him for dismissioun thairof in the townis favouris, and thairfore gevis full commissioun and power to Henry Nesbet, William Littill, and Alexander Owsteane to pas and mak ane fynall end and agriement with him thairaneut."

The deputation appears to have settled the matter with Pont, as his Contract (page 53), as has already been seen, was dated on 26th April 1585—being about five weeks thereafter. The Report of the deputation is contained in the following Minute :—

"16. *June* 1585.—The foresaids, bailyes, dene of gild and [council] in consideratioun that it wes agreit to mak ane fynall appoyntment with maister Robert Pont, twicheing his rycht of the prouestrie of the Trinitie College, according to ane act maid the xxv day of Marche last, and be the report of the persouns appoyntet to mak the said agrement that it is fynallie endet be word with him, to the setting doun of the sam in writt, and that thair suld be payet to him the sowme iij^{c} merk at the ending of the contract, and yeirlie induring his lyfetyme the sowme of [*blank*]; quhilk at lenth will be ane mater verray proffitabill to the town and helpfull to the College, and yit hes been neglectit sen the said day; thairfor fynds it most expedient that the sam be endit in writt within a xv dayes; and gevis commissioun to William Fairlie, Dauid Williamsoun, and George Smyth to caus forme the contract, and ordanis James Ros, thesaurer, to avance and deburse the said sowm of iij^{c} merk to the said maister Robert, at the ending of the said contract, quhilk sall be allowet in his compts; and ordanis the deykins to be wairnit agane Setterday after the prayers to heir the said contract, and gif thair consent thairto, and for taking ordour to send the sam to the said maister Robert, and to gett ane gift of the Provestrie subscryuit be the King's Grace."

An agreement having been come to between the parties, the next step was the passing of the following Minute of the Town Council :—

"28. *July* 1585.—Ordanis William Fairly to caus send to Henry Nesbet, bailyie, to Saynctandrois the procuratioun for dismissioun of the Provestrie of the Trinitie College, in favouris of the guid town, that the said Henry may gett the rychtis thairof past and owtred; and ordanis James Ros, thesaurer, to pay to the said maister Robert Pont the sowme of thrie hundredth merkis promittet to him for the said dismissioun, according to the contract maid betuix him and the guid towne."

The annual allowance to Pont having now been adjusted, it was desirable that all properties or titles or documents which he possessed should be handed over to the Corporation. Two Minutes of the Town Council of the period seem specially to refer to this matter. The first of these is as follows :—

"25. *March* 1585.—For dyuers consideratiouns moving thame, renunceis the instance of the actioun and precept persewet be thame and thair procuratour fiscall aganis the beidmen of the Trinitie College, for productioun before thame as superioures of the town of Leyth of all infeftments and euidents that the saidis prebendares and beidmen hes of any lands within the town of Leyth, and passis fra the persute of the said actioun intentit be thame *pro loco et tempore;* and ar content that the commoun kist of the said College, and euidents contenit thairin sall remayne in custody and keping of maister Robert Pont, provest of the said College till forther ordour be tayne concerning the said mater be commouning betuix him and thame. And this continuatioun to indure for the space of ane yeir, quhil maters may be amicablie composit amangs thame but proces of law.

"9. *February* 1586.—Gevis commissioun to Andrew Sclater, Alexander Vddert, Jhonn Jhonestoun, Henry Chairters, maister Alexander Guthre, to pas, visy, and mak inventour of the euidents in the charter kist of the Trinitie College, quhilk is in the hands of maister Robert Pont, and to present the sam the nixt counsall day."

The charter kist in the possession of Pont was delivered up, and intimation of the same was duly made to the Town Council on the 16th day of February 1586. The terms of the Minute are to the following effect :—"Grantet and confest thame to haif resauet fra maister Robert Pont, sumtyme provest of the Trinity College, the commoun euidents of the said College and commoun kist thairof, according to ane inventour maid thairof and subscryuet be the said maister Robert [Pont] and Andrew Sclater, bailye, and thairfore exonerat and dischairget the said maister Robert Pont of the samyn; quhilk kist, euidents and inventour wes delyuerit to Jhone Jhonestoun, collectour, to be sichtit and orderet be him that forther ordour may be tayne thairwith agayne this day aucht dayes."

The Provost was not the only official the Magistrates and Town Council had to reckon with. The prebendaries had claims and the beidmen had also to be bought up. All this was no doubt a question of time. The following Minute of Council may serve somewhat to illustrate this :—

"28. *November* 1582.—Appoyntit and agreit with maister Jhonn Manderstoun, ane of the prebendares of the Trinity College, anent his title and richt to ane yaird in the said College as followes, to witt: In respect the proffitt of the haill yairds cumis to the vse of the puir in the hospitale of the said College, thairfore ordanis the maisters of the said hospitall to pay to the said maister Jhonn the sowm of fourty schillings in full contentatioun of the haill byrun proffeitts quhilk the said maister Jhone may clame for his yaird; and the maisteris of the said hospitall present and to cum to pay to him yeirly and termely the sowm of fourty schillings induring his lyfetyme, begynnand the first termes payment at Whitsounday nixt; for the quhilk caus the said maister John renunces all rycht, title and kyndnes quhilk he hes or may pretend to haif to ony of the saidis yairds in tyme cuming, togidder with the byrun proffeits thairof.

After Pont's resignation, the Magistrates and Town Council appointed Henry Charteris, merchant, to act in the place of the Provost, to consult with the prebendaries in the management of the affairs of the College. In other words, to look after the revenues and disbursements, so long as they had a local habitation there. The words of the Minute are as follows :—

"22. *April* 1586.—Appoyntis and nominats Henry Chairteris, merchant, for thame and in thair names, as haveand the place of the provestrie of the Trinitie College be donatioun of our Soucrane Lord, to convene with the prebendares and chapter of the said College at thair ordinare conventiouns and all vther tymes neidfull, and thair to intreatt, vote, ressoun and concludo vpoun the commoun effaires of the samyn to be proponit in the said conventioun in and be all things as appertenis to the office of the provest of the said college; gevand vnto him thair full power and commissioun to that effect be thir presents, to indure ay and quhill the sam be expreslie revoket and discharget; provyding alwayes that in all materis that may concerne the said provest and bailyeis and counsall in thair rycht of the said provestric and patronage of the said Colledge that he mak thame be aduertist thairof before the sam be concludet in the said chapter and tak thair avyse thairvpoun."

Professor Norman Macpherson in his voluminous Report, an abstract of which appears in the Appendix to this volume, writes as follows (page 4 of the print lodged in the Court of Session):—"In the early days of the Hospital, there was an intimate relation between the Town Council and the Kirk, or the Session of the Kirk, from which, to a large extent, the funds for supporting the Hospital were at that time derived. There seemed to be in existence no separate minutes of the Kirk or Session; but the results of their deliberations with the Town Council are frequently recorded in the Minutes of the latter, and the Kirk Treasurer's accounts are instructive on the subject of the management of the general poor, as are also the city accounts kept by the Town Treasurer." Here the learned Professor seems to confound two things, viz.—the relation of the Kirk Treasurer to the poor, and the clergy's relation to Trinity Hospital. It is quite true that for generations, as can be proved, the Dean of Guild funds were dispensed by the Town Council to those in somewhat needy circumstances, and the Kirk Treasurer was frequently made the medium of these benefactions being bestowed. It is also true that there was an office of Session Clerk who until some ten years ago, or so, was regarded as Clerk of the Sessions of the Kirk, and claimed a monopoly of the fees in regard to the proclamation of bans over the whole area of the ancient and extended royalty. But when the learned Professor tries to make out that there was a Presbytery interest in the charity of Trinity Hospital, he makes an entire mistake. A reference to the first code of regulations will show that the two Ministers of the Trinity College Church of the period who were governors of the Hospital * were led therefore, with their elders and deacons, who were also the nominees of the Town Council at that period, to take a special interest in the Hospital, and to make recommendations, from time to time, as to masters and beidmen; and the following extracts are to be read in that light :—

The following are examples :—"Leet given in by the Kirk Session to the Council of the Good Town for the election of two masters for the Hospital,—annexed in minutes of appointments dated 21st October 1614." But long previous to that entry the same remark is applicable, *e.g.* :—On 10th January 1581, "the provest, baillies, and counsale, and . . . deykins of craftis, grantis, gevis, and disponis to Mr Gilbert Grott, noter, the place and beidmanship now vacant and in their hands, and beand at their dispositioun be deceis of . . . last possessour thereof, with proffeitts and casualties belonging thairto.' There is also a ratification of the same, which is as follows :—"7 February 1581,—With avyse of the ministers, elders, and deaconis of the Kirk, grants ane place, bed and room in the new hospitale, induring thair willis, to Mr Gilbert Grot, sumtyme writter."

While the Town Council was endeavouring to obtain the resignation of Provost Pont of Trinity College, they considered it to be their duty to select two masters to preside over the affairs of the Hospital. One of these was a merchant of the town, while the other was a craftsman or master tradesman. They also drew up a Code of Regulations for the

* *Vide* Footnote containing No. 1 of the Regulations for conducting the Trinity Hospital, in which out of the three leets of seven, constituting the twenty-one Governors, comprises "the Deacon-Convener, the two Ministers of the College Church for the time being, and the four tradesmen to be appointed by the Town Council."

government of the charity.* On the 14th day of February 1578, William Lytill and Jhonne Harwood were called upon to fulfil the duties until Michaelmas next, and they had to take an oath that they would be faithful "for diligent *cura* and laubouris to be taikin thairupoun bayth for the pure and caussis concerning the said hospitale to the said day."

The first persons on record who became inmates under the

* The following were the regulations for conducting the affairs of Trinity Hospital passed by the Governors, at an early date:—

1. The Hospital shall be governed by a Council of Governors, consisting of twenty-one persons, whereof the Lord Provost, the four Bailies, the Dean of Guild, and the Treasurer of the City of Edinburgh, during their continuance in office, shall be seven; the persons who sit in the Town Council in the character of Old Magistrates, during their continuance in the Town Council in that character, shall be seven more; and the Deacon Convener, the two Ministers of the College Church for the time being, and four Tradesmen to be chosen by the Town Council, shall be the other seven.

2. The Council of Governors mentioned in the foregoing statutes, whereof eleven are declared to be a quorum, shall meet four times in the year in the Hospital, *viz.*, on the third *Monday* of *October* second *Monday* of *January*, second *Monday* of *April*, and second *Monday* of *July*; and as often at other times as the Hospital shall require; and shall have power and authority to govern the Hospital; censure, punish, and extrude the persons entertained in it; to chuse, censure, and dismiss all officers and servants, as occasion requires; to direct its œconomy within and without doors; to act with the Treasurer; and, in general, to order all its affairs, determining and concluding by a majority of votes.

3. The persons to be admitted into, and maintained in the Hospital, shall be no other than old men or old women, burgess' wives, or children of burgesses, not married, nor under the age of fifty years; or shall be persons of the age and state of life before mentioned, presented by the donators of Two Hundred and Fifty Pounds *Sterling*; and the number of the persons to be constantly entertained shall be so many as the revenue of the Hospital can conveniently maintain, after the deduction of the charge of management and of maintaining the fabrick.

4. The donor of the sum of Two Hundred Pounds *Sterling* shall be privileged to present any person whatsoever, of the age and state forementioned, to be admitted into and maintained in the Hospital, at the end of six months after payment of the respective sums before mentioned, and the privileges shall descend to heirs and successors whatsoever. Providing, nevertheless, that no person be presented upon the decease of another, till twelve months are elapsed after the last person's decease.

direction and patronage of the Council were Robert Murdoch, James Kelly, John Muir, James Wright, John Weatherspoones, Isabel Bernard, and Janet Gate. This was prior to the time already alluded to, when twelve new beds were supplied, and after the two masters named had been appointed.

---

5. All persons admitted into the Hospital shall be provided with decent apparel, wholesome food, and convenient lodgings, furnished with clean linnen, bed and bed-cloaths; shall have such allowance paid them weekly for petty incident expenses, as the Council of Governors shall think fit, and shall be decently buried at the Hospital's expence. But, each person shall bring into the Hospital, at their admission, a bed and bed-cloaths for their own use, and shall sign a writ, by which they transfer and dispone to the Masters for behoof of the Hospital, all the goods and gear, money or effects, they are possessed of at their admission. And they shall further solemnly promise before the Council, to demean themselves orderly in the Hospital, to be obedient to the orders of the Council, and to obey the Governor and Governess in all their just and lawful commands.

6. The officers and servants imployed in the Hospital shall be—two Masters, the one a merchant and the other a tradesman; a Clerk, a Governess, a Caterer or Cateress, a Porter or Messenger, and as many maid servants as the exigence of the Hospital shall require. Upon the death, demission, or removal of any thereof, the Council shall proceed to chuse others in their places, within fourteen days thereafter.

7. The joint business of the two Masters shall be frequently to visit the Hospital, in order to inspect the conduct and behaviour of all the officers, servants, and persons entertained in it; to report to the Council what they observe to be amiss; and to summon meetings of the Council as occasion requires. But it shall be the particular province of the Merchant Master to serve as Treasurer to the Hospital by receiving the revenue, and defraying the expence of it, and keeping regular books of accompts, in the form to be prescribed to him by the Council. And, of the Tradesman Master, to inspect the behaviour of the people in the Hospital in a particular manner, and see to the execution of the Council's orders.

8. The office of the Clerk shall be, to attend all Meetings and Committees, to keep an exact Sederunt-book of Transactions, and Register-book of all persons admitted into the Hospital; to write all committees' reports; to draw all writs and evidents which concern the Hospital's affairs; to keep all the papers belonging to the Hospital in a safe place, and in due order; and, further, to do what the Council shall, from time to time, direct in his sphere. His salary shall be such as the Council shall appoint, not exceeding Ten Pounds *Sterling* yearly.

9. The province of the Governor shall be, to inspect the manners and behaviour of all

Although a very beneficent institution, and thoroughly appreciated by many of those who enjoyed its comforts, free from the cares and vicissitudes of life,—even at a comparatively early stage its management became a matter of some anxiety and worry to the Corporation.

---

persons in the Hospital, particularly of the men, and to report what he finds amiss to the Masters; to discourse with them, council, advise, and reprove them, as occasion requires; to sit at table when the men eat; to officiate as chaplain, by praying with them in the morning and evening, asking God's blessing and returning Him thanks at meat; and, further, to do what else the Council shall from time to time direct regarding his office. He shall be maintained in the Hospital at bed and board, and his salary, out of which he is to provide himself with decent cloaths, shall be such as the Council shall appoint, not exceeding Twenty-five Pounds *Sterling* yearly.

10. The business of the Governess shall be to inspect the manner and behaviour of all persons in the Hospital, particularly of the women; and to report what she finds amiss to the Masters; and officiate as Steward, taking charge of the provisions of meat and drink brought into the Hospital; overseeing the dressing and disposal thereof; and accompting for it to the Masters; to comptroll the Caterer, or Cateress, and accompt with him or her; and sit at the head of the table, where the women eat; and, further, to do whatever the Council shall, from time to time direct, concerning her office. She shall be maintained, and intertained in the Hospital; and her Salary for providing cloaths, and defraying personal charges, shall be such as the Council shall appoint, not exceeding Twelve Pounds *Sterling* yearly.

11. The Caterer, or Cateress' business shall be to go to the Mercat, and buy the victuals, accompting to the Governess for his or her intromissions; and, if a Cateress, to assist in dressing of them, and doing other parts of a Servant's Work in the Hospital, his or her Fee, and the fee of the other servant maids shall be such as the Governess shall agree upon with them, by advice of the Masters. And the Porter, or Messenger's business shall be, to open and lock the gates regularly, delivering the keys every night to the Governor, and receive them back from him in the morning; to summon the Governors to all meetings; and further, to do what the Masters, or the Governor or Governess shall direct, consistent with the rules of œconomy in the Hospital. They shall be maintained and intertained in the Hospital; and the porter or messenger's salary shall be what the Council shall appoint, not exceeding Three Pounds *Sterling* yearly.

After these laws follows the form of Oath, to be taken by the Governors of the Trinity Hospital, as well as by the Masters; but as these were in no way altered, when subsequent regulations were enacted in 1730, it does not seem requisite to quote them at this time.

The annual revenues of the Hospital, when Maitland reported upon them in 1753, were £637, 11s. 1d. They are now, in this year of grace 1896, more than ten times that amount.

At the time when the old beidmen were resident within its walls, there were to be found cases of insubordination continually cropping up. For example :—

Council Records, Vol. VIII. folio 214, 4th March 1573, W. Synclare, beidman, is decernit to pay to Thomas Libertoun, viiis., quilk he his awand for the mending of William Youngaris heid quilk he brake within xx dayis.

So early as the 26th February 1584, steps had been adopted to put "ordour to all enormities within the said Hospital," and for "depriving and putting forth of sic puir as troubles the rest"—thus on 14th May 1589 an order was issued "not to pay the dues of beidmanship in time to come to James Staynes, in respect of his manifold misdemeanours, and mainly towards his wife."

On the 29th day of Febuary 1660, an Act of the Town Council was passed—that, "with the ministers and masters to purge the Hospital of scandolous persouns," and, with this view, that "one was worthy to be extrudit," a second was to be "sharplie rebuikit," and others were to be "purged furth thairof."

The offences chiefly complained of were "habitual cursing, calling bad names, creating disturbances in the house, and getting drunk."

A minor offence seems to have consisted of beginning their meals, or carrying off the same, before the blessing had been asked, with the punishment of forfeiting their dinner during the next day.

Catherine Aitkenhead's offences were habitual cursing, giving bad names, creating disturbances in the family and getting drunk. Many reasons existed for expelling inmates down to so recent a period as 1834, when Mr Young was removed from the Hospital for making false reports as to the inmates being neglected, aggravated by his misconduct during a solemn admonition administered by one of the

Magistrates, in the presence of the whole inmates who had been convened for the occasion.

But there were also other trival matters that involved punishment. These chiefly were when any of the inmates sold for a price or gave away for the benefit of others, any meal or bread which the Hospital had provided to them for their own sustenance.

Notwithstanding that there fell to be occasional expulsions from the misconduct of wicked persons, the Hospital was highly appreciated by the majority of the inmates. Nay it is a fact that there was a great desire on the part of many persons to obtain admission to the House, by the payment of a sum of money for the privilege, either on the part of themselves or their friends or relatives. In the year 1653, Catherine Edglie was admitted as an inmate, on her having assigned to "the hospitall fyve hundredth merkis of good debtis, and two hundredth merkis of desperat;" Sophia Bennet was admitted in 1745, on a friend of hers own becoming bound to pay £10 a year for her in advance.

The Sacrament of the Lord's Supper was from time to time celebrated within the walls of the Hospital. The following Minute of the Town Council bears upon this point:—"9th January 1579.—It being found gude be the ministeris and kirk that the taibill of the Lord suld be celebrated vpon Sonday nixt in the Hospitall of the Trinatie College to the bedrellis thair and sic vtheris as sall resort that day resaving thair tikketis conform to the ordour, they ordane Lucas Wilson, dene of gild, to prepair for the said taibill all thingis necessar."

Before proceeding further in the narrative, it may be well to explain that in May 1592, Sophia Ruthven, the young Duchess of Lennox, was buried, with great solemnity at the east end of the Church of Trinity College. She was a daughter of the luckless Earl of Gowrie, who died in 1584, and was forcibly abducted from a house in Easter Wemyss, wherein she had been secluded to secure her from the violence of the Duke's wrath. But he carried her off on his own horse during the night, and married her in defiance of King and Kirk. These were the days of ancient chivalry. This occurred on the 19th day of April 1591, consequently she did not very long survive her abduction.

Lady Jane Hamilton, likewise, on the 18th December 1596, by her dying testimony, dated the 9th day of the said month, bequeathed 100 merks to the Trinity College Church, for a "buriall place" there. She was the youngest daughter of the Duke of Chatelherault, and Countess of the Earl of Eglinton, from whom she was divorced, because of the parties standing in the fourth degree of consanguinity. She died at Edinburgh, on the 18th of December 1596, nine days after her will had been made and signed.

CHAPTER X.

TOWN COUNCIL CONTROL,—*continued.*

THE word "beidmen," although a relic of pre-Reformation times, seems to have been in use for nearly a century and a-half afterwards. It was also made applicable to the female inmates, who were designated "beidwomen." This is made evident by the following extract from the Town Council Minutes. The meeting seems to have taken place within the walls of the Hospital. The Minute is as follows:—

"At the Trinity Hospitall, the 20th June 1689.—Sederunt of the Hospitall Councell. P. Sir John Hall; Old B., B. Chartres; B. M'Lurg, B. Bruce, D. Gild, Tho. Crawfurd; Thesr. Wm. Menzies; D. Stirling, D. Reid, D. Thomsone; Old Thesr. Muir; Wm. Wilson, Thesr. of the Hospitall.

"The which day the haill beidmen and beidwomen being called upon, the Councell appoynts the Thesaurer of the Hospitall to call for James Lindsey, Robert Dun, Ion Kello, and Ion Nicolson, their Burges tickets who ar beidmen of the Hospitall; as also Christian

Robertsone to produce her husband's Burges ticket to the Thesaurer of the Hospitall befor the nixt meiting of the Councell; as also to inquyre what Ryght the rest of them hes.

"Mr William Halkhead, Chaplane of the Hospitall being called upon and Inquyred at, if he frequently examines the beidmen, beid-women, and servants in the Hospitall, and giff he uses exerceise in the Hospital? He answered that he only examines the family twyse befor the Administrating of the Sacrament of the Lord's Supper, and uses exerceise in the familly morning and evening continually. And being also Inquyred at, if he gives obedience to the Law anent his frequent praying publicly for King William and Queen Mary? He answered, that he uses frequently publickly to pray for the King and Queen, bot he never named King William and Queen Mary, bot the King and Queen that were established by Law. And being desyred to explaine his meaning,—whether he meaned King William and Queen Mary? He desyred Wedinsday to give answer."

What the answer was, when Wednesday did arrive, it has not been possible to find out.

"The Councell appoynts the origionall Rights of the Hospitall to be inspected and the tenents' tacks of the Hospitall to be delyvered to the present Thesaurer of the Hospitall."

In 1611, the number of beneficiaries in the house was 35; by 1628, it had reached to 50. A gradual reduction then took place, when efforts were being made to repair the Hospital, and pay off debt which had been incurred in the investment of the Hospital funds in the acquisition of landed properties. These investments showed great insight on the part of the Trinity Hospital Governors of the day, which are now yielding an annual return of more than was originally paid for them. At the time referred to, there were few on the roll, and these few were boarded out.

The Magistrates and Town Council, at this juncture, carried on the affairs of the Hospital, chiefly through donations and bequests on the part of benevolent citizens; and having frequently made powerful appeals for aid, they seem to have been fairly successful in these appeals to the public.

Professor Macpherson frankly acknowledges this. He states (page 15 of his Report) :—"The charity seems always to have occupied much of the attention of the Magistrates; and from the continuous flow of donations and bequests, larger or smaller, it seems also to have enjoyed the confidence of the community." Again, he says "The institution seems to have been eminently useful in providing for poor people of all conditions, who were (or were related to) burgesses, and the number of applications for the benefit of the charity seems to have been largely in excess of its means of meeting them. The result was a constant struggle between the desire on the one hand to extend the usefulness of the charity, and on the other to keep the expenditure within due limits. The manner of checking excessive expenditure was occasionally somewhat arbitrary. Thus in 1672, there were thirty-three inmates, said to be more than the rents could support, so four were expelled—one for being of 'a bad carriage and behaviour,' being frequently drunken, but the other three for no graver offence than happening to be married. The remedy generally adopted was milder. Thus on 30th May 1688, it was resolved to fill no vacancies till the number was reduced from thirty-two then in the Hospital to twenty-eight, 'as the annual rents of the principal due to the Hospital is not able to maintain any more.' Notwithstanding this, a Minute of 10th April 1700 shows that there were fifty-one persons in the Hospital."

There are many entries in the Town Council's Minutes, bearing upon the sums which the Corporation had to spend in the way of buildings and repair. A few extracts will suffice to make this plain.

19. *May* 1581.—Because it was meanit be certane eldares of the Kirk, that the ruif of the hospitale in the Trinity College is faillaud and habill to decay gif remeid be nocht haistely fund thairto, fyndis it guid that the nychtbouris and inhabiteris of this burgh be requyrit and travellet with for thair help to the reparatioun thairof, and thairfoir appoyntis and nominatis Alexander Owsteane and Edward Galbrayth to speik the deykinis and thair craftis, Jhone Adamesoun and Jhone Dury, minister, to speik the men of law, and Alexander Vddert and William Littill to speik the merchantis, and to report thair ansuer the nixt counsale day.

23. *June* 1581.—Ordanis James Nicoll, baillie, the dene of gild, William Littill, Edward Galbrayth, and Thomas Aikinheid to pas on Sonday nixt, at afternone to the hospitale, and visy the decayet pairtis thairof in the ruif and cuppillis, and to report quhair the same neidis to (be) repairit and beittit, that ordour may be tane thairanent.

22. *December* 1581.—Ordanis Jhonne Robertsoun, thesaurer, to pay to Andrew Sclater, ane of the maisteris of the new Hospitale the sowm of fourty pund debursit be him for bying of sclaittis to the theiking and reparatioun of the said hospitale.

11. *March* 1584.—Ordanis James Ros, thesaurer . . . . to big vp and repair the windowes abone the Hospitall in the Trinitie College with stayne wark or tymmer, and to enter the calsay makers in the maist necessar pairts of the town and calsayes, and to agrie with thame with the avyse of William Littill and Andrew Sclaiter.

18. *August* 1585.—Ordanis James Ros, thesaurer, to caus sett vp the ruif of the beidmenis howse of the Trinitie College, repair and theik the samyn, and intromett with the daillis being thairin quhilk ar xxvij in number, as the said thesaurer declairet, and with all vther materialles, and to put in fir geists within the samyn.

23. *December* 1586.—Ordanet James Ros, thesaurer, to caus tak the rwif of the hospitall in the Trinitie College callit . . . . . Hospitall with the daillis being thairinto, number and inventour the same, and putt thame in the loft of the townis hospitall to be keipet thair quhill the toun haif ado with the sam.

14*th November* 1587.—Fynds it expedient that ane dur (door) be strukkin throw the toun wall to serue for entres to the Trinitie College and hospitall thairof at the fute of Halkerstoun's Wynd, als weill for the clengeing of Andrew Sclaiters geir in the awld wallis of Dyngwall as for vther occasiouns quhen the town sall haif ado thairwith, and gevis commissioun to the dene of gild (and five others) to tak ordour for clengeing of the said guidis and strikking furth of the said yett or dur, and ordanet the said dene of gild to mak the expensis of strykking furth of the said dur.

The Town Council likewise from time to time appealed for funds.

On one occasion, they had to apply to the Ministers whom they blamed for not handing over to them what they considered was due to the Hospital. The Minute regarding this matter is as follows :—

15th January 1584-5.—The foresaidis bailyeis and counsall and James Wod, baxter, ane of the remanent deykins of craftis, vnderstanding that the ministers, eldares, and deaconis of the kirk hes in their hands the sowm of twa hundreth merks left til the puir of the hospitall be dyuers zealous godlie persouns and wald imploy the sam vpoun land or annuelrent, and seeing that the town hes dyuers vther sowmes gevin to the puir, thairfore amangs the rest ordanis James Ros, thesaurer, to resaue the said sowme to the vse of the town, and grantis that infefftment be gevin to the maisteris of the hospitall of this burgh and thair successouris imputt and electet be the town of ane annuelrent of sextein merkis to be tane furth of the commoun mylnis of this burgh and payet to the said maisteris of the hospitall and bestowet be thame vpoun the said puir, vnder reuersion alwayes, contenand the said sowm of twa hundreth merkis, to be maid to the town *in communi forma.* (The following is written on the margin.) *Nota.*—This tuik na effect be ressoun the kirk imployet thair money vpoun vthers.

The two following extracts from the Minutes of the Town Council have also reference to contributions to the Hospital :—

2nd August 1581.—Vnderstanding that the sowme of [*blank*] is collected and gadderit of the guid will of certane of the sessioun and guid nychtbouris of this burgh for reparatioun of the new hospitale in the Trinity College, ordanis Thomas Aikinheid and Andro Sclateris, maisteris of the said Hospitale, to resaue the said money and imploy the sam in repairing of the said hospitale, and to be comptabill thairfor to the guid towne.

13th October 1581.—Vnderstanding that the money collectit of the nychtboures for reparatioun of the hospitale wes nocht sufficient to repair the sam, for the quhilk caus and that the wark suld nocht lye idill and decay, Jhone Robertsoun, thesaurer, had lent to the maisteris of the said hospitale the sowm of ane hundreth pundis, thairfore ordainis the said sowme to be allowet to the said thesaurer in his comptis, and the saidis maisteris of the hospitall to be comptabill thairfore.

By the middle of the seventeenth century, the funds of the Hospital appear to have been in a more prosperous condition. The house had, by that time, become enlarged, a common hall, with kitchen provided, the rooms were partitioned off, so as to hold two beds each. Agreeably to Minutes of the Town Council of 20th April 1642, and 14th May 1643, with the advice of the Ministers and Kirk Session, all the beneficiaries were to live within the walls, and be clothed at the Hospital's expense. A matron was found who contracted to supply the wants of thirteen inmates. An "expectant" was also appointed to provide morning and evening exercises. The number of inmates was fixed from time to time, according to the funds at the disposal of the Governors.

About this time, however, in so far as the various documents connected with the Foundation were concerned, these seem not to have been very carefully attended to, by the officials acting under the Magistrates and Town Council. This remark was also applicable to the papers of other foundations. Possibly there was not sufficient accommodation provided at the time for their proper care. Hence the following Minute was passed on 11th April 1656.—"Forasmeikle as the haill writts of Heriot's Hospitall and the Trinitie Hospitall at the fute of Leith Wynd, ar lying scattered up and doun in several places in the inner and outter clerks chalmer, and charter hous and elsquhair, swa that the thesaurers of the said hospitallis can hardlie give accompt of the writtis and evidentis belonging thairto. Quharrforr the Counsell ordaines the haill writtis of the saidis hospitallis to be inventaried and put up in thair severall Cabinets."

The beginning of the last century (1701) seems to have been a time of great dearth and comparative poverty for the townspeople of Edinburgh. This was very much intensified by the great loss sustained by the citizens through the collapse of the Darien Scheme* in 1702.

* THE DARIEN SCHEME.—In 1695, the Darien Scheme was set on foot. A Company was started in Edinburgh for the purpose of establishing a settlement on the Isthmus of Darien, and for fitting out ships to trade with Africa and the Indies, as well as Greenland, Archangel

Nearly half-a-million of money was sacrificed in this enterprise. The Magistrates and Town Council, in their laudable endeavours to cope with the state of matters in which they found themselves placed, increased the number of inmates of the Hospital to fifty-four, besides the

---

and the Gold Coast. The large sum of £400,000 was readily subscribed. The highest anticipations were formed regarding the new adventure, and many citizens left Edinburgh, and embarked for the new settlement, in the hope of realising enormous fortunes. Apart from people of all ranks, who were contributors to the scheme, it may be mentioned that the Faculty of Advocates, the Merchant Company of the City, with Sir Robert Chieslie, the Lord Provost, the cities of Edinburgh and Perth joined it as communities; but, in the meantime, "the furious denunciations of the English Parliament proved a thorough discouragement to the project in London, and nearly the whole of the stockbrokers there silently withdrew from it." Under similar influence, the Hamburgh merchants were induced to withdraw from it, leaving Scotland to work out her own salvation in the scheme, possibly "with fear and trembling." She proceeded to do so with an amount of courage which cannot fail to be highly commended. When intelligence reached Edinburgh of the Company having succeeded in effecting a landing in Darien, and of their having successfully repulsed the attacks of the Spaniards, and planted the Scottish flag on Fort "St Andrew," it is related that thanks to Almighty Providence were offered up in St Giles' and the various churches in Edinburgh, and a general illumination, at the instance of the Magistrates, was made within the bounds of the city. The mob, however, taking advantage of the festive occasion, testified their joy by securing the city ports. They then proceeded to set fire to the door of the Old Tolbooth, and they set free those prisoners who had been incarcerated for printing seditious publications against the King and the English Court.

The scheme eventually turned out to be a great failure, all those who invested money in the enterprise lost their means. As a result, the indignation of the populace was not one whit less demonstrative when the day of adversity was announced, than they were in the day of its supposed success. The prison doors of the Tolbooth were a second time thrown open, the windows of all adherents of King William were broken; in a word, there was a general riot, in which much violence was manifested, and the Commissioners and officers of state were compelled to leave the city for several days to escape the fury of the people.

The Darien House which stood opposite to the old Charity Workhouse in the High Riggs, within the extended line of the city wall at Bristo Street, was used for many years as a pauper lunatic asylum, under the name of "Bedlam." When the City Poorshouse was removed, in 1870, to Craiglockhart, near Edinburgh, the whole ground was put into the market for feuing purposes, and the old Darien House was levelled to the ground.

Governor, Governess, and Servants, and the Corporation appealed to the public for aid, by donations and mortifications. In this they were fairly successful. It should here be noted, however, that the Union between England and Scotland having been confirmed in 1707, there was as a result a great exodus of the nobility and the wealthier classes of society from Edinburgh to London. Nevertheless, it was eventually found that the Hospital was fast running into debt. The Town Council, as Governors, were very unwilling to exclude any of the inmates from the benefit of the Institution unless they were found guilty of misdemeanours. But necessity compelled them to adopt a resolution that the number should be brought down to forty inmates in all, and that no more should be admitted.

The buildings meantime had been getting into a chronic state of decay and disrepair. In 1728, it was found unavoidable to delay the matter any longer. According to Mr Andrew Gairdner,* the Treasurer of the Hospital at the time, "The Slates were tumbling off the House, which have hazarded people's lives walking in the street, the floor in the low gallery, where the women's apartments were, and the joisting was all rot; the North-Loch ran thro' the North-end of the House, which brought the whole Nestiness (*sic*) of the North-side of the Town, and of the Butchers' Booths, through the House. There was a Thoroughfare through the House, which kept it in foul weather, both

* "An Historical Account of the OLD PEOPLE'S HOSPITAL, commonly called The *Trinity Hospital*, in *Edinburgh*; with Arguments and Motives pleading for Assistance to pay the present expensive Reparations, and to raise a Fund for maintaining many more people. To which is subjoined, Page 34, Proposals to raise a Fund for the Maintenance of *Orphans*, educating them in Religion, and bringing them up to Virtuous employments, according to their different Capacities, under the Title of a CHARITY-BANK. By ANDREW GAIRDNER, Merchant in Edinburgh, and Treasurer to the Old People's Hospital. Edinburgh, Printed in the year MDCCXXVIII."

nesty and cold. When the water did run high, it flowed through the House, and when the water was low, the foresaid Nestiness of the Town and Butchers, with that of their own Houses of Office which were in the West side, and had not Water to carry it off, lay beneath the flooring, and made it very noisom and unwholesome."

Mr Gairdner then proceeds to describe the state of the walls, which besides being in many places neither wind nor water tight, were in some parts rent from top to bottom. This was not surprising, seeing that a great portion of the walls of the buildings had stood for upwards of three hundred years.

To remedy all this state of matters, he proceeded to raise a public subscription, whereby great improvements took place on the Hospital, in its outward appearance, as well as its internal arrangements. The changes which took place contributed largely to the comfort of the inmates. Mr Gairdner in his report says :—" We have given every man and every woman, in both the high and low Galleries, a room by themselves, as being most convenient for people in their circumstances. And, because many Women, when they were admitted were in such straitened circumstances, they had much to do to provide themselves with the necessaries their rooms wanted, but were obliged to bring such things as they had alongst with them, and the House thereby was never in good order or uniform. To prevent this, for the future, we have given each of the women a new corded bed and curtains, a wainscot table and chair, and all of them except such as have a little room below the stair, a little corner cup-board, with some other little conveniences in their rooms, and some drawers in the stairs that go up to the high rooms." All these articles were understood to belong to the House and could not be removed. Their bedding and bed-clothes they were required to bring with them, and the same had to meet with the approval of the Governess.

The lighting of the House was considerably improved by additional windows and fan-lights. The garden was put into a better state of repair, and a handsome stone gateway with iron gate was erected on the North-West side. For his timely intervention, Mr Gairdner conferred an immense boon not only on the Magistrates and Town Council who were the governors; but also on the Charity itself, the inmates of the Hospital, and indeed upon the public at large.

CHAPTER XI.

STATUTES AND REGULATIONS.

THE Town Council, on the 10th day of April 1730, considered it to be their duty to revise the statutes for the government and control of the Trinity Hospital. Nearly a century and a half had passed, since they took an active interest in the administration of its affairs. It is not wonderful, therefore, that there should have been found reasons for having a revised constitution and code of regulations. During the period referred to, great experience had been no doubt gained as to a proper administration of the affairs of the charity.

The chief changes which took place, at this time, were the following :—(1.) The Ministers of the Trinity College Church were no longer included in the list of Governors, and the whole Town Council, as at that time constituted, became the governing body. (2.) The quorum of a meeting of Governors was regulated by the practice of the Town Council in its ordinary business; and as the meetings were held weekly on Wednesday, the business of the Hospital had to be transacted along with the City's business, with this exception, that a separate and distinct record was to be kept of the Hospital's affairs, apart from the Council's ordinary Minutes. Other meetings of the Town Council, as Governors of the Hospital, might be held, if required. (3.) A sum of £300 was required as a donation, to give a right of presentation. This was an advance of £50 upon the sum formerly arranged. (4.) The functions of the two Masters seem to have been dispensed with. The Treasurer, who appears to have been then constituted the highest officer, was required before entering upon his office to find caution to the satisfaction of the Town Council, to the amount of £400 sterling, for his intromissions, and the fourteen days' restriction as to choosing other officials seems to have been removed. (5.) The duty of the two masters was devolved upon the Treasurer, who was required to inspect the conduct and behaviour of all the officers, servants, and inmates; to report to the Governors what he saw amiss; to receive the revenue and defray the expenses; and have these embodied in carefully kept books, in the form prescribed by the Town Council. (6.) The House Governor had the same duties assigned to him as were contained in the original Regulations, with one exception, viz., that he had to report to the Treasurer, in place of the two Masters. (7.) In regard to the Governess (or Mistress) the same remark applies, as in the previous case. She was to report to the Treasurer. (8.) In reference to the Caterer or Cateress, and the other servants of the establishment, the Treasurer was made to undertake the duties of the two Masters.

The following are the regulations at that time (1730), approved of by the Lord Provost, Magistrates and Town Council :—

INTRODUCTION.*

SEEING the welfare and prosperity of all societies depend upon the regular and steady administration of their affairs in a conformity to the fundamental rules of their con- *Argument for compiling statutes.*

* Printed by A. Murray & J. Cochrane, Edinburgh. 1772.

stitution; and that such is the instability and fluctuancy of human affairs, arising from men's different ways of thinking and acting, that regular and steady administration cannot in any measure be ascertained, without laying down rules or statutes: And seeing the mismanagement of an hospital, and misapplication of its funds, are, by the common consent of mankind, deemed crimes equal in wickedness to sacrilege; and that it is highly expedient for preventing these evils, and for establishing and maintaining good order and œconomy, that rules and statutes be laid down, and that the Governors of Hospitals should come under sacred and solemn obligations to observe and obey them, and to act honestly and disinterestedly: Therefore the following statutes are enacted:—

STATUTE I.

Council of Governors.

The sole Governors of the said Hospital are, and shall be, the Lord Provost, Magistrates, and Town Council, of Edinburgh, with the Deacons of Crafts, Ordinary and Extraordinary, in Council assembled.

STATUTE II.

Powers of the Council, place and time of meeting.

The Council of Governors (whereof a quorum is declared to be the same as the quorum of the Town-Council by the sett) shall have power and authority to govern the hospital; to censure, punish, and extrude, the persons entertained in it; to chuse, censure, and dismiss, all officers and servants; to direct its œconomy within and without doors; to act with the treasurer; and, in general, to order all its affairs, as occasion requires, determining and concluding by majority of votes. And as the ordinary stated meetings of the Town-Council are on Wednesday weekly, all business respecting the Hospital shall be then and there transacted, and a separate and distinct record thereof kept, as at present; but prejudice to the Governors to meet oftener, or at other times, as they shall see cause.

STATUTE III.

The persons to be admitted into the Hospital described by their number.

The persons intitled to be admitted into and maintained in the Hospital shall be no other than Burgesses, Wives of Burgesses, and Children of Burgesses, not married, nor under the age of fifty years; and the number of persons to be constantly entertained shall be so many as the revenue of the Hospital can conveniently maintain, after deduction of the charge of management, and of maintaining the fabrick.

STATUTE IV.

The donor of the sum of L. 300 Sterling shall be privileged to present to the Council of Governors a man or woman, qualified in all respects as in the foregoing statute; and the donor of the sum of L. 350 shall be privileged to present to the Council of Governors any person whatsoever, who is not married, nor under fifty years of age, to be admitted into and maintained in the Hospital, at the end of six months after payment of the respective sums before mentioned; and the said privilege shall descend to heirs and successors whatsover: Providing, nevertheless, that no person be presented upon the decease of another, till twelve months are elapsed.

Presentations regulated.

STATUTE V.

All persons admitted into the Hospital shall be provided with decent apparel, wholesome food, and convenient lodging, furnished with clean linen, bed and bed-cloaths, shall have such allowance paid them weekly, for petty incident charges, as the Council of Governors shall think fit, and shall be decently buried at the Hospital's expence. But each person shall bring into the Hospital, at their admission, a bed and bed-cloaths, for their own use; and shall sign a writ, by which they transfer and dispone to the Treasurer, for behoof of the Hospital, all the goods and gear, money or effects, they are possessed of at their admission: And shall further solemnly promise, before the Council, to demean themselves orderly in the Hospital, to be obedient to the orders of the Council, and to obey the Household Governor and Mistress, in all their just and lawful commands.

The manner of entertaining and matters to be performed by the persons admitted into the Hospital, laid down.

STATUTE VI.

That in all time coming, the treasurer shall, before entering upon his office, find caution, to the satisfaction of the Council, to the amount of L. 400 Sterling, for the faithful discharge of his trust; and that he, the Household Governor or Chaplain, Mistress, and other officers and servants, shall be appointed by the Council, as the exigencies of the Hospital require. Upon the death, demission, or removal, of any whereof, the Council shall proceed to chuse others in their places.

The officers and servants to be employed.

STATUTE VII.

The business of the Treasurer shall be, frequently to visit the Hospital, in order to inspect the conduct and behaviour of all the officers, servants, and persons entertained in it; to report to the Council what he may observe amiss; to receive the revenue, and

The office of the Treasurer.

defray the expence of the Hospital, and keep regular books of accounts, in the form to be prescribed to him by the Council; to inspect the behaviour of the people in the Hospital, in a particular manner, and see to the execution of the Council's orders; and keep all the papers belonging to the Hospital, in the charter-house, in due order.

STATUTE VIII.

The Governor's sphere and salary.

The province of the Household Governor shall be, to inspect the manners and behaviour of all the persons in the Hospital, particularly of the men, and to report what he finds amiss to the Treasurer; to discourse with them, counsel, advise, and reprove them, as occasion requires; to sit at table where the men eat; to officiate as chaplain, by praying with them in the morning and evening, asking God's blessing, and returning him thanks, at meat; and further to do what else the Council shall from time to time direct concerning his office. He shall be maintained and entertained in the Hospital at bed and board; and his salary, out of which he is to provide himself with decent cloaths, shall be such as the Council shall appoint, not exceeding L. 25 Sterling yearly.

STATUTE IX.

The Governess's business and salary.

The business of the Governess or Mistress shall be, to inspect the manners and behaviour of all persons in the Hospital, particularly of the women, and to report what she finds amiss, and officiate as steward, taking charge of the provisions of meat and drink brought into the Hospital, overseeing the dressing, and disposing thereof, and accounting for it to the Treasurer; to comptrol the Caterer or Cateress, and account with him or her, and to sit at the head of the table where the women eat; and further to do whatever the Council shall from time to time direct concerning her office. She shall be maintained and entertained in the Hospital; and her salary for providing cloaths, and defraying personal charges, shall be such as the Council shall appoint, not exceeding L. 12 Sterling yearly.

STATUTE X.

The Caterer or Cateress's Maid - servants, Porter or Messenger, their duty and fees laid down and fixed.

The Caterer or Cateress's business shall be, to go to the market and buy the victuals, accounting to the Governess for her or his intromissions; and if a Cateress, to assist in dressing of them, and doing the other parts of a servant's work in the Hospital. His or her fee, and the fee of the other maid-servants, shall be such as the Governess shall agree upon with them, by the advice of the Treasurer. And the Porter or Messenger's business shall be, to open and lock the gates regularly, delivering the keys every night to the Governor, and receiving them back from him in the morning; and further to do what the Treasurer and Governess shall direct, consistent with the rules of œconomy in the Hospital. They shall be maintained and entertained in the Hospital; and the Porter or Messenger's salary shall be what the Council shall appoint, not exceeding L.3 Sterling yearly.

STATUTE XI.

Every Governor shall, at his admission, and before he enter upon the exercise of his office, take the following oath, to be administered to him by the clerk, viz.

Oath to be taken by the Governor and officers.

"I A. B. do faithfully promise, and solemnly swear, That I will punctually "observe the statutes of this Hospital, and demean myself uprightly, disinterestedly, "and honestly, in the choice of officers and servants, and in all other matters which "concern the Hospital; and if I, at any time, find any person attempting or endeavour-"ing to embezzle its revenue, or defraud it in any manner, I will vigorously oppose him, "and reveal it to the Council. This I promise, and swear, by God, and as I shall "answer to him at the great day."

Every Treasurer shall in like manner, before he enter upon the exercise of his office, take the following oath, viz.

"I A. B. now appointed Treasurer of the Trinity Hospital, do faithfully promise, "and solemnly swear, That I shall faithfully and honestly perform all that is required of "me by the Statutes of this Hospital, by God, and as I shall answer to him at the "great day."

And the same oath, *mutatis mutandis*, shall be taken by the Household Governor and by the Mistress.

CONCLUSION.

The use of statutes and oaths.

The administration of the Hospital's affairs being thus settled, and the faithful execution of these rules being charged home upon the conscience of every Governor and Officer, it is to be hoped, that, by the blessing of Heaven, the pious and laudable ends of this charitable foundation will be fully attained, to the comfort of the poor, and the honour of those who now are, and in all future time shall be, concerned in the management of its affairs.

FINIS.

These statutes were afterwards revised in 1782, when the following resolutions were adopted by the Town Council, and the terms thereof were incorporated as the Rules of the Institution.* The effect of the same seems to have been to vest in the Town Council as a body several powers previously exercised by the officials.

At Edinburgh, the Tenth day of April in the year One thousand seven hundred and thirty.

1730.

WHICH day the Honourable the Magistrates and Council, with the Deacons of Crafts, ordinary and extraordinary, of the City of Edinburgh, Governors and Administrators of the Trinity Hospital, being assembled; taking into their serious consideration that, by the decreet-arbitral pronounced by the Right Honourable Archibald Earl of Islay, recorded in the Council minutes, the eighth instant, it is found and declared, That the Council could not delegate their power of the government and administration of the Trinity Hospital to others. And being resolved to conform themselves to all things determined by the said decreet, do unanimously agree, that the sole government of the said Hospital, and its affairs, shall be from this time forth in the Town Council ordinary and extraordinary only, and no longer remain in the Council of twenty-one persons, to which the power of the government and administration thereof was delegated by the Town Council's act, the twenty-sixth day of August, one thousand seven hundred and twenty years, and where it has remained till now; and therefore the said act is hereby rescinded. And furder, considering that the flourishing of this Hospital does (under God) very much depend on a regular and steady administration; which, considering the changeableness of the administrators, cannot be so well ascertained as by settling rules and statutes for the management of the rents and funds of the said Hospital without doors, and for the regular economy of all matters and things within the house; the Council unanimously agree to govern all the affairs of the aforesaid Hospital by rules and statutes. Therefore, the Council authorise and appoint the present and old Magistrates, Deacon Conveener, Deacon Nimmo, and Deacon Ogilvy, as a committee to compose these rules and statutes, and report the same to the Council for their approbation. Extracted from the Records of Council of the city of Edinburgh, by

Sole government of the Hospital vested in the Town Council ordinary and extraordinary.

Affairs of the Hospital to be governed by rules and statutes.

Committee to compose rules and statutes.

(Signed) JOHN GRAY, Clk.

* Printed by Alex. Smellie, Edinburgh. 1803.

Nota, By different acts, the treasurer is directed, on occasion of vacancies happening by death or otherwise, to report the same to the council of Governors.

Treasurer to report vacancies to the Governors.

At Edinburgh, the Eighth day of February, in the year One thousand seven hundred and forty-four. 1744

Which day the Right Honourable the Lord Provost, Magistrates, and Council of the city of Edinburgh, Governors and Administrators of the Trinity Hospital, in council assembled, enact, statute, and ordain, That all grants, powers, and privileges of exhibiting and presenting Hospitallers, to be made and granted to whatever person or persons, who, in consideration thereof shall gift or mortify any sum or sums of money to the use of the said Hospital, shall in all time coming be with and under the following condition, viz. That, in case that at any time hereafter, the interest or annualrent of money shall be by law reduced to a lower rate than five *per cent.* upon the death or removal of any poor person or hospitaller, who shall be exhibited and presented in virtue of any such powers and privileges (after annualrent or interest shall be so diminished) his or her room and place shall be and remain vacant and unfilled up, until the annualrent arising, and falling due upon such principal sums as shall be so gifted and mortified, shall run up to a sum, which, when conjoined with the principal sums, shall produce an annualrent or interest equal to what such principal sums would produce, at the rate of five *per cent.* Extracted from the record of the said Hospital, by

Act relative to preventing Hospitallers, in the event of interest on money falling below 5 *per cent.*

John Gray, Clk.

At Edinburgh, the Fifth day of September, in the year One thousand seven hundred and fifty-nine, 1759.

Which day the Right Honourable the Lord Provost, Magistrates, and Council of the city of Edinburgh, with the Deacons of Crafts, ordinary and extraordinary, of the City of Edinburgh, Governors and Administrators of Trinity Hospital, being assembled, Bailie Andrew Simpson from the committee on the Hospital affairs reported, that, according to a list given in to them, it appeared there were fourteen persons who were out-pensioners of the said Hospital, therefore were of opinion, that allowing the funds of the Hospital to be bestowed in that way, gives encouragement to many persons to apply for the said charity that would otherwise not do it, if they were obliged to go into the Hospital; therefore enacted, statuted, and ordained, that no person in time coming shall be admitted as an out-pensioner of the said Hospital; and that all and

Act against admitting of out-pensioners.

every one admitted as members of the said Hospital, shall reside, and be entertained therein in the ordinary way. Extracted from the records of the said Hospital, by

(Signed) JOHN GRAY, Clk.

At Edinburgh, the Twenty-second day of April, in the year One thousand seven hundred and seventy-two,

1772.

WHICH day the Right Honourable the Lord Provost, the Magistrates, and Council, with the Deacons of Crafts ordinary and extraordinary of the City of Edinburgh, Governors and Administrators of the Trinity Hospital, being assembled, Bailie Hamilton produced in Council a scroll of Statutes made up by his committee, in obedience to the order of Council of the 25th of March last. Which, being read in Council, were unanimously approven of, and whereof the tenor follows.

Statutes for the establishment of good order and economy in the Hospital.

INTRODUCTION.

Introduction.

Seeing the welfare and prosperity of all societies depend upon the regular and steady administration of their affairs in a conformity to the fundamental rules of their constitution; and that such is the instability and fluctuancy of human affairs, arising from men's different ways of thinking and acting, that regular and steady administration cannot in any measure be ascertained, without laying down rules or statutes: And seeing the mismanagement of an hospital and misapplication of its funds are, by the common consent of mankind, deemed crimes equal in wickedness to sacrilege; and that it is highly expedient, for preventing these evils, and for establishing and maintaining good order and oeconomy, that rules and statutes be laid down, and that the governors of hospitals should come under sacred and solemn obligations to observe and obey them, and to act honestly and disinterestedly: Therefore, the following statutes are enacted.

STATUTE I.

Governors of the Hospital.

The sole Governors of the Hospital are and shall be, the Lord Provost, Magistrates, and Town Council of Edinburgh, with the Deacons of Crafts ordinary and extraordinary, in Council assembled.

STATUTE II.

Quorum the same as the quorum of the Town Council.

Powers of the Governors.

The Council of Governors (whereof a quorum is declared to be the same as the quorum of the Town Council, by the sett) shall have power and authority to govern the Hospital; to censure, punish, and extrude the persons entertained in it; to chuse, censure, and dismiss all officers and servants; to direct its economy within and without doors; to act with the treasurer; and, in general, to order all its affairs as occasion requires, determining and concluding by majority of votes. And, as the ordinary stated meetings of the Town Council are on Wednesday weekly, all business respecting the Hospital shall be then and there transacted, and a separate and distinct record thereof kept, as at present; but prejudice to the Governors to meet oftener, or at other times, as they shall see cause.

Business of the Hospital to be done at the Council Meetings on Wednesday, weekly. Separate record to be kept, but Governors may meet oftener.

STATUTE III.

The persons entitled to be admitted into, and maintained in the Hospital, shall be no other than Burgesses, wives of Burgesses, and children of Burgesses not married, nor under the age of fifty years; and the number of persons to be constantly entertained shall be so many as the revenue of the Hospital can conveniently maintain, after deduction of the charge of management, and of maintaining the fabric.

Persons entitled to be admitted to the Hospital.

STATUTE IV.

The donor of the sum of three hundred pounds Sterling shall be privileged to present to the Council of Governors a man or woman qualified in all respects as in the foregoing statute; and the donor of the sum of three hundred and fifty pounds, shall be privileged to present to the Council of Governors any person whatsoever, who is not married, nor under fifty years of age, to be admitted into and maintained in the Hospital, at the end of six months after payment of the respective sums before mentioned; and the said privilege shall descend to heirs and successors whatsoever, providing nevertheless that no person be presented, upon the decease of another, till twelve months are elapsed.

Sums to be paid for rights of presentation. N.B. This part of the Statutes altered. See Act of Council 17th May 1797.

No person to be admitted on decease of another till twelve months are elapsed.

STATUTE V.

All persons admitted into the Hospital shall be provided with decent apparel, wholesome food, and convenient lodging, furnished with clean linen, bed and bed-clothes; shall have such allowance paid them weekly for petty incident charges as the Council of Governors shall think fit; and shall be decently buried at the Hospital's expence. And each person shall bring into the Hospital, at their admission, a bed and bed-clothes for their own use; and shall solemnly promise before the Council to demean themselves orderly in the Hospital, to be obedient to the orders of the Council, and to obey the household-governor and Mistress, in all their just and lawful commands: And shall sign a writ, by which they transfer and dispone to the treasurer, for behoof of the Hospital, all the goods and gear, money, or effects they are possessed of at their admis-

Apparel and other provision for those admitted.

To bring in at their admission a bed and bed-clothes.

To promise obedience to the orders of the Council, Governor, and Mistress.

To dispone their effects to the Hospital, Act of Council 2d September 1795.

sion : And, moreover, in terms of the act of Council 2d September 1795, they shall likewise in the same deed bind and oblige themselves, in the event of their succeeding to any heritable or moveable subjects, other than what they were possessed of at the period of their admission, to assign and dispone at least so much thereof, as will compleatly reimburse the Hospital of every charge and expence its revenue may have been put to, on such member happening to succeed to, or acquire any future accession of fortune, whether heritable or moveable ; and upon refusing to comply with the above, such person or persons shall forfeit the benefit of the Hospital, and be dismissed therefrom ; and that in their stead, needy persons shall be admitted from time to time. Ordered, that this regulation shall be intimated and read to every person who shall in future obtain the benefit of the Hospital, previous to their admission thereto. It being always understood, that this regulation is meant only to extend to those to be admitted by the Governors on the Burgess fund, and not to affect persons admitted in consequence of presentations from the representatives of those who purchased rights of presentation.

STATUTE VI.

Treasurer to find caution to extent of 400l. Sterling.

That, in all time coming, the treasurer shall, before entering on his office, find caution to the satisfaction of the Council, to the amount of four hundred pounds Sterling, for the faithful discharge of his trust ; and that he, the household governor, or chaplain, mistress, and other officers, and servants, shall be appointed by the Council, as the exigencies of the Hospital require ; upon the death, demission, or removal of any whereof, the Council shall proceed to chuse others in their places.

STATUTE VII.

Business or province of the Treasurer.

The business of the Treasurer shall be frequently to visit the Hospital, in order to inspect the conduct and behaviour of all the officers, servants, and persons entertained in it ; to report to the Council what he may observe amiss ; to receive the revenue, and to defray the expence of the Hospital, and to keep regular books of accounts in the form to be prescribed to him by the Council ; to inspect the behaviour of the people in the Hospital in a particular manner, and see to the execution of the Council's orders, and keep all the papers belonging to the Hospital in the charter house in due order.

STATUTE VIII.

Province of the Household Governor.

The province of the Household Governor shall be to inspect the manners and behaviour of all the persons in the Hospital, particularly of the men, and to report what he finds amiss to the treasurer; to discourse with them, counsel, advise, and reprove them, as occasion requires; to sit at table where the men eat; to officiate as chaplain, by praying with them in the morning and evening, asking God's blessing, and returning Him thanks at meat; and further to do what else the Council shall from time to time direct concerning his office. He shall be maintained and entertained in the Hospital at bed and board; and his salary, out of which he is to provide himself with decent cloaths, shall be such as the Council shall appoint, not exceeding twenty five pounds Sterling yearly. Salary.

STATUTE IX.

The business of the Governess or Mistress shall be to inspect the manners and behaviour of all persons in the Hospital, particularly of the women, and to report what she finds amiss, and officiate as steward, taking charge of the provisions of meat and drink brought into the Hospital, overseeing the dressing and disposing thereof, and accounting for it to the treasurer; to controul the caterer or cateress, and account with him or her, and sit at the head of the table, where the women eat; and further to do whatever the Council shall from time to time direct concerning her office. She shall be maintained and entertained in the Hospital; and her salary for providing cloaths, and defraying personal charges, shall be such as the Council shall appoint, not exceeding twelve Pounds Sterling yearly. Province of the Governess. Salary.

STATUTE X.

The Caterer or Cateress's business shall be, to go to the market, and buy the victuals, accounting to the governess for his or her intromissions; and, if a cateress, to assist in dressing of them, and doing the other parts of a servant's work in the Hospital. His or her fee, and the fee of the other maid servants, shall be such as the Governess shall agree upon with them, by the advice of the treasurer. And the Porter or Messenger's business shall be, to open and lock the gates regularly, delivering the keys every night to the Governor, and receiving them back from him in the morning: and further to do what the Treasurer and Governess shall direct, consistent with the rules of oeconomy in the Hospital. They shall be maintained and entertained in the Hospital; and the porter or messenger's salary shall be what the Council shall appoint, not exceeding three pounds Sterling yearly. Province of the Caterer or Cateress. Province of the Porter.

STATUTE XI.

Every Governor shall, at his admission, and before he enter upon the exercise of his office, take the following oath, to be administered to him by the clerk, viz.

Oath to be taken by every Governor at his admission.

"I do faithfully promise and solemnly swear, that I will punctually "observe the statutes of this Hospital, and demean myself uprightly, disinterestedly, "and honestly in the choice of officers and servants, and in all other matters which concern "the Hospital. And if I at any time find any person attempting or endeavouring to "embezzle its revenue, or defraud it in any manner, I will vigorously oppose him, and "reveal it to the Council. This I promise and swear by God, and as I shall answer to "him at the great day."

Every Treasurer shall in like manner, before he enter upon the exercise of his office, take the following oath, viz.

Oath by the Treasurer, and

"I now appointed Treasurer of the Trinity Hospital, do faithfully "promise and solemnly swear, that I shall faithfully and honestly perform all that is "required of me by the Statutes of this Hospital, by God, and as I shall answer to him "at the great day."

Household Governor and Mistress.

And the same oath, *mutatis mutandis*, shall be taken by the Household Governor, and by the Mistress.

CONCLUSION.

Conclusion.

The adminstration of the Hospital's affairs being thus settled, and the faithful execution of these rules being charged home upon the conscience of every Governor and officer, it is to be hoped that by the blessing of Heaven, the pious and laudable ends of this charitable foundation will be fully attained to the comfort of the poor, and the honour of those who now are, and in all future times shall be concerned in the management of its affairs.

Clerks to tender the oath to the Council on 1st Wednesday of October yearly.

Appoint the clerks, on the first Wednesday of October yearly, to tender to the several members of Council the oath appointed to be taken by the Governors as mentioned in the foregoing statutes. Extracted from the records of the said Hospital, by

JOHN GRAY, *Clk.*

1777.

At Edinburgh, the Third day of December, in the year One thousand seven hundred and seventy-seven.

WHICH day the Right Honourable the Lord Provost, the Magistrates, and Council of the City of Edinburgh, with the Deacons of Crafts, ordinary and extraordinary, of the

City of Edinburgh, being assembled, they did, amongst other things, on report from the committee on the affairs of Trinity Hospital, for the better internal government of the Hospital, order and appoint, that all the members should be obliged to attend prayers, evening and morning, except in the case of sickness; and that the names of such persons as did not attend should be marked in a book, and reported to the Treasurer of the Hospital, in order that he may lay the same before the Committee. And the Council, for the more regular conduct of the affairs of the Hospital, and of the several members within the same, vested the Committee with full powers, and recommended to them to meet monthly at the Hospital, or oftener, as they shall find necessary, for the better ordering of the affairs of the said Hospital. Extracted from the records of said Hospital, by (Signed) JOHN GRAY, *Clk.*

Members to attend prayers.

Committee vested with powers.

At Edinburgh, the twenty-ninth day of July in the year One thousand seven hundred and seventy-eight, 1778.

WHICH day the Right Honourable the Lord Provost, Magistrates, and Council of the City of Edinburgh, with the Deacons of Crafts, ordinary and extraordinary, of the said City, Governors and administrators of the Trinity Hospital, being assembled, Bailie Thomas Cleghorn, pursuant to the remit with full powers to him and his Committee as mentioned in the Council's Act, the third day of December, one thousand seven hundred and seventy-seven, produced in Council a report made up by the said Committee, whereby they give it as their opinion, that in order to remedy sundry abuses, the Council should strictly enjoin the Treasurer to visit the Hospital as frequently as directed by the statutes, and punctually to execute every part of his office in person; and, wherever any difficulties arise, to apply to the Committee for assistance, in enforcing his orders. The same injunctions ought also to be given to the house governor and governess, with regard to their different departments, as pointed out by the statutes, and immediate dismission should be the consequence of their failure or neglect.

Injunctions to Treasurer.

To Governor and Governess.

That the house may be kept clean and in good order, the victuals properly dressed, and everything within the house completely executed, an additional allowance ought to be made to the wages stipulated for the different servants, conform to the situation of the present times, as what is specified by the statutes is no way adequate to the labour of such servants as are qualified to do their duty in that house with fidelity;—and the

Anent the servants' wages, &c.

committee submit to the Council, if it would not be proper to give the servant who acts as cook and cateress, four pounds *per annum*, one of the other two servants three pounds ten shillings, and the other three pounds Sterling of yearly wages.

Members to dine at one common table, &c.

Hour of dining.

That all the members in the house should dine at one common table, the governor and governess to preside thereat in their order; and no person to be excused, nor the victuals allowed to be sent to their own apartments, except in the case of sickness, to be certified by the governor or governess; and the hour of dining shall be at one o'clock, as at present. The committee took into consideration what would be the proper allowance for dinner to each person at the public table, having in their eye the regulations tenth April one thousand seven hundred and twenty-one, and propose to the Council that the dinners for each day of the week should be as follows:

Daily provisions to the members.

Monday—Each man to get twopence, each woman one penny halfpenny, as at present.

Tuesday—A rump of beef boiled with barley and roots, or greens, according to the season; half a pound of beef, and one and one half ounce of barley, to be allowed for each person; the roots or greens not to exceed three-pence.

Wednesday—Beef or mutton roasted, allowing half a pound for each person, with roots of the season, or greens, not exceeding eightpence.

Thursday—Beef flanks boiled with barley, roots, or greens, as upon Tuesday.

Friday—Eggs and butter, barley and milk, or potatoes, according to the season, and half allowance of meat. If eggs and butter, each person to be allowed two eggs, and not exceeding half a pound of butter to six. If barley and milk, a pound of second barley, and five mutchkins of milk, and two ounces of brown sugar for four persons. If potatoes, one half of the ordinary allowance of meat, the expence upon the whole not exceeding that of the egg dinner.

Saturday—A rump of beef boiled with barley, roots, or greens, as upon Tuesday.

Sunday—Roast beef or mutton, with roots or greens, as upon Wednesday.

Allowance of ale.

Allowance of meal and bread, &c. for breakfast, dinner, and supper

or money in lieu thereof.

That the allowance for ale should be continued as at present, that is, one pint a day for each man, and three mutchkins for each woman; and they should also be allowed two pounds of meal each per week, for making porridge for breakfast, and twelve ounces of bread for dinner and supper. But, if they rather chuse money for their breakfast and supper ale and meal, they should each of them, in lieu of these receive ninepence per week; in which case they are only to be allowed a mutchkin of ale each for dinner, and twelve ounces of bread, and no meal; or they may take money for their breakfast ale and meal, and then they will be allowed sixpence per week, the men three mutchkins, and the women a chopen of ale each for dinner and supper, twelve ounces of bread, and no meal.

That no person be allowed to carry off or dispose of provisions of any kind, under the penalty of extrusion if a member, and of immediate dismission if a servant, and forfeiture of their bygone wages. The same restrictions to take place with respect to the governor and governess. No provisions to be carried off.

That all the members shall be in the house by eight o'clock at night in winter, and nine o'clock in summer; the bell to be rung at these hours, the roll to be called, and the persons absent to be marked in a book to be kept by the governor for that purpose, to be shown to the treasurer and committee, when called for; the doors to be locked at these hours, and none to be admitted into, or to go out of the house thereafter, without the express permission of the governor or the governess. Members to be in the House by 8 at night in winter, and 9 in summer, and doors to be locked at these hours.

That all the wards and apartments be cleaned and aired by the servants of the house every day, as well as the public rooms; and the surgeon of the hospital to report the state of the patients, and the manner they are treated, to the treasurer or committee once every month. Wards to be cleaned and aired every day. Surgeon to report the state of the patients monthly.

That the present custom of allowing out-pensioners, being contrary to the statutes, should be discontinued, where the Town has a right to present, without prejudice to private patrons; as the committee are of opinion that the savings from the regulations above proposed, would produce a fund sufficient for admitting an additional number of house-members. Out-pensioners discontinued.

The committee are further of opinion, that persons admitted into the Hospital ought to bring with them a feather bed and bedding of cloaths, in terms of the condition in their act of admission, and ought to reside in the Hospital; and that sending out provisions to those who do not comply with this condition, or to those who leave the Hospital, after they come into it, is highly irregular and improper, and should be discharged in all time coming. Persons admitted to bring with them a feather bed and bedding. No provisions to be sent out of the house.

Which being considered by the Magistrates and Council, they, with the extraordinary Deacons, approve of the said report, and did, and hereby do statute, enact, and declare accordingly; and ordain the said regulations to be strictly observed in time coming, during the Council's pleasure; and resolve that the same shall take place from and after this date, recommending to the said committee to see the same put to due execution.—Certified from the records of said Hospital, by

John Gray, *Clk.*

At Edinburgh, the sixteenth day of March, in the year One thousand seven hundred and ninety-one,

1791.

WHICH day the Right Honourable the Lord Provost, Magistrates, and Council, with the Deacons of Crafts ordinary and extraordinary, of the City of Edinburgh, Governors and Administrators of the Trinity Hospital, being in Council assembled, on motion by the Lord Provost, the Council resolved that in time coming, no motion, petition, &c. relating to the Trinity Hospital, shall be made or read in Council, until the ordinary business is finished, and announced by the clerks to be so. Extracted from the records of Council, by JOHN GRAY, *Clk.*

No business relative to the Hospital to be done until the ordinary business is finished.

At Edinburgh, the seventeenth day of May, in the year One thousand seven hundred and ninety-seven,

1797.

Act fixing the sums to be paid for rights of presentation to the Hospital.

WHICH day the Right Honourable the Lord Provost, Magistrates and Council of the City of Edinburgh, governors and administrators of Trinity Hospital, being assembled, —read representation by Bailie Coulter, bearing, that on the twenty-fifth day of March one thousand seven hundred and seventy-two, the following sums were fixed for the rights of presentation to the Trinity Hospital, to wit, for a right of presentation at large, three hundred and fifty pounds Sterling, and for a restricted presentation for a burgess or guild-brother, burgess or guild-brother's widow or child, three hundred pounds Sterling,—That it is now found that the interest arising from the above sums is inadequate to the expence of supporting a member in the Hospital at present, owing to the high prices of all the necessaries of life; and, after consulting the Treasurer of the Hospital, the representer was of opinion, and moved, That the Governors should pass an act, declaring and ordaining, that in future, the sum to be paid for a presentation at large, shall be the sum of four hundred pounds Sterling; and for a restricted presentation, to wit, for a Burgess or Guild-Brother, Burgess or Guild-Brother's widow or child, the sum of three hundred and fifty pounds Sterling. Which representation and motion having been seconded, the same was unanimously approved of; and the Council ordained, that the respective sums before mentioned shall be paid for rights of presentation to the Trinity Hospital, from and after this date; and that this act shall continue in force until the same shall be altered by the Magistrates and Council. And ordered, that the same shall make part of the statutes of said Hospital. Extracted from the records of the said Hospital by JOHN GRAY, *Clk.*

FINIS.

The last to which reference requires to be made is in the year 1821, when the following Regulations were passed.* The chief matter dealt with seems to have been to permit the practice of bestowing of out-door pensions, which former Governors condemned. The decision of the Town Council was likewise in favour of increasing the qualification of those who wished to present pensioners to the Hospital, to a capital sum of £350 and £450. A surgeon is also to be appointed to report as to the health of the inmates.

At Edinburgh, the Twenty-second day of August, in the year One thousand eight hundred and twenty-one, 1821.

WHICH day the Right Honourable the Lord Provost, Magistrates, and Council of the City of Edinburgh, Governors and Administrators of the Trinity Hospital of Edinburgh, being assembled, there was read the following Report by the Committee appointed on the first day of November last, to revise the Statutes of the Hospital.

REPORT of the Special Committee appointed by the Governors on the first of November 1820, to revise the Statutes of the Trinity Hospital.

Your Committee having met on the 20th of November last to proceed in the matter remitted to them, found, that various opinions were entertained, not only as to the powers of the Governors, in the administration of their trust, to grant out-pensions, but also as to their right to alter the statutes of the Hospital. In order, therefore, to put an end to all doubts on these important points, it was deemed proper to have legal advice; and your Committee "Resolved, that a case be laid before counsel in order to "ascertain whether the Governors can legally grant pensions to persons not residing in "the house, and can alter the statutes of the Hospital, from time to time, as they shall "see fit."

A case was accordingly prepared, and the opinion of the Solicitor-General obtained. To these your Committee beg leave to refer, as ingrossed in the records; and, in terms of this opinion, they hold it to be clear,—

* Printed by Alex. Smellie, Edinburgh. 1803.

1st, That, if the revenue exceeds what is necessary for supporting those whom the house is capable of maintaining, the Governors are entitled to grant pensions to out-pensioners; and,

2d, That the Rules for the general management of the Hospital may be so altered and modified, from time to time, as a change of circumstances may render necessary and beneficial in extending its benefits.

Your Committee being convinced that, by the granting of out-pensions, the benefits of the institution are greatly extended; and that the predecessors of the Governors, in passing acts against the granting of these, must either have acted under a mistake in regard to their powers, or upon erroneous views, have no hesitation in recommending that the Acts 5th September 1759, and 29th July 1778, so far as these relate to out-pensioners, be rescinded.

Your Committee are farther of opinion, that it is improper to attempt to regulate the order and economy of an establishment of this nature by specific regulations applicable to every case: And that it is better to make general regulations for the government of the Institution, and to trust to the efficiency of the officers and controul of the permanent committee for the due administration of these.

Your committee, in going over the present statutes and existing acts of the Governors, with a view to adapt them to the present times, have not found much to alter. They have endeavoured to embody, in the following Statutes, such detailed rules as at present stand on the authority of acts of the Governors passed since the Statutes were framed; and, in presenting the Regulations underwritten for their consideration, the Committee beg leave to suggest, that, if the Governors shall think fit to adopt them, it will be necessary to suspend the operation of all the acts of the Governors containing separate regulations, and which are henceforward to be considered as superseded by the following

STATUTES.

I. The sole Governors of the Hospital are, and shall be, the Lord Provost, Magistrates, and Town Council of Edinburgh, with the deacons of crafts, ordinary and extraordinary, in council assembled.

II. The council of Governors (whereof a quorum is declared to be the same as the quorum of the town council, by the sett) shall have power and authority to govern the Hospital; to censure, punish, and expel persons entertained in it; to chuse, censure, and dismiss all officers and servants; to direct its economy within and without doors; to act with the Treasurer; and, in general, to order all its affairs as occasiou requires, determining and concluding by majority of votes. And, as the ordinary stated meetings of the town council are on Wednesday weekly, all business respecting the Hospital shall be then and there transacted, and a separate and distinct record thereof kept as at present without prejudice to the Governors to meet oftener, or at other times and places, as they shall see cause.

III. The persons entitled to be admitted into, and maintained in the Hospital, or to receive an out-pension, shall be either burgesses, wives of burgesses, or children of burgesses, not married, nor under the age of fifty years; and the number of persons to be constantly entertained shall be so many as the revenue of the Hospital can maintain, after deduction of the charge of management, and of supporting the fabric.

IV. The donor of the sum of three hundred and fifty pounds sterling shall be entitled to present to the Council of Governors a man or woman qualified in all respects as in the foregoing statute; and the donor of the sum of four hundred and fifty pounds shall be entitled to present to the Council of Governors any person whatsoever, who is not married, nor under fifty years of age, to be admitted into and maintained in the Hospital, at the end of six months after payment of the respective sums before mentioned; and the said privilege shall descend to heirs and successors whatsoever, providing, nevertheless, that no person be presented upon the decease of another, till twelve months shall have elapsed.

V. All persons admitted into the Hospital shall be provided with decent apparel, wholesome food, and convenient lodging, and furnished with clean linen, bed and bedclothes; they shall have such allowance paid them weekly for petty incident charges as the Council of Governors shall think fit; and shall be decently buried at the Hospital's expence. And each person shall solemnly promise to demean themselves orderly in the Hospital, to be obedient to the orders of the Governors, and to obey the Treasurer, Chaplain and Mistress, in all their just and lawful commands: And shall sign a deed, by which they transfer and dispone to the Treasurer, for behoof of the Hospital, all the goods and gear, money or effects they are possessed of at their admission: And, moreover, in terms of the act of the Governors, 2d September 1795, they shall likewise, in the same deed, bind and oblige themselves, in the event of their succeeding to, or acquiring any heritable or moveable subjects, other than what they were possessed of at the period of their admission, to assign and dispone at least so much thereof as will completely reimburse the Hospital of every charge and expence its revenue may have been put to on their account; and, upon refusing to comply with the above, such person or persons shall forfeit the benefit of the Hospital, and be dismissed therefrom; and that, in their stead, needy persons shall be admitted from time to time: And it is ordered, that this regulation shall be intimated and read to every person who shall in future obtain the benefit of the Hospital, previous to their admission thereto: It being always understood, that this regulation is meant only to extend to those to be admitted by the Governors, and not to affect persons admitted in consequence of presentations from the representatives of those who purchased rights of presentation.

VI. That a Treasurer shall be appointed with a suitable salary; and, in all time coming, he shall, before entering on his office, find caution to the satisfaction of the Governors, to the extent of five hundred pounds, for the faithful discharge of his trust; and that he, a Chaplain, Mistress, and other officers and servants, shall be appointed by the Council, as the exigencies of the Hospital require.

VII. The business of the Treasurer shall be frequently to visit the Hospital, in order to inspect the conduct and behaviour of all the officers, servants, and persons entertained in it; to report to the Governors what he may observe amiss; to receive the revenue; and, in general, to perform the whole duties of a factor; to defray the expence of the Hospital; and to keep regular books of accounts in the form to be prescribed to him by the Governors; to inspect the behaviour of the people in the Hospital in a particular manner; to superintend the execution of the Governors' orders, and keep all the papers belonging to the Hospital in the Charter-house, in due order.

VIII. The province of the Chaplain shall be to inspect the manners and behaviour of all the persons in the Hospital, particularly of the men, and to report what he finds amiss to the Treasurer; to discourse with them, counsel, advise, and reprove them, as occasion requires; to officiate, by praying with them in the morning and evening, asking God's blessing, and returning Him thanks at meals: And, further, to do what else the Governor shall, from time to time, direct concerning his office. He shall be maintained and entertained in the Hospital at bed and board; and his salary shall be such as the Governors shall appoint.

IX. The business of the Mistress shall be to inspect the manners and behaviour of all persons in the Hospital, particularly of the women, and to report what she finds amiss, and officiate as house-keeper, taking charge of the provisions of meat and drink brought into the Hospital, overseeing the dressing and disposing thereof, and accounting for it to the Treasurer; and, further, to do whatever the Governors shall, from time to time, direct concerning her office. She shall be maintained and entertained in the Hospital; and her salary shall be such as the Governors shall appoint.

X. That the Surgeon shall make a monthly report of the state of health of the inmates; and, before any person presented to the Hospital shall be admitted to the House, the Surgeon shall be required to see them, and to report to the Treasurer whether the person presented labours under any disease that may render it dangerous or improper to receive him or her into the House; and, in the event of the report of the Surgeon being against the admission of any person, the Treasurer shall immediately bring the matter under the notice of the Governors.

XI. All the members of the Establishment shall be obliged to attend prayers evening and morning, except in case of sickness; and the names of absentees shall be marked in a book, and reported to the Treasurer, in order that he may lay the same before the Governors.

XII. That all the inmates shall be in the House by eight o'clock at night both in winter and summer. The bell to be rung at that hour, the roll to be called, and the persons absent to be marked in a book to be kept by the Chaplain for that purpose. The doors to be locked at the above hour, and none to be admitted into, or go out of the House thereafter, without the express permission of the Chaplain or Mistress.

XIII. Every Governor shall, at his admission, and before he enter upon the exercise of his office, take the following oath, to be administered to him by the Clerk, viz.—

"I do faithfully promise, and solemnly swear, that I will punctually "observe the Statutes of this Hospital, and demean myself uprightly, disinterestedly, "and honestly, in the choice of officers and servants, and in all other matters which "concern the Hospital. And if I, at any time, find any person attempting or en- "deavouring to embezzle its revenue, or defraud it in any manner, I will vigorously "oppose him, and reveal it to the Council of Governors. This I promise and swear by "God, as I shall answer to him at the Great Day."

Every Treasurer shall, in like manner, before he enter upon the exercise of his office, take the following oath, viz.—

"I now appointed Treasurer of the Trinity Hospital, do faithfully "promise, and solemnly swear, that I shall faithfully and honestly perform all that is "required of me by the Statutes of this Hospital, by God, and as I shall answer to him "at the Great Day."

And the same oath, *mutatis mutandis*, shall be taken by the Chaplain and by the Mistress.—

(Signed) JOHN TURNBULL, *Preses.*

The Governors, having considered the foregoing Report, Statutes and Regulations, approved of the same; enacted and declared, in terms thereof; directed the same to be printed for the use of the Governors; and ordered the Memorial, with the opinion of the Solicitor-General above referred to, to be engrossed in the Records.—Extracted from the Records of the said Hospital, by

C. CUNINGHAM, *Conj^t. Clk.*

To face page [illegible]

VIEW OF TRINITY HOSPITAL AND GROUNDS—DRYING CLOTHES.

CHAPTER XII.

RETROSPECTIVE GLIMPSE OF HOUSE AFFAIRS.

IT may be interesting to enquire how the affairs of the Hospital were conducted during the last century. It may be taken for granted, that there was likely to be little or no change upon the policy of the governing body, or the management of the affairs of the charity, during most of that period, especially after the revisal of of the Regulations of 1730. The inmates were undoubtedly a class superior to those who were to be found in the City Poorshouse. The latter institution was begun in 1743, for the reception of the ordinary or common poor of the town. It was then popularly known as "the Charity Workhouse." It was built on a space of ground, formerly denominated as the "High Riggs," being about 200 feet to the south-west of the place where Bristo Port stood. It was bounded on the north by the burial ground belonging to the Grayfriars' Church, on the south by the city wall, and on the west by the ground known at the time as the "New Burying Ground," also a part of the High Riggs. It was erected by voluntary contributions by the inhabitants. The annual outlay for maintaining each person at that time was £4, 10s.

At first the expenses were borne by a tax of two per cent. which was laid upon the valued rents of the old city parish, half of the profits of the ladies' assembly rooms were devoted to the same purpose, and one half of the church door collections were bestowed upon the same object, as well as the results of voluntary contributions among the citizens. The gentlemen of the legal profession refused to be assessed; but eventually they had to succumb, and pay their rates to assist in providing for the support of the poor. The same exemption was claimed by the Lawyers in regard to the Annuity Tax, a cess laid upon the Ancient and Extended Royalty, for at least one hundred years, to help to pay the Stipends of the City clergy, a tax regarding which a passing allusion will fall to be made at a future stage.

The Royal Infirmary of Edinburgh had even previous to that time been established, viz., in 1729, for the curable sick, from whatever part of the world they came, without the slightest restriction. The sick poor were, therefore, at that date provided for, by another and a much more thoroughly-equipped institution, with the same or even better relief than that which they formerly enjoyed within the Hospital of the Holy Trinity.

It was, therefore, for the maintenance of decayed burgesses, their wives and families, that the uses of the Hospital were, during most of that century, exclusively devoted.

After the Union, which occurred in the year 1707, Edinburgh seems to have been in a state of absolute poverty. The great bulk of the citizens could not fail to have suffered severely from the exodus to London, as well as from the total collapse of the Darien Scheme, to which a direct reference has already been made in these pages. Canongate appears to have had the greatest transformation scene effected on its highways and byeways. The poet Allan Ramsay—looking back upon its gay days, before the King and Court were transferred to England, and when in place of the braw lads and lassies that paraded on the Canongate pavement in the days of yore—he found the sturdy artizan and the hardy labourer frequenting its streets, and that they were the tenants of, as well as were living in, those tenements which were previously the resort of the gay and the noble of the land, was constrained thus to write :—

"Oh! Cannigate, puir elrich hole,
What loss, what crosses dost thou thole!
London and death gar thee look droll
And hang thy head;
Wow but thou hast e'en a cauld coal
To blaw indeed."

This state of affairs was not confined to the Canongate, but it seemed to be the condition of the city generally. The many benefactions which were then bestowed upon respectable citizens, or their dependants, who might have been thought to have occupied a superior position in Society, would seem to imply that a great proportion of the inhabitants had nothing better to look to at that time than what may, with all truthfulness, be described as "a-hand-to-mouth" state of subsistence. The Dean of Guild's Book of Pensions,* which, in so far as yet published, dates from July 20, 1554, to June 13, 1744, gives abundant proof of this. At that time there was practically no parochial relief. The Dean of Guild was almoner in Edinburgh for the Church of Scotland, and the Clerk of the Sessions. As an example, there may be quoted the following entries :—"Nov. 20, 1719. To Margaret Piggot, relict of Mr John Goodall, Professor of Hebrew in the College of this citie, on account of her indigent condition, and to pay her

* Colston's Guildry of Edinburgh, page 119.

husband's funeral charges, £25 sterg. as the current half-year's sallarie." "Dec. 11, 1719. To Anne Campbell, relict of Mr Joseph Foord, late preacher of the Gospel in Skinners' Hall, of this citie, for several great and weighty reasons, £25 sterg." There are many other such quotations to which reference might be made; but these may suffice. They were grants or gifts to people, of even a superior class, when compared with the majority of those who were usually included in the Trinity Hospital benefaction.

The late Mr Andrew Gairdner, to whom a previous reference has been made (page 80) was, for a considerable time, the Treasurer of the Hospital. He was appointed to the office in 1727, and he died in 1739, twelve years thereafter. He was a man of a most benevolent character. He was continually engaged in doing good. He found the house in a state of great disrepair, and he immediately set to work to issue a short Historical Account of the Charity, and to request subscriptions from the public, to enable the Governors to have it put in a creditable state of repair. In this step he was eminently successful. The good services he rendered to the charity during his life time, were highly appreciated by the Town Council and the public. And it is proper to state, that he himself, under his will, left a sum of £200 to the Hospital, in virtue of which the Governors, on 31st July 1745, granted to his son (the then Treasurer of the Hospital in succession to his father) and to his heirs, the power and privilege of presenting a member of the Trinity Hospital from time to time, qualified in all respects. In a pamphlet (already referred to) published at Mr Gairdner's instance,* in which he strongly

* Mr Gairdner, having had his attention directed to the large number of orphan children in Edinburgh, as well as in other parts of Scotland, who were left in destitute circumstances, and exposed to all the evils which are inseparable from a state of idleness and ignorance—

TRINITY HOSPITAL STAIRCASE.

To face page 135.

urges the foundation of a Hospital for Orphan Children, which resulted in the Orphan Hospital of the present day being begun, of which institution he was unquestionably the projector and founder,—he thus refers to the feeling of satisfaction which, in his time, seemed to pervade the inmates of Trinity Hospital as to the ample provision made for them, and the comforts which they enjoyed, as well as the immunity from domestic or business cares and worries, of which they were relieved. The speaker he refers to, is made to say :—" I always

looking upon them, moreover, as in precisely the same condition as those who were the recipients of the Trinity Hospital benefit, with this one exception, that they had youth on their side and a long vista of the future before them—set his heart on providing an institution for this neglected class of the community.

To assist him in his work he published two pamphlets. The former of these was entitled "A Looking Glass for Rich People, or a Plea for the Poor," while the other was a reprint of a German work, viz., "Pietas Hallensis, or a History of the Orphan House at Glauca, in Saxony, by A. H. Frank, Professor of Divinity in the University of Halle." This he intended to be understood by the public as a model of the proposed new Hospital. Both of these were published prior to the appeal already referred to in 1734.

A balance of £218, 13s. 5d., after having repaired the Old People's (Trinity) Hospital, was the nucleus of the foundation of the Orphan Hospital. Many other subscriptions began to flow in. It is right, however, to state, that in his exertions Mr Gairdner was assisted by several well-disposed and benevolent inhabitants. In the beginning of the year 1733 they communicated their design to the Society in Scotland for Promoting Christian Knowledge and several persons of distinction. The proposal got great encouragement, a plan was agreed upon, and a constitution was framed for the government of the Hospital. In the month of September of the same year, a house in Bailie Fyfe's Close, belonging to Mr Trotter of Morton, was hired at a rent of £12 per annum, furniture procured to the value of £15, thirty children were elected to the benefits of ehe Institution, a matron or mistress was appointed, and Mr George Brown, one of the teachers of the aforesaid Society, at the Bridge of Kelty, near Dunblane, was chosen master, the Society agreeing to pay his salary, as well as to furnish all the books required by the children for their education.

In 1734, a general collection was taken in all the churches and meeting houses of the city, as well as in the surrounding districts, on behalf of the Hospital ; and so well did the public respond to the appeal that Mr Gairdner and his friends were enabled to feu a piece of ground, called the Dingwall Park, belonging to the Trinity Hospital, on which the house of Dingwall Castle used to stand, adjacent to the western end of Trinity or College Church.

used to dread the terms of Whitsunday or Martinmas, especially if I was not ready with my rent. But now I can look both of these fellows in the face, and as they have nothing to expect from me, I can say straight either to Mr Whitsunday or Mr Martinmas,—How do you do, this morning, gentlemen?"

Nevertheless, quarrels and even riots did frequently take place among the inmates. This state of matters was not, therefore, confined to the time when the beidmen had a local habitation, but it extended even to the beginning of the present century. The attention of the

---

The foundation-stone was laid on the 28th day of June of the same year, and the edifice was erected in accordance with plans designed by Mr William Adam, one of the most celebrated architects of his day, and brother of Robert Adam, the architect of our University. As an illustration of the popular feeling exhibited at the time, on behalf of the Hospital, 24 journeymen wrights of their own free accord, subscribed a paper agreeing to work gratuitously for 140 days in the erection of the house; the candlemakers resolved to give to the Hospital every year large donations of candles, amounting to 13 stones; an anonymous friend was at the expense of a marble frontispiece, with inscription, bearing the date of the foundation of the Hospital, to be put over the entrance. Other benefactions followed afterwards—viz., Dr Glen, of Edinburgh, presented a clock; John Young gave the dial plate, John Bonar painted it, and Thomas M'Innes put it up. Notwithstanding all these benefactions, the cost of the building was upwards of £800.

In 1735, the children were removed to the new building. During the same year the Town Council granted a seal of cause to the Hospital, which continued to receive an accession to its funds by subscriptions, legacies, and church collections. In 1739, when Mr Gairdner died, there were 74 orphans maintained and educated in the Hospital, and the funds which the Managers had received were invested in the purchase of land near Inveresk.

At the time the Hospital was built, the New Town and the grand scheme of Provost Drummond's—viz., the North Bridge—had not been contemplated. A few houses leading up by Calton Street to what was then designated "Multrees Hill" (now St James' Square) were the only neighbouring buildings, and the whole ground to the north and west was a continuous line of fields, part of which at the time bore the name of "Bearford's Parks." In 1768 a vigorous but unsuccessful attempt was made to prevent the erection of the theatre on a part of Forglen's Park, adjacent to the Hospital, the site on which the present General Post Office stands. Other innovations were stoutly resisted by the Managers of the Hospital; but the opposition was generally ineffectual.

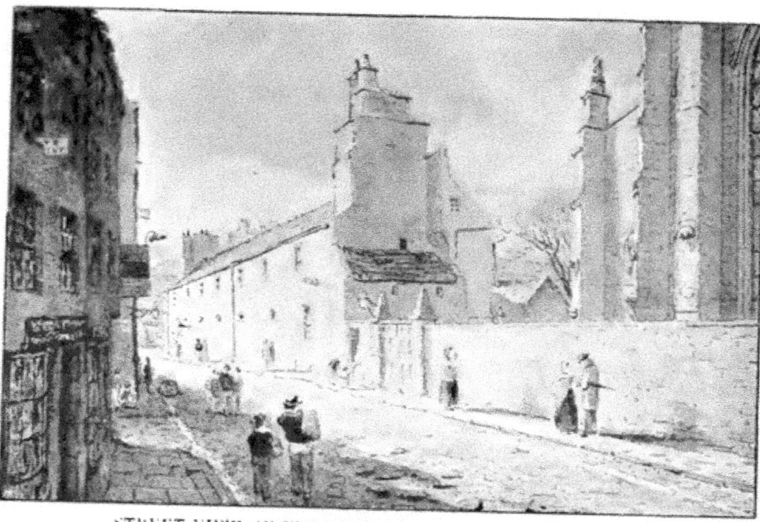

STREET VIEW OF TRINITY HOSPITAL. ENTRANCE GATE.

[Between pages [illegible]]

SOUTH-EAST CORNER OF TRINITY HOSPITAL.

[Between pages 156-7.]

Governors had been frequently directed to this subject, though the inmates of the House were wont to meet only at meals and at worship.

Alluding to the behaviour of the inmates (Council Register, 29th July 1778), Arnot writing in 1780 (4to page, 563) says—"The behaviour of the persons maintained in the hospital, although they are a class above the vulgar, and are so comfortably subsisted, supports the argument against maintaining the poor in a congregate body, and public poors-house. The quarrels and riots among them were so frequent, the selling of victuals allowed them, and applying the price to improper purposes, and their nasty way of living (to which the poor people in Scotland are exceedingly addicted) has aroused very lately the attention of the Governors, endeavouring to correct their abuses. Indeed the mob seems a monster so little affected by reason, and so powerfully influenced by religion, that frequent ablutions ought to be inculcated as a part of the Christian, as it has been of the Jewish and Mahometan religions."

Each of the inmates had a convenient room. The male inmates were annually allowed a hat, a pair of breeches, a pair of shoes, two shirts and two neckcloths. Every second year, each one was provided with a coat and a waistcoat or vest. The female inmates had yearly a pair of shoes, a pair of stockings, and two shifts. Every second year they were each awarded a gown and petticoat. The cap or "mutch" which they were in the habit of wearing, seems to have been provided by themselves.

For the purchase of petty necessaries,—the men were allowed eight shillings and eightpence a year. This must have been for snuff or tobacco, which were largely in demand in those days. For a somewhat similar reason, the women had an annual allowance of six shillings and sixpence. Regarding food, each inmate had a daily supply of twelve ounces of household bread; of ale, the men had an imperial Scots pint, while the women had two-thirds of a pint, which was at that time equal to three mutchkins of the present day. For breakfast, they had oatmeal porridge (hasty pudding as it has been designated); and for dinner, they had, during four days in the week, broth and boiled beef; while, for two days, they had roast meat, and on Monday, in lieu of flesh meat, the men had allotted to them the sum of twopence, and the women one penny half-penny to spend as they themselves thought best.

A reference to the Minutes of the Town Council of the period, as well as a perusal of the House-books, throw strange side-lights, or even foot-lights, on the practice of the time. There is no doubt that the management of the Hospital was conducted on most economical principles. The prices of the various commodities which were then supplied, will bear favourable comparison with those of the present day. It will no doubt be a surprise to the reader, to be informed that three pounds' weight of beef or mutton could at that time be obtained for the sum of fivepence, and that a good leg of lamb could be bought for the small silver coin denominated "one sixpence." The House-book, which was very specific, not only detailed the number of "sows' hedds" that were consumed on the premises, but in the desire of the Town Council of the period, for every scrap of information, as to expenditure, they required to have it duly intimated to them as to the number of "brats" (coarse pinafores or aprons) which were used by the domestics.

Although the usual weekly menu is specified above, there were occasional departures from the same recorded. The common sense of those in charge would take care to have occasional changes of diet largely dependent upon the particular seasons. For example, a fish diet was from time to time provided every Friday. Possibly this might with all due propriety be called "a Lent day,"—reminding the reader of the old couplet—

"The Monks of Melrose brewed good ale,
On Fridays, when they fasted."

The fish diet consisted of dried, or "hard fish," with butter and mustard, or "green (fresh) fish," with pepper and ale for sauce.

There were two public tables in the Hospital, where the various beneficiaries sat down. The one was a table for the females, and the other a table for the males. At the head of the former, the Governess or Mistress presided, while at the latter the Chaplain was accustomed to rule. There were no dinners provided on Sunday. A supper took the place of dinner.

The religious services of the House were conducted by the Chaplain twice a-day, viz.:—on morning and evening, while, on the Sunday, there were three services. In addition to their having to listen to the ministerial exhortations, they were, according to the old parochial system of "catechising" required not only to conform to the rules, but to be subjected to the examination of the Chaplain, by observing the custom of their "repetting (repeating) the sermons."

As regards the custom of "catechising" in Scotland, as it was practised long ago, induces the writer to refer to a story that was told many years ago regarding the late Lord Jeffrey. That eminent judge and literary critic was at one time resident in a most secluded part of the West Highlands of Scotland, enjoying his holiday retreat. One afternoon, he received a message from the parish minister, which was conveyed to him by the parish beadle (or betherel) that the clergyman intended next day, at a certain hour, to pay his Lordship a pastoral visit. Lord Jeffrey was only too pleased to have some person of intelligence to talk to, in his retirement from the busy scenes of life, letters, and industry. When the parson arrived, and was ushered into the drawing-room, his Lordship engaged him in a most animated conversation as to all the surroundings of the district and as to their respective proprietors, which somewhat disconcerted the worthy pastor. At last, recovering himself the latter said, "My Lord, you are aware that I could not presume to wait upon your Lordship, but for the fact that you are temporarily one of my parishioners, and that it is incumbent on me to call for your Lordship and the family in my pastoral capacity. I have to ask you, therefore, to summon Mrs Jeffrey and the whole household to 'their exercises.'" Lord Jeffrey at once rang the bell, and the butler was told that all the inmates were to meet without delay in the drawing-room, when a big family Bible was placed before the clergyman. The parish minister addressing Lord Jeffrey, with the utmost feelings of respect, spoke thus, "My Lord" (strong emphasis on the *my*), "since I became the pastor of this parish, now upwards of forty years ago, I have never failed to adopt the wholesome system of 'catechising,' which I think is productive of most excellent results; and, as I always include all my parishioners in my examination, and invariably begin with the head of the household,—May I ask your Lordship, what is Effectual Calling?" Never was an Edinburgh Reviewer more puzzled at a question. His Lordship had many years before forgotten what was popularly known as "his carritches." Nevertheless he was not to be outdone, and he volunteered the following answer — "Well, I would say that the man performs his calling most effectually, who does it with ability and success." The minister accepted the answer, and passed on to Mrs Jeffrey. Perhaps he did not quite realise the scope of the answer; possibly he did not wish to show his Lordship's ignorance of the orthodox

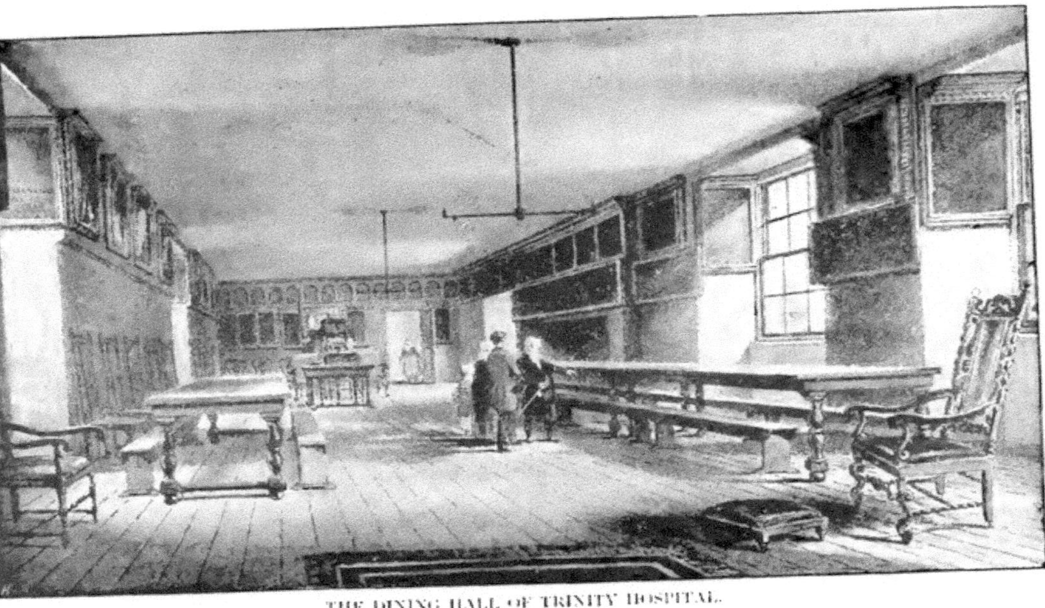

THE DINING HALL OF TRINITY HOSPITAL.

Between pages [illegible]

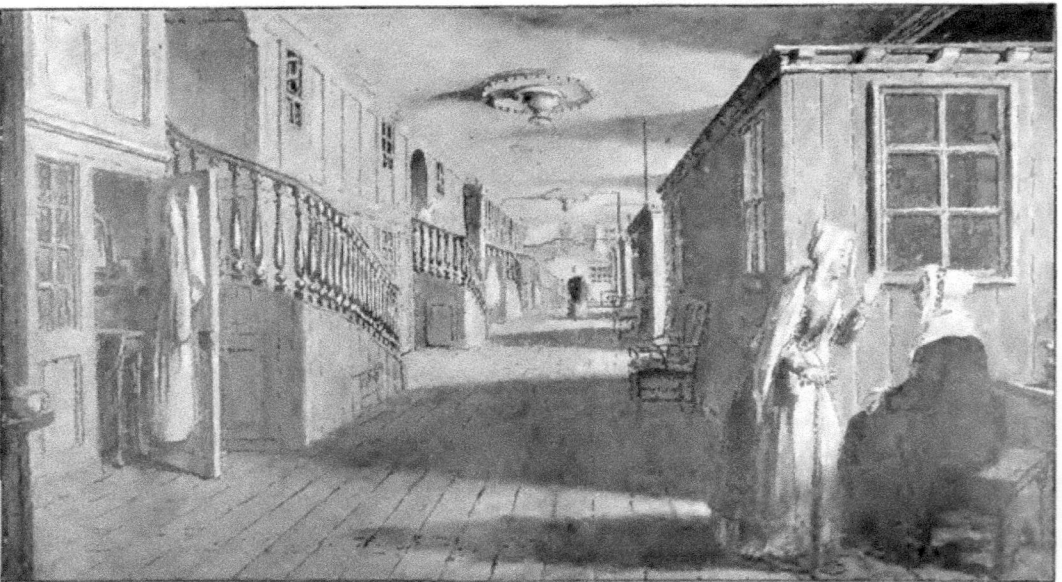

THE CORRIDOR OR HALL OF TRINITY HOSPITAL.

[Between pages [illegible].]

answer as it is given in the Assembly's Shorter Catechism; but more probably he did not desire to get into an intricate discussion with the learned judge, in which he might have come off second best. When the minister came to examine the domestics, he found they were better prepared for his questions. They had youth on their side; and several of them had not many years before emerged from a Parish or a Sunday School, where that Manual of Christian instruction which had been drawn up by the Assembly of Divines at Westminster was as a rule regularly taught to the rising generation, with "the proofs" attached thereto. But to return.

Whatever came of the Chaplain's examination of the inmates, there were other rules, which were most strictly observed. After the Reformation, the blue gown was dispensed with, and a sombre purple robe eventually took its place. The refusal to wear this garment subjected the individual to pains and penalties: *e.g.*—One inmate was ordered to remove from the premises, for refusal to wear a vestiture of "sad purple cullored cloth" which the Governors had selected by way of a livery for the beneficiaries.

As bearing upon the class of persons who from time to time were admitted to the Hospital, the following quotation may be referred to:— The late Lord Cockburn, writing at so comparatively recent a date as 1840, says:—"One of the present female pensioners is ninety-six. She was sitting beside her own fire. The Chaplain shook her kindly by the hand, and asked her how she was. 'Very weel—just in my creeping ordinary.' There is one Catholic here, a merry little woman, obviously with some gentle blood in her veins, and delighted to allude to it. This book she got from Sir John Something; her great friend had been Lady something Cunningham; and her spinet was the oldest that had ever been made; to convince me of which she opened it, and pointed exultingly to the year 1776. Neither she, nor the ninety-six-year-old was in an ark, but in a small room. On overhearing my name, she said she was once at Miss Brandon's boarding-school in Bristo Street, with a Miss Matilda Cockburn, 'a pretty little girl.' I told her that I remembered that school quite well, and that the little girl was my sister; and then I added as a joke, that all the girls at that school were said to have been pretty, and all light headed, and given to flirtation; the tumult revived in the vestal's veins. Delighted with the imputation, she rubbed her hands together, and giggled till she wept." It has been said that the octogenarian to whom Lord Cockburn refers was a Miss Gibb, and she was nearly the last of the old inmates of the Hospital.

Another illustration of the superior class of inmates who occasionally found the Hospital a pleasant place of abode, on their retirement from social life, may be illustrated by the following entry:—Miss Violet Maitland, who was resident in the Hospital in 1842, having received a considerable legacy,—did not fail to repay to the Governor all the money she had previously cost the Hospital, and she made a further payment to the Treasurer, on condition that she should be permitted to enjoy the privilege of remaining still as one of the inmates. This was about one year before the Imperial Parliament had doomed the destruction of the old Hospital building.

It was a rule of the House that on the death of any of the inmates, the Charity should make provision for his or her decent interment. About the middle of last century, the sums allowed for a funeral were as follow:—

Two dozen of clay Tobacco Pipes, .	£0	0	4
Dead Chist (Coffin), . . .	0	10	0
Dead Linnens (Clothes), . .	0	10	0
Gravemen's Dues, ...	0	2	6
Morte Cloth, *gratis*, . . .	0	0	0
Total,	£1	2	10

But this, apparently, did not exhaust the charges. If pipes were supplied, then something was required to put into them. Hence among some other charges, one was found for tobacco :—

Six gallons Ale, . . .	£0	6	0
A peck of Flour in shortbread,	0	2	0
A pint of Brandy, . .	0	3	0
A pound of Tobacco, .	0	1	6
Together,	£0	12	6

The total expenses of a funeral worked out, therefore, at £1, 15s. 4d.

The building was, before it was taken down, two storeys high, and it formed two sides of a square. It was not by any means ornamental. It had a quaint old-fashioned appearance, and was certainly not a very attractive residence. The windows were narrow and deep, especially in the lower floor. In fact it had a most dismal and repelling aspect; it was certainly not a house to induce people to resort to it.

Along the interior of the upper floor, there was a corridor, about half the width of the house. It was lighted from the west, and it served as a library and a place of promenade. The library had several important missals and old Bibles at the time of the house being dismantled. Most of these have gone amissing, and there now remain chiefly a large number of works of Divinity, dry-as-dust. Opening upon this corridor, were to be found a range of little rooms, used as bedrooms, which once formed the resort of the prebendaries in former times. The other parts of the House were of more modern construction, and these were fitted up when the Hospital came to be used solely for the support of the decayed burgesses of Edinburgh, and their wives and children, upwards of fifty years of age.

This restriction of the inmates was enacted by a Minute of the

Town Council, of date 24th May 1643, and was not by any means in accordance with the terms of the foundation. There seemed to be no such restrictions in the Hospital Charters.

It was, therefore, a Resolution of the Corporation, pure and simple, on behalf of the burgesses of the period and their relatives, on account of important services rendered by them and their ancestors to the community at large.

THE MATRON'S ROOM.

Between pages 144-5.]

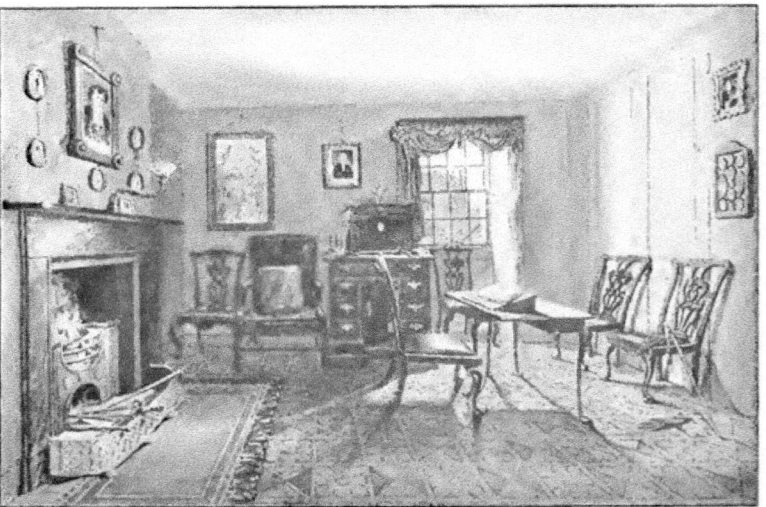

THE CHAPLAIN'S ROOM.

[Between pages 144-5.]

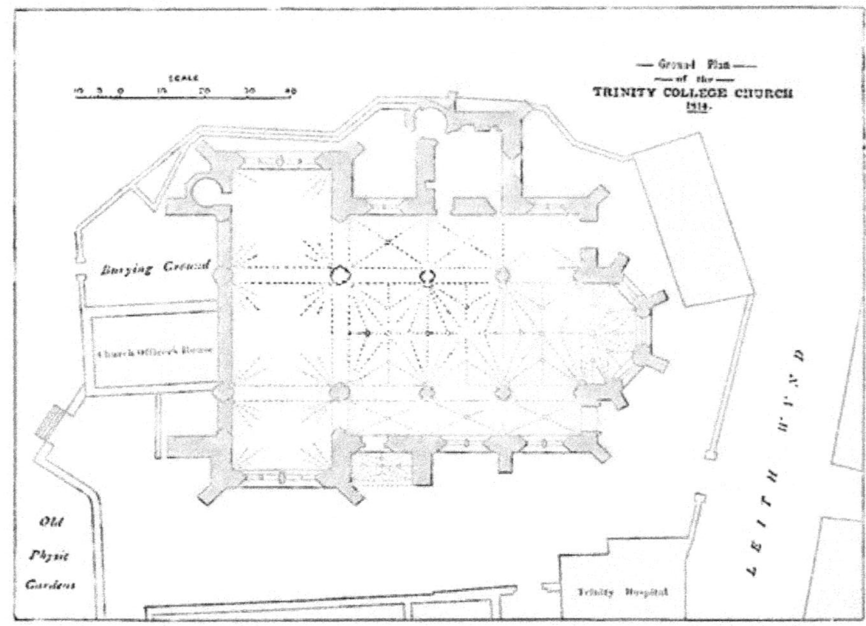

GROUND PLAN OF THE TRINITY COLLEGE CHURCH (1844).

To face page 145.]

CHAPTER XIII.

THE TRINITY COLLEGE CHURCH.

T may safely be assumed, that the Trinity College Church was, in 1844, undoubtedly the finest specimen of Gothic ecclesiastical architecture within the City of Edinburgh. Whatever were the original designs,—and these, in consequence of a variety of circumstances to which a passing allusion has already been made, were never entirely carried out,—it is, nevertheless, true, that this place of worship, as it appeared, at the beginning of the present century, was justly regarded as a most beautiful and very rare specimen of architecture, which gave to the antiquarian and to the man of taste a great deal to think upon and to mentally digest. It is right, however, to state that the nave was never built. This state of matters is capable of explanation. It was not unusual for devout persons, in that age of church building, to erect as much as they were able to do in their own day, and then leave the completion of the work to posterity, like the Cathedral of Cologne, which having been begun many centuries ago, has been finished only within the last few years.

As the building of Trinity College Church stood, at the time, it consisted of a choir and transepts, while the central tower was only partially built; and the same appeared to have been brought to a sudden termination, through its having been finished by crow-stepped gables and a slanted roof.

The ornamental accessories, with which the edifice seemed copiously to abound, did not fail to exhibit many varieties of design, notwithstanding that that most destroying demon, denominated "Time," had wrought his own fair share of destruction among them. The figure of the Monkey, which has always been regarded as a most fit representation of "the Devil," appeared very frequently in a variety of phases and positions in the gurgoyles. Why his Satanic Majesty should have been called upon to play so conspicuous a part, in a building most religiously dedicated to Christian Worship, is one of those things which possibly no one would be well able to understand, unless it had been on the unalterable principle recorded in Holy Writ, wherein we are advised most carefully, sedulously, and strenuously, to resist the Devil, and not under any circumstances to flee before or from him.

Why the Devil should not have appeared to the Trinitarians, in the garb of the more Biblical simile, of a "roaring Lion, seeking whom he may devour," seems equally strange. It could not certainly have been as a representative of the monkey race, and a first development of the human species, in consequence of any Darwinian theory as to evolution or human progression, in the origin of mankind generally, that he was brought to the front. That most speculative theory had not had, for many generations thereafter, a place and principle of local habitation in the human heart or intellect. Possibly the best excuse that can be made for its somewhat peculiar appearance or apparition, in regard to its being tolerated in a house dedicated to the worship of the Almighty God, where Christians were from time to time accustomed to resort for the purpose of religious worship was, that the image of the Monkey happened to be of frequent occurrence in the ecclesiastical buildings which were erected here and elsewhere, during the fifteenth and sixteenth centuries. It was, therefore, a matter of fashion or custom,—the outcome of the ideas or tastes of the period.

The ornamental details with which the interior of the Trinity College Church was so richly invested, were exceedingly varied and of the most quaint description. There were numerous armorial designs, which adorned many parts of the edifice. These were usually to be found towards the east end of the Choir.

The various, and equally varied, corbels, represented here and there an angelic form, or some other such beautiful device. But these were of more rare occurrence. The fashion of the day seems to have been to exhibit the contest continually going on between good and evil, as it is so aptly represented in the church of *Notre Dame* in Paris. The evil passions were demonstrated in a variety of ways, representing the most hideous and grotesque forms of extraordinary monsters, great or small, broad or tall—forms celestial, terrestrial or speculative—as should be supposed by the spectator to be designed for the purpose of bearing or carrying the enormous burdens, which, from their position in the building, they were to be understood to support, on the same principle as Atlas was represented, of old, to carry the Globe on his back.

One heraldic device has been described by both Maitland and Arnot, as being the arms of Queen Mary of Gueldres, the Foundress of the College and Hospital. It was situated on the side of a buttress at the west angle of the south transept, and it was in excellent preservation at the time of the edifice being taken down. A closer inspection and subsequent research have, however, proved it to be the "Coat of Arms" of Alexander, Duke of Albany, the brother-in-law of the Foundress, who, at the time of her death, was resident at the Court of the Duke of Gueldres. In respect of her own "Coat of Arms," these have now generally been supposed to have been carved out upon the north-east buttress of what was then "the vestry," near to the place where it was generally understood her mortal remains were deposited at the time of her decease in 1463.

The vestry, according to the late Sir Daniel Wilson, in his most admirable work entitled "Memorials of Edinburgh in the Olden Time," 1847 (Vol. II. page 176), "afforded externally a fine specimen of the old Scottish method of 'theiking with stone,'" with which the whole church, except the central tower, was roofed, till about the year 1814, when it was replaced with slates. The vestry also exhibited a rare specimen of an ancient Gothic chimney, an object of some interest to the architect, as being one of the few specimens of domestic architecture in that style which escaped the general destruction of the religious houses in Scotland.

The centre aisle of the Trinity College Church was very lofty. The groining was excessively rich in design. There was a most beautiful and handsomely symmetrical doorway, which, being placed under a well-proportioned porch, with firmly-groined roof, gave access to the south aisle of the choir, while a similar, though somewhat smaller one, many previous years before, would appear to have existed immediately under the Great Window of the north transept.

According to the late Mr James Grant (in his work entitled "Cassell's Old and New Edinburgh," Division II. page 303), "the choir of this church from the apse to the west enclosure of the rood tower was 90 feet long, and 70 feet from transept to transept window; the north aisle was 12 feet broad, and the south 9 feet. It is a tradition in masonry, that the north aisles of all Catholic churches were wider than the south, to commemorate the alleged circumstance of the Saviour's head on the Cross falling on His right shoulder. In digging the foundation of the Scott Monument, an old quarry, 40 feet deep, was discovered; and from it the stones from which the church was built were taken. With the exception of Holyrood, it was the finest example of decorated English Gothic architecture in the city, with many of the peculiarities of the age to which it belonged."

The Trinity College Church, not very long after the Reformation, was used as, and constituted, one of the parish churches of the City of Edinburgh. So early as 1584,—only about seventeen years after the Town Council had obtained from Sir Simon Preston the transference of his right to the Church and pertinents, and just about the time of the deed of agreement with Robert Pont, already referred to (page 47), the Lord Provost, Magistrates, and Town Council resolved to divide the town into four parishes, each to have a church. One of these parishes was designated the North-East and the Canongate-Head Parish, and to it was allocated the Trinity College Church.* Again,

* The Minute of the Town Council is to the following effect, and it not only divides the town into parishes, but also provides for the election of elders and deacons. It thus casts a side light on the religious policy and government of the day :—

"14. *October* 1584.—For establissing ane guid ordour and pollicie within the kirk, and execution of the disciplyne thairof, hes agreitt and condiscendit to the heids sett down be the persouns nominat to that effect in maner following, to witt,—The haill towne to be deuydet in foure parochins, according to thair quarters as thai presentlie stand, and euerie parochein to haif thair paroche kirk, according to thair quantitie, the grittest parochein to the grittest kirk, viz. St Geillis Kirk for the sowth west quarter; the Magdalein Chaipell for the sowth eist within the ports, the New Kirk for the north west, and the Trinity College for the north eist and the Cannogait heid without the port, and to this effect the said college to be incloset within the town, and ane yett to be strikkin furth in the town wall at the fute of Halkerstoun's Wynd, to serue for a passage to the said kirk. Attour, euerie ane of thir paroche kirkis to haif thair awin particulare reidare, and euery parochiner to cum to the prayers, communion, repentance, baptisme, and mariage in his awin paroche kirk. And, last, the provest, bailyies, counsall and deykins, with avyse of the ministers, to elect furth of euerie parochein thre elders and four deaconis, quha sall convene all togidder ilk Thurisday, with twa bailyeis and four of the counsall of the town, to tak ordour with the effairis belanging to their charge, to witt, the correctioun of the maners and support of the puir. And the names of the said eldaris and deaconis to be gevin to the ministers, and intimat be thame to the pepill, that gif any personis haif to say aganes the saidis persouns

in 1635, in conformity with an arrangement with King Charles, and in obedience to an Act of the Lords of Secret Council of 1st November, and for fulfilling the agreement with King Charles, the Town Council "divided and distinguished the whole town, including the West Port, Cowgate Street, and Head of Canongate and inhabitants thereof into four parochins," and appointed the limits of each. One of these parochins or quarters was the North-East quarter, and for this quarter the Council appointed the "College Kirk." Again in 1641, the Town Council divided the burgh into six parishes, appointing the churches and ministers respectively to each. The third of these parishes was thereby appointed the North-East Parish, and to it was appointed the church, "pertening of auld to the Trinitie Colledge, commonly called the 'Colledge Church.'" Various other divisions were made from time to time; but from the commencement of the Magistrates and Town Council's right in and management of the Trinity College Church, it had always been appropriated to, and been used as, one of the city churches; and it had been invariably allocated to the parish designated as that of the Trinity College. Ministers have always been appointed thereto, by the Corporation, in virtue of the right of patronage conferred upon them; the ministers have been recognised and dealt with by the Presbytery, and by other superior church courts, by Parliamentary enactments, by the courts of law, and otherwise, as of the city ministers, and as having right with their other brethren in the city ministry to the status and the funds which pertained to the city clergy. The whole ecclesiastical arrangements of the city have invariably been made and

may compeir, and his complaynt beand fund of trewth and resonabill, ane vther to be electit in place of that eldar or deacon. And ordanis the haill deykins of crafts to be warnet agane Fryday nixt to gif thair consent to the present ordour."

sanctioned by the Presbytery. Those arrangements have likewise been acknowledged by the courts of law and other judicatories, civil and ecclesiastical, and have been acquiesced in by every body, on the footing of Trinity College Church having been one of the recognised city churches. The seat rents were applied in the same way as the other city churches, and the expenses connected therewith were provided for and paid in the same manner.

As has already been stated, when the Church and College buildings, with the Hospital came into the hands of the Town Council, all of them had suffered more or less at the hands of Argyle and his followers. The Provost, Magistrates and Town Council had, therefore, to appeal for subscriptions from their fellow citizens to aid them. A building which has been allowed to get into decay, is not as a rule treated with great respect by the populace. In those days the lads and boys of the town were as mischievous as they are at the present time. Their conduct drew the attention of the authorities to them; hence there is a Minute of the Town Council to the following effect:—25. *June* 1589.—Understanding that the apprentices and children of the bonnet-maker craft, carries on their occupation daily furth of their masters' houses, "under Craigingatt and in the hie streets," and under pretence of that liberty, "casts staynes and brekis the glas windois in the Kirk of the Trinitie College," therefore ordains them and their masters to be admonished hereof, and charged to keep themselves within their booths and workhouses, and not to be found working either at the said craig or in the streets, and that the Deacon of the craft cause the same to be attended to, and the officers to help him in bringing the transgressors to punishment.

There are several Minutes of the Town Council bearing upon the subject of monetary help being required, which it may be proper to quote.

EXTRACTS FROM TOWN COUNCIL RECORDS:—

"20. *May* 1586.—William Littill, provest, the bailyeis, thesaurer and ane pairt of the counsale being convenit, Jhonn Jhonestoun, collectour, producet the sowme of fyftie merk in name of ane persone quhome he thocht nocht expedient to nominat, gevin be the said persoun of benevolence to the reparatioun of the Kirk in the Trinity College. Quhilk money wes delyuerit instantly to Alexander Vddart in name of the towne, and he, and Johnn Adamsoun, James Inglis, Andro Cairny, with ane bailyie, appoyntet to pas and seik the benevolence of the nichtboures to that wark, and als the Townes College foundet in the Kirk of Feyld; and ordanes ane lettre to be pennit to thame to schaw the nichtbouris the mater with the townis guid-will to thais wark lattet throw inhabilitie.

"22. *March* 1587-8.—Jhonn Jhonestoun, collectour, producet and delyuerit to Alexander Vddert, in name of the guid toun, ane Portugall ducatt, by and attour the fyftie merk gevin of before to the help of the reparatioun of the Trinity College Kirk, boyth gevin be ane certane persoun of godlie zeal to that vse.

"21. *February* 1588-9.—Gevis and disponis to the reparatioun of the Kirk in the Trinity College, the sowm of four hunder merk awand to the toun be the Flemyng websters, quha ar past to Sanctandrois (St Andrews), and be their souerties, to be imployet at the sicht and discretioun of the ministers, eldares, and deaconis of the kirk of this burgh.

"7. *March* 1588-9.—For better avancement of the wark to be begun be the sessioun in repayring of the Kirk of the Trinity College, and that the vyce of fornication may be supprest, and the vnlaws thairof mair exactly vpliftet nor thai haif bene heirtofore, and for dyuers vther guid caussis and consideratiouns moving thame, gevis and disponis to the said wark all the vnlawes and penalteis of sic as transgressis the townis acts and ordinances maid aganis the fornicatouris, and sic as huirds, concellis, and resaitts thame in thair howssis; and makis and constituts Alexander Speir, writter, collectour, vplifter, and persewar of the samyn, vpoun compt and rekning, to be maid by him to the Sessioun of the Kirk of the samyn, and this present act to stand induring the townis will allanerly.

"26. *March* 1589.—Gevis and grantis to the help of the reparatioun of the Kirk of the Trinity College ane competent number of the reddiest and lowsest staynis of the Hospital of St Pawles Wark, and consentis to the dountaking thairof, to be applyet to the said wark."

It may be requisite at this stage that a passing allusion should be made to a matter of considerable importance in connection with Scottish ecclesiastical history, in which the incumbent of the Trinity College Church did not obey the behests of his clerical superiors, or even of his Majesty King Charles I. Sunday, the 23d day of July 1637, has for many generations been noted, as the particular occasion, when George Hannay, Dean of Edinburgh, officiated in St Giles, and when there were present a large gathering of dignitaries. It is related, that Spottiswoode, the Archbishop of St Andrews was there, the Bishop of Edinburgh, the Lord Provost and Magistrates of the City, the Judges of the Court of Session, the Members of the Privy Council, and a great concourse of people. The occasion of the gathering was the fact that, by command of the King, Laud's Liturgy was to take the place of the more simple one of John Knox. The fact of its being "a new-fangled liturgy," imported from England, and that it had more Popish tendencies than the usual English liturgy, which it was designed to take the place of, did not at all commend it to the Scottish mind. Besides, it had never been approved of either by Parliament or the General Assembly, but was being forced upon the Edinburgers by the arbitrary command of the Crown. The people of Edinburgh would have none of it. When Dean Hannay opened the new service book, a storm of tumult prevailed; and a woman of great courage, well-known to posterity by the name of "Jenny Geddes," at once seized her camp stool and hurled it at the head of the offending Dean. Her example was soon followed, and stools and books were being pitched about promiscuously across the place of worship, like snow balls in a snow-ball riot. The indefatigable Jenny Geddes, having heard some one near her join in the response of "Amen," at once struck him in the face, calling out "Traitor, dost thou dare to say Mass at ma lug?" Jenny Geddes in her zeal for the Protestant faith earned for herself a name in history as a daring and successful reformer.* In St Giles Church, the circumstance is duly recorded. On one of the pillars there is a brass plate which states the fact of Dean Hannay's work on that occasion. But there is another brass plate not far from it which practically says "*audi alteram partem.*" The wording of it is to the following effect:—

> "Constant oral tradition affirms that, near this spot, a brave Scotch woman, Janet Geddes, on the 23d July 1637, strvck the first blow in the great strvggle for freedom of conscience, which, after a conflict of nearly half a centvry, ended in the establishment of civil and religiovs liberty."

It is currently reported that the late Right Hon. John Inglis of Glencorse, Lord President of the Court of Session, is responsible for the latter.

History records the fact that, on the same Sunday, a lesser riot took place in the Church of the Grayfriars, James Fairly having undertaken to brave the popular storm. His senior colleague in the church, the Sub-Dean, Andrew Ramsay (at one time a Professor of Divinity in the University of Edinburgh, and a man of great scholarship and culture) having refused to read the service.

In the Trinity College Church, the service was not read, notwithstanding that the incumbent, Henry Rollock, had on the previous Sunday made intimation that Laud's Liturgy would on the occasion be used, and of which he stated to the congregation that he highly

* The stool of Jenny Geddes may be seen in the Museum of the Society of Antiquaries. It was gifted to the Society by James Watson, Esq., Writer, Dunse. In a communication to them, read to the Fellows on 9th December 1856, he says:—"The stool which belonged to Jenny Geddes was taken possession of by the person who had charge of the church. His daughter married a man named Pollock. She got the stool at the death of her father. A grandson of this Pollock, a surgeon, settled in Dunse about 1726. The stool was in his possession. His son, Adam Pollock, who died in 1813, has often told me its history; and, at the sale of his furniture, I attended and purchased it."

approved. During the course of the week which intervened, he saw, from the feeling of the people, that it was more prudent in him to desist. He, to all appearance, was afraid to offend the populace. The "Laye Declaration of the King" remarks "whose favour is the onely aire in which he taketh delight to breathe and live."

The following have been the Provosts and Ministers of the Trinity College Church, so long as the original building lasted, as the same can be traced, from the Kirk-Session records:—

Provosts of the Church and College, before the Reformation.

Sir Edward Boncle.
John Brady, Archdeacon of Lothian.
Sir John Dingwall.
William Cunynghame.
Robert Erskine.
Sir George Clapperton, Dean of the Chapel Royal.
Lawrence Clapperton.
Robert Pont.

Collegiate Ministers after the Reformation from 1597 *to* 1782.

1597. George Robertson.
1598. Walter Balcanqual
1625. John Maxwell, A.M.
1626. Thomas Sydserf, Dean of Edinburgh.
1628. Haric Rollock, A.M.
1635. James Elliot, D.D.
1639. William Colville, A.M.
1641. William Bennet.
1644. Robert Laurie.
1648. John Smith, A.M.
1649. Hew Mackail.
1661. John Glendie.
1662. Joshua Meldrome, A.M.
1663. Alexander Carneross, A.M.
1669. John Macqueene, A.M., Sub-Dean of the Chapel Royal.
1673. Andrew Cant.
1674. Robert Laurie, A.M., Bishop of Brechin.
1679. Andrew Cant, junr., A.M.
1689. Hugh Kennedy, A.M., Moderator of General Assembly of 1690.
1692. John Moncrieff.
1701. Archibald Riddell, A.M.
1710. James Grierson, Moderator of General Assembly of 1719.
1714. James Bannatine, do. 1739.
1732. George Logan, do. 1740.
1758. Robert Dick, A.M.
1758. Henry Lundie.

Ministers of the Trinity College Church since it became a single charge in 1782.

799. David Dickson, D.D., afterwards translated to St Cuthbert's.
1802. Robert Anderson.
1801. Thomas Macknight, D.D., Moderator of General Assembly of 1820.
1810. Andrew Grant, D.D. Dean of the Chapel Royal.
1813. Walter Tait, A.M.
1834. William Cunningham, D.D., afterwards Principal of the New College, Edinburgh, and Moderator of the Free Church Assembly of 1859.
1843. William Steven, D.D.

The late Rev. Walter Tait was shortly after the beginning of the present century the incumbent of the charge. Having been ordained in 1795, he was called to Trinity College Church in 1813. He had a large and influential congregation. It was partly composed of dwellers in the New Town, and residents of the Old Town, with a wholesome admixture of Canigotians. He was very popular as a preacher. About the year 1833, however, he had imbibed new notions regarding Christian tenets, and he was compelled to resign his charge in consequence of his departure from the doctrinal standards of the Church of Scotland. The very few that seceded with him, were for many years denominated in Edinburgh as "the Taitites."

The Rev. Mr Tait was a believer in, and a follower of, a much abler man, the celebrated Rev. Edward Irving. The latter, born in the burgh of Annan, was first of all, after his being licensed to preach the gospel, assistant to the great Rev. Dr Chalmers in St John's Church, Glasgow. From there, he proceeded to London, and preached to Scottish Presbyterians, in the Caledonian Asylum, Cross Street, Hatton Garden. The novelty of his style, and the force and eloquence of his discourses, soon rendered him the most popular preacher of his day, and the singularity of his appearance and gesticulation attracted very large congregations. The principal orators and statesmen of the day crowded to hear him; he literally became quite "the rage" among the wealthy and fashionable of the Metropolis, and his chapel doors were thronged with carriages, so that it was found necessary to grant admittance only by tickets. About 1827, the chapel in Hatton Garden, already referred to, was found too small to contain the large concourse of persons who continued to throng to it. A subscription was forthwith entered into, for the purpose of erecting a larger and more commodious church; and the handsome edifice in Regent Square (which is now very well known by most Scotsmen resident for a short time in the Metropolis, as the church of the late Rev. Dr James Hamilton, the present Rev. Professor Oswald Dykes, and latterly of the Rev. John Macneill) was completed in 1829. In the beginning of 1830, Irving's supposed heretical views were brought before the Scottish Church in London, and he was ordained to stand his trial before the Presbytery of the said church, who were charged to examine and report upon his "Work on Christ's Humanity." The libel charged him with holding Christ subject to original and actual sin, and with denying the doctrines of atonement, satisfaction, imputation, and substitution. The exhibition of the "unknown tongues" uttered by some designing or deluded members of his congregation, chiefly females, and pronounced by Mr Irving from the pulpit to be the "manifestations of the Holy Ghost," next occupied public attention. The trustees of the National Scottish Church, Regent Square, at last found it necessary to prefer charges against him, in addition to those already before the Presbytery. On May 2, 1832, the London Presbytery unanimously found him guilty of heresy, and dispossessed him of his charge as minister of the church in Regent Square; and the Presbytery of Annan, of which he was a member, on March 13, 1833, formally deposed him from the ministry of the Church of Scotland. He died at Glasgow in 1834, about one year after his deposition from the Church of his Fathers. He was only in the forty-second year of his age at the date of his death, although he looked much older. His long grey hair and his wrinkled brow gave him a more aged appearance. It has been stated that "there can be no doubt but that the melancholy errors and extravagances, into which he was betrayed in the latter years of his life, were the effects of a diseased imagination, arising from that morbid love of the marvellous, and that craving for notoriety for which he was so remarkable, and to which he at last fell a victim." With all his eccentricities, however, and even although his immediate successor in Regent Square Church has well remarked, in the analysis of his character which he has given forth to the public is to the following effect—"his practical wisdom did not keep pace with his discursive powers—the might of his genius, and the grandeur of his views, and the prevailing solemnity of his spirit" left a deep impression on his hearers and contemporaries, and Edward Irving became the founder of a sect. In Britain, they were first popularly known as "the Irvingites." They subsequently assumed the name of the "Holy Catholic Apostolic Church," and in London, Edinburgh and Glasgow, from the wealth and influential character of some of the members, they have been enabled to build very large and imposing structures in these cities for their peculiar mode of worship.

But to return. The Rev. Mr Tait was obliged to surrender his charge of Trinity College Church. The appointment of the Town Council of the day fell upon the Rev. William Cunningham of Greenock, a most able theologian, and who was afterwards well known as the successor to Dr Chalmers in the Principalship of the Free Church or New College in Edinburgh. Mr Cunningham came to Edinburgh under very favourable circumstances. He had great personal ability and public reputation. It has been frequently stated that, for some time after his induction, the demand for sittings in the Trinity College

Church was so great, that the vacant seats had to be balloted for. Nevertheless it did not always continue to be so. Cunningham was a most powerful debater in the Church Courts. He had a purely logical mind. He was a Calvinist of the most pronounced type, and he did not try to reconcile his peculiar views with the fashion of the world, in its daily intercourse with society at large. His congregation became "smaller by degrees and beautifully less," and at the time of the Disruption of the Church of Scotland in 1843, it was given up by the Free Church as a separate charge—most of the members going into the fold of the late Rev. Dr John Bruce, who was then the seceding minister from the parish church of St Andrew. The Rev. Dr William Steven, who had previously been for several years House Governor in George Heriot's Hospital, was appointed to the vacant charge in the Established Church during 1843. When the congregation was called upon to find other quarters, they worshipped within the building then known as the Calton Convening Rooms, which is now utilised as the Burgh Assessor's Office. The congregation, during Dr Steven's pastorate, was never a large one, being composed of between 70 and 80 members. On his death, which occurred in 1857, he was succeeded by the late Rev. William Smith, D.D., afterwards translated to the Parish Church of North Leith. During Dr Smith's incumbency, the congregation had so increased in numbers, that other provision had to be made for them. This was done by the Town Council obtaining a lease of Free John Knox's Church, in the east side of the High Street, for a few years. The Rev. Robert Wallace, D.D., became Dr Smith's successor, and the Annuity Tax Bill of 1860 having extinguished the Old Church as one of the City Charges, the congregation of Trinity College Church found accommodation therein. Dr Wallace was nine years thereafter translated to the charge of Old Grayfriars, in succession to the late Dr Robert Lee, and he was appointed Professor of

Church History in the University of Edinburgh. He subsequently laid down his "holy orders," by resigning his charge and chair, became an English barrister, and has for three successive periods been elected Member of Parliament for the Eastern Division of the City. In 1869, Dr Cornelius Giffen was appointed successor to Dr Wallace, until he was translated to the parish church of St Mary's in 1872. During that year the Rev. Dr Gentles was appointed in succession to Dr Giffen, and he again got translated to the Abbey Church, Paisley, in 1879, when the Rev. Alexander Kennedy was called to the vacant charge of Trinity College Church. He is still the incumbent of the parish.

CHAPTER XIV.

THE SALE OF THE CHURCH AND HOSPITAL BUILDINGS.

THE doom of the ancient fabrics of Trinity College Church and Trinity Hospital was now written. In the inexorable decrees of fate, both edifices were bound to go; and the ground space they occupied was destined to be taken advantage of for other and possibly more utilitarian purposes.

The projectors of the North British Railway—which at that time consisted merely of a proposal to construct a line between the City of Edinburgh and the good old town of Berwick-upon-Tweed—had duly made announcement of their intentions in the newspapers of the day, about the middle of the month of November 1843, all in conformity with the Standing Orders of the Houses of Parliament in regard to private bills. The Book of Reference and Relative Plans had been as usual deposited with the proper officials on the last day of the month. Although at first, it seemed to be a comparatively limited proposal, involving the construction of about sixty miles of railway,—it was well known that the line was being formed with the view of its being joined to sundry other contributory lines of railway, in order to constitute a grand trunk line to London, by way of Newcastle, Darlington, York, Selby, Doncaster, Grantham, and Peterborough—denominated "the East Coast Route."

Prior to the formation of the railway system, all communication between Edinburgh and London was either by the Royal Mail Coach (the land service), or by the steamers sailing from Leith or Granton (the sea service). In both cases, about three days were consumed in the journey. The arrival of the London Mail Coach* about three o'clock in the afternoon, was an event which, in the writer's memory, is still a very vivid recollection, as a record of the past. At the sound of the bugle-horn of the red-coated Guard, every vehicle or machine in transit got quickly out of the way, as the four-in-hand Mail Coach came tearing along Nicolson Street, down the South and North Bridges, past the Old Theatre Royal to the then General Post Office in Waterloo Place, and which is now occupied as the New Waverley Hotel. At very rare times the Mail Coach was the depositarian of some fugitive from justice; and the vehicle, all bespattered with mud as it usually behoved

* The Royal Mail Coach as it existed at that time, was not a very ancient institution. The "Sun" newspaper, a London bi-weekly, on Wednesday, June 5, 1799, contains the following announcement, which is here copied *verbatim et literatim*.—"MAIL COACHES.—The advantages which the public have derived from the establishment of Mail Coaches has long been felt and acknowledged; and it is with pleasure that we hear that it is now determined on, to extend that benefit north to Inverness, for which place a coach is to commence running on the first day of July next."

It is requisite to explain that, for the purposes of the post-service, there were no relays of post-boys, or horses, at different stages; one man and one horse accomplishing the whole ride and taking the necessary rests by the way. For example, the post between Edinburgh and Aberdeen stopped one night at Dundee, and another at Montrose. This system continued in Scotland until well on in the last century. Up till 1763, the communication between London and Edinburgh was only three times a week; but by that time it was made to be five times a week. At first, the mail was 85 hours in travelling from London to Edinburgh, and 131 hours in returning. Until 1788, there was no direct mail to Glasgow. Previous to that time, the post was sent round by way of Edinburgh, and it took the whole of five days in transit.

One of the most remarkable steps which the General Post Office took at that time was the adoption of the late Mr Palmer's celebrated plan in 1784. The chief part of this plan

to be, after the mail bags had been duly delivered at the Post Office, was then driven along to the entrance to the Edinburgh Jail, which at that time and until very recently was opposite to the steps leading up to the Calton Hill. Within the precincts of the prison-house, the culprit was safely and securely deposited, in the presence of a wondering crowd of spectators who thronged the doorway, to get a passing glance of the prisoner as he passed in.

The departure of the Mail Coach for London was a sight not less interesting. The stowing away of the bags was witnessed every day by a considerable crowd of wondering spectators. But the depositing of the protecting blunderbuss and the pair of pistols was the last duty to be discharged by the Guard, before he took his place at the back of the Mail Coach. As is recorded of an old Edinburgh character, who

was to have the mail coaches in charge of an armed guard, by way of stage coaches,—(which thus became mail coaches), instead of the mails being conveyed as formerly, by a boy in mailcart or on horseback. Mr Palmer's merit consisted in this, that a greater degree of regularity and of speed in post conveyance was possible; and in catching the hint from the stage coaches which nobody saw but himself. The advantage of employing stage coaches which subserved other purposes, was a species of economy, when taken in contrast with the mail curricles which were exclusively devoted to the duty of only carrying the mails.

Mr Palmer was afterwards, because of his merits, appointed Comptroller of the Post Office, in which capacity he is understood to have made several important changes in the internal details and arrangements of the office.

The first mail coaches on Mr Palmer's principle were the Bath and Bristol in 1784. Previous to this plan having been adopted, the ordinary speed of the post bags was 3½ miles per hour. On the new plan, the speed became at least doubled. In later times, the average speed of the Royal Mails was usually 8 miles 7 furlongs, while the highest reached not unfrequently 10 miles 5 furlongs.

Royal Mails were first conveyed between Liverpool and Manchester by railway in 1828. When a railway service was established in 1835, between London, Liverpool, Birmingham and Manchester, the service was utilised so far as it could be made available to facilitate the Scottish and Irish service. It was upwards of twelve years thereafter that the Royal Mail Coach ceased to be known on the streets of Edinburgh.

went by the name of "Bailie Duff," and whose peculiar hobby was to precede all funerals during his lifetime, with two streamers of crape two yards long, suspended from the back of his hat; so the Mail Coach had in Edinburgh a character of the name of Wishart, whose daily habit it was regularly to attend at Waterloo Place and see the Mail Coach start on its southern journeys.

But the idea of the old building of Trinity Hospital being about to be taken down, and unquestionably the finest specimen of Gothic architecture in ecclesiastical buildings being about to be for ever removed, did not fail to create quite a sensation in the "Modern Athens," more particularly in antiquarian circles. In those days, the Parliamentary Bar had not got that distinction to which in more modern times it has attained, and which is owing very much to the extraordinary development of the railway system all over the Kingdom. At the time referred to, and for many years previous, learned counsel were rarely employed in regard to local bills. The parties, who were promoting the same, usually appeared before the Committee to which the matter had been relegated *in propriâ personâ*, along with their agents; and they explained to the Members of the Committee the various details of the project, while those who came in opposition were attended by their respective agents, and were heard for their interest. It was so, when the late Mr Duncan M'Laren, as Treasurer of the City of Edinburgh, attended in London in regard to the City Agreement Act of 1838, including a Settlement as to the Leith Docks, the University and Schools revenues, and an Arrangement with the City Creditors. It was equally so, when the late Mr Adam Black, as Lord Provost of the City, went to London, for the purpose of meeting before a Parliamentary Committee, the projectors of the North British Railway and their engineers and agents. In a letter sent at the time to his senior bailie (the College Bailie of the period), Mr William

Duncan of Danevale, who was afterwards a son-in-law of Mr Black's, that gentleman very recently informed the writer that Mr Black had sent down instructions to him to send up the late Mr John Sinclair (at that time Keeper of the Council Records, and afterwards Conjunct Town Clerk of the City), to bring with him all the documents that would be required to prove their case. Mr Sinclair was duly despatched, and arrived in London with his books and writs. In another letter the Lord Provost duly announced his satisfaction at Mr Sinclair being beside him; and writing on the morning when the case was to come before the Parliamentary Committee, he jocularly added—"I feel this morning very much like unto Robinson Crusoe of old, with Sinclair as my man Friday, going forth to fight the savages!"

It is, however, right to state at this stage, that it would be a great excess of folly in the present day for any local authority, interested in any vexed question before the Legislature to appear otherwise, in the progress of any Parliamentary Private Bill, except through the most direct, though somewhat expensive, course of employing learned counsel. It has become so much a custom in Westminster, that an attempted recourse to the former method, would certainly prove abortive to any man, or body of men, who were so foolish as to try it. We now live in a different age, and under very different conditions and surroundings. As the old mediæval Latin hexameter expresses it:—*Tempora mutantur, nos et mutamur in illis*—The times are changed, and we have changed along with them. We now live practically in a new state of things—in an age of railways and tramways, of morning daily newspapers as well as evening daily newspapers, of telegrams and telephones,—and he would be a most daring and rather adventurous man who would counsel a return to the former practice, and would seek to imitate those who lived in a byegone age, when other circumstances and different arrangements prevailed. He would certainly be found at a discount. One must seek in public business to keep abreast of the times, otherwise he is sure to be pronounced "a waster." It is, however, a great drawback of the present system, that three or four members of the Bar require to be employed in any great case, if due attention is to be given to it. Even when these arrangements are made, it not unfrequently happens, that none of them can be got to put in an appearance, when required,—being engaged in other Committee Rooms. This has been found to be a great drawback, and somewhat of a scandal. Besides the time which an enquiry may take is so uncertain, as frequently to cause considerable and quite unprofitable expense, in agents and professional and other witnesses waiting on for many days for the case in which they are interested. This has led to a movement in regard to enquiries as to private bills being taken upon the spot. Whether the measure proposed will be successful, is a matter of some dubiety. There is no doubt, however, that some modification of the present arrangements is likely to take place. But, after so long an experience, it will be rather a difficult matter wholly to do away with the Westminster enquiry in most cases.

Nevertheless, in the former times, as has been stated, counsel rarely appeared. Mr Adam Black, as Lord Provost of the City of Edinburgh, somewhat successfully fought the promoters of the North British Railway. He obtained for the Corporation of Edinburgh, as the Governors of Trinity Hospital, the sum of £6000 for the hospital buildings and site; and that sum, at the present time, forms part of the capital stock of the Trinity Hospital fund.

It was otherwise, however, with the Trinity College Church. That was a subject not quite so easily disposed of, and settled. The power to obtain the site and to take down the College Church, after a great deal of negotiation, was thus adjusted in the North British Railway Act, 9 and 10 Vic. cap. 74. The clause is to the following effect:—" It shall not be lawful for the said North British Railway Company to make any alterations on, or to use for the purposes of the said railway, the additional land in the parishes of Trinity College, St Andrew and Canongate, which by this Act they are authorised to purchase for a terminus in Edinburgh, until they shall have agreed with the Lord Provost, Magistrates and Town Council of the said City, on a plan for the removal and rebuilding, at the expense of the Company, on another site, either within the said parish of Trinity College, or as near thereto as conveniently may be, of a new church, with equal convenience of access and accommodation to that already existing in the said parish; and that, in such agreement, provision shall be made for the adoption of the same style and model with the existing church, providing always that any difference of opinion between the parties regarding the plan and site of the said new church, shall be subject to the arbitration of the Sheriff of Edinburgh, declaring that it shall be competent to the Railway Company to offer, and the said Magistrates and Council are hereby authorised to accept of, a sum of money as compensation for the said church and in lieu of the foresaid obligation."

It would have saved the Town Council many a weary debate, and a great deal of litigation, extending over a long period of years, as well as the electors of the city many a contested election in the various wards, if they had most sedulously confined themselves to the former proposition of the North British Railway Company; and which, briefly interpreted, was "a church for a church, in or near the district or parish, on the old and well-known model." The Town Council did not fail to profit by its experience at a later stage on quite another matter. It was not then a question of "kirk," but one of "market."

When the North British Railway directors came to the resolution to extend their station-house westwards, which in its initial stage was south of what used to be known as Shakspeare Square, immediately behind the Old Theatre Royal, the site of the present General Post Office; and when they desired to include the area at the foot of Canal Street and adjacent buildings, at that time well known as the Fruit and Vegetable Market—(a market which had been opened during the civic reign of Lord Provost John Manderston, druggist, East Rose Street, in 1819, and whose name was wont to appear carved on the gateway, which, for railway purposes had afterwards to be removed)—so as to make the site of the Waverley Bridge the new terminus, with the old Edinburgh and Glasgow Railway on the one side of the Station-house, and the North British on the other side; the former having deposited a Bill in Parliament to extend the line from Haymarket through the West Princes Street Gardens and East Princes Street grounds to the aforesaid site,—the Town Council of the day resisted the proposals of both these companies. In this, however, they were unsuccessful. Parliament, in its wisdom, deemed it proper to grant the concession to both the Railway Companies in the interest of the public, and for the purpose of affording to the community greater facilities and expedition in travelling; although many citizens of taste inveighed against the barbarism of allowing a railway service through the beautiful garden and valley which had taken the place of the old North Loch. In one respect, however, the Town Council was successful. In regard to the North British Railway, and its appropriation of the Fruit and Vegetable Market, it came to an Agreement with the Railway Company, that it should, in place of accepting any sum of money, be provided with another market in lieu of the one which by the Bill was taken from the Town. For many years thereafter, the market continued to be regularly held on an area which formed part of the Old Physic Gardens to the east of the middle and large southern arches of the North Bridge. But the exigencies of the Railway Company, through its greatly increased and increasing traffic, required more additional space; and numerous and varied were the proposals from time to time, on the part of the Railway Directors, to get rid of their obligations under the Act, by converting their responsibilities into the payment of a sum of money. From £21,000 to £25,000 was something like the amount offered. It was a tedious and much deferred battle. The Town Council's never-varying demand, however, was "Market for market." Many correspondents in the newspaper press supported the Railway Company as against the Corporation. This was likely to be the case, when there was a large body of interested shareholders. Nevertheless the Town Council remained obdurate; and in this they were right. When the North British Railway Company resolved to shut up the Scotland Street Tunnel, which was the old access by the Edinburgh and Granton Railway to Fife and the North, and no further traffic was in future to be taken that way, a much easier route having been provided, in the opening of the Abbey Hill and Leith Walk Stations,—a solution of the difficulty was then found. The present site of the Waverley Market was conceded to, and accepted by, the Town Council; and the improvements which the Corporation have since effected on the site after it came into their hands, have tended greatly to enhance the value of the Market, which, placed as it is in so central and accessible a situation, could not fail to render it a place of continual resort, as well as to make it adaptable to many useful purposes in the public interest.

It was otherwise, however, in regard to the arrangement as to Trinity College Church. On the 4th day of May 1848, the Town Council had agreed with the North British Railway Directors,* to accept

* The following is the Deed of Agreement referred to:—

It is agreed upon between the parties following, viz., The Lord Provost, Magistrates and Council of the City of Edinburgh, of the first part, and the North British Railway Company, incorporated by Act of Parliament, of the second part; that is to say a sum of money in lieu of the obligations on the part of the latter to find another site and to rebuild the Church. Possibly the Railway Directors saw many complications looming in the distance, which might have a tendency to give them worry, and to produce dissatisfaction. Hence the Deed of Agreement of 4th May 1848. As has been stated, there had been previously received from the Railway Company the sum of £6000 for the Hospital buildings and site. Under the first

whereas by an Act of the 10th Victoria, caput 74, intituled, "An Act to authorize the construction of several Branch Railways, and other Works in connexion with the North British Railway," the said second parties acquired power to purchase certain additional property in the parishes of Trinity College, Saint Andrew, and Canongate, in the city of Edinburgh, including Trinity College Church, and the ground on which it stands, for the purposes of the said railway; and it is thereby provided, that it should not be lawful for the said second parties to make any alteration on, or to use for the purposes of the said railway, the said additional land, until they should have agreed with the said first parties on a plan for the removal and rebuilding, at the expense of the said second parties, of a new church, in manner therein mentioned; but it is by the said Act declared, that it should be competent for the said second parties to offer, and the said first parties are thereby authorised to accept of, a sum of money as compensation for the said church, and in lieu of the foresaid obligation; and whereas the said first parties applied for and obtained an interdict against the said second parties making any alterations on or using for the purposes of the said railway the said additional land, until the said condition should be satisfied; and whereas certain proceedings took place before the sheriff of Edinburgh in reference to sites and plans for the new church, and latterly, a site, on ground acquired by the said second parties, with relative plans proposed by them, were approved of by the sheriff, under a reference to him, in terms of the provisions of the Act; and whereas the ground so fixed on for a site * was subject to a restriction against building in favour of the said first parties as superiors thereof, and having been considered by them to be unsuitable for the said church, they objected thereto, and declined to discharge the said servitude or restriction; but the said second parties maintain that the said restriction is not now in force; and the said parties being desirous to put an end to all questions, disputes, and differences, in regard to the said matters, have agreed as follows; videlicet,—

* Ireland's Woodyard, at foot of Leith Wynd.

head of the agreement, Mr Rhind, architect, fixed £16,371, 9s. 6d. as the estimated expense of rebuilding Trinity College Church, and it was provided that for this purpose the Railway Company should grant promissory notes; while, under the fourth head of the agreement, immediate payment should be made of £800 as the price of the site of the Old Church, and £500 for a discharge of the Hospital of a restriction against building on ground to the south of the Old Hospital proposed

First. The said second parties do hereby offer, and the said first parties do hereby accept of, the sum of money which shall be fixed by David Rhind, esquire, architect, from estimates to be procured by himself, without challenge or interference by either party, as the actual cost of erecting and completing for occupation a church on the site and in exact accordance with the plans approved of by the sheriff as aforesaid, including architect's fees, clerk of works' allowance, and all other necessary charges, and that as compensation for the said church, and in lieu of the obligation on the said second parties under the said Act of Parliament in reference to said church.

Second. The said sum shall be payable at the term of Whitsunday 1849, with interest at the rate of five per cent. from the term of Whitsunday 1848, and thereafter during the not payment.

Third. The said second parties shall immediately deliver to the said first parties a promissory note at 12 months' date by [*blank*] of the directors of the said railway company, for the sum of 15,000*l.* sterling, which promissory note, when paid, or whatever portion of the sum thereby due shall be recovered, shall, when so paid, be imputed *pro tanto* of the sum offered and accepted as aforesaid, it being hereby declared that the said promissory note shall not operate as a novation of the claim of the said first parties against the said second parties for implement of the obligation imposed on them in regard to the building of a new church for said parish; but in the event of said promissory note, or any part of the sum therein contained, not being paid when the said promissory note becomes due, the said first parties shall have recourse against the said second parties and the property of the company for enforcing performance of that obligation.

Fourth. The said second parties shall make immediate payment to the said first parties of the sum of 1,300*l.*, that is to say, of the sum of 800*l.* as the price of the site of the present Trinity College Church, and of the sum of 500*l.* for a discharge of the restriction against building on the ground proposed for the site of a new church as aforesaid.

Fifth. If the expense of erecting the new church, as the same may be estimated by Mr

as the site of the New Church. The sums of £800 and £500 were received on 9th May 1848. At the same time, there was received from the Railway Company a promissory note for £15,000, and on the 17th August 1848, a further note for £1371, 9s. 6d.,—making up the £16,371, 9s. 6d., as the estimated expense of rebuilding the Church. The promissory notes were partially renewed from time to time, and

Rhind, together with the foresaid sum of 1,300*l.*, shall be less than 15,000*l.* in all, the said first parties shall repay the difference to the said second parties on receiving Mr Rhind's estimate; and if, on the other hand, the total expense shall exceed 15,000*l.*, then the difference shall, on the said estimate being received, be paid by the said second parties to the said first parties, either in cash, or by a bill, with interest from its date, to be granted by the said directors at 12 months, in the option of the said directors.

Sixth. All expenses connected with the transaction and with the proceedings before the sheriff and the Court of Session shall be defrayed, and the expenses already incurred by the said first parties shall be immediately paid to them by the said second parties.

Seventh. The said first parties on receiving delivery of the said promissory note, and on payment of the foresaid sum of 1,300*l.* and expenses as aforesaid, agree to withdraw the foresaid interdict at their instance, and consent to the said second parties immediately taking possession of and using the additional property acquired by them under the said Act, including the present Trinity College Church and the grounds whereon it is erected, in the same manner as if the obligation relative to the rebuilding of a new church had been already implemented by them.

Eighth. The said first parties bind and oblige themselves, whenever required, to execute and deliver to the said second parties, at the expense of the latter, a conveyance in terms of the said second parties' acts, of the said Trinity College Church and site thereof, together with a discharge of the foresaid restriction; and upon the foresaid promissory note being retired and payment being made of any other sums that may be due under this arrangement, a discharge of the obligation incumbent on the said second parties by the said act in regard to the erection of a new church for said parish, and generally of all claims and demands competent to them in the premises. In witness whereof these presents, written upon stamped paper by Peter Young Black, clerk to Messrs. Smith and Kinnear, writers to the Signet, are subscribed (under this declaration, that the words "and have since purchased," on the fourth and fifth lines, and the words "the obligation imposed," on the 32d line, counting from the top, were deleted before subscription) as follows: viz., by the Right honourable Adam Black, Lord Provost of the city of Edinburgh, for himself, and as taking burden on him for the

were fully paid up and discharged, with £1643, 11s. 5d. of periodical interest, up to 17th May 1852.

Having made this arrangement with the Railway Company, the Magistrates and Town Council as a Corporation and as Governors of Trinity Hospital were not long in finding themselves involved in a perfect "sea of troubles," out of which they did not emerge for upwards of a quarter of a century thereafter.

---

magistrates and council of the said city, at Edinburgh, the 4th day of May 1848, before these witnesses,—Patrick Graham, writer to the Signet, and Joshua Wilson Coomb, apprentice to the said Right honourable Adam Black; and by John Learmonth, esquire, of Dean, George Hamilton Bell, esquire, Fellow of the Royal College of Surgeons, Edinburgh, and Sir James Forrest, of Comiston, baronet, three of the directors of the said North British Railway Company, as follows; viz. by the said John Learmonth and George Hamilton Bell, at Edinburgh, the said 4th day of May and year last mentioned, before these witnesses,—David Smith, writer to the Signet, and William Balfour Reid, clerk to the said Smith and Kinnear; and by the said Sir James Forrest, also at Edinburgh, the same day, before these witnesses,—John Forrest, esquire, residing in the Royal Circus, Edinburgh, and Alexander Brown, coachman to the said Sir James Forrest; and sealed with the corporate seal of the said company, place and date last above mentioned; this testing clause, from and including the words "these presents" to the end being written by Alexander James Taylor, clerk to the said Smith and Kinnear, by whom the words "At Edinburgh" have been interlined between the sixth and seventh lines counting from the bottom hereof.

(signed) *Adam Black*, Lord Provost,
John Learmonth, Director.
George Ham. Bell, Director.
James Forrest, Director.

CHAPTER XV.

CONCERNING THE HOSPITAL'S REVENUES.

IT would be a mistake to suppose that the charitable institution, called "The Trinity Hospital," derived pecuniary benefit from those revenues, which, in the Royal Charters, already enumerated and described, were set forth as the emoluments of the respective Provosts, Prebendaries, Choiristers, and Beidmen under the old dispensation. The Hospital, as such, acquired none of these old church revenues. It is desirable that this fact should be made sufficiently plain, at this particular stage of the history of the Charity.

The Town Council after the Reformation, being desirous, as we have seen, to make proper provision for the maintenance of the ministry of the Protestant Church, as well as for the College of Edinburgh, the Schools, and the Poor within the city, did appeal to Mary Queen of Scots, and her son, King James VI., for grants of some of the old Kirk livings or Church benefices in the country. By numerous Royal Charters, and Acts of the Scottish Parliament, several grants of considerable value at the time were made, and confirmed to the City, during the course of the half century subsequent to 1560. These revenues, which were derived by the Provost, Magistrates, and Town Council, under the before-mentioned charters, were at the first devoted to the three objects already specified, viz., towards the support of the clergy, of education in the higher sense of the term, and the poor or helpless.

The Town Council, on the 9th day of February 1586, elected James Henrysoun, notary, to be the collector of the rents of the Provostry of the Trinity College, "and the beidmen thairof." A year after, they appointed Jhonn Jhonestoun to be their procurator, factor, and collector of the Kirk Annuals of the Burgh, and to have the oversight of the Town's College or University. The minute of his appointment is in the following terms:—

11. *February* 1587.—Considerand that the commoun rent vnderwritten is nocht habill to be governet and brocht to ane perfectioun be thair ordinare (officers), the dene of gild and thesaurer, quha hes alreaddy gritter chairge and burding than thai ar habill to owertak, bot will requyre greitt lawbouris and travell of the maist expert that may be fund, leving him na vther thing to do, and heavand lang pruif and experience in tyme past of the zeall, guid will and qualificatioun of thair belouit nichthour, Jhonn Jhonestoun, brother germayne to the laird of Elphinstoun, thairfore thai haif maid, creatt and constitute, and be thir presents makis, creats and constitutes the said Jhonn Johnnstoun their verray lawfull and vndowtet procuratour, actor, factour and collectour, gevand, grantand and committand vnto him thair full playne power and commissioun, with expres mandment and chairge to collect, inbring and resave, in name and behalff of the guid towne and to the vitility and proffeitt thairof, all and quhatsumeuir annuellis, mailles, fermes, grissumes, fruits, teynds, and emoluments, pertening to the personage and vicarage of Currie, callit the archideynrie of Lowthiane, and to the provestrie of the Trinitie College, siclyke to the personage of Dumberny, Poltie and Moncrief, now pertening to the saidis provest, bailyies, counsall and deykins of crafts and thair successouris, and als of the kirk annuellis of this burgh qulilkis ar nocht alreddy evictet and recoverit be decreitt, and of the few fermes of the new sett furth pairts of the Commoun Mwir . . . and als the said Jhonn to haif the ower-sicht, cuir and governament of the effaires of the College laitly foundet and erectet be the guid toun in the Kirk of Feyld, and of the place, maisteris and students thairof, as his lasour and tyme may serue according to the necessitie of the said effaires thairof, and as he shall be commandet to

do be the guid toun; and sielyk to haif the administratioun and seruice of the effaires of the Commoun Mwir and of the Seynis and landis quhilk sumtyme pertenet thairto and is now recoverit be the toun. . . . For the quhilk caus thay haif gevin and grantit vnto him ane yeirlie stipend of the soum of thre hundreth merks money.

During the year 1640, a separate system of accounting was established, for the purpose of bringing out clearly the revenues of the University, including the revenue from the country Kirk-livings, in so far as these had not been appropriated to the augmentation of the stipends of the established clergy in the country. The arrangement at that time entered into, continued until the year 1861, when, in virtue of an Act of Parliament, passed during that session, the available revenues derived from the old grants by Queen Mary and King James VI. were directed to be applied towards the endowment of the High School of Edinburgh.

The grants of the country church livings, or benefices—including the benefices anciently attached to the Trinity College Church and Hospital, did not deal with, or dispose of, the fabrics of the Trinity College Church and Hospital, and their precincts or grounds in the immediate neighbourhood of the same. No doubt, the Collegiate Church of the Holy Trinity, with the churchyard, houses, buildings, orchards, yards and pertinents thereof, which were formerly occupied, or possessed, by the Provost and the Prebendaries of the said Collegiate Church, together with the place (site) and part of the buildings and yards of Trinity Hospital, lying contiguous thereto, with the land lying on the west side thereof, were granted for the building and construction of an Hospital thereon, for the maintenance of such honest, poor, and impotent persons, aged and advanced in years, or sick indwellers and inhabitants within the said burgh, and also for such other old, indigent, and impotent people as should be found fit for receiving such benefit and charity in the said Hospital so to be founded.

By the Charter in 1587 referred to already, King James VI. empowered the Town Council to sustain within the Hospital, recently built and repaired by them, within a part of Trinity College Church, as many poor persons as could be conveniently sustained upon the rents of the Hospital of Trinity College, and to apply Trinity Hospital, which was then in a ruinous condition, to whatever other profitable use as should seem most expedient.

Thus, at the close of the sixteenth century, there was substituted, in place of the Trinity Hospital of the old foundation, the newly-founded and formed Trinity Hospital, under the administration and fostering care of the "Provost, Bailies, Councillors and community of our said burgh of Edinburgh for the time being," but endowed only with the Church and Hospital, and the immediately surrounding grounds of moderate extent, and left therefore largely dependent, for the means wherewith to support the beneficiaries of the Hospital, upon the pious liberality of the citizens of Edinburgh.

That such liberality was expected and encouraged, is manifest by the phraseology made use of in some of the old Acts of the Scottish Parliament, *e.g.* (1579, cap. 51), "Act in favour of the Hospital of Edinburgh.—Moreover because there are divers persons, godly and zealously moved, pitying the miserable state of the poor, and delighting in that godly work of erection of an Hospital within the said burgh, to be annexed thereto for the entertainment of the poor, weak, aged, and sick persons, to be sustained therein; therefore our sovereign Lord, with advice of his three estates, gives and grants licence to all persons who may be moved to support the said Hospital in lands, tenements, or annual rents, within the said burgh, so to do."

In the management and control of the new or post-Reformation Hospital, the Magistrates and Town Council were assisted by two Hospital Masters, annually appointed. The one, as we have seen, belonged to the Merchant class, and the other was one of the Craftsmen of the town. It was a part of the duty of these officers to receive and disburse the revenues of the Hospital. The earliest existing account of the Hospital Masters' intromissions is for the year to 11th November 1612, being about twenty-seven years after Pont demitted his duties as the Provost of the Trinity College.

The accumulated capital in the previous year (1611), which had been derived from donations, legacies, and mortifications or bequests, amounted to about £24,440 of Scots money. The revenue for the year 1611-12 (including £2070 of annual rent, or interest, generally calculated in those days at 10 per cent.) was £2223, and the disbursements amounted to £1894, shewing thereby a surplus income of £329. There were received during the period 1611-12, legacies amounting to £999, in addition to a balance of £398, in the hands of the previous year's masters. These were added to the capital sum, which was lent out at interest, making, therefore, the gross sum of the capital £26,200 at the close of the year.

In 1612, there were 35 beneficiaries resident in the Hospital. For several subsequent years, the numbers were respectively as follows:—viz., 32 in 1613, 35 in 1614, 34 in 1615, 36 in 1616, 45 in 1617, 40 in 1618, 38 in 1619, and 35 in 1620.

The accounts of 1611-12 shew that, at that time, the Hospital did not possess any real or heritable estate, other than the Trinity College Church and the Hospital buildings, together with the site on which these stood and the adjacent grounds. The capital sums already quoted were lent out at interest, and they serve to show that there was a progressive accumulation of the funds. By means of donations and bequests to the Hospital, amounting to about £10,000, during the period from 1612 to 1744, the Town Council, as governors of the charity, purchased, on its behalf, various lands in the neighbourhood of the city. They acquired, in 1628, the lands of Coatfield, at the price of £3250 0 0

They afterwards purchased 22 additional acres of Coatfield for	864	13	4
While, in 1641, they bought 16 acres of land at . Nether Quarryholes for . . .	527	15	7
In 1679, they secured 3 additional acres of the above for	86	13	4
Sum paid for Coatfield and Quarryholes, . .	£4729	2	3
Again, in 1739, they purchased part of the estate of Dean (viz.:—Dean Parks and Blinkbonny) at the price of . .	3651	1	4
Making the total of their purchases of land,	£8380	3	7

To show the advantages of these most judicious investments, and the great value to any Corporation in having their funds laid out in land, where in course of time the benefit of the unearned increment comes in, to play a most important part as a factor for good, it may be shewn by the progressive increase of the said subjects down to 1889, that this will be made sufficiently plain.

It may be here stated, that these landed properties form still the chief portion of the Hospital's heritable estate. The results of the income derived from such investments, from time to time, has been as follows:—

In the year 1612, .	£ 6	18	10
" 1644, .	298	2	5
" 1744, .	445	2	9
" 1845, .	1971	8	7
" 1873, .	2408	13	3
" 1889, .	4463	18	4

In 1612, the whole ordinary income of the charity was £185 per annum of sterling money, of which about £7 was derived from heritage, while £173 was from interest, and £5 from other sources. In 1889, the whole ordinary income of the charity (including the income of the Alexander Bequest) was £6435, 4s. 4d., of which £4463, 18s. 4d. was derived from rents and feu-duties of lands and heritages, £1870, 4s. 6d. was from interest on moneys lent out, and £101, 1s. 6d. was from other sources.

In 1612, the number of the beneficiaries was, as we have already seen, 35; while the amount expended on their maintenance was £158. In 1889, the number of the beneficiaries was 193, while the amount of payments made to them, or on their account, was £4120. In 1890, the number of beneficiaries was increased by 40, at an annual charge of £600 for pensions, making the total number of the pensioners at that time 233, and the yearly charge therefor £4700.

These figures, therefore, shew the progressive development of the means and estate of the Trinity Hospital charity, and the continued extension of its benefits within the last 300 years. The growth has been on the one hand largely due to the generous liberality of benevolent citizens in Edinburgh, and on the other, to the wise forethought of the Magistrates and Town Council, as the Governors of the charity, in acquiring for the Hospital, the now very valuable estates of Coatfield and Quarryholes, to the north-east of the city, and which is intersected by the Easter Road, in a direct line to Leith; and also the lands of Dean Parks and Blinkbonny, in the north-west outskirts of the city. While the former-mentioned lands are at present being quickly utilised for feuing purposes, the latter are still let off as agricultural subjects; but the rapid extension of the city in that direction, leaves little doubt that early in the next decade, the grounds of Dean Parks owned by the Governors will be speedily built upon, and will yield a greatly increased revenue.

To show the benefits that have been derived from the proper utilisation of the Governors' property in the east of Edinburgh, it may be stated that, on the motion of the writer, the Town Council, in 1875, resolved to terminate the lease of Quarryholes farm, consisting of about 100 acres, and which had been ten years before granted on a lease of twenty-one years, at the annual rent of £745, terminable in the year 1886. In consequence of the lease having to be relinquished, the tenants of the farm, as a matter of course, made heavy claims upon the Governors. These were submitted to arbitration. The result of the whole was that the Governors had to pay a capital sum of £11,000 by way of compensation to the lessees, and for the laying out of the grounds for feuing purposes, through the formation of roads and drains, and other works.

Notwithstanding of this large sum having been spent, the result has been extremely satisfactory. The net rents derived from the unfeued

grounds, which are chiefly let as grass parks, amount to	£430	0	0
The new feu-duties payable are	1920	0	0
Total, .	£2350	0	0
Whereas, as stated above, the old farm rent was	745	0	0
Thereby shewing, in the year 1890, an increased annual rent of . . .	£1605	0	0

Since that time, several large portions of the ground have been feued off; and, while these pages are passing through the press, the disposal of a large amount of ground is in course of negotiation with the Caledonian and North British Railway Companies, the result of which will be referred to at a future stage.

One other matter the writer considers it to be his duty to notice. When the proposal was made to construct the Regent

Bridge, a scheme carried out in 1818, whereby a new and most beautiful access was obtained to the city, the matter came under the attention of the Governors of Heriot's Hospital on the one hand and the Town Council as the Governors of Trinity Hospital on the other,—as to the probable effects upon their lands for feuing purposes being opened up and developed. The former had a considerable number of acres to the south-west of what is now known as the Easter Road. The latter had a still larger holding of land to the north-west and east of the said road. The new bridge implied the formation of the Regent Road, a direct access to Piershill and Portobello, as well as a most important access by the Easter Road to the Town of Leith. Heriot's Hospital Governors contributed £13,000 towards the undertaking; while the Town Council subscribed £8000, of which amount it was resolved that the Trinity Hospital should be debited with one-half, viz., £4000. This was in the year 1813. It is a notable fact that the Minute of the Finance and Property Committee of the Heriot's Hospital Governors recommending the same, was signed by the late Rev. Dr John Inglis, as chairman of the said Committee. He was minister of the Old Grayfriars Church, and he was the worthy father of the much respected late Right Hon. John Inglis (Lord Glencorse), President of the Court of Session. No one has ever questioned or impugned the validity of the action of the Heriot Governors of that time, whose contribution was upwards of three times that of the Governors of Trinity Hospital.

It fared otherwise, however, with the Town Council. In a Parliamentary paper entitled "General Report of the Commissioners appointed to enquire into the state of Municipal Corporations in Scotland, presented to both Houses of Parliament, by command of His Majesty" (page 38), there is the following entry:—"In some burghs the funds vested in the magistrates and town council for charitable purposes, which are usually called mortifications, have not been properly administered. Mention has already been made of the gross mismanagement in Edinburgh and Aberdeen, and of the practice of the magistrates or council borrowing in their corporate capacity, the funds vested in them as trustees. A striking example of malversation, with relation to the property of Trinity Hospital in Edinburgh has been observed. The Town Council of Edinburgh are the administrators, and they consented to the imposition on its funds of a debt of £4000 for making a road, and building a bridge near the city, by neither of which any part of the property of the Hospital has been benefited."* The reporters were seven legal gentlemen of high position in the city, and their opinion is entitled to that respect which is their due; but, beyond expressing their own opinion, they do not seem to have taken the opinion of any practical men on the subject. Nevertheless, it may be matter of opinion whether there is not another aspect of the question. The borrowing of money from trusts of which a town council has the management, for municipal purposes, is not now regarded as either wrong, illegal, or inexpedient. It has now the high sanction of the Imperial Parliament, in most of the Corporation Bills which are being yearly passed by both Houses. In regard to the benefit to the feuing ground, which is the property of the Trinity Hospital Governors, and which is intersected by the Easter Road, he would be a bold man, who at the present time would dare to assert, that the bridge-making and the road-forming referred to, have not essentially benefited the funds both of Heriot's and Trinity Hospitals. Indeed it is a well-known fact that when

* London: Printed by William Clowes and Sons, Stamford Street, for His Majesty's Stationery Office.—1835.

the learned Reporter (Professor Macpherson) advised adversely to the Town Council's contention, he had great difficulty in getting any master-builder to agree with him, although it is quite true that he eventually succeeded in obtaining one. The First Division of the Court of Session (Lord President Inglis presiding) by interlocutor, dated 19th March 1878, adopted the recommendation of Professor Macpherson, and echoed in even stronger language the views of the Parliamentary Commissioners. They ordered that the £4000 should be restored to the funds of the Trinity Hospital, by the Town Council, from out of the Common Good fund of the City, with four per cent. interest from 15th July 1874, until the principal sum was paid. This was accordingly done. The Trinity Hospital has therefore practically got the benefit of better accesses to its grounds for nothing. This has greatly enhanced the value of the lands. It is now reaping a good harvest. Possibly in consideration of its charitable purposes, and on account of the enormous demand by the poor to obtain a place on the roll, it is a condition of affairs not very much to be regretted. But it may still form a debatable question, on which a good deal might be said or written, whether the Town Councillors were not absolutely right in the main, and whether they had better notions than the legal gentlemen as to the ultimate results, as also whether the strictures passed upon them at the time when these observations were made, were strictly correct.

It is quite possible that the seed had to lie a considerable time before the harvest appeared. And yet, at the time when this great improvement was projected, the City of Edinburgh, in so far as building operations were concerned, was in the full blow of prosperity. A joint plan by the late Mr Robert Adam, architect, had been prepared by the consent of Heriot's Hospital Governors and the Town Council, for a great new suburb to the north-east of the city; and they had obtained the concurrence of the adjacent proprietors of land, to join with them in the enterprise. But the collapse of the building trades in 1822, consequent upon the depressed state of business all over the country, put an end to the rapid increase of the city for nearly half a century. The tide of affairs in this respect has during the last twenty years turned; the progress and extension of the city have been marvellous; and if Trinity Hospital funds suffered for many years through no return upon the sum of money advanced, that has now been well repaid in the fact that it is receiving a fourfold return at the present time by the uses to which the ground is now put, and the greatly enhanced prices now obtained, when compared with what would have been received fifty years ago. The Trinity Hospital charity is, therefore, deriving full advantage from the Regent Road and Bridge improvement, to which, as has already been seen, by the decision of the Court it was not practically a contributor, while the other charity of George Heriot's Hospital continued to be a large contributor to the enterprise.

CHAPTER XVI.

THE RE-BURIAL OF MARY OF GUELDRES.

WHEN the Hospital and Church of the Holy Trinity were doomed to destruction, the late Sir Daniel Wilson occupied at the time the honorary position of Secretary to the Society of Antiquaries of Scotland. His great influence as well as his pen were speedily, though ineffectually, engaged in remonstrances against what was regarded, in many quarters, as so great an act of vandalism, viz.—the removal, from the view of the citizens of Edinburgh, of the ancient, historic, and beautiful structure of the Trinity College Church. He used every effort in his power to avert, if it had been possible, all traces of this ancient royal foundation being removed from the site.

In his somewhat recently published work,* he thus writes:—"On Sunday, May 14, 1848, I witnessed the last religious services within the walls of the ancient Church. The City Magistrates, who had sold it to

* *Reminiscences of Old Edinburgh*, by Daniel Wilson. Vol. ii. pages 8-10. Edinburgh: David Douglas, 1878.

the spoilers, with incongruous ostentation, attended in their official robes, much as they were wont of old to preside over a public execution.* The quaint richly-carved capitals, the beautiful roof, with its sculptured bosses of varied design, the pier-shafts rising from corbels ingeniously grotesque, and leading the eye up to the fan-like ribs of the groined ceiling, all seemed to have only received their perfecting touch in the harmonious tintings of time, since the remains of the Royal Foundress were laid beneath the flooring, where they still rested in peace. The Rev. Dr Steven, the incumbent of the parish, entering into the feelings which the occasion was calculated to awaken, chose his text from Matthew xxiv. 2, 'Verily I say unto you, There shall not be left here one stone upon another that shall not be thrown down.' The words were appropriate; yet they seemed to sound with a bitter irony in the presence of those by whom this very verdict had been decreed, and from the lips of one who had been no unwilling party to it. I still recall the mingled feelings of mortification and pain with which I quitted for the last time the sacred edifice as such. I was in it many a time thereafter, when it had ceased to be a place of worship, but still retained all its attractive details, tempting the pencil to make some record of them before its last stone was thrown down."

Sir Daniel Wilson writes possibly somewhat too strongly on the subject; but it is wholly from the antiquarian point of view. He blames both the Town Council and the preacher; whereas he ought to have borne in mind that they were altogether powerless in the hands of the Houses of the Imperial Parliament, who alone were invested with the power of preserving the edifice.

* In this the learned writer is wrong. The two junior Magistrates are the only members of the Corporation whose attendance is required for this function; and their duty is to deliver over to the executioner the *corpus* of the culprit, and to give a receipt for the body after the execution.

The representations which were at the time made to the Town Council, as well as the terms of the North British Railway Act, already referred to—induced the Corporation to take steps to have the edifice rebuilt as it originally stood; but it behoved to be on another site. With this view, they at once gave instructions to the late Mr David Bryce, architect, that every stone of the old church should be carefully numbered, and should be safely deposited on the lower part of the Calton Hill—now converted into a public pleasure ground—between the south side of the Regent Road and the line of the North British Railway. This work was entrusted to the late Mr Lawrence, and the papers connected with it are in the possession of his son, Mr Peter Lawrence of this city. There, for many years, the stones remained, during the discussion of the much-vexed question of site, and various other questions of law, which cropped up from time to time to trouble the already much-vexed members of the Corporation. It will excite little surprise when it is mentioned that that well-known cairn of stones was not likely to remain long in an undisturbed condition.

Individual antiquarian tastes always long to be satisfied, as well as the cupidity of curiosity collectors who have not even the antiquarian hobby in their constitution, but have the desire to possess something rare or peculiar—hence, many of the very finest of the stone and other carvings of the Trinity College Church were, usually under the cloud of night, quietly but surely carried away to various parts of the suburbs of the city, which were at the time rapidly extending in what may, for want of a better phrase, be designated 'Villadom,' and these carvings were utilised as a rule in the construction of various rockeries and other fantastic garden erections, in connection with private houses. A better colour might have been given to such selfish and wilful misappropriation, if it could have been stated on its behalf that the vandalism proceeded from a mistaken feeling of religious enthusiasm—if the sentiment could have been recorded of the depredators:

> "Thy saints take pleasure in her stones,
> Her very dust to them is dear."

But no such moving spirit could either in truth or veriest justice be ascribed to them in the matter. The carrying away of these relics was regarded at the time as purely and absolutely cases of the most unmitigated covetousness, implying a gross breach of both the eighth and tenth commandments.

No doubt, when all the facts and circumstances of the case came in the course of years to be adjusted and finally disposed of, it turned out that it would have been impossible for the Town Council to have complied with the desires of the antiquarians, as well as the terms of the North British Railway Act, in regard to the proposed scheme of restoration. The sum eventually adjudicated by the House of Lords was entirely prohibitory of this being done. But that fact gave no valid excuse at the time for the somewhat scandalous spoliation of a vast number of the quaintest, most grotesque, yet beautiful and much valued carvings, which from time to time were taken away, in the manner already stated.

When the fabric of the Church came to be removed, the Society of Antiquaries demanded that a search should forthwith be made for the remains of the Royal Foundress.

The following minute of the Society refers to this subject:—

3. April 1848.—Mr Laing laid before the Meeting copies of the correspondence with the Lord Provost, the City Clerk, and the Hon. Board of Commissioners of Her Majesty's Woods and Forests, relative to the search for the remains of Queen Mary of Gueldres and their

removal to Holyrood Chapel. The following were appointed a committee to take such steps as may be necessary in furtherance of this object, and to report, Messrs Chambers, Laing, Macdonald and the Secretaries. The Secretary was directed meanwhile to write to the Chairman of the Board of Directors of the North British Railway, requesting that as the demolition of the Ancient Collegiate Church of the Holy Trinity was now decided on, the carved stones, armorial bearings, etc., might be reserved for the Society's museum.

In the prosecution of this work, Sir Daniel Wilson took a most lively interest, along with his friend the late Dr David Laing of the Signet Library. The officers of Her Majesty's Board of Works, under the direction of the late Mr Robert Matheson, and his able assistant the late Mr Kerr, began their operations on the 22d day of May 1848. The place where it was understood the Queen's mortal remains were deposited was, as has been already stated, a space under the north aisle, in the centre of the lady's chapel, or sacristy, or, as it was latterly called, "the vestry." *

* The following Report is extracted from the Minute Book of the Society of Antiquaries of Scotland. It was submitted to a meeting of the Council of the Society held on the 24th day of May 1848, and a copy of it was directed to be transmitted to the Honble. Board of Commissioners of Her Majesty's Woods and Forests. It is as follows:—

"MARY OF GUELDRES. On Monday, the 21st of May, at seven A.M., the officers of Her Majesty's Board of Works commenced their search for the remains of Queen Mary of Gueldres, within the Collegiate Church of the Holy Trinity, of which she was the Foundress. The first excavations were made in the North Aisle of the Choir, where a finely-carved Credence Table and other features indicated the site of some of the Altars of the Church. The search afforded evidence that the whole Aisle had been used as a place of sepulture, but nothing was found worthy of special notice, as indicative of the rank of those who had been buried, or of great antiquity in the remains. Attention was then directed to the Aisle, latterly used as the Vestry of the Church, where the existence of a very fine Piscina affords undoubted evidence of its having been a chapel of some importance. After excavating in various directions, on digging right down in the centre of the area, the workmen came upon portions of glazed floor tiles, about the level of the old floor, which was fully three feet beneath that of the old

In the centre of this place, was found an ancient coffin containing the skeleton of a female. A reference was made to the late Mr John Goodsir, an eminent surgeon and the well-known Professor of Anatomy

---

Vestry. Most of the tiles were of an orange colour; but one nearly whole, and several fragments of others, were dark purple, suggesting the probability that the floor had been paved with these in alternate squares, or according to some other regular pattern. Underneath this, a mass of very solid concrete was found, near the west wall, and, a little lower down, towards the centre of the floor, the workmen exposed the arm bone of a skeleton.

"On discovering distinct evidence of human remains, on a spot generally assigned by tradition as the place of sepulture of the Royal Foundress, a flat stone was laid above them, and the workmen were set to clear out the length of the grave. On the whole being levelled to the proper depth, the edge of an oak coffin was exposed, which proved, on being further uncovered, to be in a state of extreme decay. There were no remains of the lid of the coffin; but, on the end, at the feet, being cleared, it was found to be narrower at bottom than top, and rising so as to form the segment of a circle on the upper edge, showing that the lid of the coffin had been rounded at the top.

"The coffin measured five feet, eleven inches, in length; the sides were straight, and the breadth, both at the head and foot, eighteen inches. It appeared to have been very shallow, and more so at the feet than the head; but the extremely decayed state of the wood prevented exact measurements being taken. It may be added that, when the body was removed on the following day, the bottom of the coffin was found to be made of oak planks laid length-ways (contrary to modern practice), and a single transverse bar was fastened across the centre. The whole was secured with iron nails, having very large heads, but otherwise too much corroded to enable any opinion to be formed of their original shape. It should be added that a slightly constructed drain crossed the grave obliquely, and the whole soil was so saturated with moisture, as abundantly to account for the extreme state of decay of the coffin and its enclosed remains.

"On the skeleton being completely exposed, it was found lying in its natural position, with the bones undisturbed. The skull was turned round on the left cheek, and the spine exhibited a remarkable degree of curvature. In this state, the whole was covered over with boards, and left under the care of three trusty workmen of Her Majesty's Board of Works, by whom the place was watched all night.

"On the following morning, shortly after ten o'clock, the skeleton was examined by Mr John Goodsir, Professor of Anatomy in the University of Edinburgh, in presence of Mr Matheson and Mr Kerr of the Woods and Forests Office, several members of the Council of the Society of Antiquaries, some of the Directors of the North British Railway, the Right Rev. Bishop Gillies, and others. On examining the skull, the Professor pronounced it to be

in the University of Edinburgh. He very soon pronounced the remains to be those of a female of about thirty years of age. His report was to the following effect:—"The skull was characterised by great

that of a female, though unusually short, and broad behind for a female head. The cheek bones are very delicately formed, the teeth small and regular, and the nose very prominent. The head altogether affords evidence, in his opinion, of a woman of decided character.

"The examination of the pelvis completely confirmed the evidence of its being a female skeleton. The bones of the legs and arms were also examined, and referred to by the Professor as characterised by feminine delicacy of formation. The marked curvature of the spine, Mr Goodsir stated, was such as must have elevated the right shoulder, but not to such an extent as would amount to a deformity which might not easily be concealed by the dress. The curvature was towards the right breast, with a corresponding return of the lower part of the spine towards the left side. The Professor remarked that such was of very common occurrence in the female skeleton, though not often to so great a degree. The effect it would have on the figure would be to give the appearance of a short body and long limbs.

"After Professor Goodsir had completed the examination, careful measurements were taken of the exact position of the coffin. The body lay directly east and west, with the feet towards the east. The breadth of the Chapel from north to south, is sixteen feet, four inches; and the centre of the head of the coffin was found to measure exactly eight feet, two inches from either wall. The Chapel measures, from east to west, fifteen feet, six inches; and the head of the coffin was found to be five and a half feet from the west wall, leaving the space from the foot to the east wall of four feet, one inch. On this side, however, the deeply splayed recess of the window affords great additional breadth, where, in all probability the Altar of the Chapel stood.

"Under the direction of John Henderson, Esquire, Queen's Remembrancer, and in presence of those who had witnessed the previous examination, with the addition of the Rev. Dr Steven, incumbent of the parish, and other gentlemen connected with the Society of Antiquaries, etc., the remains were carefully removed from the grave; and after being wrapped in cloth, were deposited in a lead coffin provided for the purpose. This was secured under the direction of Mr Henderson, and sealed with the Exchequer Seal. The remains of the coffin with the earth enclosed in it, were also wrapped up with it and placed in a separate box, which was likewise fastened up and sealed; after which both were removed in a hearse to the Exchequer Chambers, Parliament Square.

"It is worthy of notice that the top edge of the coffin was little more than eight or nine inches below the original floor; so that it was, in all probability covered with a flat slab, decorated, it may be, with a brass, or bearing an inscription and sculptured device. The disappearance of all remains of the coffin lid, afforded evidence that the tomb had been opened

delicacy, especially in the cheek bones and the lower jaw, which also indicated a well-formed chin. The teeth were small and regular, the forehead was broad, but not high, and the nasal bones indicated a well-defined and probably slightly-hooked nose."

before, and this seemed to be further confirmed by the absence of nearly all the finger bones, notwithstanding the most careful search for them; so that it seems not improbable that gold or jewelled rings may have tempted the cupidity of the spoilers who invaded the resting place of the dead. The extreme dampness of the soil, however, may possibly account for the absence of these bones, by the ordinary process of decay. A mass of very solid concrete which remained at the head and foot, had probably covered the whole coffin originally, and been the sub-structure on which the paving rested. This had been broken through, but the general state of the skeleton left no room to doubt that the body had been moved from its original position.

"Mary of Gueldres, the consort of James Second, King of Scotland, died 16th November 1463. According to the concurring testimony of all early Scottish Historical Writers, the Queen was interred in the Church of the Holy Trinity, near Edinburgh, which she had founded shortly before her death; but which from the early death of the Royal Foundress, was never completed according to the original design.

"That the remains thus discovered in the Chapel attached to the Church of the Holy Trinity are those of Mary of Gueldres, Queen of Scotland, the wife of James Second and mother of James Third, appears conclusively and satisfactorily established. On the buttress at the north-east angle of this Chapel, a highly-decorated niche (more ornamental than any other on the whole of the Church) is surrounded by a Tablet, bearing apparently the Royal Arms now greatly defaced and time-worn. The richly-sculptured Piscina in the interior has already been referred to; and in the south wall separating it from the North Aisle of the Church, and from which it is approached by a highly-decorated doorway, a squint, or hagioscope, has been discovered in the course of the recent investigations, through which a person seated at the Tomb could see the High Altar.

"It is provided in the Foundation Charter, that 'whenever any of the Prebendaries shall read High Mass, he shall repair to the Tomb of the Foundress,' and perform certain prescribed services. While this direction seems to indicate the Mortuary Chapel of the Foundress, as standing apart from the main body of the Church, it may also account for the arrangements above referred to, by which it is connected with the same.

"Exactly in the centre of this Chapel, in an oak coffin of antique form and construction, and with the feet towards the east, where the Altar of the Chapel must have stood (a practice reserved in the Catholic Church for lay persons, ecclesiastics being laid with their head towards the Altar), the remains of the Royal Foundress have been discovered, after lying

Several other members of the Society of Antiquaries took a special interest in the search. Among these were the late

Sir James Young Simpson, Bart., M.D.
Charles Kirkpatrick Sharpe, Esq., of Hoddam.
Sir George Harvey, President of the Royal Scottish Academy.
W. B. D. D. Turnbull, Esq., Advocate.
Cosmo Innes, Esq., one of the Principal Clerks of Session.
Joseph Robertson, Esq., LL.D., of H.M. Register House.
James Drummond, Esq., R.S.A.
Dr Walter Adam, George Square.
The Very Rev. Bishop Gillies, and
J. Whitefoord Mackenzie, Esq., W.S., Agent of the Convention of Royal Burghs.

A report was drawn up at the time narrating the circumstances, and conveying the impressions of those self-constituted reporters.

Sir Daniel Wilson, in his interesting work already referred to, thus writes :—" The chapel in which this ancient coffin lay entombed in the centre of the area, and directly in front of the east window, with the feet towards the site of its long-demolished altar, was entered from the north aisle of the choir by a circular-headed doorway of fine proportions

interred for nearly four centuries. The absence of any ornaments, rings, or other insignia of rank, may be but too easily accounted for, from the evident indications of the grave having been opened at some former period. Nor must it be overlooked, in reference to the apparent plainness of her sepulture, that, though a Queen, she was a widow at the time of her death; her son, King James III. was scarcely ten years of age; and while the period was one of distraction and strife, the terms in which she has been alluded to by contemporary historians, afford no less evidence of the bitterness of her enemies, than the incompleteness of her pious foundation and the lukewarmness of her friends. It may be added that, after extensive excavations in the Centre Aisle and the Transept of the Church, nothing has been found worthy of special notice, or coeval with the period of the foundation of the Church with the solitary exception of a billon penny of James Third.

"The Council of the Society of Antiquaries of Scotland, in forwarding this Report to the Honble. Board of Commissioners of Her Majesty's Woods and Forests, in accordance with the request of the Officers of the Board of Works, beg to add that it seems to them only consistent

and workmanship; and on the buttress of its north-east angle were the arms of the Foundress, Gueldres, impaled with those of Scotland. Within, it had been paved with encaustic tiles of orange and purple; and it may be assumed that, by sepulchral brass, incised slab, or altar-tomb, the precise site of the royal vault was originally indicated. But the encaustic pavement lay buried three feet under the modern flooring; and the covering of the vault of concrete appeared to have been broken through without disturbing the skeleton, which lay there in its natural state, with the bones undisplaced."

He then goes on to state:—"The head rested on its left cheek, and was regarded with all the interest which pertained to its supposed identification as that of the Queen of James II. and the mother of James III. It required no anatomical training to discern, in the delicately-formed zygomata and cheek bones, the well-developed nose and chin, and the small, regular teeth, the indications of refined and probably beautiful features. The only defect was a curvature of the spine, sufficient to have slightly elevated the right shoulder, and to which by-and-by an amusing prominence was assigned when the identity

with the rank of the Royal Foundress of the Collegiate Church of the Holy Trinity, and her direct connection with her Royal Descendant, our gracious Queen Victoria, that the remains of Queen Mary of Gueldres should be removed to the Royal Vault at Holyrood, with suitable honours, now that an Act of the British Parliament has sanctioned the demolition of the Church which she founded, and the Mortuary Chapel erected for her Tomb.

"(Signed) J. T. GIBSON-CRAIG, *Chairman*.
"D. LAING, *Treasurer*.
"DANL. WILSON, *Secretary*.

"In addition to the preceding Report, the Council directed that it should be entered on the Minutes, that the removing of the royal remains from their original resting place, and the depositing of them in the leaden coffin was accomplished by Dr Walter Adam, a member of the Royal College of Physicians, and Fellow of this Society, and he was accordingly requested to communicate to the next meeting of the Society the result of his observations on that occasion. J. T. GIBSON-CRAIG, *C.*"

of its owner came in question. Professor Goodsir, when first pointing it out, remarked that it was not rare to find such curvature in the female skeleton. It did not amount to more deformity than might easily be concealed by the dress, and such as passes unheeded in many a fair lady of modern days."

The remains of Mary of Gueldres were for a second time deposited in a handsome coffin, to be taken hence for a final resting place until the Resurrection morn. The place to which they were first conveyed was the Exchequer Chambers in Parliament Square, which at that time was also used as the office of H.M. Board of Works, and afterwards to the ancient Palace of Holyroodhouse. On a beautiful summer morning, viz.—on the 15th day of July 1848, in the royal vault of Holyrood Abbey, Her Majesty's remains were then appropriately placed. The following account of the ceremony appeared in the *Scotsman* newspaper of 19th July 1848:—

"Re-Interment of the Remains of Queen Mary of Gueldres.—The re-interment of the remains of Mary of Gueldres, Queen of James II. which were discovered some time ago in the Sacristy of Trinity College Church, of which she was the Foundress, took place on Saturday in the Chapel Royal, Holyrood, in presence of the Lord Provost, Magistrates, and Town Council, the Society of Antiquaries, and a numerous assemblage of literary and scientific gentlemen and their ladies. The coffin was conveyed to the Chapel from the Exchequer Chambers in a hearse, at half-past seven o'clock in the morning, it having been the desire of Her Majesty's Commissioners of Woods and Forests that the ceremony should be performed in a private manner. The outer coffin was covered with purple cloth, and enclosed a leaden coffin, which contained another, within which the remains of the Queen were arranged in the same position in which they were found by Professor Goodsir, embedded in plaster of Paris for preservation. The coffin bore the following inscription :—'Mary of Gueldres, Queen of James II., King of Scots, interred in the Church of the Holy Trinity, Edinburgh, A.D. 1463, removed from thence, and re-interred in the the Chapel Royal, Holyrood, 15th July 1848.' At eight o'clock, the funeral procession entered the Abbey from the Palace Gardens, the coffin being borne on the shoulders of six men. Mr Robert Rutherford, W.S., as agent of His Grace the Duke of Hamilton, and Deputy Keeper of the Palace, acted as chief mourner, walking at the head of the body, and the ribbons being held by the Lord Provost (Adam Black), Bailie Tullis, Treasurer Dick, Mr Mackenzie, W.S., Mr Matheson of the Board of Works, etc. The members of the Antiquarian Society and other gentlemen followed, and the procession slowly wound its way to the Royal Vault, at the south-east corner of the Abbey, amidst the deepest manifestations of respect and of solemn interest by the spectators, who thronged the surrounding tombs and the broken shafts of the columns in the Chapel. The coffin was then deposited in the vault, amidst the kindred remains of royalty, in presence of the company, and the assemblage soon after separated." The vault in which the royal remains have been deposited was the burying place of James V. and Magdalen of France his first Queen, and the Earl of Darnley, and other of the monarchs and royal family of Scotland. The fury of the mob, however, at the period of the Revolution, sadly impaired this royal place of sepulture, which has since been allowed to remain in a state of dilapidation and decay, and the leaden coffins which at no distant date enclosed the remains of the "illustrious dead" have been entirely carried away, with portions of the skulls and other bones. A cast of the head of the Queen was taken the day before the funeral, in presence of the Council of the Society of Antiquaries and the gentlemen above named, and is still preserved in the Society's Museum.

Before closing this chapter, the writer considers it his duty to bring before the readers' attention another matter of some importance in connection with Trinity Hospital and Trinity Church, as well as the Royal Foundress, for which he is again indebted to Sir Daniel Wilson. He thus writes :—"By a curious coincidence, at the very time when historical students were mourning the destruction of this fine architectural memorial of the fifteenth century, the transference from Hampton Court to Holyrood* of a painting long recognised as containing portraits of James III. and his Queen, Margaret of Denmark, led to its identification by Mr David Laing, as the original altar-piece of the Collegiate Church, founded by the mother of that king. It is a work of art of singular interest, as the only example of a Scottish pre-Reformation altar-piece known to exist, and includes portraits of great historical value. It is a diptych, painted on both sides of its two leaves. The two exterior compartments are thus filled up: On the one is King James III. with his son, 'The Flodden King,' as a youth of about twelve years of age. The two are represented as kneeling, with St Andrew, the patron saint of Scotland, behind them; on the other, is the Queen, and a figure in armour, with an aureole—possibly designed for St Olave of Denmark—holding over her a banner, inscribed Ave Maria. On the right inner compartment is the Trinity: the Divine Father, enthroned in glory, sustaining the Redeemer in His passion; while the Holy Spirit rests on Him in the form of a dove. This clearly points to the dedication of the Church; while, on the left compartment, the beautiful Foundress, as it has been assumed, is represented in the character of St Cecilia playing on an organ. An angel who looks out from behind has been surmised by Mr Laing as possibly representing her daughter. The arms of the Queen, impaled

* *Reminiscences of Old Edinburgh*, by Daniel Wilson. Vol. ii. pages 8-10. Edinburgh: David Douglas, 1878.

in a lozenge with the royal arms of Scotland, place beyond doubt the identity of the principal characters; and another shield is equally confirmatory of the relation of the whole to the Collegiate Church, founded by Mary of Gueldres. In front of the organ at which St Cecilia presides, is a kneeling ecclesiastic, with marked features, strongly indicative of individual portraiture; and, as appears from the arms blazoned alongside of him on the organ stool, this is Sir Edward Boukil, first provost of the church, and confessor of its Foundress."

Sir Daniel then goes on to say, "The historical interest of this picture is greatly increased from the means it supplies of judging of the actual condition of art in Scotland, at a time when the King, James III., was charged with keeping low company; because he preferred the society of artists and musicians to that of the rude barons of his realm; and even made of his two chief artistic favourites, Cochrane and Ramsay, his advisers in state affairs. Alike in drawing and execution, the merits of the painting are great; as historical portraits, its picturings are invaluable; and Pinkerton has justly said of it that 'hardly can any kingdom in Europe boast of a more noble family picture of this early epoch.' The features of St Cecilia are not of that idealised cast of beauty which would become the mere saint, but are rather suggestive of individual portraiture. The temptation is great to recognise in them the likeness of the deceased Queen, and to trace in her avocation a possible reference to special musical tastes, so that James III. may have inherited from his mother his passionate love for music. But it may be noted that the name Mary is the only baptismal one which, according to the usage of the medieval church cannot be changed at confirmation; and had the features of Mary of Gueldres been represented in beatified saintship, there would have been a special aptness in the introduction of the Virgin Mother, as the counterpart to the Trinity. There is, indeed, a certain incongruity in the design, in which the Provost, Sir Edward Bonkil, plays so prominent part, as the companion piece to the conventional representation of the Holy Trinity, which tempts us to look for an explanation in some events of the time. It is worthy of note that so early as 1474, proposals were made for the betrothal of the Princess Cecilia, the daughter of Edward IV., to the Prince James of Scotland, then only two years old; and this proposed alliance was not finally abandoned till 1483,* when the City of Edinburgh acquired its peculiar constitution as a distinct county, or sheriffdom, in return for advancing the money to refund to England the Princess Cecilia's dowry. To one of the latest stages of this proposed alliance with the House of York,

* In *Wilson's Memorials of Edinburgh* (page 19), the following narrative is given of the circumstances; and as these are more fully related therein, it has been deemed advisable to reproduce it:—"William Bertraham, the provost of Edinburgh, and with him the whole fellowship of merchants, burgesses, and community of the said town, loyally and generously obliged themselves to repay to the King of England, under certain circumstances, the dowry to his daughter, the Lady Cecil; or otherwise, 'undertook for the King of Scotland, their Sovereign Lord, that he should concur in his former obligations, provided he or they, the said provost and merchants, were informed of the King of England's pleasure by the next feast of All Saints;' which obligations they afterwards fulfilled, repaying the money, amounting to 6000 merks sterling, upon the demand of Garter King-of-Arms, the King of England's messenger. In acknowledgment of this loyal service, the King granted to the city a deed in 1492, by which the provost and bailies were created sheriffs, within all the bounds of their own territories, and rewarded with other important privileges contained in that patent, which is known by the name of the Golden Charter. He also conferred upon the craftsmen the famous banner, long the rallying point of the burger ward in every civil commotion, or muster for war, which is still preserved by the Incorporated Trades, and known by the popular name of the Blue Blanket." [Wilson is wrong as to the Golden Charter. The important deed so known, was as we have seen (page 58) the work of James VI. on the 15th March 1630. Pennecuik also refers to the transaction in his Work published in 1722. Wilson's account is much the same as Pennecuik's, but the latter gives the date as 1482, and he makes no reference to the Banner of the Crafts at this time. On the other hand, he seeks to trace the Blue Blanket to a much earlier period in history, viz., to the "Origine of the Croisade, from whence he asserts that it undoubtedly had its rise."]

THE HOLY TRINITY. (*From Painting in Holyrood House.*)

(1) [Between pages 200-1.

JAMES III. OF SCOTLAND AND HIS SON, AFTERWARDS JAMES IV. (*circa*) 1484. SAINT ANDREW CROWNING THE KING. (*From Painting in Holyrood House.*)

(*)

[Between pages [illegible].

QUEEN MARY OF GUELDRES REPRESENTED AS ST CECILIA, WITH SIR EDWARD BONCLE, FIRST PROVOST OF TRINITY COLLEGE. *(From Painting in Holyrood House.)*

(·) [Between pages 200-1

MARGARET OF DENMARK, QUEEN OF SCOTLAND
(*circa*) 1484. (*From Painting in Holyrood House.*)

(4)

[Between pages 200-1.

may possibly be due, the curious intermingling of sacred allegory and portraiture in this altar-piece of the Collegiate Church—even if we suppose St Cecilia to preserve the portraiture of the Royal Foundress, and assume the attendant angel to represent the affianced princess of the House of York.

"In truth, if the stories of old chroniclers are to be relied upon, the Queen was no saint. The Church which she founded was, in more ways than one, a curious historical memorial of her age; and its sculptures—from which many of the tail-pieces of these chapters have been selected—furnished some singular disclosures relative to the faith of the times."

CHAPTER XVII.

A SURPRISE, AND WHAT IT LED TO.

THIS world has been called "one of surprises." Although it does sometimes occur that "the unlooked-for happens," the old adage is nevertheless true, that "exception proves the rule."

The event which has just been recorded, as to the mortal remains of Mary of Gueldres, was not likely to pass away without some new sensation taking possession of the minds of a certain class of the community, whose chief attribute seems to consist in their objectiveness. The *Athenæum* (a well-known London publication) declared two months thereafter that the remains of the right Queen had turned up, and among other proofs of the veracity of their informant or reporter, it was added that, "There is a lateral curve on the spine which corresponds with a report that Mary had a vertebral deformity." All the newspaper press of the day was ablaze; and, according to some of these journals, it was foolishly stated that this must be the real Queen, because there was found a crown upon her head, rings on her fingers, and the royal arms wrought in silver on her coffin. Any amount of gullibility that would tend to amaze the public and sell the newspapers was resorted to. The primary cause of the sensation was as follows :—

The late Dr David Laing had invited to dinner, on the 20th September of the same year, to his house in Portobello, a few antiquarian friends. It need not be said that at such a gathering there was likely to be "a feast of reason and a flow of soul." But this suddenly terminated when the announcement was made that another Queen Mary had been dug up from among the ruins that very day. The late James Ballantine, poet and painter, who was present, declared that he had seen the exhumed remains,—that it had been found in the centre of the apse, in a lead coffin, with a rounded projection for the head, and that from the perpendicular and antero-posterior extent of the frontal region of the head, the very small cerebral space, the unsymmetrical, contracted and undeveloped state of the base, and the retarded condition of the wisdom teeth, the remains were those of one of feeble or deficient intellect. This was the opposite of what had been always written regarding Mary of Gueldres.

In all probability, the remains at that time found, were either those of the young Duchess of Lennox, or the Countess of Eglinton, referred to in pp. 96-97 of this volume.

"A little spark often causes muckle wark." Such is the old saying, and such was the effect of the "new find" having got abroad. One very notable feature was afterwards found out in the case. It has already been stated, that, in the latter skeleton, the top of the skull had been sawn off. When opened for examination, the two consulted professors discovered "in the exposed interior, certain bony *spiculæ* protruding into the cerebral region," which in the opinion of Professor Simpson, suggested the probability that the owner had been subject to epileptic fits. All the circumstances seemed to indicate that the female remains referred to had been buried about a century later than Mary of Gueldres. That fact would serve to support the theory that they were the remains of one of the noble ladies previously mentioned. The antiquaries and their friends were therefore reassured that they had deposited the proper remains in the Royal Vault.

The following is the official report by Professor J. Y. Simpson, M.D., Professor of Midwifery in the University of Edinburgh, and John Goodsir, Esq., Professor of Anatomy and Physiology in the same University, upon the female remains recently discovered in the choir of Trinity College Church, as it was read at a meeting of the Society of Antiquaries of Scotland, on the 9th day of November 1848; and the same was ordered to be engrossed in their minutes. It was as follows:—

"EDINBURGH, 2 *November* 1848.

"We have examined the skeleton found in a leaden coffin, under the High Altar of Trinity College Church, and we are of opinion, that the female to which it belonged was of a feeble frame; and more particularly from the weak and delicate condition of the skeleton generally; but especially of the spine, the long bones of the limbs, and of the skull.

"We are also of opinion that from the small perpendicular and antero-posterior extent of the frontal region of the head; the very small cerebral space; the unsymmetrical, contracted, and undeveloped state of the base; the retarded condition of the wisdom teeth (and the skull having been opened for examination); this female who certainly was above twenty, but below thirty years of age, was of feeble or deficient intellect. (Signed) "J. Y. SIMPSON.

"JOHN GOODSIR."

The Secretary was instructed to send a copy of this report to H.M. Board of Works, and to add that the place of interment of these remains indicate those of a person of such rank that propriety would seem to dictate their re-interment in Holyrood Chapel if not in the Royal Vault.

At a previous meeting of the Society of Antiquaries, Dr Walter Adam of George Square, son of the celebrated Dr Alexander Adam, Rector of the High School, under whom Sir Walter Scott, Lords Brougham, Cockburn, and Jeffrey, the Messrs Francis and Leonard Horner, and the great galaxy of illustrious Scotsmen, who flourished at the end of last century and the beginning of the present were educated, was requested by the Society to act for them in this matter, and he was further asked to submit a report on the subject to a future meeting.

The meeting was held on June 1st, 1848, when a report was read and approved of. Mr C. Trotter moved, seconded by Mr Turnbull, special thanks to the Secretary. The thanks of the Society were also voted to Messrs Matheson and Kerr, for their great courtesy and ready co-operation.

At the request of the Society, Dr Walter Adam having furnished the following Report on the subject, the same was submitted to the meeting:—

EDINBURGH, 29 *May* 1848.

In compliance with the desire of the Council of the Society of Antiquaries of Scotland, I beg to submit to the Society the following Report of what I actually did and observed during the exhumation of the remains of Mary of Gueldres, Queen Dowager of Scotland, within Trinity College Church, Edinburgh, on Tuesday, the 23d of May 1848.

1. Being within the said Trinity College Church, by invitation from Dr Steven, the clergyman thereof, about half-past eleven o'clock on the forenoon of the 23d of May 1848, and learning that no other individual then present was acquainted with the human structure, I made offer to John Henderson, Esquire, Remembrancer of Her Majesty's Exchequer, to remove from their resting place, the bones which I understood had been discovered on the evening of the 22d of May, and which had earlier on the forenoon of the said 23d day of May, been inspected by Professor Goodsir.

2. Having accordingly descended into the grave, I found the head, collar-bones, and spine exposed to view: the spine showing a great degree of curvature, while there was a perfect continuity of all the vertebræ.

3. The bones were imbedded in a dark red, moist, and tenacious soil. They were inclosed at the sides by thin boards of nearly black, and much softened wood, and they rested on a floor of similar wood.

4. The head, the collar-bones, and the vertebræ of the neck, I found to be free from all injury or decay; the other bones partaking of the colour of the soil, and tending to decomposition.

5. The small bones of the hands and feet had in great part disappeared; and, with the exception of a few nails, I could not after the most diligent search, perceive a trace of any metallic substance.

6. The bones having been partially arranged on boards, I, as carefully as time and situation permitted, and without attempting to free the bones from the adherent soil, wrapped them in thin woollen and cotton cloth. I then placed them all together, at the broad end of the leaden coffin which had been provided for their reception—said coffin having been thereafter sealed with the Exchequer seal. I saw it safely conveyed from the Church to the hearse outside the churchyard.

7. So far as it may be proper to add any expression of opinion, I should say:—

First.—That from relative appearances, it may be inferred that the head and neck had been effectually protected from those influences which had altered the hue and the firmness of the other bones of the body.

Secondly.—That whatever invasion there may have been of the Royal Tomb, the absence of any displacement of the vertebræ warrants the belief that the spine itself had never been disturbed.

8. In conclusion, I would suggest that the future preservation of those bones cannot be more effectually secured, than by their being, previously to re-interment, inclosed in a vase of strong glass.

Also.—That before the hollow, now open, is filled up, a block of durable stone should be laid in the very place which had been so long occupied by the remains of Mary of Gueldres.

All which I hereby report to the Antiquarian Society.

(Signed) Walter Adam.

But the occasion of the surprise referred to in this chapter did not pass away without a certain amount of fun, and some pleasant literature being circulated.

At a Conversazione of the Society of Antiquaries held on the 20th day of December 1848, an antique document, printed in black letter, was freely circulated among those present. It was said to be the composition of *Maister D. Doubleyowe*, which puzzled not a few as to its authorship. The well-known initials of the accomplished Secretary (D. W.) only too plainly revealed the fact. It is herewith reproduced :—

ANE AULD PROPHECIE, bot doubte be
Merlyne or Thomas of Erceldoune,
fundin under ye altar-stane of ye
Quenyis College of ye Haly Trinitie
besyde Edenburgh, AND diligentlie
comparit with ye Cronyclis and
auld Wrytingis quhilk yairto effeir,
be Maister D. Doubleyowe, ane
Brither of ye Auncient
Fraternitie of ye
Antiquaries.

Quhar-for of swylk Antyqwyteys
Thai yat set hale yare delyte
Gest or Story for to wryte,
Owyir in Metyre, or in Prose,
Flurysyde fayrly yaire purpose
Wyth queynt and curyous circumstance,
To rays hartis in plesance.

quod Androw of Wyntown.

Quene Mary of Scotlande, ye Duik of Gillirlandis douchter, and sisteris douchter to ye Duik of Burgone, spousit in the yer of God m.cccc.xlix. to King James ye secund with ye fierie face, Hyr unerdyng fra hyr awn College besyde Edenburgh, quhilk sho hyr self fundit biggit and dotit. Also of ane awesum and merwalous Demone quha sete hys herte on hyr banes, and of ane haly and pyous Fraternitie quha unerdit the samyn in spyte of hys tethe, and of ye twa valiand Knychtis quha discomfytit the monstrous beste, and strak him doune, and pushionit hym incontinent wyth hys awin malyce. ALSO of some quha lookit maist stout and rycht cocke-sure at ye begynin, quha lookit blae yineuch gin ye hynderende.

Ane Ballat of Olde Quene Moll; as sung be ye Menstrallis to ye plesand Tune of "Olde Kyng Cole," with bariationes.

There lived a Quene in the Olden Time,
And a pious Quene was she,
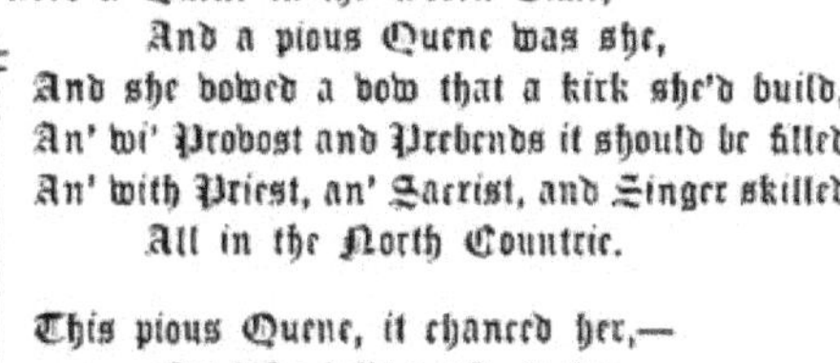
And she bowed a bow that a kirk she'd build,
An' wi' Probost and Prebends it should be filled,
An' with Priest, an' Sacrist, and Singer skilled,
All in the North Countrie.

This pious Quene, it chanced her,—
For wha wilt not?—to dee;
An', for a' her tokens o' pietie,
Folk bowed sair penance she maun dree,
For they ca'd her nae better than she should be,
All in the North Countrie.

But the Priests they chaunted the haly mass,
And the Clerks they sang, perdie;
An' ilk Prebend the "De profundis" said,
As wi' haly water he sprynkeled
The through-stane whaur the Quene was laid,
All in the Sacristie.

An' years gaed by, and changes wore,
An' times nane thought to see;
There cam' a Demon, the Demon o' Steam;
The Dragon o' Wantly was naething to him,
He gobled down churches like strawberries and cream,
Or a caup o' flummerie!

This truculent Demon a longing took,
When hungry he chanced to be,
To mak' a snack o' her pious bones,—
Kirk, transept, vestry, steeple, and roans,

We'd swallow, and make no bones o' the stones;—
    All in the Sacristie.

But, as good luck would have it, there chanced the while,
    Ane pious Fraternitie,
An auld-warld, monkish race o' freres,
Wha ilka lang-kisted bane reveres
As a saunted relic o' bye-gane years,
    All in the North Countrie.

An' they bowed a bow, an' they sained a sign,
    An they sware fu' piouslie;
An' never a man o' them a' was afear'd,
For they grippit the Steam Demon by his beard,
An' they howkit the Quene frae the mouldy yird,
    All in the Sacristie.

An' they dighted their specs, an they rubbit their een,
    An' they vowed the Quene was she;
An' they took a cast o' her pious skull,
An' they kisted her banes in a leaden shell,
An' they cirded her under a velvet pall,
    All in the Rood Abbie.

The Demon had set his heart on her banes,
    An' an angry Demon was he;
He took the auld kirk in his hungry maw,
An' he crunched it doun betwixt tooth and jaw,
An' he lickt his chops, and chuckled, haw! haw!
    We shall see—what we shall see!

For it chanced 'mong the auld-warld dead were laid
    In the Kirk fu' peacefullie,
He turned up, whar ance the altar stood,
Wi' its mystic host and its haly rood,
Some rotten banes lapp'd in lead and wood,
    All in the Sacratie.

An' fu' loud he shriekit an elritch laugh,
An' revenged he wad be;
He sent in haste for the Queen's Remembrancer,
And bad him cook up the banes instanter,
An' swear them to ilk antiquarian haunter,
The Quene's banes in veritie.

The Queen's Remembrancer he cam post haste,
An' wi' him ilk Antiquarie;
The Curator look'd red, the Treasurer look'd blue,
The Secretary sniffed, but he only said, Whew!
And the President groaned out, What shall we do?
For it stinkit maist villainouslie!

Next there cam in hot haste, as best they might,
Some wha foremost afore maun be;
An' each stood bolt up, like an innocent man,
For they suddenly remembered—let wha will ban,—
They never had believed the auld Quene was the one,
Frae the first they never had—not they!

Besides 'twas as plain as a beggar's pike-staff—
As they suddenly cam to see,—
That a pious Quene, in her mouldie bed,
Was always known by being lapp'd in lead,—
Tho' such logic, 'tis certain, made some shake their head,
Baith in North and South Countrie!

By good luck there chanced, on the nonce, riding by,
Twa Knights o' the lancet, perdie;
I warrant, at the sight, the Secretarie,
Vice-president, Treasurer, and all, you might see
Look as though such lead-logic they thought might weigh
Somewhat short of the veritie.

There was John o' the Bone, a right Good-sir,
And Sir James o' Midwiferie;
The tane, a bright, fat, fodgel chield,
Wi' somewhat o' rare auld Grose's build,
The tother was lang as his lance, afield
Baith Knights o' gude degree.

The Demon, aghast, belched smoke and steam
At the threat o' sic enmitie;
But on catching a glower o' their dauntless een,
He lookit first red, then yellow and green,
Till at last, in a fit o' o'ermaisterfu' spleen,
He dwam'd awa' utterlie.

They prickit his hide, and bowed wi' the banes
That pushionit he should be;
They took up the skull, and the one said, Faugh!
A Quene! quoth the other,—sic a Quene I ne'er saw—
As he thrust a thigh-bane in the Demon's maw,—
But the Quene o' Bedlamie!

The Demon he groaned, and coughed, and choked,
And sputtered maist furiouslie;
But some that were there, I can warrant you,
Durst scarce show their faces, they looked sae blue,
And the Secretarie bowed, and Vice-president too,
'Twas the rarest mare's-nest ever on view
All in the North Countrie.

Moral.

Now all you Antiquaries beware how you swear
  To a Quene's identitie,
Unless in the case it should chance, indeed,
That the ladye turns up well lappt in lead,
With a crook in her spine, and a cleft in her head,
Which, as everybody knows, are the marks agreed
  For a Quene in the North Countrie!

The colophon of the original black-letter edition of fifty copies bore that it was "imprented be *Andrew Jack*, prenter to y^e^ Quenis Maiesties leiges, dwelland at y^e^ fit of Niddryes Wynde, in y^e^ *Quenis Hie Gaite*, aneist y^e^ *Chapele of Sanct Mary* in y^e^ *Cow-Gaite* fundit be *Elizabeth*, Countess of Ross of auld, in Edenburgh, in ye yere of Grace clↄ Iↄ cccxl. ix."

The following satire referred to the edifice :—

A fane it was where sculpture's curious wile,
  And all the grace of mediæval art,
Were richly blended in the ornate style
  Of that old century; whereof a part,
  Thus fossilised, lived on within the heart
Of the succeeding centuries, as one
  Trustworthy chronicle
In lasting characters of graven stone.

An honest chronicle it was of facts
    Such as fond lovers of those good old times
Scarce look for record of 'mid pious acts
    Of royal devotion; trail of shameless crimes
    And follies wherewith still the Devil limes
To catch weak mortals:—but no prurient taint
    Is to be dreamt of 'neath
The modish piety of ancient saint!

It was, in truth, with its grotesque, and grave.
    And leering drollery, from corbel, boss,
And capital, and gurgoyle; and with nave
    Shorn of its purposed graces; a most gross.
    Plain-spoken petrifaction of the loose
And sensual guise of that old century's faith;
    Like motley mingling with
The solemn shroud and smileless gaze of death.

Yet had it, too, its look of the divine
    And earnest faith that claimed in that old creed
Such place as golden chalice in the shrine
    Honoured to hold both bones of sainted dead,
    And paten, emblem of Christ's living bread:—
A fitting chantry for such queenly saint
    To vow and fashion thus
With mystic imagery and sculpture quaint.

The Secretary was not pleased with the Town Council of the day, although, as already explained, they had only to follow the orders of the Imperial Parliament. He had also a grudge at the Rev. Dr Steven, the minister of the parish. Hence he penned the following lines:—

THE PROVOST AND THE COAL BUNKER.

O SICAN a Provost as Embrugh has got,
An' sican a Council an' Bailies an' a',
For the camstrary bodies, nae body kens how,
Hae pawn'd ane o' the kirks, an' there's sic an ado,

What wi' writers and clergy, sic hullabaloo,
    Folk wunna hear tell o't ava.

A gousty auld rickle o' sticks an' stanes,
    Yet some cankered carles wunna let it gae;
Sin' the kirk's stood already 'boon four hunder year,
They threep it might stan' for four hunder mair;
An' they've measured and skeitched it frae riggin' to flair,
    Just as tho' it were worth a strae!

An' then they uphaud as a matter o' taste—
    A queer thrawn taste I trow they maun hae,—
That the skeely wark o' the auld Papist loons
Is worth mair nor a fee o' gude Scots pouns,
An' its sculptur has value beyond a' bounds,
    Just for its antiquitie!

Auld Knox, I jalouse, taught us better a wheen;
    An' a credit to the gude town 'twad be,
Gin the parish session would tak the pains,
An' put sic fule booers to stocks and stanes
In the cutty-stool sark, for the kirk's amends,
    An' the cure o' sic Papistrie.

Gudesakes! the auld kirk stood out o' the way;
    Was't Sundays or Mondays made unco sma' matter:
Gin the folk stayed at hame 'twasna want o' room,
Mass John, worthy man, little fashed his thoom;
Though the laigh pews were scant, and the galleries toom,
    He aye wailed his best screed o' dreich clatter.

But our Provost has ettled a lucky thought;
    An eident chield, as right sould, was he.
Some new neighbours hard by had drawn in their stools
And they wanted a bunker to haud some coals,
Ye may guess the clanjamfry o' rogues and fules
    O' a railway companie!

The kirk, though 'twas auld, was stout and strang,
As four-hunder-year wark behoved to be;
For sic neebors he thought it weel worth a ware,
Sae our slee pawkie Provost bespak them fair,
Aughteen thousand punds—neither less nor mair,—
An' the kirk-fauld sould weir the colliery.

Some folk wad hae thought him gane gyte in his mind—
In fact clean wud-mad and demented!—
Or maybe his Lordship did but droll!
Aughteen thousand punds down for a stance, an' the whole
For nae purpose on earth but to haud a wheen coal
To stan' by just until they be wanted!

But the slee pawkie loon kent his customers weel,
Sican gentry are chancey o' reference—
Mair for token the siller, when a's come and gane,
Wared on sic a dooms rickle o' timmer an' stane,
Turns out to've been ither folks 'stead o' their ain,—
Whilk ye'll own maks a wonderfu' difference!

Mass John—though ye'd hardly expeckit the thing,—
Made a grane o' a mane—sican blethers!
He owned to sair doubts how the bargain would tell;
An', somehow, the auld kirk and he sorted fu' weel;
Then to gie up, free haun', to the muckle black deil—
Or neist thing to't—the kirk o' our faithers!

But our Provost can whistle in a'body's lug;
Quo' he, "Ye're your ain light, my man, in;
Yer Rev'rence maun lippen for ance to advice,
I hae gien a slee hint to a skeely man, Bryce,
And he'll rig up a braw bran-new kirk in a trice
Whar the crowds scarce'll find room for stanin'!"

The auld kirk's lang doun, an' the coal-fauld's in use,
An' precisely aneuch paid the feeing;

What's thought now o' the bargain is ither folk's wark,
But Mass John maun byde on for his braw-fashioned kirk,
An' the crowds he was promised, frae mornin' till mirk,
 For I sair doubt our Provost's a slee ane.

O sican a Provost as Embrugh has got,
 An' sican a Council, an' Bailies an' a'!
They wad wyle the auld lark frae the lift sae hie,
An' the swan frae the loch, and the gled frae the tree,
An' a minister's sell frae his pulpit sae slee,
 An' a' wi' a wink an' a blaw!

CHAPTER XVIII.

DIFFICULTY OF THE SITUATION—THE ANNUITY TAX.

WHEN the Houses of Parliament ordained that the Trinity Hospital, and the Trinity Church and College buildings, which had, notwithstanding occasional devastations and spoliations of the times, survived more than three and a half centuries, —should be levelled with the dust,—it is not surprising to find that there were a considerable number of objectors, who most strenuously resisted the supposed sacrilege. Objectors are to be found everywhere, and in every variety of circumstances.

The very idea of removing, and still more of possibly obliterating from mortal vision, the most beautiful specimen of Gothic architecture in the capital of Scotland, was a matter not to be tolerated under any circumstances. When the Town Council, in an evil hour, took upon itself the choice of a site, and the restoration of the old building of Trinity College Church, it subjected its members, for many long years, to an amount of hostile criticism and obloquy, that it could not by any possibility have foreseen, otherwise it would certainly never have sought to place them, for so long a time, in the very unenviable position to which they were undoubtedly exposed.

Denominational jealousy, in the City of Edinburgh, was never more exhibited than it was about the period referred to. The Church of Scotland had been rent in twain by the much-to-be-regretted Disruption. In fact, religious jealousy dominated the ancient capital. By far the larger number of the Edinburgh Established Church clergymen had resigned their charges, when the secession took place; and the bulk of the people, who were attached to their ministers, and connected with their respective congregations, went out along with them, and joining the Free Church of Scotland. With the exception of St Stephen's, Greenside, and Lady Yester's, the churches presented little else than an array of empty benches. In so far as the three churches mentioned were concerned, their success was attributable to the fact that their respective pastors considered it to be their duty to remain in "the auld Kirk." The strongest ecclesiastical and political feeling seemed to pervade the minds and hearts of all classes of the community. The feelings engendered at the time seemed even to enter into the purely business relations of the town. Free Church people sought out those who were of the same communion in the distribution of their patronage, and the same remark may be likewise said to apply to the members of the Established Church. In addition to the causes of the Disruption, and its effects, there was at the time the old burning sore of what was known as "the Annuity Tax,"* a heavy tax which all the rate-

* THE ANNUITY TAX.—This tax was originally proposed by King Charles I. He sent certain proposals to the Magistrates of Edinburgh in 1625. The Magistrates answered these proposals, and some further negotiations followed between the Crown and the Magistrates, in consequence of which an Act of the Privy Council was passed in 1634. The

payers in the ancient and extended royalty, with the exception of the lawyers (members of the College of Justice), were called on to pay for the support of the city clergy. So long as the Church of

Privy Council acted under powers received from Parliament. By that Act of the Privy Council, power was given to levy a tax not exceeding 1200 merks of Scots money for behoof of the ministers; but it excepted from the tax the Lords of Council and Session. This went on until the year 1649, when a proposal was made to increase the number of ministers, and to levy an additional sum of money, in order to pay the stipends of the larger number. By an Act of Parliament passed on 2d March 1649, authority was given to lay on a tax of five per cent. for the purpose of enabling the Magistrates to raise a sum of 19,000 merks for the payment of six ministers. This rate, however, was not found sufficient for the purpose. A further Act was passed raising the rate to six per cent. in June 1661. The next Act was 106 years thereafter, viz. in 1767. Under that Act, the Magistrates obtained power to extend the royalty, and to levy within the area of extension the same taxes as they were authorised to levy within the ancient royalty. Subsequent extensions took place by Acts of Parliament in 1785, 1786, and 1809 respectively. By the Act of 1661, the tax provided for only six ministers; whereas that of 1809 was made applicable to the payment of all the ministers. Shortly thereafter a question arose between the Magistrates and the ministers as to the distribution of the funds. The Magistrates maintained that the Annuity Tax was a fund out of which they were entitled to allocate such stipends as they thought fit for the behoof of the ministers: in point of fact they argued, in the law proceedings which commenced in 1810, that the ministers were mere stipendiaries; that the Magistrates received the whole funds applicable to the payment of the ministers' stipends, paid the same into the hands of the City Chamberlain, and allocated from time to time to the ministers such stipends as they thought the circumstances of the case required. The ministers, on the other hand, maintained that the whole produce of the Annuity Tax was their exclusive property, and that they were not to remain, as they had hitherto been, the mere stipendiaries of the Magistrates. The ministers, therefore, raised an action of declarator in the Court of Session, for the purpose of having their rights determined by a decree of the Supreme Court.

The law plea, which was begun in 1810, ended in 1814. The judges were at first equally divided upon the point:—three were in favour of the contention of the Magistrates, and three in favour of the ministers. They, therefore, pronounced no decision, but ordered additional pleadings. The case came a second time before the Court, when only five judges were present. Of these, three supported the ministers, and two supported the Magistrates. The final decision was, therefore, in favour of the ministers. There was no appeal taken. The case was taken out of Court by a minute of compromise between the parties.

Scotland was by far the most numerous religious body in the city, the Voluntary or Nonconformist element had quietly to submit, although there were several who yearly showed their entire dis-

The members of the legal fraternity claimed exemption from the tax from the time the Act of 1661 was passed. It is stated by Fountainhall, that the exemption of the College of Justice had not been pleaded till a short time before 1678. In 1687, the Court of Session declared "the members of the College of Justice exempt from payment of the ministers' stipends, as also from watching, warding, and all impositions for the same ;" and, in 1778, the members of the College of Justice were found exempted from the payment of poor's money, and other taxations imposed by the Magistrates.

When the law case above referred to was taken out of Court, a contract was entered into between the Magistrates of the city on the one hand, and the ministers on the other, whereby the latter assigned all their rights to the former, and the Magistrates continued to collect the revenues applicable to the payment of the ministers' stipend just as they had done before the lawsuit, engaging to pay to each of the ministers a stipend of £520 each per annum. The contract was to subsist from 1814 to 1820. When the ministers ceased to be stipendiaries of the Magistrates in 1820, the formidable opposition to the tax on the part of a large portion of the public began. The Magistrates, however, did not continue to disburse the funds. They appointed a Collector, who found caution to them for his intromissions, and who was ordered to put the whole proceeds of his collection into a chartered bank, and a committee of the ministers superintended the distribution of the funds. They had a factor or law agent of their own, so soon as they ceased to be stipendiaries. By a decision of the Court of Session, afterwards ratified by the House of Lords, the Magistrates were held not to be responsible for any defalcations on the part of the Collector, after he had found proper caution for his intromissions. This was made final against an appeal by the ministers to have it ordained to be found otherwise. The annual value of the various taxable subjects was at that time decided by a body of Stentmasters (in number 30) appointed by the Town Council. This was before the passing of the Public Statute in regard to the Valuation of Lands and Heritages in Scotland.

It may be proper here to state one or two facts in connection with the history of this much hated tax. The Act of the Privy Council of Scotland, dated the 18th day of March 1634, gives the following as the reason for its being imposed :—"For sa meikle as there is nothing more consonant to equitie and reason, than that all such persouns that dailie enjoy in plentie that blessing of the word of God, and heares the same preached, and does perticipat in the benefit of the clergy, should contribute to the maintenance of the ministri in these places where they take the foresaid benifit." Then the Act of Parliament in 1649 narrates :— "That the provyding and maintaining of the sex ministeris doth concern the worship of God,

approbation at their having to pay what they termed "Tribute to Cæsar," and that too in strict opposition to what was their conscientious convictions. Several of them went the length of a passive

and tend to the propagating and maintaining thereof in the chief citie of this Kingdom, from which non that are partakers of so great a benefit will in conscience withdraw or exaim themselves, without great guiltiness before God." Again the Act of 1661 says:—"That the common good and patrimonie thairof is exhausted and overburthened, and upon the considerations foresaid are the inhabitants of the said burgh, who hes the comfort and benefit of preaching of the Gospel and ministerie within the same be the space of divers years vntil this tyme hes been in use to pay for the provision and stipend of sex of the ministeris of the said burgh," etc. All these Statutes are clear evidence, that the heritors and others, having a right to the houses, were not liable to the tax, unless they did occupy or inhabit the same; and this principle was embodied in all the Statutes passed for the extension of the royalty of the city. The Act of 1767 reserved the teinds payable from the lands over which the royalty was extended to the owners of those teinds, and left the lands subject to the burdens incident to them, in so far at least as the parishes from which they were disjoined and annexed to the royalty were concerned. For example, the lands which formed the extended royalty continued to be subject to teinds in the parishes of St Cuthbert and South Leith respectively, while the inhabitants of the houses built upon lands in these districts paid, so long as it continued to be exacted, the old Annuity Tax.

The opposition to the Annuity Tax began in 1820, when the ministers ceased to be stipendiaries of the Magistracy, and commenced to take the full benefit of the revenues, as they thought, of the fund provided for their support. The difficulties which then arose proceeded chiefly from a spirit of discontent, because of the invidious privilege of the lawyers. One person, a respectable publisher, and belonging to the Established Church, was apprehended and incarcerated as a debtor. The gentleman referred to was Mr William Tait of Prior Bank, Melrose, the originator and publisher of "Tait's Magazine," and a brother-in-law of the late Mr Adam Black. After remaining for a time in prison, the debt was paid, but the liberation of the person so incarcerated, assumed the form of a triumphal procession through the public streets, leading to his dwelling-house. Thousands of the inhabitants were witnesses of the scene; and, probably as his reward, he was returned to the Town Council, as a member of the Corporation, under the election which took place after the Reform Bill was passed. A period of quiet afterwards arose; very much because little was at that time done to enforce payment. Arrears accumulated, resistance to attempts to sell the effects of the debtors assumed a more decided shape; and when it was found that the attempts of public sales of goods were hopeless, one of the Magistrates of the day, the late Mr Joseph Hood Stott, along with another citizen who had conscientiously

resistance, and allowed their goods to be distrained, rather than of their own motive to pay what they called "the Obnoxious Tax."

In such instances, there were always to be found a class of

refused to pay the tax, preferred to go into prison, where they both remained for the period of three weeks. The result, however, was, that the law was vindicated, and the tax was paid. One-third of the amount levied could not be collected. There was yearly from £2000 to £3000 of arrears. Indeed, between 1844 and 1850 inclusive, the arrears were £19,672, 13s. 11d. A select committee of the House of Commons was appointed on the 6th of May 1851, who heard voluminous evidence on the subject, and two months thereafter their report was ordered to be printed. The result of that report was that they recommended that the stipends of the eighteen ministers be fixed at £600 per annum, viz. £10,800; and that the two ministers of Canongate receive, in addition to the seat-rents, £250 each, viz. £500=£11,300 as a total charge. This they proposed to provide for in the following manner:—From the Leith Docks £2000, from seat-rents £2000, from interest on balance of Trinity Church Fund, after setting apart £10,000 for the immediate erection of a new church £250, from the revenues of the Deans of the Chapel Royal to be transferred to the Queen's Remembrancer for Scotland and appropriated towards payment of the ministers' stipend, the Corporation giving up to the Government the patronage of three of the city churches, £2300; and to be paid out of the proceeds of a municipal tax, not exceeding three per cent. on the police rental of the ancient and extended royalties of the City of Edinburgh, and that part of the Canongate subject to the assessment.

The proposals of the Parliamentary Committee were not entertained. The late Baron Moncreiff was instrumental in 1860 in carrying a Bill which made considerable modifications on the incidence of the tax. Briefly stated, it was to this effect:—That several of the double charges should be made single charges, as the incumbents died out; that the members of the College of Justice should be taxed equally with their fellow citizens; that there should be no separate rating for the substitute for the Annuity Tax, but that 3d. per £ extra should be levied in respect of watching, lighting and cleansing within the boundary of the ancient and extended royalty, with one penny per £ on the southern and outward districts; also that the seat-rents of the churches should be applied to redemption of the tax, fixing the calculated amount at £2000 per annum. The Bill became law. While it modified greatly the rate levied on those who had previously paid the tax, it caused a larger amount of opposition than ever, chiefly on account of the new tax of one penny per £ on the southern districts of the town. Agitation still continued, and partial payments were resorted to, so that a new and modified Bill was brought in by Lord Advocate Young, whereby the levying of any rate should be restricted to a certain number of years. This was the merit of the Act of 1870, which restored peace in the city, in so far as "Roups for Ministers' Stipends" were concerned.

political agitators, who did not fail to get it duly published to their fellow-citizens, when a sale by auction of this kind was announced, that it was a "Roup for Ministers' Stipend." This, as a matter of course, produced a large and infuriated mob, who hustled and jostled the auctioneer, and those who were prepared to go in for a bargain and purchase the effects. To so great an extent did this prevail, that no auctioneer in the city could be got to undertake any roup for failure to pay the Annuity Tax. On one occasion, a member of the fraternity from Glasgow was so bold as to come through to make the attempt. He tried to be courteous and civil, without effect. He was simply jeered at, and sneered at. The first sale, which was in Frederick Street, was a failure; and the second, which took place, during the afternoon, in Hanover Street, led to something approaching to a riot, to which the military were called out. Indeed so great was the increasing popular feeling against the tax, that it was found absolutely requisite to find a remedy. After a great deal of legislation, it got a satisfactory solution towards the end of the year 1870, when an arrangement was made by which the Public Loan Commissioners advanced a sum of £56,500 to the Corporation for payment to the Representatives of the City Churches (the Ecclesiastical Commissioners) in addition to sums from other sources which had been previously given over for the support of the city clergy —in all £90,000. The sum advanced by the Loan Commissioners was repaid by an assessment levied over the City Parish and Canongate Parish in terms of Young's Act of 1870, which extinguished the debt in about nine years. During the time that this tax was a direct levy on the ratepayers, it had the effect of materially lessening the influence of the Church of Scotland in the city. It helped to cause the Church of Christ to be spoken of as a reproach and a bye-word among a very numerous and respectable body of the community. The immunity which the Church of Scotland received from scathing public criticism, at the time when this unfortunate question of public taxation was satisfactorily settled, has told greatly in favour of Church Establishment. At the present time, the Established Church in Edinburgh is by far the most powerful and the strongest of all the religious denominations in the city, and every year it is obtaining a greater and more abiding hold on the sympathies and support of the community at large.

It may be said, that it formed no part of the duty of the writer, in compiling a History of Trinity Hospital and Trinity College, to diverge into so lengthened an account of the ecclesiastical struggles of the period, and specially to refer to that, for so long a time, vexed question of the Annuity Tax. Nevertheless, it would be very difficult indeed, when called upon to write a history of the subsequent phases of this question of Trinity College Church, and especially as to the long-disputed question of a site, without bringing into view the ecclesiastical, political, and even social, surroundings of the period.

When the question of the site came to be discussed, it was clear that, in the obviously-divided state of opinion, there was not much prospect of harmony being arrived at. There were undoubtedly a Church party and an Anti-church party in the Town Council. The followers of the former were desirous of having the old church erected on some site near to, or in, the New Town; while the other party desired, on the lines of the agreement with the North British Railway Company, to have the edifice erected as near the site of the former church as was possible, and particularly within the parish, if this arrangement could by any means be effected. Five sites were at the time suggested, viz.:—

1. A site at the corner of the Calton Hill, adjoining the stairs which lead to the hill, and immediately to the east of what used to be known as the Calton Convening Rooms.

2. A site to the east of the Burns Monument, opposite to the west-end of Regent Terrace, and adjoining to the New Calton Burial Ground.

3. A site to the south-east of the East Princes Street Gardens, immediately opposite to what is now the publishing office of the *Edinburgh Evening News*.

4. A site in Market Street near to the Bank of Scotland, where the Imperial Hotel now stands. And

5. A site for many years well known as "Ireland's Woodyard," at the west side of the foot of Leith Wynd, and within the parish of the Trinity College Church.

The four sites last named obtained the favour and support of the Church party, while the latter was strenuously upheld and supported by the Nonconformist section of the Town Council. It also obtained the approval of the Sheriff. It would seem to be a work of supererogation to relate the various meetings which took place regarding both sides of the question, and the amount of bitter sectarian and political hatred and schism to which it led. All these are now things of the past, and had better be relegated to that region of oblivion, which is possibly the best place to which they can be consigned.

The site adjoining the Burns Monument was departed from. The same remark may be applied to the East Princes Street Garden one, and to the Market Street site. The only two that held their place in the competition, were Calton Hill site on the one hand and Ireland's Woodyard on the other.

The Calton Hill stance was the favourite one with the Church party in the Council as well as with the Antiquaries. But it would appear from the evidence of the late Sir William Johnston, the Lord Provost of the time, before a Parliamentary Committee as to the Annuity Tax in 1851 (Report, page 16) that there were difficulties in the way of having the building of the Church proceeded with. His words were :—"The Presbytery applied to the Town Council some time ago to proceed with the building of the Church. At that time there were difficulties in the way. The Town Council purchased a site to which they could not get access, from the heir or the person owning the land not being of age; and even yet we have not got the site which was purchased; it is not in our hands." Sir William, who was a Free Churchman, expressed his opinion in favour of the site when it could be utilised. He likewise said that he was in favour of the old building being restored stone by stone. He explained that in order to carry out this idea all the stones had been marked and numbered. The leading members of the Town Council in favour of this site were the late Bailies Forrester and Cassels. The latter was at the time one of the elders of the Trinity College Church.

But there was on the other hand a Nonconformist party in the Town Council to be reckoned with. They took up the position that all that was required was that a church suitable for the parish, and on a site in or near the parish, was what was incumbent on the Town Council. The site of Ireland's Woodyard, therefore, presented to their minds the best solution of the question.

The late Bailie Andrew Fyfe may be quoted as a representative of the Nonconformist class. Before the same Parliamentary Committee he had occasion to express his views, which (page 220) were as follow :—"I have examined the transactions regarding the Trinity College Church, and the result of that examination is to produce a conviction on my mind that the Town Council is under no legal obligation to rebuild or restore the old Church, or to expend the whole fund which they received from the Railway Company in rebuilding that Church. That is the result of my examination of the whole of the documents which have passed between the Town Council and the

Railway Company. I think that the only obligation upon them is to rebuild such a church as will afford adequate accommodation to the parish." In answer to the Judge Advocate, and other Members of Committee, Mr Fyfe stated that was the opinion he had formed not only from the construction of the clause in the Act of Parliament, but also from the terms of the agreement entered into subsequently by the Town Council and the Railway Company. In reply to a question put by the late Sir William Gibson Craig, Bart., viz.,—"Supposing the Town Council were to build a sufficient church for the accommodation of the congregation for £6000, what power do you consider they have with reference to the appropriation of the residue of the money?" Mr Fyfe's reply was to the following effect :—"I consider that they are entitled to appropriate it, in such a way as they may consider most advantageous for the interests of the community, seeing that out of the ordinary revenue or common good, large sums of money for building churches have been expended by the City. It has been found by the final decision of the Court of Session, in an action regarding the seat-rents of the city churches, that the Town Council are entitled to reimbursement of the money so expended: The amount of that fund will not be less than £50,000. Hence I hold it is quite clear that the Town Council is not only legally, but equitably, entitled to apply such portion of the price of Trinity College Church as they may consider necessary to any purpose to which they might apply the ordinary revenues of the city." Mr Fyfe would not have objected even if the money had been applied in part redemption of the Annuity Tax. He seemed altogether to neglect the interests of the beneficiaries in his own views of religious and church policy. Happily, however, there were those who, though they were Nonconformists, took a different view of the question,—being deeply impressed with the thought contained in the two lines—

"Blessed is he that wisely doth
The poor man's case consider."

The matter which had been so long debated reached a climax in the November of 1856. It was, during this year, that the city's boundaries had been extended so as to be co-equal with the Parliamentary area. The baronies of Canongate, Calton, Portsburgh, and Broughton ceased to exist, and were to form part of the city. The Southern Districts, which, up to that time had had a separate jurisdiction, became also directly under the municipal control. The Commissioners of Police, who for many years had been elected by the ratepayers to attend to the departments of watching, lighting, and cleansing, were, by the same Bill, abolished—their functions in future devolving upon the Municipal Corporation. The Town Council, which previously consisted of thirty-one elected members, with the Dean of Guild and the Convener of Trades, was now enlarged to forty-one, being eight additional elected members, or thirty-nine in all, and the other two members already referred to. The city was divided into thirteen wards, with three representatives to each. Although the boundaries of the city have since been greatly enlarged, no additional members have been added to the Town Council,—a re-adjustment of the various areas of the municipal districts having met the exigencies of the occasion.

The re-construction of the Town Council in 1856 told sorely against the Church party. Prior to the November election, they were in a decided majority, and had carried a resolution during that very year, to apply the whole of the Railway money to the rebuilding of the Trinity College Church. This resolution was not carried out, in consequence of an action of declarator having been raised in the Court of Session, to which special reference will fall to be made in the next chapter. In the meantime, however, it may be mentioned that, in consequence of the changed aspect of the constitution of the Council, it was proposed in 1858, and carried by a majority (the minority of course dissenting and protesting) that only a sum of about £7000 should be devoted to the building, and that it should not be in the same style and model of the previous edifice.

CHAPTER XIX.

THE BENEFICIARIES' LAW PLEA.

WHILE the question of a site for the Trinity College Church was agitating the community, and occasioning great diversity of opinion not only among Town Councillors and dissenters on the one hand, and the Established Presbytery, churchmen, and antiquaries on the other, and when the Town Council by a majority had come to the conclusion to devote the whole of the money to the rebuilding of the Church on the site at the south-west corner of the Calton Hill, an important step was being taken to circumvent all their views, and which, when propounded, filled many minds with consternation.

This was an action of declarator raised, chiefly on the instigation of the late Professor William Dick (Founder of the Royal Edinburgh Veterinary College), the late Dr John Renton, and several other Radical members of the Town Council. The late Mr William Wotherspoon, W.S., acted as agent in the case, which was called on the 8th day of August 1856. It was an action in the Court of Session, at the instance of eleven of the Hospital Beneficiaries. As most of them were somewhat advanced in life, it was thought desirable that as many as could be found to act as "our levites," should appear as *pursuers*. Most of them did not survive to see their case practically successful. Margaret Hume, residing in No. 40 Candlemaker Row, whose name appeared first on the list, did not live to see the result. But Margaret Clephane of 15 Buccleuch Street (the second name mentioned) seems to have enjoyed a better lease of life, and was therefore cognisant of the termination of the legal fight in which for years her name was prominently brought before the Law Courts of the country.

The action was laid against (1) the Lord Provost, Magistrates and Town Council, both as representing the community of the said city, and as trustees, administrators, and governors for the time being of the said Trinity Hospital of Edinburgh, and for themselves and their successors in office; (2) as also, against the Reverend William Steven, doctor of divinity, then one of the ministers of the City of Edinburgh, and claiming to be the minister of the parish or district of the said City of Edinburgh, known by the name of Trinity College Parish, for any interest competent to him or his successors in office in the premises; (3) as also, against the Reverend the Moderator of the Presbytery of Edinburgh, and all the individual members thereof, whose names are all duly recorded (as well as those of the Town Council)—being all members, or claiming to be members, of the said Presbytery of Edinburgh, or the major part thereof, and for themselves and their successors in office, as representing the said Presbytery for any right or interest they or the said Presbytery have in the premises—*defenders*.

The contention was, that the church or building known by the name of Trinity College Church, and which was situated near the foot of Leith Wynd, Edinburgh, together with the building known as Trinity Hospital, Edinburgh, situated adjoining to the said Church, with the ground pertaining thereto, belonged to and were vested in the Lord Provost, Magistrates, and Town Council of the City of Edinburgh, as trustees and administrators, solely and exclusively for the ends, uses, and purposes mentioned and contained in a charter by King James VI. of Scotland, with consent of the Lord Regent and of the Lords of the Secret Council, in favour of the said Provost, Magistrates, Council, and Community of the said burgh, dated 12th November 1567, and which charter was ratified, approved, and confirmed by various subsequent charters, grants, and Acts of Parliament. It was contended that said charter was still a valid and subsisting grant, and that the defenders, the Lord Provost, Magistrates, and Town Council were bound thereby, and by the terms and conditions thereof, in all points, and were not entitled to use and apply the property thereby conveyed, or the produce or prices thereof, in any other manner, or for any other uses and purposes, than the uses and purposes contained in the said charter. It was likewise contended, that the Magistrates and Town Council were bound to apply the sum of £17,671, 9s. 6d. received by them from the North British Railway Company, as the price of, or compensation for, the said Trinity College Church, and ground pertaining thereto, and for other rights of property or servitude belonging to the said defenders, as trustees and administrators of Trinity Hospital, or whatever sum they received for the said church and property, and interest thereon, solely and exclusively for the use and behoof of Trinity Hospital, and "for the building and construction of the said Hospital, houses, yards, and policies thereof, and for the maintenance of the poor and sick to be placed therein, and for no other use whatever," all in terms of the said charter of 12th November 1567. It was specially contended that the Lord Provost, Magistrates, and Town Council were not entitled to apply the sum received as the price or compensation for the church and property taken by the North British Railway Company, or any part thereof, to any use and purpose which would not be for behoof of, or beneficial to, or in furtherance of, the purposes of the said Trinity Hospital; and particularly that the defenders were not entitled to apply the said sum, or any part thereof, in the purchase of ground or site for, or in the erection of, a church to be used as one of the city churches of Edinburgh, or for any other purpose not conducive to the use and benefit of the said Trinity Hospital. Interdict was also asked against the Town Council using or applying the sum received from the Railway Company as compensation for the church and site, or for any other use or purpose than for the benefit and behoof of the foresaid charity; and interdict was further asked against the application of the whole or any part of the money being devoted to the purchase of a site for, or in the erection of, any church whatever, whether to be used as one of the city churches of Edinburgh, or otherwise.

As the summons concluded for expenses against any, or all of the defenders compearing, and as the Town Council undertook to defend, no appearance seems to have been made by the Rev. Dr Steven, the incumbent, or by the Presbytery of Edinburgh as such.

The Town Council on the other hand contended that Trinity College Church formed no part of the property of the Hospital applicable for the support of the poor, but that, before it came into the hands of the Magistrates and Council, it was used as a church in terms of the original foundation for Divine Worship; and that after it was acquired by the Magistrates and Council, it was used as one of the city churches, for the use of the Trinity College Parish, until it was taken down by the North British Railway Company. No rent was ever paid to the Hospital for or in respect of the church, nor was any of the expenses of the repair of the church laid against the funds of the Hospital. The entire expenses of maintaining and repairing the fabric were defrayed out of the funds belonging to the common good of the city. The Council, however, admitted that no seat-rents were ever charged against the officials or the inmates of the Hospital for their accommodation in the church. They averred that the city had from time to time been divided into districts or parishes, and different churches had been appropriated for the use of the inhabitants of the localities in which they were situated. They referred to the fact which has been already brought out, that so early as 1584, about seventeen years after the Town Council obtained the transfer from Sir Simon Prestoun of his reversionary right to the Trinity College and pertinents, and after the agreement with Robert Pont, apparently with the view of securing a proper title to the church—the Magistrates and Town Council resolved to divide the city into four divisions or parochins. Again, this arrangement was ratified in 1625, in conformity with an arrangement with King Charles I. In 1641, the Town Council divided the city into six parishes, appointing churches and ministers thereto. Various other divisions took place from time to time. The Town Council maintained that, from the very beginning of their management of the Trinity College Church and Hospital, the church had been allocated to the Trinity College Parish, and been utilised as one of the city churches; that all the ministers of the same had been appointed by them, in virtue of the right of patronage conferred upon them; that the ministers of the said church have been recognised and dealt with by the Presbytery and by the other Church Courts, by Parliamentary enactments, by the Courts of Law and otherwise, as city ministers, and as having right with the other city ministers to the status and funds provided for the city clergy; that the whole ecclesiastical arrangements in the city have invariably been made, sanctioned by the Presbytery, acknowledged by the Courts of Law and other judicatories, civil and ecclesiastical, and acquiesced in by every body on the footing of Trinity College being one of the city churches;

that the seat-rents had been applied, and the expenses connected therewith had been provided for in accordance therewith. The Town Council further referred to the fact that in 1810, an action was instituted by the then ministers of Edinburgh, including the minister of the Trinity College Church, against the Magistrates and Town Council, in which, founding on the charter of 1566 by Queen Mary, and subsequent charters already adverted to, they claimed right to the church lands and revenues thereby conveyed, on the ground that these were vested in the Magistrates and Council, to be applied to the support of the ministers of the city, and other ecclesiastical purposes. The Town Council, however, maintained in defence, that these were destined to various other purposes besides payment of the ministers' stipends. After a great deal of procedure, the Magistrates and Council were assoilzied from this part of the conclusions of the action of 1810, and ever since the Trinity College Church has been dealt with, as previously, as one of the city churches. They explained that during all the time they had charge of the charity, the funds of Trinity Hospital had been received and administered by a separate treasurer. The Town goes on further to explain that, according to the Act of Parliament, the Directors of the Railway Company were themselves taken bound to erect a new church, after the style and model of the one taken down, on a site as near as possible to the old one; but that there was a stipulation that that agreement might be set aside by a payment of money; that as the money had been accepted by the Town Council, the latter were bound under their contract with the former, and in obedience to the Act of Parliament, to erect a suitable building on the best site they could obtain to supply the place of the former church. They further denied the right of the pursuers, being only beneficiaries or pensioners, enjoying the benefits of Trinity Hospital, to appear against their governors—the Magistrates and Town Council of the city.

The late Mr Adam Gifford, Advocate (afterwards Lord Gifford), appeared for the pursuers or beneficiaries, and Mr George Young, Advocate (now Lord Young), appeared for the Town Council as Governors of the Hospital, who both addressed the Court at great length on the subject. The case was heard before the late Lord Ardmillan (James Craufurd) as one of the Lords Ordinary in the Outer House. The following was his Lordship's decision on the various points raised:—

"Edinburgh, 29th January 1859.—The Lord Ordinary having heard counsel for the parties, and made avizandum, and considered the closed record, productions, and whole process—Finds that the pursuers, Margaret Hume and others, have sufficient title to institute and pursue this action, and accordingly repels the first plea in law stated for the defenders: Finds on the merits that, having regard to the charters and titles and documents in process, to the admitted fact of the long unbroken and unquestioned possession and use of the Trinity College Church, and to the provisions of the Act of Parliament, 9 and 10 Vict. cap. 74, the pursuers are not entitled to decree as concluded for against the defenders, the Lord Provost and Magistrates of Edinburgh, to the effect that the said defenders are bound to apply the whole sum received by them from the North British Railway Company, under the provisions of the said Act, 'solely and exclusively for the use and behoof of the Trinity Hospital, and for the building and construction of said hospital, houses, etc., and for the maintenance of the poor and sick to be placed therein, and for no other use whatever,' and that the pursuers are not entitled to decree as concluded for, to the effect that the defenders are not entitled 'to apply the said sum or any part thereof, in the purchase of ground or site for, or in the erection of, a church to be used as one of the city churches of Edinburgh,' and that the pursuers are not entitled to interdict as craved: Finds that the first and second conclusions for declarator are only introductory and ancillary to the leading conclusions to which the above findings apply. Therefore assoilzies the defenders from the conclusions of the action, and decerns: Finds the pursuers liable to the defenders in expenses; allows an account thereof to be given in, and remits the same, when lodged, to the auditor to tax and report."

The pursuers, however, did not allow the matter to rest. They reclaimed against the above judgment to the Lords of the First Division. The reclaiming petition was sent to the debate roll on the 8th day of February 1859.

This was not, however, the only difficulty in which the Town Council was placed. By the election of 1856, and the reconstruction and enlargement of the Council, a new generation of civic rulers had arisen who refused to carry out the decision that had been arrived at a few months previously, and declared that £7000 was quite sufficient to expend on the building of a new church. This did not please Bailie Forrester and others, who had previously led the Corporation in the matter. The result was that an action of declarator was raised in the Court of Session on the 22d February 1858, at the instance of William Forrester, one of the bailies, Thomas Murray and others, Town Councillors, being a minority of the Magistrates and Town Council, with consent and concurrence of Robert Chambers, publisher, and others, residing in and citizens of Edinburgh, against the Lord Provost, Magistrates, and Town Council of the City of Edinburgh, concluding as follows:—Therefore it ought and should be found and declared, that the sum of £17,671, 9s. 6d. received by the defenders or their predecessors, as on the 15th day of May 1848, from the North British Railway Company, under and by virtue of the Act 9 and 10 Vict. cap. 74, with the interest which has accrued, or may hereafter accrue thereon, is held by them in trust for the erection of a new church, within the parish of Trinity College, or as near thereto as conveniently may be, with equal convenience of access and accommodation to that formerly, and at the date of the said Act, existed in the said parish, and of the same style and model: And the said defenders ought and should be decerned and ordained, by decree foresaid, to execute the purposes of said trust, and forthwith to build, or cause to be built, within the said parish of Trinity College, or as near thereto as conveniently may be, a new church, with equal convenience of access and accommodation, and of the same style and model as the church formerly existing in said parish, at the date of said Act, all agreeably to a plan, to be approved of and authorised by our said Lords in the course of the process to follow hereon: And the said defenders ought and should be interdicted, prohibited, and discharged, by decree of the said Lords, from employing the funds held by them in trust, as aforesaid, in the erection of any other church than a church of the construction, accommodation, style, and model before described, or otherwise than as before set forth.

In their condescendence, the pursuers stated that Trinity College Church had, since 1587, been used and dealt with in every respect by the defenders, their predecessors, and all parties, as one of the parish churches of Edinburgh. It was a very ancient building, the most perfect specimen of the particular order of architecture to which it belonged, an object of interest to historians, architects, antiquarians, and the citizens. In the Bill which the Railway Company introduced into Parliament, they asked power to acquire the said church on the ordinary footing, leaving the compensation to be regulated by the Lands Clauses Consolidation Act. The proposed destruction of the church by the Railway Company excited great discontent among the citizens, and accordingly the Bill was opposed on behalf of the citizens. Protracted discussions took place before the Committee of the House of Commons appointed to consider the Bill. They inserted in the Bill a clause in the following terms:—(For this clause, *vide* page 166). After the above clause was inserted, the Bill passed both Houses of Parliament, and received the royal assent on 26th June 1846, and it now forms the Act 9 and 10 Vict. cap. 74, and the said clause forms section 8 of this Act.

In carrying out this clause, the Railway Company and the Magistrates and Town Council differed both upon the site and the plans for the new church; whereupon, in terms of the Statute, they applied to the Sheriff, before whom a variety of procedure took place. Ultimately, on 11th September 1847, the Sheriff approved of a certain site, provided that the Railway Company could give a clear title to it, and, on 26th February 1848, the Sheriff aproved of a report by Mr David Rhind, architect, and relative plans, as the plans for the New Trinity College Church. Instead of the Railway Company building the church, in conformity with the plan thus approved of, an agreement, dated 4th May 1848, was entered into between the Lord Provost and Magistrates, or by the then Lord Provost for their behoof, on the first part, and the said Railway Company on the second part, wherein the foresaid 8th clause was recited, and it was set forth that,—"Whereas certain proceedings took place before the Sheriff of Edinburgh, in reference to the sites and plans for the new church, and latterly a site on ground acquired by the second parties, with relative plans proposed by them, were approved of by the Sheriff, under a reference to him, in terms of the provisions of the said Act; and whereas the ground so fixed on for a site was subject to a restriction against building, in favour of the said first parties as superiors thereof, and having been considered by them to be unsuitable for the said church, they objected thereto, and declined to discharge the said servitude or restriction; but the said second parties maintain that the said restriction is not now in force;" and they "agreed that the second parties did thereby offer, and the said first parties did thereby accept of the sum of money, which shall be fixed by David Rhind, Esq., architect, from estimates to be procured by himself, without challenge or interference by either party, as the actual cost of erecting and completing for occupation, a church on the site, and in exact accordance with the plans approved of by the Sheriff as aforesaid, including architects' fees, clerks of works' allowance, and all other necessary charges, and that as compensation for the said Church, and in lieu of the obligation on the said second parties under the said Act of Parliament in reference to the said Church." The sum thus to be fixed was to be payable at the term of Whitsunday 1849, with interest at the rate of five per cent. from the term of Whitsunday 1848, and the second parties were also to make immediate payment to the said first parties of the further sum of £1300; that is to say, of the sum of £800 as the price of the site of the then Trinity Church, and of the sum of £500 for a discharge of the restriction against building on the ground proposed for the site of the new church, as therein mentioned. Under, and in accordance with the agreement then made, Mr Rhind ascertained and fixed the sum to be paid by the Railway Company, in addition to the £1300 before mentioned, at £16,371, 9s. 6d., composed of the particulars specified in his report, dated 15th July 1848. The £16,371, 9s. 6d. thus fixed, added to the £1300, made in all £17,671, 9s. 6d. The sum of £16,371, 9s. 6d. was the exact amount of the actual cost, as calculated by Mr Rhind, which would have been incurred by the construction of the Church, according to the plans approved of by the Sheriff. These sums were therefore paid, in accordance with this agreement. Very soon after the 4th May 1848, the old church was taken down, and the site has ever since been occupied by the Railway Company. The Lord Provost, Magistrates, and Town Council did not execute the plans so approved of; and, after a delay of many years, have now resolved (the pursuers and others dissenting and protesting) to expend only £7000 on the erection of a church. They have called for plans of a new church, and have refused to require that they shall be of the same style and model as the church formerly existing,—requiring merely that it shall be a suitable church for the parish. The church which the defenders propose to erect, is not a church of the style and model of the old Trinity College Church. No church capable of meeting the statutory requirements can be constructed for the sum which the defenders propose to apply to the purpose. Hence the present action.

The defenders' (the Lord Provost, Magistrates, and Town Council) statement was to the following effect:—The defenders narrated (1) the particulars connected with the foundation by Mary of Gueldres of the College or Collegiate Church, with its provost, prebendaries, choiristers, etc., as these are fully detailed in Chapter I. of this volume. (2) They narrated the duties of the various officials and the means by which they were supported, or by which their livings were provided. And (3) they recapitulated the allowance which was given to the beidmen, apart from the revenues of those beneficiaries which have been already mentioned.

They then declare (6) that after the Reformation, the Magistrates and Town Council of the city passed an Act of Council (on April 23, 1561), setting forth that "it is thocht gude that the rentis, annuellis, and utheris emolumentis, quilkis of before was payit furth of landis and tenementis within yis burt, to papestis, priests, freries, monks, nonnis and utheris of yat wicket sort, for maintenying of idolatrie and vain superstitioune, seeing it has plesit ye Almichtie to oppin ye eis of all peiple, and give yame ye knowlege of sic vain abusis,—Therefore, yat ye saidis rentis and emolumentis be applyit to mair profitable and godlie uses, sic as for susteuying of the true ministereis of Goddis word, and biging of hospitals for the pure, and colleges for leirnying and upbringing of ye zouth, and sic uther godlie wurkis." (7) On August 27, 1561, they presented a supplication to Queen Mary, praying for a grant of the situation where the Blackfriars had been, with their yards that they might build an hospital, and of the Kirk-of-Field for a school, offering to pay a reasonable price therefor, and of certain rents of chaplainries, then in Her Majesty's hands, for sustaining of the Hospital and School. Queen Mary in 1562 (March 16) granted a charter in favour of the Magistrates and Town Council of the piece of ground so asked, for the construction and plantation of an hospital for support of the poor.

(8) On January 3, 1566, King James gave a letter to the Council setting forth the terms of the above charter, and authorised the Magistrates and Town Council to use and dispose of the subjects so conveyed to them at their discretion, but so that the annual profit and return should be applied for the sustenance of the poor in the hospital.

(9) About two months thereafter (March 13, 1566), Queen Mary made a grant in favour of the Corporation of a number of ecclesiastical subjects and revenues which are specified (10 and 11). Sir Simon Preston's conveyance to the Council, and charter of King James's approval, and transference of the same, quoted at large (12, 13, 14, 15, 16, 17, and 18). Allusion is made to the Town Council's control of the Church and Hospital, to Pont's resignation of ecclesiastical subjects and revenues, to further grants from the Crown for the foundation of the Edinburgh or Town's College, the School, etc., down to the time when King James attained majority. (19) The Act passed by the Scottish Parliament, ratifying all these arrangements is next

referred to. (20) The Golden Charter is then quoted from. (21) King Charles's Charter is introduced. (22) The division of the town into four parochines or quarters, and the subsequent division into six is next explained. (23) The Magistrates and Council deny that the College Church was a parish church in the ordinary sense, although they had used it as such. (24) The Hospital derived no revenue from the Church. The Council made use of it as a convenient practical arrangement, and the fabric was maintained by grants from the common good fund of the burgh. (27) Reference is made to the other action pending in the case (*Clephane, etc.*), in which it was contended that the money belonged to the charity, and there was no need to build the Church at all. The Magistrates and Council then add—After much discussion and deliberation, the defenders came to be of opinion that the most reasonable, expedient, and proper course, with reference to the legitimate interests of all parties, was to erect a suitable church for the use of the district or parish of Trinity College, and to apply so much of the money in question as might be requisite for that purpose. They resolved, accordingly, by a majority. The resolution was opposed by the pursuers, who constituted the minority. The defenders were advised that if a balance should remain after providing for a suitable church, that it must be used in their discretion with reference to the purposes of the Royal Charters, to which reference has been made. The Magistrates and Council have not as yet adopted any resolution in regard to the disposal of any such balance. (29) The defenders are of opinion that the true interests of the district and parish, and of the congregation attached to it, will be better consulted, and provided for, by the erection of a suitable church, constructed with reference to the convenience of a Presbyterian congregation, and the Presbyterian form of worship, than by the reconstruction of the old church, which, as already stated, was not adapted to the purpose for which it was applied.

The pursuers (*Forrester and Others*) pleaded: That under a just construction of the Act of Parliament 9 and 10 Vict. cap. 74, in reference to the facts detailed in the record, the sum received by the defenders from the Railway Company does not belong absolutely to the Magistrates and Council, but is held by them in trust for the erection of a church, within the parish of Trinity College, or as near thereto as conveniently may be, with equal convenience of access and accommodation, and of the same style and model as the church which formerly existed at and previous to the date of the said Act.

The defenders (*Magistrates and Town Council*) pleaded: That the pursuers' averments were insufficient in law to support the action. That it was quite lawful for the Corporation to apply the money in question, in conformity with the resolution of the majority, to which resolution no legal objection existed. That the provisions of the Act 9 and 10 Vict. cap. 74 did not import any legal obligation on the defenders to apply the money in question in the manner specified in the conclusions of the summons. Neither were they so bound by virtue of the Act or agreement with the Railway Company referred to in the summons, or otherwise.

There were thus two different actions to be disposed of; and it was deemed advisable that they should be heard together.

The two cases came before the Court of Session, during the month of June 1860. The judgment of the Court was pronounced on the 26th day of the month. On the Bench were the Lord President (Inglis), Lord Ivory, Lord Curriehill, and Lord Deas. Lord Ivory differed from his brethren in the view their Lordships took of the position of affairs. The majority of the Bench supported their decision, at great length; but in view of after events, it does not seem to the writer requisite to have these embodied in this work, other than the reasons given by the Lord President Inglis.

The LORD PRESIDENT said—This action at the instance of certain members of the Town Council against certain other members of the Town Council, concludes to have it found and declared "that the sum of £17,671, 9s. 6d. received by the defenders or their predecessors, on 15th May 1848, from the North British Railway Company, under and by virtue of the Act 9 and 10 Victoria, cap. 74, with the interest which has accrued, or hereafter may accrue thereon, is held by them in trust for the erection of a new church within the parish of Trinity College, or as near thereto as conveniently may be, with equal convenience of access and accommodation to that formerly, and at the date of the said Act, existing in said parish, and of the same style and model;" and that they should be ordained "to execute the purposes of the trust, and forthwith to build, or cause to be built, within the said parish of Trinity College, or as near thereto as conveniently may be, a new church, with equal convenience of access and accommodation, and of the same style and model as the Church formerly existing in said parish at the date of said Act;" and that they ought to be interdicted from employing the funds held by them in trust, "in the erection of any other church than a church of the construction, accommodation, style, and model before described." The pursuers rest their contention in support of these conclusions upon the Act of Parliament 9 and 10 Victoria, cap. 74, and upon the circumstances under which that provision of the Act was passed by the Legislature. It appears that this Trinity College Church was part of subjects that had been held by the Magistrates for a great length of time, and held by them under a charter—I need not go further back than the charter of 1567—which gave right to Trinity College Church, and to certain subjects in the neighbourhood of it. That Church appears to have been used as a church, so far as it was used at all, from that time downwards until 1846, when this Act of Parliament was passed. It would appear that the Railway Company require to get possession of the subjects, belonging to Trinity Hospital, or to the Magistrates—whoever might be the proprietors of them—that were in that locality, and the Legislature appears to have dealt with the Church which stood there differently from the other subjects that were there. The provision in the Act is—"That it shall not be lawful for the said North British Railway Company to make any alterations on, or to use for the purposes of said railway, the additional land in the parishes of Trinity College, St Andrew, and Canongate, which by this Act they are authorised to purchase for a terminus in

Edinburgh, until they shall have agreed with the Lord Provost, Magistrates, and Town Council of the said city on a plan for the removal and rebuilding, at the expense of the company, on another site, either within the said parish of Trinity College, or as near thereto as conveniently may be, of a new church, with equal convenience of access and accommodation to that already existing in the said parish; and that in such agreement provision shall be made for the adoption of the same style and model with the existing church." That is the leading provision. I have not the Act of Parliament before me, but I believe it is not disputed that this property was scheduled in the Act, and the Magistrates were represented as the proprietors. I do not know whether that remark is applicable to other portions of the property disposed of—whether the whole of the property connected with Trinity Hospital was scheduled in the same way. That has not been explained to us. But the Magistrates were inserted as the proprietors of that portion of the property now in question. The clause which I have read is the leading part of the provision, but there is a proviso as to any differences that may arise regarding the plan or site; these are to be subject to the arbitration of the Sheriff; and there is a declaration "that it shall be competent to the Railway Company to offer, and the said Magistrates and Town Council are hereby authorised to accept of a sum of money as compensation for the said Church, and in lieu of the foregoing obligation." I understand the fact to be, that the sum paid by the Railway Company to the Magistrates under that provision of the Statute, was made up of three elements: one—the larger one—was the sum which was estimated as the cost of replacing the Church on a site selected, or to be selected; another was the value of the site of the old Church; and a third was the value of a certain servitude against building, that was possessed over certain ground in that locality. It did not comprehend the value of other lands or property, nor the site of the Church. The question now arises as to the application of the fund which has been so received by the Magistrates. They appear to have at one time contemplated the execution of the purpose which the present pursuers contend was the proper purpose, viz., the erection of a church similar to the former one; but they afterwards came to entertain a different opinion as to their duties and rights, and their present statement to us is, that they consider that they ought not to go to the expense of erecting a fabric of such a costly character as would be a church in the style and model of that which existed. They do not tell us what they propose to do with the balance. They state that they have a discretionary power as to the management of this fund. I do not know exactly upon what principle. It was not very clearly explained whether they claim the same discretionary power in regard to it, which they have in regard to all funds belonging to the Corporation, or whether it is a discretion within certain limits which the Act of Parliament has imposed upon them, or whether it is a discretion within certain limits imposed upon them by the titles under which they formerly held the property. That has not been made clear; but I do not find that there is, on the part of the Magistrates, any statement or admission of unwillingness to erect a church. On the contrary, I understand their contention to be that they are entitled to erect a church, and have some intention of doing so; but that they think it would be a waste of the money, to employ so much of it in the erection of a fabric of the style and model of the Church formerly existing, and that it would be a sounder exercise of discretion, and a more proper execution of the duties devolved upon them, that they should apply part of that sum to other objects connected either with the Hospital, or with educational purposes generally, or otherwise. It appears to me that, in this action, there is an indication of the same views and the same contention as in the other action which we are going to deal with, at the instance of the persons interested in the Hospital; and, though that is not the immediate case I am speaking to, yet I may mention in regard to the matter there involved, that I am not disposed, in anything that I may say in this case, or in anything that I may say in that other case, to interfere in any degree, or to concur in any judgment that in my opinion will interfere in any degree, with the general principle, that when money is devoted to a particular purpose, and especially to a charitable purpose, and where the title upon which that is given, and the objects for which it is destined, are expressed unambiguously, it is incompetent for the parties who are administrators of the trust to divert it to other purposes. There are cases which I think go very decidedly to that effect, and some of them of comparatively recent occurrence. There is the case of Heriot's Hospital, there is the case of Dundee, and there is perhaps as clear an exposition as any in the case of the Ramsay bursaries at St Andrews. But, while that is my opinion, it does not exclude this consideration which may come into some of those questions, viz., whether when the title under which the property is held, or the deed which is appealed to as constituting the trust to the parties holding it is not unambiguous, whether in that case what has all along been done in reference to the execution of the trust may not be taken as construing and establishing the true character and nature of the trust, and the proper mode of administering it. I observe, in reference to this particular property, that it was conveyed to the Magistrates in the form of a church. There was the Trinity Collegiate Church, there were certain gardens connected with it, and there was the Hospital and certain grounds connected with it; the property being divided as the Magistrates state, and as all the parties state, into these separate portions.

The portion which we are now dealing with is the Church—the Church, and the ground merely upon which the Church stood, and not any of the other subjects. Now, that particular subject so conveyed as a church, remained always as a church, while in the possession of the Magistrates. It may be that the Trinity Hospital had certain interests in that Church. I think it so appears from the statement, which I do not understand to be contradicted, that the beneficiaries of the Hospital derived certain benefits from that Church, by accommodation within the Church without payment. I do not understand that the beneficiaries of the Hospital were ever charged for that accommodation. They obtained seats within that Church, administration of service within that Church, and of course these benefits could not be obtained for them without certain expenses connected with obtaining them. I do not desire at present to go into any question as to how any surplus, after providing for them these benefits—any surplus that may have been derived from the seat-rents—should have been applied, or how they may have applied; and, in the case that is now before us, I do not see that the conclusions of the action contain anything as to the uses that are to be made of the new Church, or of the interests that are to exist in that church after it is erected. It is simply an action to obtain the erection of a church, within the locality described by the Act of Parliament, and of the style and model prescribed by the Act of Parliament. The question, then, arises—whether that demand is well founded, or whether the defence that is maintained against it is well founded? It appears to me that the demand is well founded. I think, in the first place, that it is impossible to read the clause in the Act of Parliament, without seeing that this property was dealt with in a manner totally different from the ordinary rights and interests that parties promoting public works have under the Lands Clauses Act. It is made matter of legislative stipulation, not that the property shall be valued, but that a certain Church shall be erected in lieu of the old Church. It is not the mere passing of a Bill allowing the matter to proceed in the ordinary way, allowing the parties to prove the value of the masonry as it stands, or of the interest which they derive, or could have derived from letting the seats, they upholding the fabric and providing the preacher, or for letting the entire building as a church for rent. It is not that. It is the introduction of an anxious stipulation that something shall be done, which is now said to be unnecessary, and to be a mere waste of money on costly ornament; but still it is a dealing with that subject out of the ordinary way, because there is a provision that the Railway Company are not to be entitled to take the ground, unless or until they provide a church within that locality which is specified, and of the same style and model with the existing Church. There is a declaration that it shall be competent to the Railway Company to offer, and to the Town

Council to accept of, a sum of money, as compensation for the Church, and in lieu of the foregoing obligation. It is not that in lieu of the obligation they are to receive a sum as compensation for the loss of the Church; but that they are to receive a sum as compensation for the Church, and as the price of relieving the Railway Company from the obligation to take upon themselves the duty of erecting the Church of the same costly style and model. There is the sum to be paid for the cost of erecting after that particular style and model, apart from or in addition to the intrinsic value of the property, or the price which could be obtained for it. I attach great importance to that. I think it shows that the sum we are now dealing with, is a sum that comes not merely in lieu of what might have been the assessed value of the property if the matter had been proceeded with in the ordinary course of going to a jury, and assessing the value according to the Lands Clauses Act, but it is a sum that comes in lieu of an obligation to do another thing which is quite different—a thing implying cost for ornament and otherwise. It was foreseen that it might be inconvenient for the Railway Company to delay their occupation of the ground till they did that thing themselves; and it was provided that they might implement their obligation, and be allowed access to the ground by handing over to the Magistrates the requisite sum for doing the thing which they themselves were to have done. I cannot read this clause in any other sense, than that the Magistrates hold this money as having come in lieu of that obligation which was on the Railway Company, and as a sum to be applied to the fulfilment of that obligation, as far as necessary for the accomplishment of that which the Legislature required to be done. I therefore think that the true meaning of this clause is, that that money is to be so applied, in so far as it is necessary for the accomplishment of that object. It may be—and I do not wish to pronounce anything upon that just now—it may be that the object that is required by the Legislature to be accomplished—the erection of a church of the same style and model with the Church then existing—may be attained without the expenditure of all this money, and the interest that is now accumulating. That is a possible case. I do not know how that may be; and, if the Church shall be erected, and a surplus shall exist, I do not wish at present to pronounce anything as to how that surplus is to be disposed of. All the demand now made is, that the Church shall be erected, and that the money shall be so expended, as far as is necessary for that object. If additional ornament is demanded beyond what was upon the ancient Church, it may be a question whether the surplus ought to be appropriated to that, or would be more properly appropriated to something else. It may remain a question after this Church is erected, what are to be the interests in any revenues that are to be derived from it? I do not desire to decide that question now. It is not raised. All the length I propose to go, is to decide that the Magistrates are bound to erect that Church, *ante omnia*, to erect the Church. That is what is asked. It may be that, after it is erected, it may be found that the Trinity Hospital have material interests, such as to have seats in it, or other interests. That is possible. But the first question is, is that Church to be erected? I think the Act of Parliament cannot be avoided in that particular, and I think that the whole history of the Church, and the use that has been made of it from the beginning as a church, shows very clearly that it was a fitting shape in which to retain that part of the property. I do not at present go into questions that may be raised hereafter. I reserve my opinion on the question that may be raised as to other interests that are said to exist in that Church apart from those of the Hospital, as to other uses to which it has been applied, and may be applied. The conclusion at which I arrive, then, is, that the substance of the Lord Ordinary's interlocutor in this first case is right as to the erection of the Church. I also think that, before ordering the parties to erect the Church, some steps ought to be taken, such as the Lord Ordinary points at, in regard to the obtaining of plans and estimates, and the adjustment of a site. I am, however, disposed to think that the phraseology of the Lord Ordinary's interlocutor ought to be a little altered, and that the sum be corrected, and should not comprehend the estimated price of the servitude. I would, therefore, recall the interlocutor, and pronounce another substantially the same.

Then, in regard to the other case at the instance of Reid and Others, I have already stated generally my view as to trusts of this kind. I think that where there is no ambiguity, the parties in possession cannot be heard to plead anything against the plain and obvious and unquestionable meaning of the trust. On the other hand, where there is room for construction, I think that, in the matter of construction, great light might be derived from usage. But the view I take of this case does not require me to deal with that point. I think that this action has for its object and purpose substantially, as exhibited in its conclusions, taking them as a whole, to have the Magistrates prevented from building any church at all. The first conclusions as to declaration of the trust are of a general character, and introductory, I think, to what follows. Then there is a conclusion that it "should be found and declared, by decree foresaid, that the defenders, the said Lord Provost, Magistrates, and Town Council of Edinburgh, are bound to apply the sum of £17,671, 9s. 6d. received by them from the North British Railway Company, as the price of, or compensation for, the said Trinity College Church and ground pertaining thereto, and for other rights of property or servitude belonging to the said defenders as trustees and administrators of Trinity Hospital, or whatever sum they received for the said Church and property, and interest thereon, solely and exclusively for the use and behoof of Trinity Hospital," and "for the building and construction of the said Hospital, houses, yards, and policies thereof, and for the maintenance of the poor and sick to be placed therein, and for no other use whatever." That is the first operative conclusion of the summons. Now, I would read that conclusion, standing by itself, as meaning that the whole of the money is to be applied for the building and construction of said Hospital, houses, yards, and policies thereof, and for the maintenance of the poor and sick to be placed therein, which would necessarily exclude the rebuilding of the Church. That which I regard as the natural reading of this primary conclusion is, I think, made clear by the final conclusion, which seeks to prohibit the defenders from doing certain things,—"and, in particular, they should be prohibited and interdicted from applying the whole or any part of the said sum in the purchase of a site for, or in the erection of, any church whatever, whether to be used as one of the city churches of Edinburgh, or otherwise." The argument submitted to us on the part of the pursuers was to the same effect, and directed to the same end. Now, I am of opinion, that, in the position in which the Magistrates are placed, it is their duty to build a church, of the same style and model with that which previously existed; and I cannot sustain an action which has, for its object and scope, the interposing and preventing them from doing that which I think is their duty under the Statute, in execution of the trust which they hold under the Statute, now that the money is in their hands. Such being my view of their duty, I cannot give effect to these conclusions. There are other conclusions in the action, but they are all mixed up with this, its leading object, and I cannot take the action to pieces and re-arrange or reconstruct it, or deal with it bit by bit in a fragmentary way. I am for assoilzieing the defenders from this action, but I do not wish to preclude the pursuers from bringing any other action which may be more suitable for the clearing of their interests. I do not wish to preclude them from bringing any other action which may make more clear their construction of the trust, or their interest in the Church, or in any surplus of the fund. I do not wish to decide anything against them in that respect. I would leave that open to them. But I think that the plain object and scope of this action—its primary and its final conclusions, are for the preventing of the erection of any church, or, in other words, to prevent the Magistrates from doing that which I consider it to be their duty to do, under the Act of Parliament I am, therefore, on that ground, against sustaining this action. I am for assoilzieing the defenders. I do not throw out of sight any of the cases that have been decided as to the duty of trustees. I think that the principle I have stated in regard to that matter is clear, and I do not interfere with it; but I do not think that this action brings out that principle purely. I think it is directed to an object which is not a proper one in reference to the trust which the Magistrates have undertaken, and therefore I am for assoilzieing the defenders from it.

The Court pronounced the following Interlocutors :—

In the action at the instance of William Forrester and Others :—The Lords having considered the Reclaiming Note, No. 25 of process, and having heard counsel for the parties thereon, and on the whole cause, Recall the interlocutor reclaimed against, and in place thereof, find that the sums of £16,371, 9s. 6d. and £800 mentioned in the record, and making together a sum of £17,171, 9s. 6d. received by the defenders or their predecessors, as on the 15th day of May 1848, from the North British Railway Company, under and by virtue of the Act 9 and 10 Victoria, chapter 74, with the interest which has accrued, or may hereafter accrue thereon, is held by them in trust for the erection of a new church, within the locality designated in the said Act as the parish of Trinity College, or as near thereto as conveniently may be, with equal convenience of access and accommodation, and of the same style and model as the Church formerly, and at the date of the said Act existing: Find that the defenders are bound to build, or cause to be built, and to expend the said sum of £17,171, 9s. 6d. and interest, or as much thereof as may be necessary, in acquiring the site and in the erection of the said new Church as aforesaid: To the above extent and effect, Repel the pleas in law for the defenders, and decern and declare in terms of the declaratory conclusions of the libel;—And, with a view to the adjustment of the site and plan of the new Church, and the carrying of the above findings into effect, and the disposal of the further conclusions of the action, Remit to the Lord Ordinary to proceed with the cause: Find the defenders liable to the pursuers in expenses hitherto incurred, both in the Outer House and Inner House, without prejudice to, but reserving all questions of ultimate liability and relief between the defenders, the Lord Provost, Magistrates, and Town Council of the City of Edinburgh, and all or any of the individual defenders or others whatsoever; Allow an account of expenses to be given in, and remit the account, when lodged, to the Auditor of Court, to tax the same and report; Appoint the report to be made to the Lord Ordinary, and Remit to his Lordship to decern for the taxed amount thereof.

In the action at the instance of the pensioners in Trinity Hospital:—The Lords having considered the reclaiming note for Mary Ann Reid and Others, No. 16 of process, and heard counsel for the parties thereon, and on the whole cause, Recall the interlocutor of the Lord Ordinary reclaimed against; and, in place thereof, find that the sums of £16,371, 9s. 6d. and £800 mentioned in the record, making together a sum of £17,171, 9s. 6d. received by the defenders or their predecessors, as on the 15th day of May 1848, from the North British Railway Company, under and by virtue of the Act 9 and 10 of Victoria, chapter 74, with the interest which has accrued or may accrue thereon, is applicable to the acquiring of a site, and the erection of a church, within the locality designated in the said Act, as the parish of Trinity College, or as near thereto as conveniently may be, with equal convenience of access and accommodation, and of the same style and model as the Church formerly, and at the date of said Act, existing, and that the defenders are bound so to apply the said sum and interest, or as much thereof as may be necessary, for the accomplishment of the above purposes: Find that the present action is directed substantially and specifically against the said sum and interest or any part thereof, to the said purposes, or any of them; and that the other or more general conclusions contained in the summons are so libelled as to be merely introductory and ancillary to the said operative conclusions, which have for their object to prevent the said sum and interest, or any part thereof, from being applied as aforesaid—therefore Assoilzie the defenders from the conclusions of the action, in so far as directed against the application to these purposes of the said sum and interest; and, *quoad ultra*, Dismiss the action, reserving all questions as to the rights and interests of parties in the said Church when erected, and as to the uses and purposes to which the same may be applied, and the rights and interests of parties in the surplus, if any, which may remain of said sum and interest, after the Church has been erected, and all other questions *hinc inde* between the parties, to be disposed of in any other action as accords of law, and Decern: Find no expenses due to either party.

Lord Ivory's reasons for not concurring, may be briefly stated. His Lordship said he took little interest in the feud raging between the Town Councillors as to church and site. He viewed the question from the interests of the trust and charity. He regarded the Church as part of the charity, and not as the property of the city or as a parish church. He doubted whether the actions as laid, were conceived in the best shape for a well matured, and precise, and exhaustive judgment of the most important questions involved in them. He thought that some more extended inquisition into the facts, and some more deliberate analysis and dissection of titles and evidence would be necessary. Fortunately his difficulties were not shared by the rest of the Court, and he had the comfort of feeling that what he had to say would not affect the judgment to be pronounced. Referring to the charters, his Lordship said, "There is not a word from beginning to end of all this which points at keeping up the edifice, or for directing it to any different purpose or use from the locality contiguous, which was given along with it. Both were given *simul et semel*, and both equally given for the one eleemosynary purpose which was so energetically set forth above, and for no other use. There is not a word from beginning to end which points at an ecclesiastical endowment." . . . "There was no grant of the Church to the City—to be endowed out of the City funds, or to be appropriated as a city church. . . . Judging from the elements we possess, I have no sort of doubt, that, in the outset, and on the face of the original grant, the intent was very clearly to apply it for the beneficial uses of the charity, and so far as I have yet been able to discover, I cannot satisfy my mind that it was ever legally or effectively diverted from these objects. . . . The trust title being the only title which the City have, and it being set forth on the very face of that title what was the specific purpose for which they received it, and there being no conflicting title in the person of anybody since, it appears to me that no length of mere use could prescribe a contrary right; and therefore that the Church remains substantially a trust property as much as ever. . . . If a church were to be held even as a proper accessory to the charity, so far as necessary for the accommodation of its members, the ends of the trust, in this respect, would seem to have been fully answered, by confining the re-erection to the measure of want which was thus indicated; and as to the surplus, throwing it into the general estate of the charity for the more peculiar ends for which itself had been created." . . . His Lordship, in winding up his observations, referred to a proposal in certain quarters to use the money in a settlement of the Annuity Tax question; or to have it applied for some civic purpose. He added, "I am decidedly against giving the least countenance to such an abuse of the trust, which the defenders are bound to execute in the interests exclusively of the charity. It might have been enough in this view, to give the pursuers' contention in this second action a simple absolvitor. But as your Lordships have arrived at a different conclusion generally, it is needless to speculate upon what might have been done under a different view."

The learned Counsel and Agents who represented the parties, were as follows :—

For William Forrester and Others—Mr Patton and Mr A. Rutherfurd Clark. Agent—Mr James Webster, S.S.C.

For Mary Ann Reid and Others (afterwards Clephane, etc.)—Mr Moir and Mr Adam Gifford. Agents—Messrs Wotherspoon and Morrison, W.S.

For the Lord Provost, Magistrates, and Town Council of Edinburgh—Mr George Young and Mr A. B. Shand. Agent—Mr Patrick Graham, W.S.

Lord Ivory, though he stood alone, had taken a firmer and more judicious grip of the question than his learned colleagues on the Bench. He had viewed the matter not from a parochial, as well as judicial, point of view, but from the broad and catholic basis as to what was best to be done in the circumstances for the charity of Trinity Hospital.

CHAPTER XX.

AN APPEAL TO THE HOUSE OF LORDS.

THE decision of the Court of Session in both actions narrated in the last chapter was appealed to the House of Lords. In the case of Clephane there was no difficulty found. But in regard to the judgment in that of Forrester and Others, on the strong advice of Mr George Young (now Lord Young) appearance was made on behalf of the Corporation as respondents. The judgment of the House of Lords was wholly adverse to the opinion of the Court below, and the speeches of the Appellate Lords are so interesting and instructive, that it has been considered advisable to reproduce them *verbatim et literatim.*

Messrs Anderson, Q.C., and C. Grey Wotherspoon appeared as counsel for Clephane and Others, along with Messrs Deans and Stein, Westminster, and Messrs Wotherspoon and Mack, W.S., Edinburgh.

Mr Rolt, Q.C., and Sir Henry Cairns, Q.C., appeared as counsel for the Magistrates of Edinburgh, along with Messrs Maitland and Graham, Westminster, and Messrs Graham and Johnston, W.S., Edinburgh.

The Attorney-General (Palmer) and Selwyn, Q.C., appeared as counsel for Forrester and Others, along with Messrs Loch and Maclaurin, Westminster, and Mr James Webster, S.S.C., Edinburgh.

After hearing counsel—

The LORD CHANCELLOR (WESTBURY) said—My Lords, I think it desirable to call your Lorships' attention particularly to this case, the circumstances of which I will carefully review, in the hope that not only the grounds of your Lordships' decision may be fully stated and well understood, but also in the hope, which I am almost afraid to entertain, that further litigation in this matter may be prevented.

The case is one of very great simplicity, and, to a mind acquainted with the subject, and with the principles which ought to govern the administration of charities, it can present no possible difficulty. The material facts are these: Anterior to the Reformation, and from a foundation made in the fifteenth century, there was established in Scotland, immediately without the precincts of the City of Edinburgh, but now, I believe, included within these precincts, a College, or, as we should call it in England, a chantry of priests, to which an alms-house or Hospital was annexed. It appears that the ecclesiastical part of this eleemosynary foundation consisted of a provost, eight prebendaries, and two choiristers. The purely eleemosynary part of it consisted apparently of thirteen beidmen, poor men. There was attached to the College a Church, apparently built in a very beautiful manner, and presenting, though imperfect, a fine specimen of the order of architecture according to which it was erected. The Church consisted merely of a choir, and of what is called in Scotland a cross, or by us more frequently a transept. It was undoubtedly of dimensions far beyond what was required by the priests and by the beidmen; and, therefore, it is reasonable to infer, that it afforded accommodation to the neighbouring residents. In this state of things, the Reformation swept over Scotland. The priests were driven out of the place, the beidmen apparently were permitted to remain there. It would seem that the Church was disused for some time before the grant of the charter of 1567, and part of the Hospital appears to have fallen into a state of ruin.

In this condition of things, during the infancy of King James I. (*i.e.* of England but VI. of Scotland), the charter of 1567 was granted. It is unnecessary to call your Lordships' attention to that charter, in any considerable detail. Your Lordships will find, that, for charitable purposes, a grant is made by King James to Sir Simon

Prestoun, who was at that time Provost of the City of Edinburgh, being a grant of the whole of the Church called "Collegiate Church of the Trinity," with the churchyard, buildings, and so forth, appertaining thereto, and also the Hospital at that time denominated "Trinity Hospital." The whole of this is granted to the Provost and Magistrates of Edinburgh. The purposes of the grant appear to be these: an obligation is thrown upon the Magistrates to rebuild or construct the Hospital, and to support the poor and the sick, who were the objects of the charity; and it is provided that the whole of the property so granted shall be devoted to these uses and to none other.

It would seem that the Master of the Hospital, that is, the superintendent of the poor men, continued to reside in the Hospital at the time of the grant; and accordingly we find a contract, that was made between the Magistrates of Edinburgh and the Master of the Hospital, a person of the name of Robert Pont, which it is material only to advert to, for the purpose of pointing out, that Mr Pont surrendered into the hands of the Crown, for the benefit of the grantees, namely the Magistrates of Edinburgh, the benefice of Trinity College, and all the things appertaining to it; and that, in consideration of this transfer, the Magistrates paid to Mr Pont a sum of money, and the Magistrates also contracted to pay Mr Pont the sum of £160 Scots yearly, during his lifetime. I advert to this only for the purpose of pointing out, that it is reasonable to infer, that some money was paid by the Magistrates, probably out of their own funds, for the purpose of this charity.

In that state of things, another grant was made by King James I. (VI. of Scotland) to which it is material to refer. It appears to be dated in the month of June 1585. Its materiality, as bearing upon the present subject of enquiry, lies in the fuller description which it contains of the objects of the Hospital. After a more full and ample description of the objects of the grant, it is declared, that it should be taken and held by the Provost and Magistrates of the city *pro sustentatione*, and so forth; for the maintenance of the aged decrepit men, orphans, and poor within the Hospital, and poor scholars within the College and Schools, at all times thereafter. The charter also proceeded to authorise the Magistrates and Council to rebuild the Hospital, which was then in a ruinous condition, in a more convenient situation at or near the College.

A little anterior to this particular grant, in the year 1584, the Magistrates appear to have divided the Town or City of Edinburgh into four districts or parishes. And your Lordships will find, that on the 14th October 1584, a resolution or order was made by the Town Council, by which the Trinity College Church, that is, the Church of this charity, was appropriated for the accommodation of the north-east parish or district. I wish particularly, therefore, to point out, that, from the very earliest times, and as soon as it could be supposed that the grantees took possession of the subject of the grant, there was a dedication of the Collegiate Church, so far as it could be applied without prejudice, to the use of the Hospital, for the accommodation and service of the inhabitants of the district.

Your Lordships will find, from the subsequent charter, that the Hospital was rebuilt by the Magistrates of Edinburgh; and then come two important charters of May and July 1587, to which I will, for a moment, direct attention. The important part of them appears to be a statement by the King in the charter of May 1587, that it shall be lawful for the Provost and Magistrates and their successors to use the old Hospital, in order that they may be able (it is printed very inaccurately, but your Lordships will be able to make the necessary corrections) to support the poor within the Hospital, which has been recently repaired by them, by means of the rents of the said Hospital, in a convenient manner.

Then, in a subsequent charter, your Lordships will find a declaration made, that the grant is made for the support of the ministers and the poor, and for the entertainment of the said College (that I suppose means for the preservation or the maintaining of the said College) lately erected by them, that is the Magistrates. Then follows a provision, that the Provost and community, and their successors, shall be bound to support the ministers serving at the Churches.

To that may be added an Act of Parliament, which was passed in 1592, which also recognises the position of the Council and Magistrates with respect to the charity.

I have troubled you at this length with these details, for the purpose of showing that, at that time, by an order made in October 1584, the Church had been dedicated to the purposes of the district, so far as it was not required for the Hospital; that that use of the Church, which must have been then perfectly well known, is nowhere adverted to as being at variance with the purposes of the charity, and must therefore be taken to be sanctioned and confirmed by the subsequent grants to which I have adverted.

In that state of things, your Lordships will find a further statement, which is material, in which it is stated and appears to have been admitted, that Trinity College parish, or Trinity College district, was well known as one of the districts into which the city was divided, and that the building therein used as the Church has been constantly treated as if it were the Parish Church of the district.

Now, from these facts, therefore, I submit to your Lordships that two conclusions may with propriety be drawn. First, that the permitting Trinity Church to be used as a place of worship for the inhabitants of the district, after reserving full accommodation for the poor and the officers of the Hospital, was not a breach of trust, but was perfectly consistent with the purposes of the charitable grant. And, secondly, that inasmuch as such user has continued uninterruptedly from the foundation of the charity to the present time, it must be considered, that the maintenance of the Church for the use of the Hospital and the inhabitants of the adjoining district is one of the lawful purposes of this charity. These being, as I conceive, just conclusions to draw from the facts to which I have referred, I now pass on to the transactions which have subsequently occurred, and which have given rise to this litigation.

The North British Railway Company was empowered by its Act of Parliament to take, for the purposes of its railway and for the purpose of constructing a station for that railway, the piece of land on which this Collegiate Church stood; and, of course, it was a matter of great importance that the terms and conditions on which the Railway Company should be permitted to take this land should be accurately and clearly defined in their Act of Parliament. I desire you to pause for a minute to consider what is the object of one of these Railway Acts of Parliament. The object of an Act of Parliament of that kind is, to define the manner in which the Railway Company shall be bound to make compensation to the owner of the property taken, but it is not a part of the object of such an Act of Parliament, to interfere at all with the title to that property, or to lay down any rule affecting the ownership of the property, or the manner in which the money to be given to the owner of the property shall be employed. To do any such thing would be greatly beyond the proper scope and limits of that description of legislation.

Now, with that general observation, I will beg attention to the clause in the North British Railway Act, which is the 8th section of the 9 and 10 Vict. cap. 74, upon the particular language of which a great part of this legislation is founded. And, indeed, on the construction proposed to be given to that section, the whole of the second suit, brought by Forrester and Others, is entirely based. Now, the section (reading it shortly) may be divided into three parts. The first portion of it enables the Company to restore and rebuild the Church, which they purpose to take down; and, in the event of their doing that, the obligation is carefully imposed upon the Company of restoring and rebuilding it exactly as they found it, at the time they took possession of it. And, in order to meet any questions that might arise in the course of that operation, a tribunal or arbiter is provided, namely the Sheriff of Edinburgh, to whom any differences of opinion arising in the course of that operation might be referred.

Then the section concludes with an alternative, which it is put in the power of the Railway Company to adopt, namely, that in lieu of the obligation which has been thus carefully described, to rebuild the Church themselves, that they may give to the Magistrates and Town Council a sum of money as compensation for the Church. And by a species of refinement and subtle construction, which I regret that any person has been found to entertain, because it has produced years of litigation, and has been an impediment to the use and application of the money belonging to this charity, it appears to have been thought, that it was possible to construe the clause in such a manner as to attach to the money to be paid by the Railway Company, an obligation of application precisely to the same effect as that which the Railway Company would have been bound to observe, in the event of their adopting the first alternative of undertaking to restore the Church.

I think it impossible that any such ingenious subtlety should receive any kind of acceptance. One of your Lordships (LORD CRANWORTH) suggested what is the true interpretation, as I humbly think, of these words:—in lieu of the said obligation, namely, the obligation of restoration, which is described in the first part of the clause. If it be not the alternative embraced by the Company, it is still to be the measure of the amount of compensation, so that, in point of fact, the object of the clause is this: that if the Company did not undertake to restore the Church actually, they were bound to pay to the Magistrates, as trustees of the charity, such a sum of money as they would have required to expend, as if the first alternative had been embraced by them. That is a reasonable interpretation to give to the clause, and it gives a standard of the compensation to be paid.

It appears that practically this was the construction which the parties put upon the clause. For proceedings were taken for the purpose of ascertaining what ought to be done in order to restore the Church, and they were prosecuted so far as to enable the referee to determine exactly the sum of money which the Railway Company would have to expend, if they had entered upon and completed the work of restoration. The Railway Company very wisely preferred to pay the money, rather than to undertake the duty of seeing to its expenditure, and presiding over the restoration of the Church; and that sum of money, which is very considerable, amounting altogether, I think, to £17,000, was actually paid over to the trustees of the Hospital in the month of May 1848.

Now, that money, when received by the trustees of the Hospital, was part of the general funds of the charity, applicable for the purpose of re-instating the Church in a reasonable time, precisely in the same condition in which it stood at the time when the Church was taken away by the Railway Company. But it would be ridiculous to suppose, for a moment, that it was the object of the Act of Parliament, or that there can be any principle of law, or any suggestion of reason or common sense, that would lead the mind to the conclusion, that this money, when received by the Magistrates and Town Council, was received under an obligation to have it expended entirely, or the greater part of it, in the actual re-production, with all its architectural decorations, of that exact building which was taken by the Railway Company. It is a lamentable thing that such a suggestion was ever made; it is as unfounded in law, as it has been lamentable in consequences. I hope your Lordships will not yield the smallest countenance to any such contention, which ought not to have been entertained by any reasonable mind, and which would be utterly repudiated by anyone knowing well the principles upon which charities ought to be administered.

This leads at once to the conclusion, that the whole of that suit, instituted by Forrester and Others, and which was brought expressly for the purpose of maintaining the proposition, that the whole of the money paid by the Railway Company should be dedicated to the purpose of an exact reproduction of the original building, is founded upon an entire misconception and erroneous construction of the clause of the Act of Parliament; and, therefore, I have not the smallest hesitation in advising your Lordships, that the whole of the interlocutors in that suit which have been appealed from should be reversed; that the defenders shall be absolved from the conclusions of the summons, and the summons itself be dismissed. I am very sorry to be obliged to add, in consequence of the countenance that has been given to that suit, that I cannot individually advise your Lordships to go further than to dismiss it without expenses.

Then, that suit having been cleared away, we come to the consideration of the other suit, originally instituted by persons having a direct interest in the charity, as being some of the objects of that charity. To that suit, the Magistrates and Town Council of Edinburgh are called as defenders, in their capacity of trustees of this Hospital, and although there has been a good deal of criticism upon the conclusions of that summons, and although it is true that some of the conclusions are rather directed to an end that would be inconsistent with the re-erection of a Church sufficient for the accommodation of the inhabitants who would resort to the old Church, yet I think the conclusions of that summons, fairly construed, especially in a charity case, might well have warranted the Court of Session in taking upon themselves, to pronounce in that suit the order which I think common sense and reason imperatively required should be pronounced, in some suit or other directed to the end of effecting the proper administration of this charity-property, and the proper application of this sum of money which has been allowed to remain so long unappropriated.

Therefore, I shall not hesitate to recommend your Lordships to reverse the interlocutors which are appealed from in that suit, and further, I shall recommend your Lordships to make that suit the basis or foundation of an order which I trust, if your Lordships approve of it, will be found to comprehend all the material objects that are now required to be provided for, in the hope of securing a just and reasonable administration of the charity.

It is material to observe, that the Magistrates suggested that a sum of £7000 only was required for the acquisition of a site, and for the erection of a new Church of sufficient capacity to provide for the wants of the inmates of the Hospital, in the enlarged scale on which I hope it will be established, and also for the accommodation of the neighbouring inhabitants. I wish I could add to that what I have looked for with anxiety, a clear and definite expression on the part of the Magistrates, of their willingness to have this fund devoted to the purpose of the proper augmentation and re-establishment of this charity, after deducting so much as should be required for erecting the new Church. But what I have found not so clearly expressed in the pleadings has been supplied by the Counsel for the Magistrates at the Bar, and I understand from their counsel, that they are quite willing, as it is their duty to be, that the whole of this fund, *minus* the sum that shall be absolutely required for the rebuilding of the Church, shall be at once applied in the augmentation of the charity.

In the hope, therefore, of providing for these ends, which, as I observed during the argument, at the first blush of the thing must have presented themselves, as being the clear objects to be attained by a Court of Justice in this case, I have at some length perused the order which I will submit to your Lordships, as the proper order to be pronounced under the circumstances of the case. I propose that the order of your Lordships' House in both appeals should run thus:—

Reverse all the interlocutors in the second suit, that is, the suit by Forrester and Others; Assoilzie the defenders from the conclusions of the summons, and Dismiss the same, but without expenses; and, in the first suit, that of Clephane and Others, Reverse the interlocutors appealed from, and declare that, under the circumstances of the case, and having regard to the usage which has uniformly prevailed since the establishment of the charity, it is fit and proper that so much of the money received by the defenders from the North British Railway Company, as will be sufficient for the purpose, but not exceeding £7000, shall be applied to the purchase of a site and in building a Church, which, after reserving full accommodation for all the inmates of the Hospital and persons connected therewith, will afford to the inhabitants of the district as much accommodation as was afforded by the Collegiate Church which has been removed; and declare, that such Church ought to be built in connection with the Hospital, or on a site as near thereto as can be conveniently obtained; and declare, that the duty of building such Church belongs to the defenders as trustees of the charity, and that they will not be under any obligation to observe or follow the style or model of the old Church in such new building; and declare that such Church will be the property of the charity, subject to its being used, and if so used, then to its being kept in repair, and maintained in like manner as the old Church was before its removal by the Railway Company, and that the defenders forthwith bring in and lodge with the Court below, a minute showing the site and plan of the building of such new Church, and the building is not to proceed until such plan and site have been approved of by the Court; and declare that all the residue of the money received from the Railway Company, and all interest thereon, and all the rest of the property of the Hospital is applicable to the enlargement and maintenance of the charity, as declared and established by the charter of May 1567 and November 1587, according to a scheme to be settled for that purpose (I may say in passing, that the reason in my mind for introducing both charters is this, that your Lordships will find in the charter of November 1587 a rather more full description of the objects of the charity than is contained in the charter of 1567); and refer it to the Court below to settle and approve of such scheme accordingly; and let the Court inquire and ascertain of what the property of the Hospital consists, and in what manner the money received from the Railway Company has been invested by the defenders, and when such investments were made, and what sums have been received for interest thereon, and by whom and how such sums have been applied; and declare, that the expenses properly incurred by the pursuers and defenders in the suit of Clephane and Others ought to be paid out of the funds of the charity, and let the same be duly taxed, and the amounts paid out of such parts of the funds of the charity as the Court of Session shall deem most fit to be applied for that purpose.

I humbly submit to your Lordships that this order will, as far as we can now foresee, provide for the immediate necessities of the case; and I trust that there will be found, in carrying this order into effect, a conscientious spirit that shall recognise the religious and moral duty that rests upon these parties no longer to keep the charity fund in abeyance, but to apply it as it ought fifteen or sixteen years ago to have been applied, to the purposes of this useful charity.

Lord Cranworth.—My Lords, the full manner in which my noble and learned friend has gone through the details of this case, I feel, has absolved me from the necessity of adding more than a single word. In the first place, the long usage since the time of the charter, seems to me perfectly to justify this House in saying, that the maintenance of the Church as connected with the Hospital is one of its legitimate objects. That being so, supposing no Acts of Parliament had passed such as that of the North British Railway Company, but that by lapse of time, or by some accident, the Church had been burnt down or destroyed, what would have been the duty of the trustees? Clearly their duty would have been to rebuild the Church, or to build a Church with at least as good accommodation as that which existed before. But I take it to be perfectly clear, that there would have been no duty, or obligation, to rebuild it in the particular ornamental style in which the old building had been constructed. That being so, it is impossible to suppose that the Legislature, in passing a Railway Act, meant to alter the trusts which were imposed upon the trustees, of adequately discharging the duties connected with this charity. It is impossible that it could have meant to impose upon them the duty of building a Church in any particular style. The reason why that obligation was imposed upon the Railway Company, if they rebuilt the Church, is obvious. Had such an obligation not been imposed upon them, they might have built the Church in a very imperfect and improper style. It was to secure the public against that, that this provision was made. But if the alternative was adopted, which anyone looking reasonably at the subject must have known would be adopted, namely, for the Company to pay the price or the value, instead of rebuilding the Church themselves, then, when the money comes into the hands of the trustees, they have no other obligation upon them with reference to that money than would have been imposed upon them, if the Church had been in some other way destroyed and then rebuilt out of any funds which they might have in their hands for the purpose of rebuilding it. I think that the provisions which have been proposed by my noble and learned friend exhaust the subject, and I trust that they will put an end to this not very creditable litigation, which has now extended over a period of fifteen or sixteen years, and deprived both the Hospital and neighbourhood of the advantages which they have a right to derive from the use of the Church.

Lord Chelmsford.—My Lords, I concur in the view which has been taken of this case by my two noble and learned friends, and I can state the grounds of my opinion in a very few words. In order to ascertain what was the trust that attached upon this trust, and the consequent obligation upon the Corporation of Edinburgh at the time of the passing of the North British Railway Company's Act, it will be only necessary for me to advert very shortly to the terms of the charter of 1567. Now, what was the object of that charter? It is expressed very shortly in the recital to be, "to found and endow a Hospital," and for that purpose, certain property, including the Church in question, called the Collegiate Church of Trinity, was given to the Corporation of Edinburgh, for the building and construction of the said Hospital, for the maintenance of the poor and sick, to be placed by them thereon for no other use. And there is subsequently given a power to the Corporation, to dispose of this property as shall seem good, with a qualification, that they shall be bound to apply it to the foresaid use, and no other. Now, whether this means, that they were to apply the existing subjects of the grant to the purposes of the Hospital, or whether they were entitled to sell the property and apply all the proceeds to that use, it is immaterial to consider. Throughout the whole of this charter, there is nothing to bind the Corporation to maintain this Church; there is nothing to show that, either as a work of art, or for any other reason, it was such an object of interest, that it was considered desirable to preserve it. I apprehend that, under the words of the charter, it was competent to the Corporation to have applied the building itself—the Church—to the purposes of the Hospital; and there is nothing whatever to prevent their doing what they did, namely, applying the Church to the use for which it was fitted, for the purposes of divine worship. Now originally, for about seventeen years, the Church appears to have been applied exclusively for the use of the Hospital, but in 1584, and again in 1625, it was appropriated to one of the parishes into which Edinburgh was divided. Now, whether the Corporation had a right to appropriate this Church as a Parish Church, may perhaps be questioned. But, undoubtedly, as there was sufficient accommodation, not only for inmates of the Hospital, but beyond what was necessary for them, it could have been no breach of trust on the part of the Corporation to have allowed the inhabitants of the parish, that is, the inhabitants of the neighbourhood of the Hospital, to have sittings in the Church. Even if it were objectionable, there were no persons who were likely to object to it, because it seems that the inmates of the Hospital were invariably provided with the sittings, and the other persons, the inhabitants of the parish, paid for the sittings which they occupied, and all the sums received in respect of those payments were applied to the maintenance of the Church, and therefore so far the funds of the Hospital were relieved. Thus matters continued from the year 1584 down to the year 1846, and it is perfectly clear, I apprehend, that although the Corporation had applied this Church as a Parish Church, and therefore in some degree had taken it from the Hospital, yet, inasmuch as the trusts of the charter are perfectly clear, it was not competent to them to divert that Church from the uses to which it was applicable under the charter.

Therefore, in 1846, at the time of the passing of the North British Railway Act, the state of things was this, that the Church was applicable to the uses of the Hospital, and had to be maintained by the Corporation, and maintained, if you please, to the extent of the use to which it had been applied for so many years, nearly three centuries, namely, for the accommodation beyond the inmates of the Hospital of other inhabitants of the neighbourhood. Therefore, as my noble and learned friend (LORD CRANWORTH) has said, the obligation upon the Corporation, at the time of the passing of the North British Railway Act, in case the Church had been burnt down and it had been necessary to restore it, would have been merely to provide another Church with equal and similar accommodation to that which had been provided for the long period I have mentioned. Then it appears that the North British Railway Company, upon the introduction of their Bill, desired to obtain powers for the purpose of removing this Church for the construction of their railway; and if the question of compensation between them and the Corporation had been left to the ordinary provisions of the Lands Clauses Act (an Act which passed, I think, only the year before this North British Railway Act), it is perfectly clear, that all the Corporation would have been entitled to receive as compensation would have been the amount which was necessary to build a Church with similar accommodation to the one which was removed. And no jury would ever have given them what may be called a sentimental value for the Church which was to be removed, however great its architectural beauty might have been. But the Corporation were desirous of obtaining a larger sum than they could possibly have obtained by the ordinary mode of compensation, and the Company were not unwilling to give them the advantage of a larger compensation than would have been received through a jury. Therefore, I consider this 8th section of their Act to have been introduced for the purpose of providing machinery to enable the Corporation to receive a larger amount of compensation than they would otherwise receive. Now the mode which was adopted for that purpose was very plain. The Legislature provides, that the Company shall not be allowed to remove the existing Church until they shall have agreed with the Corporation on a plan for the rebuilding, at the expense of the Company, and upon another site either within the parish, or as near thereto as conveniently may be, of a new Church, and that in such agreement provision shall be made for the adoption of the same style and model as the existing Church.

Now that, as I apprehend, was the mode of ascertaining the value of the compensation which was to be paid to the Corporation. Plans, of course, could be made, and a suitable site would be ascertained, and an estimate would be made of the value of the site and of the cost of the building according to the plans which were agreed upon, and if there was any difference of opinion between the parties, the

Sheriff was to settle it. But in that mode the sum of money was ascertained as the amount of compensation which the Corporation would be entitled to receive under this clause in respect of the Church.

And then, in order to provide for this money passing into the hands of the Corporation, the Act declares that the Company shall be at liberty to offer, and the Corporation to accept, a sum of money, as compensation for the said Church, and in lieu of the foregoing obligation. It is quite clear, that the contemplation of all parties was, that the cost of the erection of the Church, according to the plans, upon a proper site having been ascertained, that that sum of money should be the amount which should be paid over by the Railway Company and received by the Corporation, as the amount of compensation to be received by the Corporation, in lieu of the obligation which was imposed upon the Railway Company. There was not the slightest intention that there should be any new obligation imposed upon the Corporation, to erect the Church in any different manner than they would have been required to do, supposing it had been left to the ordinary mode of compensation. There was not the least intention that this obligation, which was attached upon the Railway Company merely for the purpose of fixing the value, should be transferred from the Railway Company to the Corporation upon the payment of the money. If that had been intended, it would have been easy to add just a few words, and after the words in lieu of the foregoing obligation, to have said "which obligation shall then be transferred to and fulfilled by the Magistrates and Town Council." But no such obligation is imposed upon the Corporation. The money is transferred to them by this machinery which the Act has provided, and then the Corporation have only the same obligation attaching upon them which they would have had if this clause had never been introduced into the Act. They are bound to provide a Church with the same accommodation as that which previously existed, and that being so, it is quite clear, that only a portion of the sum of £17,000 would be applicable to that purpose. The sum of £7000 seems to be a very fair limit to their liability in that respect. The other £10,000, the surplus, is clearly applicable to the uses of the Hospital.

For these reasons, I entirely agree with the opinion which has been so clearly expressed by my noble and learned friend.

Sir Hugh Cairns.—Before the question is put, will your Lordship allow me to submit two considerations which perhaps your Lordships might think it right to give weight to in your order? The first relates to the costs. Your Lordships propose (as I understood) to dismiss Forrester's action without costs. I would submit to your Lordships, that provision should be made in your order for the costs of that action, and of the appeal of the Corporation, and also, that it would be necessary in point of form that provision should be made for the repetition or repayment by Forrester of the costs ordered to be paid to him, and which have been paid. And further, that in Clephane's action, in which the order which has been read by the LORD CHANCELLOR proposed to provide for the costs, the costs provided for should be not only the costs of the action, but also of the appeal which would not follow without special words. The other point I should submit to your Lordships is one which has not been referred to in the argument on either side, but which I may perhaps mention as one which your Lordships may think it right to give some attention to in the order that goes into so much detail. An Act of Parliament passed in the year 1860 (called the Annuity Tax Abolition Act), made in §§ 56 and 57, certain provisions with regard to the city and town churches of Edinburgh, and it named as one of those Trinity College Church, and it transferred to the Commissioners under that Act such rights of administration and custody as were then vested in the Town Council and Corporation, with certain provisions as to pew rents. As I understand the order which has been suggested to your Lordships as the one fit to be made in this case, I am not aware that that order will actually conflict with any of these provisions; but your Lordships might think it proper that I should now mention the Act, in order that, if your Lordships in your wisdom thought fit, some notice should be taken of it in your present order, with a view to prevent it appearing to conflict with the provisions of that Act of Parliament.

LORD CHANCELLOR.—My Lords, with regard to the last point which has been mentioned at the Bar, I would not advise your Lordships that it is either necessary to advert to it, or that it would be proper to do so—not necessary, because undoubtedly whatever may be the provisions of that Act, it will be quite competent to the Court of Session, in carrying your Lordships' directions into effect, to take the provisions of that Statute into consideration. But I should particularly object to mentioning that Act in the present order, because, although we approve of this Church, as the property of the charity, being used for the benefits of the district, yet, I apprehend, that your Lordships by no means mean to lay it down as law, that this Church when rebuilt will become a Parish Church. With regard to the other point, I must confess that I feel somewhat unwilling to go so far as to give the Magistrates of Edinburgh the whole of the expenses of this litigation, because I cannot but think that a little more energy and diligence, and a little more candour in these proceedings, would have prevented the great delay that has taken place. At the same time, I am glad to say, that the conduct of the Magistrates in the argument of this appeal has been everything that could be desired by your Lordships. And if, therefore, your Lordships desire to give the

Magistrates out of the charity fund the costs that they have been put to by reason of the proceedings in the suit of Forrester and Others, I shall entirely concur in your Lordships' views upon that matter. I think it will be necessary that the order should be so expressed, as to give to the Magistrates and to the appellants in Clephane's suit, if your Lordships approve of it, the costs of the appeal. I would therefore ask your Lordships to intimate your opinion, whether you think that the expenses of the Magistrates in Clephane's suit should come out of the funds of the charity, and I hope that your Lordships will approve of its being now distinctly stated, that, in the administration of this fund, for all the objects of the trust, the parties who are now intrusted with the carrying out of these trusts are not to consider that the Court will be justified in allowing the costs of any proceedings, except those which are conscientiously and properly directed to the just ends of administering the charity.

Lord Cranworth.—My Lords, I concur with my noble and learned friend in all that he has said. In the first place, I certainly concur with him in a very deep regret at the expenditure of what I consider a very unnecessary amount of costs in a matter that might have been more speedily and cheaply settled. But I confess I do not feel that the case is strong enough to require me to say, that, as the trustees of this fund, the Magistrates ought not to have their costs. And therefore I shall concur in my noble and learned friend's proposal, that they should have their costs out of the funds of the charity.

Lord Chelmsford.—I entirely concur with my noble and learned friends.

Sir Hugh Cairns.—With regard to the repayment of the costs paid to Forrester?

Lord Chancellor.—That would follow as a matter of course. I will put it into the order, and in that part of the order which declares that the expenses properly incurred by the pursuers and defenders, in the suit of Clephane and Others ought to be paid out of the funds of the charity. I will insert the words "including the Appeal," and also the defenders' costs in the other suit and appeal. And in the suit of Forrester and Others, I will make this addition to the order, that any sums paid by the defenders to the pursuers under the interlocutors hereby reversed, be repaid by the pursuers to the defenders.

The *Orders of the House*, as ultimately drawn up, were as follow :—

"I.—It is ordered and adjudged, by the Lords Spiritual and Temporal in Parliament assembled, that *the said interlocutors*, so far as complained of in the said appeal, be, and the same *are hereby reversed.*

And it is declared that, under the circumstances of the case, and having regard to the usage which has uniformly prevailed since the establishment of the charity in the proceedings mentioned, it is fit and proper, that so much of the money received by the defenders (respondents) from the North British Railway Company as will be sufficient for the purpose, but not exceeding £7000, should be applied in the purchase of a site, and in building a Church which, after reserving full accommodation for all the inmates of the Hospital in the said proceedings mentioned, and persons connected therewith, will afford to the inhabitants of the district in the said proceedings mentioned, as much accommodation as was afforded by the Collegiate Church in the said proceedings mentioned, which has been removed. And it is further declared, that said Church ought to be built in connection with the Hospital (if the same shall be rebuilt under the scheme hereinafter directed), or on a site as near thereto as can be conveniently obtained: And it is further declared, that the duty of building such Church belongs to the defenders (respondents), as trustees of the said charity, and that they will not be under any obligation to observe or follow the style or model of the old Church in the said proceedings mentioned, in such new building: And it is further declared, that such new Church will be the property of the said charity, subject to its being used, and if so used, then to its being kept in repair, and maintained in like manner as the said old Church was, before its removal by the said Railway Company: And it is further ordered, that the defenders (respondents) do forthwith bring in and lodge with the Court of Session a minute, showing the site and plan of building of such new Church; and the building is not to proceed until such plan and site have been approved of by the said Court: And it is further declared, that all the residue of the money received from the said Railway Company, and all interest thereon, and all the rest of the property of the said Hospital is applicable to the enlargement and maintenance of the said charity, as declared and established by the charters dated respectively the 12th November 1567 and 26th May 1587, in the said proceedings mentioned, according to a scheme to be settled for that purpose (including therein the rebuilding of the Hospital, if the same shall be deemed necessary): And it is further ordered, that it be referred to the said Court of Session to settle and approve of such scheme accordingly, and to enquire and ascertain of what the property of the said Hospital consists, and in what manner the money received from the said Railway Company has been invested by the said defenders (respondents), and when such investments were made, and what sums have been received from interest thereon, and by whom and how such sums have been applied: And it is also further declared, that the expenses properly incurred by the pursuers and defenders in this cause in the Court below, and the costs properly incurred by the said appellants and respondents in this appeal, ought to be paid out of the funds of the said charity; and it is, therefore, further ordered, that the expenses so properly incurred by the said pursuers and defenders in this cause in the Court below, and the costs so properly incurred by the said appellants and respondents in the said appeal, be duly taxed, and the amount of such taxed costs in the said cause in the Court below, and the amount certified by the Clerk of the Parliaments of such costs of the said appeal, be paid out of such parts of the funds of the said charity as the said Court of Session shall deem most fit to be applied for that purpose: And it is also further ordered, that the cause be, and is hereby, remitted back to the Court of Session in Scotland, to do therein as shall be just and consistent with these declarations and directions, and this judgment.

"II.—It is ordered and adjudged, by the Lords Spiritual and Temporal, in Parliament assembled—That the said interlocutors, so far as complained of, and the said appeal be, and the same are, hereby reversed, and that the defenders (appellants) be assoilzied from the conclusions of the summons in the proceedings mentioned: And it is declared that the expenses properly incurred by the said defenders in this cause in the Court below, and the costs properly incurred by the said appellants in this appeal, ought to be paid out of the funds of the charity in the said proceedings mentioned: And it is therefore further ordered, that the expenses so properly incurred by the said defenders in this cause in the Court below, and the costs so properly incurred by the said appellants in the said appeal, be duly taxed, and the amount of such taxed costs, in the said cause in the Court below, and the amount certified by the Clerk of the Parliaments of such costs of the said appeal, be paid out of such parts of the funds of the said charity as the said Court of Session shall deem most fit to be applied for that purpose: And it is further ordered, that any sum paid by the said defenders to the pursuers, in the said suit, under the said interlocutors hereby reversed, be repaid by the said pursuers to the said defenders: And it is also further ordered, that the cause be, and is, hereby remitted back to the Court of Session in Scotland, to do therein as shall be just and consistent, with this declaration and these directions, and this judgment."

It need hardly be stated that this decision of the House of Lords came upon the citizens of Edinburgh as a surprise. The Nonconformist or Voluntary party rejoiced; and the Established Church party along with the Antiquarians mourned the result.

The veteran Mr Adam Black came in for a fair share of abuse. But, like a brave man, as he always was, he gallantly defended himself against attack. The following correspondence will make this manifest.

"A Member of Trinity College Church" writing in the *Scotsman* of 20th February 1864, says:—

SIR,—In your article of this morning on the Trinity College Church case, there occurs the following—"We cannot pretend that we should have been inconsolable had the Church not been to be rebuilt at all. There are many more churches in Edinburgh than are well filled."

I am sure you intend no unfairness, but it is quite possible that strangers to the facts of the case may infer from your words that you would regard the re-erection of Trinity College Church in any form as an addition to the already sufficiently large number of empty churches in Edinburgh. To prevent such a misconstruction, will you allow me to state that our Church at the present moment numbers considerably above 700 communicants, and that in the old church of St Giles, temporarily lent to us by the Ecclesiastical Commissioners, every available sitting is let. Rebuilt on a suitable site, Trinity College Church runs little risk of being empty.

Will you allow me further to say how much I rejoice in your suggestion that Mr Adam Black should bring the whole matter under the notice of Parliament. If this should be done at all, it is specially proper that it should be done by him. He is as distinctly responsible for the present miserable state of matters, as the party whose name he bears is for the misery of that estate whereinto man fell. He is virtually the father of the Trinity College Church Act of 1846, and if Lord Westbury has shown anything, he has shown that that Act was not worded so as to express unmistakably its own intention. The Act, as everybody knows, in offering to the Magistrates the alternative of a sum of money in lieu of the Church, meant that they were to be held bound to build a *fac-simile* of the original Church with the money. Lord Westbury has authoritatively told us that the wording of the Act cannot be interpreted to mean this, except by a "subtle construction that cannot receive any countenance." Clearly then Mr Black must have put his foot in it. Under his auspices, Parliament, meaning one thing, has been made to say another. But surely Parliament must be allowed,—nay, is in fairness bound to correct its blunder; and on Mr Black, above all its members, lies the burden of this duty. He put Parliament wrong—he, too, should put it right. To expiate his original sin of the ill-drawn alternative clause, he is bound to do his best to get the real intention of the Legislature so expressed that not even Lord Westbury shall be able to avoid seeing its meaning.—I am, etc.

To this Mr Adam Black, M.P., replied in the *Scotsman* of 27th February :—

MR ADAM BLACK, M.P., AND TRINITY COLLEGE CHURCH.

"Oh! be his tomb like lead to lead
Upon its dull destroyer's head."

LONDON, *February* 25, 1861.

SIR,—My attention has been called to a letter which appeared in the *Scotsman* of Saturday the 20th, regarding Trinity College Church, in which the writer says that Mr Adam Black should bring the whole matter before Parliament, as "He is virtually the father of the Trinity College Church Act of 1846, and if Lord Westbury has shown anything, he has shown that that Act was not worded so as to express unmistakably its own intention." "Clearly then Mr Black must have put his foot in it. He put Parliament wrong—he, too, should put it right," etc. The writer of this letter appears to be equally ignorant of the facts of the case, and of the powers of a Committee of Parliament in the case of a private bill. It is only necessary that I should state shortly the facts, as far as I am concerned.

In 1846, when the North British Railway Company wanted Trinity College Church to be removed for the purposes of the Railway, and refused to make any reasonable arrangement with the Town Council for replacing it by another Parish Church, the Town Council in their straitened circumstances were unwilling to incur the very heavy expenses of a Parliamentary contest, and I volunteered to go, at my own expense, and conduct the case as I best could, without feeing counsel. My offer was accepted, and I received *carte blanche* to act on my own responsibility in the case. I, therefore, am bound to accept the responsibility so far, and if there was anything done wrong on the side of the Council, I take upon myself the whole blame. But how stands the fact? When I appeared before the Committee, the proposition I made was a very simple one. The Railway Company having proposed to remove the Church (which, by-the-bye, was by this time very much injured by the Railway), I consented on condition that if they took it away they should give us just such another. I think I used the word *fac-simile*, but that is of no importance, for there could be no doubt of what we asked, as we presented to the Committee lithographed views of the old Church which we urged should be restored. With the aid of the City Clerk, Mr John Sinclair, one of the shrewdest and most intelligent men I ever knew, and our London solicitors, a clause was prepared for this purpose. The very words of our proposed clause it is impossible now to give, but the sum and substance of it was, that when the Railway Company removed the old Church, they should provide us with one having equal accommodation, and in the same style and model as the one that was to be removed. The Committee did not adopt our clause, but substituted one of their own, embodying our views but making two important alterations—the first giving the Council a stringent *compulsitor* on the Railway Company, by which the Company were completely stopped in their operations till they fulfilled their obligations in regard to the Church; the other authorising the Railway Company to offer, and the Town Council to accept of, a sum of money in lieu of their obligation to build. These conditions were inserted by the Committee, not by me, and I had no power to resist them if I wished. Still, however, I thought then, as I do still, that the clause, if rightly interpreted, carried out our views, though I recollect saying to Mr Hawes, the chairman, after the Committee had decided, that I regretted the insertion of this last proviso, as I wished the responsibility of building to rest upon the Railway Company, but he said the Committee thought that by this alternative, if difficulties arose, parties might come to an arrangement. Now, sir, I affirm that the whole contest was about the building of the Church and the kind of church that was to be built by the Railway Company, or by the Town Council, provided they accepted the money for that purpose; and if the Town Council had not objected to the plan prepared by the Railway Company, every penny of that money would have been spent in building the Church for which the Railway Company had prepared plans. Notwithstanding the contempt which Lord Westbury pours upon those *who were so ridiculous as to suppose that there was any principle of law or of common sense which compelled the Magistrates to expend the money on the actual reproduction of all the fanciful decorations of the old building*, I am content to bear it in such good company when I am classed with the learned judges in our Supreme Court, whom his Lordship taunts as *adopting suggestions unfitting for any reasonable mind to entertain;* for I believe it would not only have been reasonable to have restored the Church with all its decorations, but the question in dispute between the parties having been decided by the Committee which acted as umpire in the case, I hold that, as honourable men, we were bound to fulfil our part of the contract after we received the money.

Although this letter is becoming tedious to me to write, and will be as tedious to your readers to read, I must as briefly as possible notice the principal transactions that followed in this case during my provostship. The Railway Company employed Mr Rhind, the architect, to prepare plans for building the Church in Ireland's Woodyard.

This showed their interpretation of the Act—that it was the building of a church and that it was only that which the clause provided for. The Magistrates objected to the plan, especially to the site; the Sheriff, however, decided in favour of Mr Rhind's plan; but we, having a servitude over the site, put it in force, which checkmated the Railway Company. The Directors then applied to me to see if we would take the money and build ourselves. To this I agreed, and proposed to fix the sum payable by the cost of the Church which they proposed to build. For this purpose Mr Rhind was desired to procure estimates for the completion of his plan. These amounted to above £16,000, which was paid to the Magistrates, whom I considered bound to proceed as soon as convenient to implement their part of the bargain—to build the Church in the form and model of the old one; and if it had cost more than the money received from the Railway Company for this purpose, they must have provided it. If it cost less, they would be entitled to devote the balance to any useful purpose, and I recommended that, in the event of there being a balance over, it should be expended on the repair of the Greyfriars Church. Shortly after this, Mr Bryce, the architect, made what appeared to me an excellent suggestion—that we should restore the Church stone by stone as they stood, and that where they were decayed he could easily have them replaced; that he would thus literally remove the Church as it originally stood to another locality, and at the same time complete what was unfinished of the original plan, which he estimated could be all done for from £10,000 to £12,000, and if we could have secured an appropriate site, this would have been done. But by-and-by the Spirit of Discord entered the Council, and after eighteen years of strife and heart-burnings and litigation, the bone of contention has been seized by a few old women who had the good luck to enlist Professor Dick as their *preux chevalier*.

Now that the Goths have prevailed, what is to be done? Some hint at an application to Parliament. This, I suspect, would be unconstitutional—Parliament could not reverse a decision, right or wrong, of the highest Court in the kingdom. At all events, I do not think the House of Commons would listen to any application of the kind, and to make any such attempt would be to involve ourselves in confusion worse confounded. If the Church is to be restored, I can only see one way of accomplishing it, but even of that I have no great hope—a public subscription to supplement the £7000 allowed by the Lord Chancellor; and if it could be completed at nearly Mr Bryce's estimate, this would be from £3000 to £5000.

I fear that we (I mean those who contended for the restoration of the Church) have lost all but our honour. I have often contemplated in the gay visions of the mind this fine specimen of ancient architecture adding to the embellishments of our beautiful

City; but at the Lord Chancellor's thunder I awoke, and behold it was a dream.—I am, etc.,

ADAM BLACK.

It is a somewhat singular fact, that Lord Provost Black, Mr John Sinclair, and the Society of Antiquaries, in their desire for the restoration of a rare specimen of ancient church architecture, should have so thoroughly lost sight of the chief object of the Charity, as it had been developed since the Reformation, viz.,—the support of the poor.

The result of the Trinity College Church case was known in Edinburgh on the 16th day of February 1864. It is a remarkable coincidence, that on the afternoon of that same day, at 4.30, fire was found to have broken out in the Royal Veterinary College, Clyde Street. Some wags averred that the worthy Professor had kindled a bonfire to celebrate his victory on behalf of the beneficiaries; whilst, on the other hand, it was alleged that it was the act of some evil-disposed son of the Church, who did not relish the news. The cause of the conflagration was never found out.

CHAPTER XXI.

A NEW DIFFICULTY AND A SECOND APPEAL CASE.

WHEN the judgment of the House of Lords came to be applied, as regards the case of Clephane and Others *v.* The Magistrates and Town Council of Edinburgh, before the First Division of the Court of Session (Lord President Inglis presiding), the interlocutor, pronounced by the Court on the 11th day of December 1866, contained *inter alia* the following findings :—" Further, finds that the funds so to be employed by the said defenders shall consist of £7000 of the sum of £17,671, 9s. 6d. which they received from the Railway Company as the price of the said former Church, with the interests and accumulations thereof which have accrued, or shall hereafter accrue, to the said defenders on the said sum of £7000, under deduction of such sums as have been, or shall be, paid by them in the meantime for providing accommodation for the said congregation : Further, find that it is not necessary or expedient, that the defenders should rebuild the Hospital which belonged to the said charity, and which also has been removed by the said Railway Company, and appoint the said defenders, within ten days from this date, to lodge in process a state of the foresaid fund as it is at this date, and also, within six weeks from this date, to lodge a minute, with a plan setting forth a site for, and a plan of, the church to be built as aforesaid."

A perusal of the above order will show to any candid reader, that whatever delays may from time to time occur in the tedious course which requires to be pursued in the Law Courts, there was very little consideration shown in the somewhat exacting nature of the above order, which involved the labour and time of accountants and architects, without any regard to the requirements of their ordinary avocations. The only declaration in the above judgment which gave satisfaction was the compliance with the desire expressed by the Corporation that the Hospital should not be rebuilt, but that the money given for that purpose should be capitalised, and the interest devoted to the granting of additional outdoor pensions to the many applicants who were found every half-year to be persistently knocking at the door of the Governors of the charity.

But the order of the Court of Session was put a stop to, by the pursuers (Clephane and Others) having again intimated an appeal to the House of Lords. The object of the appeal was twofold. They objected to the addition of interest on the £7000 being applied to the building of the Church, and they contended on behalf of the beneficiaries, that the Hospital should be rebuilt as well as the Church. On February 26, 1869, the appeal came before the House of Lords, when Mr James Anderson, Q.C., and Mr C. Grey Wotherspoon again appeared for the appellants. After hearing their case, it is proper to state that Sir R. Palmer, Q.C., and Mr Mellish, Q.C., who appeared for the respondents, were not called upon to reply. The following was the opinion of the Appellate Lords, which is given word for word:—

Lord Chancellor Hatherley.—My Lords, we are asked upon the present occasion to reverse an interlocutor of the Court of Session, pronounced in December 1866. It appears that this important charity (for so I must denominate it) received, in consequence of the purchase of part of its property by a Railway Company, a sum of £17,000, nearly twenty-one years ago, I think in May 1848. Then a course of procedure has taken place by which, instead of dealing with this £17,000 for the purposes and objects of the charity, a vast amount of expense has been incurred. The objects of the charity have been to a certain extent (and perhaps to a certain extent only) disregarded, whilst a contest has been going on between the Provost and Corporation of Edinburgh, and those persons who are interested in the charity, as to the exact mode in which this £17,000 shall be disposed of. The matter, however, came before your Lordships' House exactly five years ago, and the decision of your Lordships was pronounced in February 1864. It was to be hoped that the decision to which this House came, and the order which was very carefully penned upon that occasion, for the purpose of preventing all further dispute and litigation, might have had that beneficial effect. However, unfortunately, it would appear to have been far otherwise, and now in this fifth year since that order was pronounced, we are again called upon to decide in a conflict, which a little good humour, joined to the great amount of intelligence which, I have no doubt, is possessed by the parties, might have prevented; and so an end might have been put at once to this controversy, and there might have been long since built in Edinburgh the Church which your Lordships' House desired should be erected, and the rest of the fund might have been simply appropriated towards the objects of the charity.

Now, the order of your Lordships being this, that a sum not exceeding £7000 should be appropriated to the erection of a Church on the site of that which has been removed; and your Lordships having plainly declared what the exact position of the parties was, with reference to the property which had been taken, by saying that the Church, when so erected at the expense of £7000, should be appropriated for the benefit of those who were receiving the advantages of the charity; and that "subject to that it should also be appropriated for the benefit of those who, for many years previous to this litigation arising, had had the use of the Church as residents in Edinburgh," and that, after erecting the Church, at an expense and not exceeding £7000, which would be sufficient for the purpose indicated, the residue should be appropriated for the benefit of the charity, the House proceeded to direct inquiries, and the order involved, amongst other things, this direction that "all the residue of the money received from the said Railway Company, and all interest thereon, and all the rest of the property of the said Hospital, is applicable to the enlargement and maintenance of the charity, as declared and established by the charters dated respectively the 12th of November 1567, and the 26th of May 1587, in the proceedings mentioned, according to a scheme to be settled for that purpose, including therein the rebuilding of the Hospital, if the same shall be deemed necessary."

Now, I should have thought that it was plain and intelligible to every mind to which the words which I have read should be presented, and, therefore, to the appellants, that it was intended that a proper scheme and arrangement should be submitted to the Court in Scotland for the administration of the funds, and that such proper scheme, if it should be deemed necessary, but not otherwise, should include the erection of an Hospital; and that, therefore, it was remitted to those who had to consider, when brought before them in a proper manner by the submission of a scheme, and to decide whether or not they, in their judgment, deemed the erection of an Hospital necessary. If so, the whole of the learned argument to which we have this day listened, is an argument addressed to us, for the purpose of asking us to do that which it is impossible for us to do, viz.:—to reverse the decision previously come to by your Lordships' House in the year 1864. Because it appears to me, that the argument which has been used is, that it is open to us now to say, that, although it has been deemed unnecessary by those to whom the question has been referred, that the Hospital should be erected, yet we must hold not only that it is necessary, but that it was impossible for your Lordships, or for any other tribunal whatever, to exercise any discretion on the subject. That is the argument which has been addressed to us, and authorities have been cited to prove to us, that we cannot alter, and that no one but the Legislature can alter, the provisions which, it is alleged, were made by the original charter by making any use of these funds until the Hospital be first erected as a substantial building.

There one perhaps might stop, for really the whole case seems to turn upon that single point. But I think it is due to your Lordships' House to say, that it does not appear to me, that any error existed in the conclusion which was so come to. For what, after all, is the true object, purport, and intent of this charter with which we have to deal? The charter contains the following recital:—"Know ye us, and our dearest cousin, James Earl of Murray, Regent of our kingdom, moved by fervent and zealous purpose to support and assist the poverty, penuary, and want of money, and diverse aged and impotent persons, who, in their old age, have lost their means and estates, by and through the events of adverse fortune, so that they may not perish and die through extreme hunger, penuary, and want of necessary sustenance;

and, therefore, moved by piety and a good conscience, to afford them such help and assistance as their want and need require; as also understanding that this purpose cannot be properly carried into effect without our supplement and authority." That indicates the motive on the part of the Crown. The motive there is simply sustaining the poverty, penury, and want of those persons who are so afflicted, in order "that they might not perish and die through extreme hunger, penuary, and want of necessary sustenance." And then, as regards Sir Simon Preston, to whom the grant is made by the Crown, it proceeds to state what his object was :—viz., "that Sir Simon Preston has the intention and deliberate, firm and set purpose, to build, found, and with all care and diligence endow an Hospital with reasonable support, for such foresaid honest, poor, and impotent persons, aged and sick indwellers and inhabitants within our burgh of Edinburgh, and also for such other old, impotent, and indigent people as shall be found fit objects for receiving such benefits and charity in the Hospital so to be founded." Then it proceeds to say, that, in order to set the example to the subjects of good works, the Crown grants this property, which is vacant in its hands, "and at our gift and disposal, as shall be most fit and convenient for building, erecting, repairing, and reforming the said Hospital, with houses, biggings, and yards thereof, where there seems to be the greatest concourse and passage of people, as well stranger as townsman, by whose daily alms said Hospital may be benefited." Then the Crown proceeds to grant the Church, called the Collegiate Church of the Trinity, with all the buildings belonging to it; and the grant is expressed to be "for the building and construction of the said Hospital, houses, yards, and policies thereof, for the maintenance of the poor and sick, to be placed by them therein only, and for no other use."

Now I apprehend, that the real scope and scheme of the whole of that charter was this, that the primary and leading object, first of the Crown and then of Sir Simon Preston, was the relief of the poor and distressed, and providing for the necessities of the aged, and impotent, and infirm; and that, finding a place where he could conveniently erect a building for that object, he obtained from the Crown a grant to enable him to carry that primary object into effect, by the erection of a suitable building or Hospital. It is not what is ordinarily found in foundations of hospitals as such. It is not a scheme by which anything in the shape of a permanent building and a permanent staff thereto attached, or the constant continuance of the building for the purpose here described, is suggested. Nothing of that kind appears in the grant. There is no provision for a governor, or a master, or matron, or nurses, or chaplain. There is not one of those provisions, and the grant does not seem to indicate any more than what I have described, viz., that the mind of the Crown is set, and the mind of Sir Simon Preston is set, upon doing all that can be done for persons in this infirm and unhappy condition. And that which appears to have presented itself to the mind both of the Crown and Sir Simon Preston was this: Here is a place which will assist us in carrying this work into effect. Here we can erect a building, and here can place the poor, the sick, and infirm.

Now, what happened was this: Time after time the building was in a bad state of repair, and at one time it appears to have become almost ruinous. At one time there seems to have been a charter granted, which stated, that the building might be taken down and disposed of by the Corporation in such a manner as was thought most useful, and they thought it most useful to rebuild it. I refer to that passage, which is to be found in the condescendence of the appellants, simply for the purpose of showing, that the original intent and purpose and scheme of the whole charity were such as I have described, and that it was not a charity for which it was essential that a building should be provided which should be always attached to the charity, or one with regard to which any provision was made for continuing it in the shape of an Hospital, to be governed by rules, ordinances, and regulations such as those to which I have referred, and such as you find in the constitution of ordinary hospitals, founded for a special purpose of their being continued in perpetuity under the terms of the grant.

Now, that being so, what do we find in point of practice, has occurred? We find that, for more than eighty years, the course has been (and it appears to me not inconsistent with the objects either of the founders or of the Crown) to afford relief to the distressed objects mentioned in the grant outside the walls of the building. It seems to have been thought, that the existence of a substantial edifice formed no necessary part whatever of the object of the founder. Since the year 1846 or 1847, when the Hospital was taken down by the Railway Company, the charity has been continued to be wholly administered in that manner. The sick, the aged, and the poor have been relieved in a different manner from that prescribed by the charter. And so your Lordships appear to have thought it might possibly be administered hereafter; that the House was not inflexibly bound by the charter to administer it through the medium of residence within the four walls of the building, and that it was right and reasonable, that a judgment should be exercised by competent authority upon that subject, and that it was open to such authority to exercise a judgment upon it. That conclusion having been come to, your Lordships' House left it to the adjudication of those to whom the whole scheme was to be submitted. And I apprehend, that that being so, no rule of law was transgressed. And I am happy to think that the case was such;

because there had never been in our judgment anything in that decision which militated against any previous rule of law. It would undoubtedly not be competent to us at the present moment, without having that case reheard (if such a thing was possible), to reverse that decision.

The only remaining question to which I need advert, is this. It is said, if it be not necessary to erect the Hospital, why erect the Church? There, again, we are undoubtedly precluded by the order of the House, pronounced on the former occasion. But, even if it were not so precluded, I do not at all admit the justice of the argument. Many of these persons who are relieved by means of this charity may be residing in the neighbourhood. There is no reason why it should not be so; and the probability is, that many of them would have their residence in the neighbourhood of this Church, and many of them, therefore, would be partakers of the benefit which the decree of this House was intended to secure to them.

The only remaining point which occurred in the argument was the point with reference to the objections which were taken to the "states" brought in before the Court of Session. It appears to me, I confess, that there is nothing whatever of which the appellants are to complain in that respect. The only important item which they might have some ground hereafter for disputing (if the parties have not the good sense, which I trust they will have, to arrange all these matters in the manner in which charities above all things should be arranged) is under the twelfth objection, which was raised with reference to certain expenditure incurred on account of plans and surveys, and other matters of that description in connection with the Church. That is expressly reserved by the interlocutor complained of. We have, therefore, nothing to do with that part of the case. And with regard to the other objections, I see nothing of substance in them. The only alteration which appears to me necessary to be made, is with regard to what has already been suggested by one of your Lordships, namely, the omission of the interest which has occurred in the £7000 as being the sum properly applied to the erection of a Church; because it is quite clear that, by the order made upon the former occasion, £7000 was appointed as the maximum. There was no question of the interest which might arise upon the £7000, but whenever the Church is built, no more than £7000 is to be expended upon it, and it may be that not so much is necessary, at all events no more can be expended. I would, therefore, upon that point propose to your Lordships after the words £7000 in the second finding, to add the words "if so much be required."

Then, with regard to costs, in substance the appellants fail in the present appeal, and the costs must follow. The appellants sue as paupers, and, of course, as far as they are concerned, they will pay no costs. The House will not make any order with reference to the payment of costs by them. But it appears to me that, with your Lordships' sanction, no costs ought to be allowed to them in this appeal. With regard to the respondents, I confess that after what we have heard, and especially after what has last fallen from Mr Anderson, viz., that although there was a suggestion, that the question of interest should be waived, in order that fewer points might arise for argument, it was distinctly stated, that it would make no difference whatever in the appeal being prosecuted, it seems to me that the respondents are entitled to have their costs out of the charity. Therefore, what I should propose to your Lordships would be to affirm the decree, with the variations which I have suggested; to grant no costs to the appellants, and to direct that the costs of the respondents should be paid out of the charity estate.

Lord Chelmsford.—My Lords, with reference to the argument on behalf of the appellants, the only question to be determined is, whether the Magistrates of Edinburgh were bound to erect a new building to be used as an Hospital in place of that which was taken down to make room for the railway? This question depends upon the effect of the charter, and upon whether it fastens on the Magistrates of Edinburgh an irrevocable trust, that there shall always be a building to be used as an Hospital to the end of time.

Now, the primary object of the charter of James VI. in 1567, as my noble and learned friend on the Woolsack has pointed out, was the help and assistance to aged and impotent persons. There was no recital in the charter, that for those persons it was necessary to build and endow an Hospital; but all that is said is, "Understanding that this purpose cannot be properly carried into effect, without our supplement and authority," and then it goes on to recite, that "Sir Simon Preston has expressed his intention to build, found, and endow an Hospital, with reasonable support for such foresaid honest and poor and impotent persons." Then, there is a grant to the Magistrates of Edinburgh for the building and construction of the Hospital, "for the maintenance of the poor and sick, to be placed by them therein only, and for no other use," with a proviso that they shall be bound to apply "the places and others foresaid to the foresaid use, and no other." Now, I understand by that merely this, that as long as the building remains, it shall be used for the purposes of an Hospital, and for no other use or purpose, and not that there shall always be a building to be applied to the purposes of the charter. That it was not necessary that a building should always exist for this purpose, appears to me to be clear upon the words of the charter of 26th May 1587, which authorised the Magistrates to apply the old Hospital buildings which had become ruinous to whatever profitable use might seem expedient. And there is no direction whatever, that, if the ruinous building is taken down, another shall be erected in its place.

Now, if the effect of the charter was, that the Magistrates should always maintain an Hospital for the reception of poor persons, there certainly was great difficulty in justifying the former order of this House, leaving the question of the re-erection of an Hospital to depend upon whether it should be deemed necessary. But no necessity for the continuance of a building as an Hospital for ever can be deduced from the charters. This seems to me conceded by the appellants themselves; for, in the condescendence, viz. Cond. 25, they say, "In consequence of the building of the Hospital having been removed by the Railway Company, and of no new Hospital buildings having been yet erected, there are no inmates or poor persons supported or maintained in any one building or Hospital at present; but instead, pensions in weekly, monthly, or termly payments are granted to the pursuers, and to a great many other poor persons. In the event of a new Hospital being erected, the pursuers or some of them would be entitled to be received as inmates thereof." They, therefore, state it as a contingency whether a new Hospital will be erected or not. If the erection of a new Hospital had been absolutely necessary, their words would have been, "When a new Hospital is erected, the pursuers or some of them will be entitled to be received as inmates thereof."

This being so, the order of the House, upon the former occasion, was perfectly correct. It was justified by the provisions of the charter, and it is in itself conclusive of this question; because, after providing £7000 for the Church, it is declared "that all of the residue of the money received from the Railway Company, and all interest thereon, and all the rest of the property of the said Hospital, is applicable to the enlargement and maintenance of the said charity as declared and established by the charters dated respectively 12th November 1567 and 26th May 1587, in the said proceedings mentioned, according to a scheme to be settled for that purpose, including therein the rebuilding of the Hospital, if the same shall be deemed necessary. And it is further ordered, that it be referred to the Court of Session to settle and approve of such scheme accordingly."

The Court of Session by their interlocutor applied that judgment; and they directed, amongst other things, that a statement of the moneys which belonged to the property of which the Hospital consisted should be made; and also that, within four weeks, the parties should lodge a scheme showing the proposed application "of the said properties and funds." In pursuance of that interlocutor, a scheme was accordingly proposed by the trustees of the Hospital, and submitted to the Court of Session, and in that scheme there is the following statement:—"The trustees beg to state that, in their opinion, it is unnecessary and inexpedient that a new Hospital should be built. It appears to them, that the funds under their management would be more beneficially applied by continuing the out-door system of relief." Upon this, the Court of Session pronounced their interlocutor, finding "that it is not necessary or expedient that the defenders should rebuild the Hospital, which belonged to the said charity, and which has been also removed by the said Railway Company." And against this interlocutor, this appeal is made.

I think that I have already shown your Lordships sufficiently, that the order that was made by the House upon the previous occasion was well founded, and that there is no objection to it with reference to any restrictive words in that charter. I, therefore, entirely agree with my noble and learned friend upon the Woolsack, that this interlocutor must be affirmed. I also agree with him, with regard to the alteration which he has suggested, and likewise upon the subject of the costs.

Lord Westbury.—My Lords, I should hardly feel it necessary to add a word to what has been addressed to your Lordships, but for some observations which fell from the appellants' counsel, and which served to show, that the subject of the administration of charitable trusts is not yet perfectly apprehended. The jurisdiction of the Court of Session and jurisdiction of a Court of Equity in England upon the subject of the administration of charitable trusts are one and the same. Undoubtedly, in England, we have had a greater number of cases, and therefore the principles have been more fully developed. The rules which have been laid down, and the authorities in England, are of course not binding on the Court of Session, yet, as they are illustrations of the convenient mode of the application of the same principles of law, I daresay, that whenever an opportunity arises, the Court of Session will deem them entitled to respect and attention.

Now, in both Courts this principle has prevailed, namely, that there shall be a very enlarged administration of charitable trusts. You look to the charity which is intended to be created, that is to say, the benefit of the beneficiary, and you distinguish between the charity and the means which are directed to the attainment of that charity. Now, the means of necessity vary from age to age. Take a charity consisting, as it does here, of the relief of the poor. The condition of the country, or the condition of the town at the time when that charity was created, may have dictated what at that time were very convenient means for the application of the particular charity. In the progress of society, and with the greater diffusion of wealth and growth of population, the means originally indicated may become inadequate to the end, and the Courts of Equity have always exercised the power of varying the means of carrying out the charity from time to time, according as by that variation they can secure more effectually the great object of the charity, namely, the benefit of the beneficiary.

Now, it is perfectly true, that you cannot substitute one charity for another; you may substitute for a particular charity which has been defined, and which has failed, another charity *ejusdem generis*, or which approaches it in its nature and character; but it is quite true that you cannot take a charity which was intended for one purpose and apply it altogether to a different purpose. Some instances occur in our English reports upon the subject, but on an examination it will be found that what was done in those cases was not done under the ordinary authority of the Court of Equity, but that it was done in cases where the charity described failed by reason of its illegality, and where it fell to the Crown to declare what should be the form of administration to be adopted. I mention this, because our attention has been directed to the language which was used by Lord Eldon in the case of the *Attorney-General* v. *Mansfield*. That language was never intended at all to alter the law upon this subject, namely, that the means for the attainment of the end may be altered from time to time. Neither was that language intended to interfere with the settled doctrine of what is called *cyprès* application in a Court of Equity. But it was intended only to apply to such a case as this. Supposing that an attempt is made to take a charity given for the relief of the poor in a particular district, and to employ the money so dedicated for the purpose of building a bridge, or making a road, or draining a town,—those objects being quite *diversi generis* from the objects for which the charity was given,—probably those objects would not come within the powers of a Court of Equity. But the power of a Court of Equity to alter the means so as to adapt them to the end, is undoubtedly not limited.

Now, what is the case which we have to consider here? The benevolence of Sir Simon Preston, and of the Court acting at his instance, was moved on account of the condition of the poor of Edinburgh, and as one means of benefiting the condition of the poor, he was able to erect, and had land granted to him, upon which he might erect dwellings for the poor; for, although you call it an "Hospital," yet the word "Hospital" is to be considered with reference to that which is here described, and you must not derive from the word "Hospital" the idea which is frequently attached to it at the present day, namely, a particular building with a certain staff of officers, and with directions to receive annuitants therein, and to allow them certain sums of money, and to keep up a number of officers, a chaplain, and a superintendent, and so on, who are directed to be maintained in an Hospital. That is an Hospital consisting of a certain number of recipients of charity, whose interest in the charity is defined, and the Hospital is to be for them a place of permanent dwelling. But, in the direction here given, for the establishment of an Hospital, there is nothing more, so far as the charters go, than as it were the erection of an ordinary poorhouse, where the poor and the sick may be received and lodged and maintained, so long as may be necessary, and the whole seems to be left entirely to the arbitrium and discretion of the superintending authority by the founder of the charity.

Now, these buildings, such as they were, have been swept away by the authority of the law, by a Railway Company, and there is substituted for the buildings a large sum of money. Where is the necessity that that sum of money constituting the property of the charity should be dedicated to the use and service of the poor, in the same manner as that in which, at the time of the foundation of the charity, it was considered that the end of relieving the poor might be accomplished? If the end of relieving the poor can be better accomplished now, by hiring dwellings for them, or by enabling them to get lodging or cottages or dwellings of their own, the substantial object will be accomplished; and, of course, it is palpable to every one, that if we allow, for example, the laying out of £10,000 in the erection of suitable buildings for the reception of the poor, the interest of that money will be so much taken away from the number of pensions which might be given in out-door relief. Whether it should be the one, or whether it should be the other, depends on the circumstances of the time, and on what constitutes a wise and prudent and discreet administration of the funds of the charity, and that administration may alter. It does not follow that, because we approve of out-door relief to-day, the scheme continuing that form of application should have perpetual duration. Another set of circumstances may arise ten, twenty or fifty years hence, which will suggest another, and a more beneficial form of administration. And thus it is, that charity in the eye of the Court is not bound up to any absolute and no longer beneficial mode of administration; but it may receive, under these wise maxims, from time to time, that application and that administration of the fund which will best accomplish the great end in view.

I, therefore, think that these considerations would justify to the mind, not only of every lawyer, but I should hope of every wise man, who was really intent upon works of benevolence, the sort of order which was made by this House. The House undoubtedly saw no legal obligation for the erection of a building, or for the maintenance of a building, and it therefore only regarded the building as something suggested at that time with a view to an end. Whether there should be another building or not, was left to the discretion of those who were armed with the power of administering this charity, and it was accordingly settled deliberately by this House, that if they deemed a new Hospital necessary, a new Hospital should be built; but that if they deemed the building of a new Hospital unnecessary for the benefit of the poor, then there was no obligation to erect such a building.

Now, the appellants have neither here, nor in the Court of Session, presented any considerations, or any peculiar circumstances, or any facts upon which the Court of Session would have been warranted in coming to the conclusion, that it was necessary to build an Hospital. What then, have we here? We have an administration which has been exclusively directed to out-door relief for the last twenty-one years, and an administration which has consisted as to the greater portion of the funds, in out-door relief since 1785. Then, what is there to justify our departing from all that has been done, altering the course which we find to have existed, and directing so much of the funds of this charity to be laid out in what would probably be found to be a wasteful and useless form of application?

If these things had been considered, as I think they ought to have been considered below, I think we should not have observed the strange spectacle of an appeal brought here in the hopeless attempt to alter the order of the House; and I think that we might have been spared observations which were directed to show, that the order of the House was inconsistent with law and with justice. I have dwelt so much upon this point, not because I felt that the orders of your Lordships' House required to be remedied, but only to repeat the considerations which were present to the minds of my noble and learned friends, who with me heard the former appeal, and to my own mind, when that order was pronounced.

There is nothing else, I think, which remains to be said, except with regard to the variation which is proposed to be made in the interlocutor appealed from. It is quite true, that words have crept into the interlocutor, which have proceeded upon a misunderstanding of a portion of your Lordships' order. It is unnecessary to show how clear the language of that order was, and that it ought not to have been misunderstood, because the respondents very handsomely say, that it was a misunderstanding of the order, and they desire to have deleted from the order so much of the language as contains that misunderstanding. It thus becomes requisite to add to the words "£7000," in the passage which has been referred to, the words, "if so much be required," and then to delete the words which follow in italics.

With respect to the rest of the appeal, the indignation and complaint against the charges relating to plans, are answered at once by this, that there is an inquiry which is not yet exhausted. There will probably be very important questions arising upon that portion of the objections; but we, of course, do not deal with matters which are reserved by the Court of Session for further consideration.

I entirely concur with my noble and learned friend on the Woolsack, as to the manner in which he proposes to your Lordships to dispose of the costs. If, indeed, this appeal had been directed only to the erroneous part of the interlocutor, then I should have required the respondents to show, that they had been willing to abandon that erroneous part. But then they were told, that, whether they did it or not, the appeal would go forward. I think that the respondents acted with great propriety in telling the appellants:—We do not mean to maintain that part of the order; and, if you, indeed, bring it forward before the House, it is more becoming that it should be expunged by the authority of the House, than that we should make any application to the Court of Session to alter the judgment which has been pronounced.

I, therefore, think, that the respondents are entitled to their costs. But I hope and trust that this is the last we shall hear of this matter; and I rejoice the more, that we can with perfect justice refuse to the appellants their costs; because I think that it will be one of the most effective and most salutary modes of preventing further litigation. Let that be remembered, because without it I feel certain, that if hereafter there were a peg upon which an appeal could be hung, we should have that appeal brought here. Probably this matter will not be any longer a subject of litigation in this House, when the parties find that they cannot look with anything like confidence to the costs coming out of the fund.

Lord Colonsay.—My Lords, as to the question whether or not another building should be erected as an Hospital, the matters for consideration in the Court below appear to have been *first*, whether they rightly understood the judgment or deliverance of your Lordships as having dealt with that question, and *secondly*, whether if they rightly understood it as having dealt with that question, and having left it to the discretion of those who had the management of the charity, there has been anything advanced to show that that discretion has been ill-used. Now, upon both these points, I think that the case is clear. I think it very clear, from reading the judgment or deliverance of this House in 1864, that the House did deal and did intend to deal with the question, whether or not an Hospital building should be erected, and that the House dealt with it by leaving it to the discretion of those who had the management of the charity, to determine, whether it was expedient or necessary that such a building should be erected. Those parties having come to the conclusion, that it was not necessary, and that it was not expedient to erect an Hospital, but that it was more expedient and more fitting that the relief should be given to the objects of it out of doors, and nothing having been urged here as matter of discretion against that decision, I think we have no course here but to affirm the judgment of the House and of the Court below in that matter. If it had been open to us now to go into the question, whether the charters which have been read made it absolutely necessary that an Hospital should be erected, and precluded all discretion under all circumstances, we might have had a different course of proceeding to follow out. But, as far as I have been able to judge from the argument which has been submitted to us, I see no reason to doubt that the deliverance of this House in 1861, was perfectly in accordance with the principle and with the tenor of these charters.

But there is another point in this case, as to the sum which was intended to be applied to the building of a Church. I have no doubt now, after hearing what your Lordships who took part in the proceedings in 1861 have said, that the Court below have misread the judgment or deliverance of the House upon that matter. They have interpreted it in a sense in which it was not intended to be interpreted, and therefore the alteration which has been suggested in the judgment of the Court below must be made, and the amount of money to be applied to the erection of a Church must be limited to the sum of £7000. I hope, however, with regard to that matter, there will be no further delay in carrying out the direction of the House or of the Court below. As long as that matter is delayed, that sum, whatever it may be, which ought long ago to have been applied to the erection of a Church, is lying accumulating for the benefit, as it is said, of the charity, but to the detriment of those who are to have the benefit of the Church. I hope, therefore, that no impediment will be interposed to the application of that fund to the purpose to which it has been directed to be applied.

As to the notion, that, if there is to be no building of an Hospital, there is to be no Church, I think that I must regard that as more ingenious than sound. I cannot go along with the notion, that no parties are to have the benefit from the Church accommodation except the parties who reside within the buildings of the Hospital, and those parties residing in the neighbourhood of the Church, who are recipients of the fund. I think, under the interpretation which has been put upon the charters, the recipients of this charity are the parties who are primarily entitled to the benefit of accommodation in that Church, and that when the judgment of the Court below used the expression "beneficiaries," it used it properly, seeing, that in the view which that Court took, and in the view which this House has taken, there were to be no inmates. It did not follow from that, that the beneficiaries of the charity are to be deprived of Church accommodation. They are entitled to have it, and then further accommodation is to be given to the parties residing in the neighbourhood.

As to the matter of costs, I entirely concur in what has been suggested by my noble and learned friend.

The LORD CHANCELLOR put the question as follows:—That the interlocutor complained of be affirmed, with the following variations, that is to say, by inserting in the second finding the words "if so much be required" after "£7000" where they first occur in that finding, and by omitting in the same finding all the words, that follow the word "Church." And that the appellants neither receive nor pay costs of this appeal. And that the costs of the respondents be retained by them out of the charity estate.

The appellants' agents were Messrs Wotherspoon and Morrison, W.S., Edinburgh, and Messrs Simson and Wakeford, Westminster.

The respondents' agents were Messrs Millar, Allardice and Robson, W.S., Edinburgh; and Mr John Graham, Westminster.

CHAPTER XXII.

THE CARCASE AND THE EAGLES.

IT is related in the New Testament, "wheresoever the carcase is, there will the eagles be gathered together." The funds of the Trinity Hospital Charity were no exception to the rule thus laid down in holy writ.

In the year 1810, an attempt was made by the clergy of the city to obtain possession for themselves of the rich heritage, as they supposed, which had been provided for what might in all truthfulness at that time be designated "the genteel poor of Edinburgh." An action was raised by the city ministers, including the minister of Trinity College Church, to have it found and declared that, under the Charter of 1566 by Queen Mary, as well as under subsequent charters already adverted to, they were entitled to claim right to the Church lands and revenues thereby conveyed, on the ground that these were vested in the Magistrates and Town Council, for the purpose of their being applied by them to the support of the ministers of the city and other ecclesiastical purposes. The defenders, however, maintained in their defences, that the funds referred to were destined to various other purposes besides the payment of the stipends of the clergy. We have already seen that the late Bailie Andrew Fyfe would not have hesitated to have appropriated the revenues of the charity in helping to put an end to the Annuity Tax in the city, and thereby save the ratepayers' pockets. We are thus presented with the strange anomaly of the radical voluntary at a later period, practically adopting the views of the city clergy of a previous generation, though their respective motives were very different. The clergy were unsuccessful in their law suit. The Court decided adverse to their claim. After a good deal of debate and Court procedure, the Magistrates and Town Council, as Governors of Trinity Hospital, were assoilzied from the conclusions of the action at the instance of the city ministers; and, for at least half a century thereafter, the Corporation was allowed to manage the affairs of the charity after the fashion or mode that they had been accustomed to do previously.

When the question of the sale of the Trinity College Church and Hospital came to the front, chiefly in consequence of the large sum given by the Railway Company for the ecclesiastical edifice, as well as the sum allowed for the site of the Hospital and adjacent grounds, the representatives of the University authorities tried to institute proceedings against the Governors, as if they had some claim, or reason why they should be allowed to partake in some degree of the good things which they supposed were agoing at the time. They gave a considerable amount of bother, and occupied no end of time that might have been more profitably spent by the town's officials. But they found out, in due course, that their inquiries were of no avail. They had already got all that they were entitled to receive. They found out that they had no title to participate—how much soever they desired it—in what was given for, and for generations had been, the heritage of the poor burgesses of Edinburgh. In fact, with the exception of the fabrics of the Church and Hospital and the adjacent grounds, the benefactions to the charity were the result of repeated appeals to the benevolence of the public on the part of the successive bodies of Governors, as well as the pious mortifications of citizens and friends, who possessed hearts to feel for and sympathise with the sufferings and straits of their less-favoured sisters and brothers.

Another claimant, however, appeared that was not quite so easily disposed of.

This was the Parochial Board of the Parish of the City of Edinburgh, who, on the second day of October 1863, raised an action at the instance of Mr George Greig (their inspector) to have certain funds in the possession of the Town Council, for behoof of the poor of the city, transferred to them and so placed under the parochial control and dispensation. The following observations are abstracted from the Memorial which the Poor's Board laid before learned Counsel for their guidance in the matter :—

I. The Parochial Board of the City Parish of Edinburgh (which is exclusively a Burghal Parish) claims from the Magistrates and Town Council, as representing the Corporation of the City of Edinburgh, the following property and funds :—

(1.) The houses and ground now occupied by the poor, including therein right to the feu-duty of the Free New North Church (part of the Poorshouse grounds feued by the Corporation), and right to resume Forrest Road (also part of the Poorshouse grounds), for the benefit of the poor.

(2.) The City Bonds forming the residue of Paul's Work Mortification.

(3.) Trinity Hospital, and the funds thereto pertaining ; and

(4.) Delivery of all parochial titles, records, and papers.

The facts on which these claims were rested, were detailed in the printed document.

It would extend this volume to unusual dimensions, were reference made to the various documents prepared by the City Parochial Board, and submitted to learned counsel as to this claim, which in the language of the present day would be designated "a very large order."

It may be sufficient to note the demands which were made upon the Town Council, as Governors of the Trinity Hospital, and to leave the other claims to take care of themselves.

In the demands of the City Parochial Board, for the funds pertaining to the Trinity Hospital, it is right to state that these were based upon the fact that, on 12th November 1567, King James VI., moved by fervent and zealous purpose to support and assist the poverty, penury, and want of many and divers aged and impotent persons, who, in their old age have lost their means and estates by and through the events of adverse fortune, or that they may not perish and die through extreme hunger, penury, and want of sustenance; and therefore, moved by piety and good conscience to afford them such help and assistance as their want and need require (reference is then made to Sir Simon Prestoun and his resolution to found a hospital, as the same has already been duly recited in this volume); and the paper concludes with the following observations:—

What was then "our Burgh of Edinburgh" is now "the City Parish of Edinburgh." The Corporation was at that time bound to support "cruicked focke, seik focke, impotent focke, and weak focke" (*sic*); and in 1579—twelve years after this charter, the class of paupers so to be supported and housed by the Corporation, was defined by Act of Parliament, to be "all aged, pure, impotent, and decayed persons, whilkes of necessitie maun live by almes." In 1587, the Council acquired from Robert Pont, then provost of Trinity College, the provostry thereof, and its revenues; and having thus become vested in the whole subjects, applied to the Crown, and procured ratifications and confirmations thereof, and of the titles thereof, in the person of the Council. In particular, the grant of "the College Kirk, callit the Trinitie College, w[t] ye kirkyaird yairof, the mansiones the hous's and zairds yairof, ye hospitall callit ye Hospitall of ye Trinitie College, and zaird," was ratified by His Majesty in 1587 to the Council, "to ye effect zat ye said Provost, Baillies and Counsall my[t] big and erect ane hospitall upown ye samen for sustentation of ye puir, honest, aget, and decayit personis within ye said burgh, and utheris having neid of support, as the said donation and gift, of ye dait ye xii day of November, the zeir of God 1567 zeiris in lyk maner, at mair len[t] proportis." The grant of Trinity Hospital was again, with all previous grants to "the poor, aged, decripped, and indigent persons, orphans and infants destitute of parents, within the said burgh, of whatsomever dates, tenor, and contents the same be," confirmed by the Crown, on 7th August 1612, by the great charter of Kirk livings, in favour of this Council.

It will thus be seen that the poor were, by

Statute Law.	Trinity Charter, 1567.	New Grant, 1612.
1. Cruicked folk.	5. Sick.	3. Decripped.
2. Sick folk.	3. Impotent.	5. Orphans and infants destitute of parents.
3. Impotent folk.	4. Aged.	2. Aged.
4. Weak folk.	2. Poor.	1. Poor.
Act, 1579.	1. Honest Poor.	4. Indigent persons "within the said burgh,"
5. Aged.	3. Impotent.	
6. Poor.	6. Indigent people, as shall be found out, fit objects for receiving such benefits and charity.	
7. Impotent; and		
8. Decayed persons, which "of necessity, must live by alms."		

and that not one feature in the legal poor is awanting in the charter of erection, or in the confirmation thereof; all three being self-evident descriptions of one class—the common poor. While the beneficiaries under the foundation of Trinity Hospital, and the beneficiaries under the Poor Law Acts then in operation, were thus identical, the trustees were the same in both, and hence the City Parochial Board apprehends that the foundation was just one for the benefit of the common poor then resident within the City of Edinburgh. Both were poor, honest, aged, impotent, indigent indwellers, and decayed persons, within the same bounds, as shall be found to be fit subjects of charity, who, of necessity, must live by alms, or who have need of support.

From an early period, the Town Council seems to have inverted this foundation. In Maitland's "History of Edinburgh," published in 1753, page 480, the then existing Statutes of the Hospital are quoted:—Section III. of the Statutes provides,—"The persons to be admitted into, and maintained in the Hospital shall be *no other than old men*, or *old women, burgesses, wives or children of burgesses, not married*, nor under the age of *fifty years*, or shall be persons of the age and state of life, before mentioned, presented by the donators of £250 sterling, and the number of persons to be constantly entertained shall be so many as the revenue of the Hospital can conveniently maintain, after the deduction of the charge of management, and of maintaining the fabric,—so that the stock or capital always remained entire. By Section IV., donors of £200 are privileged to present any person whatsoever, of the age and state before mentioned, within twelve months of vacancies occurring. By Section V., each person, on being admitted, shall sign a writ, by which they transfer and dispone all they have, at their admission, for behoof of the Hospital.

Arnot, in his "History of Edinburgh" to the year 1780, published in 1816, page 435, refers to Maitland's Statutes, and mentions that the public had viewed the institution in so favourable a light, that it had been enriched by many pious donations, especially from the citizens of Edinburgh.

In 1823, the Statutes of the Hospital seem to have been revised and re-enacted by the Town Council, and these revised Statutes seem to be those under which the Hospital has since been administered. By the revised Statutes, the persons "entitled to be admitted into, and maintained in the Hospital, shall be either burgesses, wives of burgesses, or children of burgesses, not married, nor under the age of fifty years." Besides assigning their property at the date of admission, for behoof of the Hospital, applicants shall also dispose such property as they shall subsequently acquire, "at least so much thereof as will completely re-imburse the Hospital of every charge and expense its revenue may be put to on their account." If they refuse, they are dismissed the Hospital; and, in their stead, needy persons shall be admitted from time to time.

The schedule to be filled up by applicants requires them to answer certain questions, and among others, "(2*d*.) Is the applicant a burgess of Edinburgh, or the widow, son, or daughter of a burgess?" And from a list of applicants seeking the benefit of the Hospital at February 1861, it is seen that these are from all parts of the country, burgesses' wives or children of burgesses, all above fifty years of age, some of them as old as eighty-one.

The statement then goes on to give a synopsis of the affairs of the Hospital, and of its income and expenditure, and how that was likely to be increased from time to time; as also of the various legal cases, which had arisen and which have already been dealt with in these pages, in the hope eventually of obtaining the revenues of Trinity Hospital, with the view of reducing the amount to be annually assessed by the

City Parochial Board, upon their fellow citizens for the relief of the poor of the City Parish.

II.—Another part of the Memorial to Counsel related to the claim of the City Parochial Board to the City Bonds, which formed the residue of what was formerly known as Paul's Work Mortification.

An elaborate account is entered into, under this head, as to the origin of the charity, and the various changes which were made upon it by the Town Councils of the period; but as these have been sufficiently dealt with and explained in previous chapters, it does not seem at all necessary to recapitulate them. The only matter wherein a ray of new light is cast upon the subject, may be briefly explained:—When the proposal of the Town Council to instruct the people in the manufacture of woollen works, by William Dickson, of the city of Delft, in Holland, proved unsuccessful, the Town Council, in 1683, converted the place into a linen manufactory, in which boys were to be trained up in virtue and industry; and they entered into a tack of the work to Sir William Binny. This inversion of the mortification was questioned, in the Court of Session, but the right of the Town Council was maintained on the 22d day of November 1698, by a majority of one.

Various acts of the Town Council were recited; in particular, a statement is made that, from 26th August 1752 to 1781, the revenues from Paul's Work were accounted for to the Charity Managers. In 1787, they likewise demanded payment of arrears for Forglen's Park. A reference seems to have been made on the subject to the Hon. Henry Erskine and Bailie Galloway, one of the Magistrates, who decided in favour of the Charity Managers. The payments by the Corporation to the Managers continued until 1822, when they were temporarily withheld, in consequence of a debt claimed by the City from the Parochial Board Managers.

A long series of counter claims was the result. On the 27th July

1838, the City Agreement Act was passed by the Legislature. As the result of this, negotiations went on between the Town Council and the Charity Workhouse Governors up to the year 1851, viz., for 105 years before the passing of the Poor Law Amendment Act, and for six years thereafter. But in 1851, the Town Council, on a report by their clerk that the term for which the revenue of Paul's Work Mortification had been granted to the poor had long since elapsed, it was ordered that the revenue was to be paid and accounted for in future to Trinity Hospital, and it has been accordingly so paid and accounted for, since Lammas 1851, and the Corporation declined to listen to any claim on the part of the Board to that fund.

Reference is then made to an Act of the Town Council (of 24th March 1731) wherein they agreed to adopt this place as a Charity Workhouse, and ordained that a committee should be annually appointed for the management of the institution, the committee to consist of a certain number of the Town Council, the College of Justice, and other bodies.

Allusion is then made to the fact of the Town Council having, for so long a period of time, permitted the funds of Paul's Work to have been devoted to the objects of the Charity Workhouse; and the question is argued not as one of constitutional right, but as one of special contract, and so it was laid before learned counsel.

There are several lengthy prints on the subject, to which it is not requisite special allusion should now be made, except to state that most of these were prepared by Mr David Curror, of Wester Craigduckie, S.S.C., and that the chief counsel consulted were the late Mr Edward S. Gordon, afterwards Baron Gordon of Drumearn, and Mr William Watson, now Baron Watson of Thankerton.

As it seemed to be, as has already been stated, "a large order," it was requisite, in a history of the Trinity Hospital Charity, that the grounds of it should be sufficiently explained. But, beyond this, it may be enough to state that all these affairs were never debated in Court. They became eventually matter of mutual arrangement and agreement.

In a report of the Law Committee of the City Parochial Board on 4th July 1861, the following entry occurs :—

> "Read minute by Sub-Committee as to Mr Curror's Report. The Meeting adopt the Report as the Report of this Committee to the Board, and recommend that, as the questions at issue are between two public Boards, the Town Council should be invited to a conference with this Board, with the view to an amicable arrangement of the claims, either privately or by a reference to a counsel of eminence. Instruct the Inspector in the meantime to have the Report printed and circulated among the members of the Board, so that it may be fully before the Board, and disposed of at its next meeting.
>
> "GEORGE CAIRNS, *Convener*."

Prior to this they had received the following opinion from the learned counsel whom they had consulted :—

"We are of opinion that Trinity Hospital, and the mortifications thereto pertaining, did not pass to the Parochial Board, by virtue of the Poor Law Amendment Act.

"The foundation charter, of 12th November 1567, bears, that the Hospital is to be erected and endowed, with reasonable support, for such 'honest, poor, and impotent persons, aged and sick, indwellers and inhabitants, within our burgh of Edinburgh, and also for such other old, indigent, and impotent people as shall be found fit objects for receiving such benefit and charity in the Hospital so to be founded.' And the Act of Ratification granted by King James the Sixth to the Town Council, in the year 1587, recognises as the proper inmates of the Hospital of the Trinity College, 'Ye puir, honest, aget, and decayit personis within ye said burgh, and utheris haveing neid of support.' In both of these documents, the honest, poor, impotent, aged, sick, and decayed within the burgh of Edinburgh, are the class first indicated as the objects of the charity, but to these are added *others having need of support*. Now, if the foundation is to be construed as limited to the legal poor, then it includes the poor of other parishes than Edinburgh. If, on the other hand, it is to be read as confined to the burgh of Edinburgh, it includes others than the legal poor. On either construction, it is equally difficult to hold that the charity falls within the 52d section of the Poor Law Amendment Act. In our opinion, the provisions of that clause of the Statute do not apply, either to cases where, by the constitution of a charitable trust, property is held for the behoof of the legal poor of more than one parish or combination, or where such property is not held for the exclusive benefit of the legal poor of such parish or combination.

"Whilst we have arrived at the conclusion that Trinity Hospital, and the funds thereto pertaining, did not vest in the City Parochial Board, we still think that the Town Council cannot be held as duly administering the trust, so long as no part of the Hospital funds is devoted by them to the relief of the legal poor within the City Parish. By the foundation of the charity, such poor have, in our opinion, an undoubted right to participate in its benefits. The poor, 'within our burgh of Edinburgh' are the recipients first enumerated, both in the charter of King James, and in his Act of Ratification. And we are of opinion, that the Memorialists, and any ratepayer within the City Parish, have a good title to call the Magistrates and Council to account for their administration, and to compel them to recognise the claims of the legal poor to a share of the revenues of the Hospital. It is not easy for us to specify the exact proportion of the annual revenues which should be allotted to them. That is a matter left, in the first instance, to the discretion of the trustees, subject to the control of the Court, in the event of abuse."

In regard to Paul's Work, the learned counsel consulted said—We are of opinion that the Parochial Board are entitled to claim the whole fund which now represents the residue of Paul's Work, and the mortifications thereto pertaining, as now vested in them under the Statute. It does not clearly appear that, by the original foundation of this charity, its benefits were intended for any others than the poor of the City of Edinburgh; and from the earliest period, down to the year 1851, the legal poor of the city have uniformly been the recipients of the charity.

Acting upon the advice of counsel, the Parochial Board Managers came at last to arrange matters with the City Corporation. The following Minute, presented to the Court of Session, will make this matter sufficiently plain:—

"JOINT MINUTE for the Parties, in actions of Declarator, etc., George Greig, Inspector of the Poor of the City Parish of Edinburgh, pursuer, *against* the Lord Provost, Magistrates, and Town Council of Edinburgh, defenders. WATSON for the pursuer, and GIFFORD for the Defenders,—stated that the parties had come to an agreement in reference to the matters to which this action relates, the terms of which are expressed in a Minute of Agreement, dated 12th, and recorded in the Books of Council and Session as a probative writ, 22d January 1869, an extract of which has been lodged in process, and they therefore moved the Lord Ordinary to waken the process of consent, and to interpone his authority and sanction to said agreement, and to dismiss the action, finding neither party entitled to expenses."

The Minute of Agreement was to the following effect:—

"We, the parties after mentioned, viz., The Lord Provost, Magistrates, and Town Council of the City of Edinburgh, as representing the Community of the said City, of the first part, and the Parochial Board of the City Parish of Edinburgh, of the second part, do hereby, for ourselves, and for our respective successors in office, agree to compromise and settle the disputes and differences arising between us, in regard to the claims of the said second party embraced in a Summons raised at their instance against the said first party, in or about the month of October Eighteen hundred and sixty-three, and also in regard to the claims of the legal poor of the City Parish of Edinburgh, and of the said second party, to the lands, properties, revenues, funds, and effects held by the said first party as Trustees, Administrators and Governors of the Trinity Hospital of Edinburgh, and that upon the terms and conditions following :—

First. That the said first party shall dispone and convey to the said second party the Poorhouse of the City Parish of Edinburgh, and grounds therewith connected, mentioned in the conclusions of said Summons; with entry as at the term of Whitsunday Eighteen hundred and sixty-four, and warrandice from fact and deed allenarly.

Second. That the said first party shall dispone and convey to the said second party the Superiority of the Seven hundred and thirty-two, or thereby, square yards of ground mentioned in the conclusions of said Summons as having been feued by the said first party, or their predecessors in office, to Andrew Howden, Writer to the Signet; Archibald Gibson, Accountant, and others; together with the feu-duty and ground rent or annual of Thirty-five pounds sterling per annum thereto attached; with entry as at the term of Whitsunday Eighteen hundred and sixty-four, and warrandice from fact and deed allenarly.

Third. That the said first party shall dispone and convey and assign to, and in favour of, the said second party, the *solum* of Forrest Road or Street, so far as they have any right or interest therein; with warrandice from fact and deed allenarly, and with entry as at the term of Whitsunday Eighteen hundred and sixty-four.

Fourth. That the said second party shall assign and make over to and in favour of the said first party all and any right or claim which they have, or may be held to have, to the property, funds, or mortifications belonging to or connected with the Hospital of Saint Paul's Work, or to any of the funds mortified by Robert Johnston of the Parish of St Ann's, Blackfriars, London, or to any of the funds and mortifications included in the foresaid Summons, and that the said second party shall do whatever may be legally required, to enable the said first party to vindicate and make good the claims and rights above referred to, and shall allow the said first party to use their name in any legal proceedings for that purpose, but always at the expense of the said first party.

Fifth. That the said second party renounce and discharge, as at Whitsunday Eighteen hundred and sixty-four, all right or claim to the sum of Fifty-two pounds ten shillings, hitherto annually paid to them, and to their predecessors in the administration of the funds, for support of the poor of the City Parish of Edinburgh, by the said first party, for the burial of paupers.

Sixth. That the said second party shall assign and make over to and in favour of the said first party, all and any claims or rights which they may have, or may be held to have, to or in the lands, properties, revenues, funds, and effects presently vested in or held by the said first party, as the Trustees, Administrators, and Governors of the Trinity Hospital of Edinburgh, with warrandice from fact and deed allenarly; and that the said second party shall do whatever may be legally required to enable the said first party to vindicate and make good the claims and rights above referred to, and shall allow the said first party to use their name in any legal proceedings for that purpose, but always at the expense of the said first party.

Lastly. We, the said parties hereto, mutually bind ourselves to execute and deliver to each other all deeds necessary for the purpose of implementing and giving effect to the foregoing heads of Agreement. And in case any disputes or differences may arise between us, in regard to the meaning or effect of said heads of Agreement, or in regard to the nature or terms of the deeds which it will be necessary for us respectively to grant in implement thereof, or in regard to the expense of executing such deeds, or any other expenses herewith connected, we hereby agree to submit and refer the same to the amicable decision of Edward Strathearn Gordon, Esquire, Advocate, whom failing of Andrew Rutherfurd Clark, Esquire, Advocate, whom failing of George Monro, Equire, Advocate.—In Witness whereof these presents, written by Alexander Wright Grant, Clerk to Millar, Allardice and Robson, Law Agents and Conveyancers, Edinburgh, are subscribed in duplicate as follows, viz., by George Greig, Inspector of Poor of the City Parish of Edinburgh, for and on behalf of the Parochial Board of said Parish, at Edinburgh, upon the Thirteenth day of November Eighteen hundred and sixty-eight, before these witnesses, Andrew Ferrier, Clerk to the said Parochial Board, and William Morton, Apprentice to George Cairns, Solicitor at Law, Edinburgh, and by Peter Miller, Esquire, Bailie, and Preses, of the Town Council of Edinburgh, elected in absence of the Lord Provost, who is at present furth of Scotland, and James David Marwick, Town Clerk of Edinburgh, in name and by authority of the Magistrates and remanent members of the Town Council, present in Council at Edinburgh upon the Twelfth day of January Eighteen hundred and sixty-nine, before these witnesses, Robert Beatson, Writer in Edinburgh, and Robert Renwick, Clerk to the said James David Marwick. (Signed) P. Miller, Bailie and Preses; J. D. Marwick, Town Clerk; G. Greig, Inspr.; Rob. Beatson, Witness; Rob. Renwick, Witness; And. Ferrier, Witness; Wm. Morton, Witness.

CHAPTER XXIII.

A NOTABLE YEAR—THE CHURCH TO BE BUILT.

THE year 1869 was a notable one for the Governors of Trinity Hospital Charity. As was mentioned in the last chapter, on the 22d January of that year, the Parochial Managers had not only abandoned their claim to the management of the Charity and the control of its funds, but they allowed the mortification of Paul's Work to be utilised as a part, small though it be, of the Trinity Hospital benefaction. During the following month (February) the House of Lords had given its final decision, that no more than £7000 should be expended upon the building of the new Church, if even so much should be required. Their Lordships had also ordained that all the surplus funds and accumulations should be devoted to the charity, and they likewise concurred in the proposal that the Governors were not bound to rebuild the Hospital, but to devote the money to granting sums of out-door relief, to those who had previously the benefit of the House, or who in the meantime had been added to the roll of beneficiaries.

The Lord Provost, Magistrates, and Town Council, as Governors of Trinity Hospital, on the 21st May of the same year, presented a Petition to the Court of Session, to apply the judgment of the House of Lords, together with a minute for the said party of date 2d July 1869, and their Lordships of the First Division, on the last day of the summer session (viz. 20th July) pronounced the following interlocutor:—"Remit to Norman Macpherson, Esquire, Advocate, Professor of the Law of Scotland in the University of Edinburgh, to inquire and report—(1st) From what sources the various Funds forming the Capital of the Charity, called Trinity College, or Trinity Hospital, have been derived, and the original and present amount thereof; (2) The mode in which these Funds have been from time to time, and are at present, invested; (3) The Terms and Conditions of any Grants or Mortifications which have from time to time been made by private individuals in favour of the Charity, or of the Trustees of the Charity; (4) By whom, and in what manner, and from what class of persons, the Beneficiaries have been from time to time selected, and, in particular, whether any, and what rights of selecting or nominating Beneficiaries have been exercised, or claim to be exercised, by parties other than the Magistrates and Council as Trustees of the Charity? (5) How many out-door Pensioners have from time to time been admitted to the benefits of the Charity? (6) What allowances have from time to time been paid to such out-door Pensioners, and upon what principle such allowances appear to have been fixed; (7) What has been the Gross Annual Income of the Charity since the Old Hospital was removed; what Deductions have been made, or fall to be made, therefrom; and what has been the Free Annual Income applicable and applied for behoof of the Beneficiaries? (8) Any other fact or matter which may appear to the Reporter to be material or useful for the information of the Court in settling a Scheme for the future Administration and

Application of the Funds of the Charity. (9) What Scheme the Reporter would recommend to the Court as expedient and proper to be adopted for future application and administration, having reference to the Terms of the Charters, Grants, and Mortifications in favour of the Charity, and the judgments of this Court, and the House of Lords in the present and relative proceedings; and authorised the Reporter to take the assistance of an accountant, or other person of skill, in so far as he may find such assistance necessary for the due execution of this Remit; and to hear parties interested, who may desire to be heard, and to require production or exhibition of all writings and documents pertinent to the inquiry; and for this purpose grant diligence against havers, and commission to the Reporter to take their evidence and receive their exhibits as accords."

(Signed) "JOHN INGLIS, *I.P.D.*"

On the 15th July 1874, about five years after the above Remit, the learned Professor had his Report printed and boxed for the use of the Court of Session. It was a document of 136 quarto pages, with an Appendix of 118 pages additional. It gave rise to considerable discussion before the Court, particularly in regard to the benefaction called the Alexander Fund; and the matter was not finally adjusted until 17th February 1880. Meantime, the procedure which followed upon it was to the effect, that—

The First Division of the Court, on 18th July 1874, allowed Professor Macpherson's Report and Appendix to be seen by the defenders, the Magistrates and Town Council, and ordained them to lodge Objections by the third sederunt day in October, then next. These Objections were accordingly lodged on the 17th day of October, and, on the 20th day of the same month the Court pronounced an interlocutor, appointing Professor Macpherson's Report and Appendix thereto, with the defenders' Objections, to be put to the roll.

The case was in due course heard before the First Division of the Court, and strange to say, for a second time, on the last day of the summer session, another Trinity Hospital decision is again arrived at. On 20th July 1875,—"The Lords having resumed consideration of the Petition to apply the judgment of the House of Lords, with the Report of Professor Macpherson, and heard counsel,—Find that the funds mortified by Master James Alexander in the year 1695 have been hitherto held, administered, and applied by the petitioners, in the same way as the Funds belonging to the Trinity Hospital, and have been immixed with and dealt with as part of the funds of the said Hospital: Find that in terms of the said James Alexander's Mortification, the funds mortified by him fall to be held and administered by the Lord Provost, Magistrates, and Council of the City of Edinburgh, and the ministers of the said city, present and to come, and to be applied in the first place, in relief of poor persons of the founder's kindred; in the second place, in relief of poor persons of the name of Alexander, and lastly in relief of other persons, all as directed by his deed of mortification, dated 23d October 1695: Find that, for this purpose, it is necessary to ascertain the present amount of the capital of the said funds mortified by the said James Alexander, and to set apart the same to be administered and applied as aforesaid: Find that in the year 1700 the said funds amounted in all to £2270, and that the said funds to that amount have been immixed as aforesaid with the funds and property of the Trinity Hospital, from an early period down to the present time, and must be held to have participated proportionally with the said funds and property in the increase of value of the aggregate funds and property between the year 1700 and the year 1873: Remit of new to Professor Macpherson to ascertain the value of the whole funds and property of the said Hospital, as in the year 1700, drawing back to the said date, the value of all additional gifts and legacies received by the Hospital after the year 1700, on such terms as may seem reasonable; also to ascertain and fix the amount or value of the whole aggregate funds and property as in the year 1873, and to report what is the present amount of the said Alexander's Funds taken in the same proportion to the present value of the whole Hospital funds and property in 1700, ascertained as aforesaid: And, having considered the recommendations of the Reporter on pages 124 and 132 of the Report, and the Objections thereto, No. 73 of process,* Approve of the first four heads of the said recommendations; as regards the 5th and 6th heads, delete the words 'or Leith'; in the 7th head, vary the recommendation by declaring that the salary of the medical officer shall not be less than £105; Vary, in like manner, the 8th head, by declaring that the salary of the lady visitor shall not be less than £63; Sustain the objections to the 9th and 10th heads of the recommendations; Vary the 11th head, by striking out the words, 'subject to the general rule as to maximum income'; Sustain the objections to the 12th, 13th, and 14th heads; in place of the 17th head, substitute the words 'private rights of patronage can only be exercised after the lapse of twelve months from the death of the last presentee'; *Quoad ultra*, approve of the recommendations of the Reporter, and remit to him of new to prepare a scheme for the administration of the Trinity Hospital, and its funds and estate, and also a separate scheme for the administration of the Alexander Mortification: Appoint counsel to be heard on the question raised as to the appropriation of a sum of £4000, and also on the question whether the administration and patronage both of the Trinity Hospital and also of the Alexander Mortification ought not

* These refer to the future administration of the charity, which will fall afterwards to be specially dealt with. *Vide* page 355 of this Volume.

to be vested for the future in a Committee or Committees of the whole body of Trustees or Governors: And, in order to the due execution of the Remits aforesaid, renew the powers and authority conferred on the Reporter by the interlocutor of 29th June 1869."

(Signed) "JOHN INGLIS, *I.P.D.*"

On the 30th December 1875, the case was again heard, and the following interlocutor was pronounced:—"The Lords, having resumed consideration of the same, and heard counsel on the questions reserved by the interlocutor of 20th July 1875,—Appoint intimation to be made to the Lord Advocate, in terms of the 16th Section of the Trusts (Scotland) Act, 1867."

(Signed) "JOHN INGLIS, *I.P.D.*"

A note for the Lord Advocate was thereafter lodged on 24th January 1876, which after reciting the above interlocutor, stated that his Lordship had considered this process, and in terms of the 16th Section of the Trusts (Scotland) Act, 1867, he appears and intervenes for the interests of the charity, or any object of the trust or the public interest.

On the 8th January 1876, the Court appointed the case to be put to the Summar Roll, and on the 21st day of the said month, the case was heard, and an interlocutor pronounced relative to the sum of £4000 advanced by the Governors for the construction of Regent Bridge and Regent Road, towards the formation of an access road across the Calton Hill, when a further remit was made to Professor Macpherson on the point. The Professor lodged another Report on the subject on 3d March 1877, and on 19th March of the same year, the Court decided adversely to the Governors.*

* This matter has already been fully explained in pages 199-202 of this Volume.

Returning again to the question of the Alexander Fund, it may be stated that on 7th July 1877 Professor Macpherson lodged a third Report, dated 30th June 1877, as following out the remit made to him by the interlocutor of 20th July 1875,—(1) in regard to the present amount of the Alexander Fund; and (2) as to an amended scheme for the administration of Trinity Hospital, and likewise a separate scheme for the administration of the Alexander Fund.

On the 10th July 1877, the Court appointed the case to be put to the roll, with the Report of Professor Macpherson, and on the 19th of the same month (being time one day before the close of the summer session), an interlocutor was pronounced, allowing the defenders to lodge objections to the same. This was done on the 26th October, and the Court on the following day appointed the case to be put to the Summar Roll.

After hearing counsel, the following was the judgment of the Court of Session :—"*Edinburgh, 19th March* 1878.—The Lords, having resumed consideration of the cause, with the Report by Professor Macpherson, dated 7th July 1877, in answer to the remit contained in the interlocutor of the Court, dated 20th July 1875, and Objections thereto for the defenders, No. 123 of process, and heard counsel for the defenders,—Find that, in ascertaining the value of the whole funds and property administered by the defenders as Governors of the Hospital in 1700, no account is to be taken of the Trinity College Church, or of the Trinity College ouildings, or of any lands held and possessed by the Governors for the Hospital in the year 1700, and thereafter retained by them *in forma specifica;* and, on the other hand, find that, in ascertaining the value of said whole funds and property in the year 1873, no account is to be taken of the prices received by the defenders for the said Church and for the said Hospital buildings (including the price of a servitude in favour of the said Hospital building mentioned in the said Report), inasmuch as such prices are of known amount, and either have been kept separate, or are readily separable from the aggregate funds and property belonging to the Alexander Mortification: Find that the price or prices of parts of the lands held and possessed by the defenders in 1700, but since sold, must be included in the account of the value of the said whole funds and property in the year 1873, inasmuch as the said price or prices have been immixed with the aggregate funds and property which comprehend the funds and property of the Alexander Mortification; and, on the other hand, that in ascertaining the value of the said whole funds and property in the year 1700, the said price or prices must be drawn back to the said date, on the same terms on which additional gifts and legacies received since 1700 are to be drawn back as hereinafter directed: Find that the lands acquired by the defenders, as Governors, since the year 1700, by purchase, and not by donation or mortification, must be taken into account in ascertaining the value of the said aggregate funds and property in the year 1873: Approve of the valuation ascertained and reported by Professor Macpherson, and appoint the value of the said lands to be taken at £640 per acre in the year 1873: Find that the sum of £5730, 9s. 2d., which the defenders are appointed by interlocutor of this date to restore to the Trinity Hospital, but without interest, is to be reckoned as part of the said aggregate funds and property as existing in the year 1873: Find that the mode adopted by the Accountant, and reported by Professor Macpherson, of drawing back to the year 1700, the value of all additional gifts and legacies received by the Governors of the Hospital since 1700, and immixed with the said aggregate funds and property, is a reasonable and equitable mode, and approve thereof accordingly, as applicable not only to the said additional gifts and legacies, but also to the price or prices obtained for portions of the lands held and possessed by the Governors in 1700, and subsequently sold: Further, in accordance with the above finding, sustain the first and second objections stated by the defenders to the Report: Find that the third objection has been obviated by the above findings: Repel the other objections, and decern: Remit of new to Professor Macpherson to prepare, with the assistance of the Accountant, a state showing the amount as in 1700 of the Trinity Hospital Estate and of the Alexander Fund respectively, and the amount of the said two estates or funds respectively in the year 1873, upon the principles settled by the previous interlocutor of 20th July 1875."

(Signed on 20th March 1878) "JOHN INGLIS, *I.P.D.*"

On 5th July 1878, Professor Macpherson lodged a fourth Report, showing the amount of the Trinity Hospital Estate and the Alexander Fund, respectively, as at 1700 and at 1873, according to the principles laid down in the foregoing interlocutor. According to the Professor, the amount of the Alexander Fund at 1700 was only £2270, 0s. 8d.; while in 1873 it had attained to £30,537, 19s. 0d.

On the 9th July 1878, the Court pronounced the following interlocutor:—"The Lords allow the fourth Report of Professor Macpherson, No. 130 of process, to be seen till Thursday next, and appoint the case to be put to the Summar Roll on Friday next."

(Signed) "JOHN INGLIS, *I.P.D.*"

Another interlocutor was pronounced for hearing counsel; but further proceedings were stopped by notice having been given of an appeal to the House of Lords, in which the appellants obtained an order of service on the respondents (pursuers) and on the Lord Advocate, dated 12th July 1878. The Lord Advocate, however, intimated to the appellants that he did not intend to appear and intervene in the appeal, in order to support the judgment of the Court of Session.

The scheme for the future administration of the charity was therefore postponed, pending this Appeal.

But the decision of the House of Lords was of a dual nature. Whatever differences might arise in regard to the future management and control of the charity, it was quite otherwise in regard to the Church. The limited sum placed at the disposal of the Governors, put it quite out of the criticism of antiquaries and æsthetic gentlemen to cavil with the plans of any church which was to be erected. The Calton Hill site was dropped by its backers, and it is understood some of them lost money by the transaction.

The House of Lords had decreed that a sum of not more than £7000 should be applied to the object; and as if to preserve the funds of the charity, and keep the Governors on the safe side, it was added "if even so much be required." In applying the judgment, the Court of Session ordained that *not less than* £7000 should be spent. Such a decision might be within their powers; but it was scarcely following out the desires of the Appellate Lords.

Again the site of Ireland's Woodyard came to the front; but it was denounced as in a hollow, and in a low-lying locality, with bad service of light. Against this was quoted, by the supporters of the site, the lines from Milton's well-known poem, *Il Penseroso.*

> And love the high embowèd roof
> With antique pillars massy-proof.
> And stonèd windows richly dight
> Casting a dim religious light.
>
> There let the pealing organ blow,
> To the full-voiced quire below

NEW TRINITY COLLEGE CHURCH, JEFFREY STREET.

To face page [illegible]

THE OLD APSE OF TRINITY COLLEGE CHURCH RESTORED.

[To face page [illegible].]

In service high and anthems clear,
As may with sweetness, through mine ear,
Dissolve me into ecstasies,
And bring all Heaven before mine eyes.

It was of no use. The Lords of the First Division would have none of it. It had to be abandoned. It was not, however, a bad investment. It was purchased by the Magistrates and Town Council, as Governors of Trinity Hospital (per Disposition dated 19th April 1848, with entry to the subjects at Whitsunday 1853) for £1700. Thirty years thereafter the same subjects were sold to the North British Railway Company for £5900, or a profit of £4200. The Trinity Hospital charity was, therefore, a great gainer.

At the time referred to, Jeffrey Street was being formed, under the improvement scheme of the then Lord Provost, William Chambers. He suggested to the Town Council to offer for the approval of the Court a site in the centre of the south side of Jeffrey Street on the line of what used to be Chalmers' Close, which led from High Street to the old Physic Gardens. One merit this site possessed; it was within the parish. It began to be erected in 1872, from drawings prepared by the late Mr John Lessels, architect. It is an oblong structure, with details in the Norman Gothic style, with a tower and spire 115 feet in height. It was opened for divine service in October 1877, and it is seated for 900 persons. The ancient baptismal font that stood in the vestry of the Church of Mary of Gueldres is placed in the lobby.

In the course of the construction of the Church, Mr Lessels endeavoured to make use of as many of the old stones of the ancient edifice as could be made available for the purpose, and the old apse has been restored *in toto*. This is perhaps the most interesting and picturesque part of the whole building. But it cost the City

2 S

somewhat over £2000 beyond the sum authorised by the House of Lords. This came, as matter of course, from the Common Good Fund.

It may be mentioned that the ancient baptismal and Communion plate of the Trinity College Church are very valuable, and the former is depicted in the late Sir George Harvey's well-known picture of the "Covenanters' Baptism," and like the Communion table date from shortly after the Reformation, and have been the gifts of various pious individuals.

CHAPTER XXIV.

THE ALEXANDER CASE IN THE COURT OF SESSION.

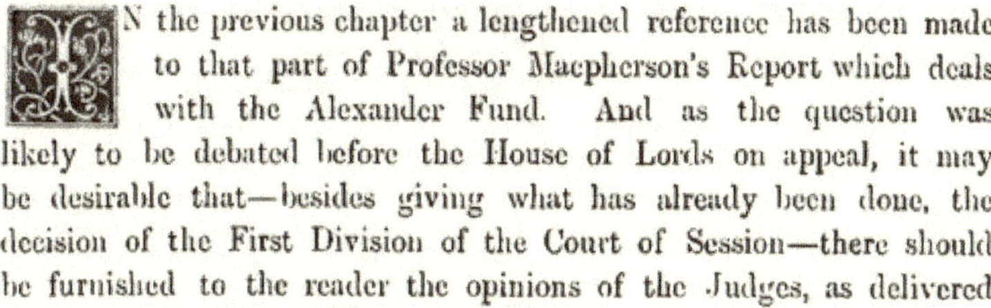

IN the previous chapter a lengthened reference has been made to that part of Professor Macpherson's Report which deals with the Alexander Fund. And as the question was likely to be debated before the House of Lords on appeal, it may be desirable that—besides giving what has already been done, the decision of the First Division of the Court of Session—there should be furnished to the reader the opinions of the Judges, as delivered by them on Tuesday, July 20, 1875 :—

THE LORD PRESIDENT (Inglis).—My Lords, the remit under which we are acting in this case is contained in a judgment of the House of Lords pronounced so long ago as 15th February 1861. A great many causes have combined to produce delay in carrying out that remit. After the cause was resumed in this Court, a further interlocutor of a very important nature was pronounced on 7th December 1866, and that again was carried to appeal; and of course during the dependence of that appeal no proceedings could take place in this Court. But in 1869 a petition was presented by the Lord Provost, Magistrates, and Council of the City of Edinburgh, and the remit set out in that petition, on which we are now proceeding, is expressed in the following terms:—"It is declared," &c. [Reads.] Upon considering this remit, we found that a very extensive inquiry into the condition of the Trinity Hospital funds at stake would be necessary, in order to enable us to carry it out; and accordingly, upon 20th July 1869, we made a remit to Professor Macpherson, and the heads of the inquiry which we directed him to make may be stated shortly. He was to inquire, first of all, of what capital fund the charity consisted, and from what sources it was derived; in the second place, the manner in which the funds are invested; in the third place, the terms and conditions of any grants or mortifications that have been made in favour of the Hospital by private individuals subsequent to the institution of the Hospital; in the fourth place, who were the beneficiaries, and how they were selected; in the fifth place, how many out-door pensioners had been admitted to the benefit of the charity; in the sixth place, what allowances had been made to them, and on what principle these were fixed; in the seventh place, what has been the gross annual income of the charity since the old Hospital has been removed, and what deductions have been made or fall to be made therefrom, and what has been the free annual income applicable to the beneficiaries. We directed him also to inquire generally into any matters that appeared to him to be necessary to enable us to frame a scheme in terms of the remit of the House of Lords, and to suggest the terms of such a scheme as occurred to him. We have now before us a very able, and necessarily also a very elaborate, report by Professor Macpherson. The questions which are thereby raised for our consideration are, fortunately, not very numerous, and I shall endeavour to notice them in the natural order in which they occur.

The most prominent and perhaps the most interesting question which is raised by this report relates to what is called the Alexander Fund. Now, that is a mortification which was made by a person of the name of Alexander, by two several deeds of gift, the first of which is dated 23d October 1695; and it is necessary to attend to the terms of that deed in order to see distinctly what is the nature and what are the conditions of the gift thereby made. [Refers in detail to the provisions of the deed.] By another deed an addition is made to this mortification, but it is not necessary to refer particularly to that, as it falls to be ruled upon precisely the same footing as the money destined by this deed.

Now, it appears that for a very long period, how far back it is very difficult to say, the funds of the Alexander Mortification have been mixed up with the other funds of the Hospital, and the income arising from the Alexander Mortification and the income of the Hospital have been administered together and for the same purpose. It would appear that the order of preference suggested by Mr Alexander has not been observed; that his own kindred and persons of the name of Alexander have not been preferred to other indigent persons; and that the income arising from the Alexander Mortification has been used just like the other funds of the Hospital, for the support of indigent persons generally. It also appears that the Lord Provost, Magistrates, and Council, as representing the community of Edinburgh, who have the sole right of administration of the funds of the Hospital proper, have assumed to themselves also the entire administration of the Alexander Fund without associating with them the ministers of Edinburgh, who are also named in this deed as jointly with them patrons and administrators and feoffees of the trust. The consequence of this has been, that the fund is no longer distinguishable in point of administration and as regards the manner in which the accounts are kept; and the referee suggests to us whether it is necessary that the funds of this Alexander Mortification should be separate, and administered as a separate trust, or whether we can sanction, what has hitherto been done, the mixing up of the Alexander Fund with the other funds of the Hospital, and allow the Lord Provost, Magistrates, and Council alone, to administer the whole. Now, my Lords, I confess I do not entertain much doubt about this. The length of time during which this has been going on, I am afraid, cannot be allowed to have any effect on this question. There can be no doubt that it was an entire departure from the deed of mortification for the Magistrates and Council alone, without the other feoffees of the trust and administrators, to take upon themselves the administration of this fund. There can be just as little doubt that it was a contravention of the deed of mortification to have no consideration for those claims of preference which might have been put forward by the kindred of the mortifier or donor, or by poor persons of the name of Alexander. And, lastly, it is just as clear—as a sequence, indeed, of those other points—that the mixing up of this fund with the funds of the Hospital generally was not in accordance with the intention and design of the founder; and that being so, it follows of necessity, I think, according to all the principles upon which we have been in use to administer charitable trusts, that this must be set right, that the Alexander Mortification must form the subject of a separate administration, and must be devoted to the purposes for which it was destined by the founder. The principles upon which we have proceeded in such cases are nowhere better expounded than they are in the case of *The Presbytery of Dundee* v. *The Magistrates of Dundee*, both in this Court and in the House of Lords, 20 Dunlop, 849; 1 Macpherson, 228; and 1 Macpherson, 483. Now, applying those principles here, the first thing we have got to ascertain is, what is or ought to be the present amount of the Alexander Mortification? and how is this to be ascertained? We are told by the reporter that the means of a precise accounting are in existence, and this appears to be so. The funds left by Mr Alexander were invested in particular securities, and those securities were not called up or changed until about the middle of the last century, and we have distinct evidence of what the amount of the fund was at that time. Now, if we proceeded upon the principle of a strict accounting against the Magistrates here as trustees, of course the way of bringing out the balance would be to charge them with this capital, as at the date when we find it in their hands, and then charge them with the income as it accrued, and let them discharge themselves the best way they could. But it rather appears to me that in a case of this kind, and looking to the nature of the trust, and the way in which it was necessarily administered, that would be too strict a principle of accounting; and while I think it is our undoubted duty to separate this Alexander Fund, and secure that it shall be administered as a separate trust in all time coming, we may deal with bygones in a way more favourable for the administrators of Trinity Hospital. The income of the fund has apparently been spent, and it has not been spent, so far as we can see, upon purposes alien to the intentions and wishes of the founder. His wishes and intentions have only been to a certain extent disregarded; that is to say, the fund has not been in the right hands of administration, and there has not been in the selection of the objects of the bounty that order of preference which he desired. But still the fair result of the evidence appears to be, that, at all events for a very long period, the income of the Alexander Fund was bestowed upon poor and indigent persons of the kind generally here contemplated. It was employed, along with the income of the other funds of the Hospital generally, for such purposes; and therefore I cannot see that there can be, especially against a shifting body of trustees like the Magistrates and Town Council of Edinburgh, any responsibility for the expenditure of that income. It is not alleged that they appropriated this fund to their own purposes as individuals, or that they appropriated it to the uses of the Corporation of the City of Edinburgh. If that had been so, it would have raised a question of a very different kind. But that does not appear to have been so, and therefore I incline to the opinion that, in so far as regards the past income of this fund, there is no room for any accounting at all.

But then the next question comes to be—How are we to ascertain what sum now in the hands of those trustees will adequately and fairly represent the capital of the Alexander Fund? Now, that is a question of some difficulty; but at the same time I think it admits of a solution. We know that the Alexander Fund was invested upon two bonds, as it was originally settled by the donor himself—the one upon the Annandale estates for £1725, 17s. 8¼d., and the other upon the Westerhall estates for £511, 13s. of sterling money; for I am speaking now of the amount as converted into sterling money and actually paid up in the course of last century. These two sums amount together to £2270. Now, the mortification was in the year 1695, and it may certainly be assumed, without any great stretch, that that money came into the hands of the Hospital Trustees by the beginning of the last century—say in the year 1700. Therefore they were possessed in 1700 of this capital sum as representing the Alexander Mortification. They were at the same time possessed of a very considerable estate belonging to the Hospital, and it is not at all difficult to ascertain what the amount of that estate was. In that way we discover what was the relative or comparative value of those two estates in the year 1700. But it is very apparent upon the face of the report before us, and the abundant information which we have on the subject, that this joint mixed estate, consisting to a large extent of the funds and estate of the Hospital proper, but also to a more limited extent of Alexander's Fund, has largely increased in amount and value between the year 1700 and the present day. Now it seems to me that this estate so jointly administered having greatly increased in value between those two dates, the Alexander Fund must be entitled to participate in that prosperity. Thus, supposing that in 1700 the estate of the Hospital proper amounted to £10,000 in value, and the Alexander Fund to £2000 in value, making together £12,000, but that at the present day the joint estate, as it appears in the hands of the administrators, amounts to £50,000 in value, then that £50,000 must be apportioned between the same funds in the same proportion that they bore to each other in the year 1700; that is, as 10 to 2. I am taking the figures I have mentioned as entirely suppositious, not supposing they represent the entire value, by any means. On the contrary, the value, as we see, is very much greater. Now there may be some little difficulty in adjusting the precise way in which this result is to be brought about. In the first place, the Alexander Fund in 1700 consisted of money lent out on heritable security; but the Hospital estate consisted to a very considerable extent of heritable property, and therefore to institute any proper comparison between the two estates in the year 1700, it would be necessary to convert the heritable estate of the Hospital into money, and that must be done upon some fixed rate. That, however, is not a matter of very great difficulty. But then there occurs also this consideration: The Hospital estate proper has increased very much in amount in the interval between 1700 and the present day by additional gifts and mortifications, and therefore it would not be fair to the Hospital to compare its estate as it stood in 1700 with the Alexander estate as it stood at that time, and then to take that proportion for dividing the fund as it now stands, because the Hospital estate has been added to very largely by benefactions of other individuals, whereas the Alexander estate has been stationary. Then it is not possible to take in those additional sums which the Hospital estate has received at different times as of precisely the amount which they were at the time they were received. It is necessary, in order to bring out a proper comparison such as I am suggesting, that the value of those additional donations to the Hospital shall be taken as at 1700, and so it becomes necessary to draw back to the year 1700 the value of the additional mortifications and gifts, and it would be necessary in that way to fix at what rate of interest that drawback is to be made, and also whether the interest is to be simple interest or compound interest. It is obvious that, so far as the Hospital is concerned, and the interest of its inmates and beneficiaries, the larger its estate can be made in the year 1700, the better for it now in this question with the Alexander Fund; and on the other hand, that, so far as the Alexander Fund is concerned, the more the value of the Hospital funds can be brought down in the year 1700, the greater will be the share of the present joint estate to which the Alexander Fund would be entitled in a division at the present day. Therefore the fixing of these things,—first of all, the rate of conversion of the heritable estate into money as at 1700; and secondly, the rate of interest at which the additional donations are to be drawn back to 1700, and whether that is to be simple or compound interest,—are questions of very great importance, and upon which it is not desirable to come to any premature or rash decision. I am only for the present endeavouring to explain the principles upon which this ascertainment of the Alexander Fund is to be made; therefore what I should suggest would be that we should fix some period, say the year 1873, or some recent period of that kind, at which the division of the existing aggregate estate is to be made, and that we should arrive at the result, when we have once got the requisite materials, simply by a sum in proportion; because, as the Hospital funds stood to the Alexander Fund in 1700, so they should stand in 1873; and the only matter we require in order to get our result, is to fix the different figures which shall enter into that proportion. The fund being ascertained, it appears to be, and I believe it to be, that for the future it must be administered, not by the Lord Provost, Magistrates, and Council alone, but by those trustees, with the addition of the ministers of Edinburgh, who are named in the deed. The circumstance that the ministers of Edinburgh have never claimed to be conjoined in this administration, is of no consequence. No persons of an official character can give away the rights of their successors in office under a trust of this kind, and therefore the trust must be constituted and administered now as provided by the truster in his deed of mortification; and this fund, which is to be placed in their hands, and administered by them for the future, must be administered not as part of the Hospital estate, but precisely in terms of the directions of Mr Alexander in his deed of mortification. There must be a preference for his kindred, if there be any living; there must be a preference for indigent persons of the name of Alexander, if any such apply, in terms of the deed; and it is only after the fulfilment of those requirements that the remainder of the fund can be used for indigent persons generally.

Now, that seems to be all that it is necessary for us to determine at the present stage, because until we have the precise figures before us, enabling us to fix the amount of the Alexander Fund, we cannot proceed any further.

There is another matter of very considerable importance, but about which, although it is distinctly stated in the report of Professor Macpherson, we did not hear any observations from the counsel for the Magistrates. I refer to a sum of £4000, which is said to have been expended in payment, *pro parte*, of the new road across the Calton Hill, in the year 1813. Now, this sum stands in a very peculiar position. I am not at present going to give any opinion as to what should be done about it, because I think that would be wrong, without giving the Magistrates and Council an opportunity of being heard on the matter. But as the point is stated on page 107 of Professor Macpherson's Report, it seems from it that the Magistrates were under obligation by an Act of Parliament to spend a certain sum of money—apparently £8000—out of the Corporation funds, for the promotion of an improvement consisting of the making of this road, the building of the new jail, and some other things, and that of that £8000 they made the Trinity Hospital contribute £4000. Now, if that be so, it is not very easy to see how the indigent persons who were to be maintained out of the Hospital funds were to be benefited by the making of a new road across the Calton Hill; and if by the expenditure of that sum of £4000 out of the Trinity Hospital funds the estate of the Corporation of the City of Edinburgh was to that extent benefited, it would seem to follow from the ordinary principles applicable to such cases that the Corporation must be answerable to replace that sum. However, I do not wish to be understood as giving any opinion upon that subject at present. It is a very important point, and obviously must be a point involving pretty large liability; and we should desire, before disposing of it, to have all the assistance we possibly can have from the counsel for the Magistrates.

These are the only two matters of very general importance, I think, that it is necessary to determine, as raised by Professor Macpherson's Report; but there are certain matters besides, connected with this scheme, which the reporter has suggested, to which objections have been lodged by the Magistrates, and I shall endeavour to state as shortly as I can the conclusions I have arrived at on these. The suggestions of the reporter begin on page 124 of his report. They are recommendations as to the future application and administration of the charity—that is, the Trinity Hospital funds, of course, apart from the Alexander Fund. The first four of these suggestions are not objected to at all on the part of the Magistrates, and they seem to be very well judged. But the fifth and sixth heads of the recommendations seem to be liable to an objection in respect of the introduction of the reference to Leith, and the Magistrates say that that implies an extension of the benefits of the charity to persons in Leith as well as in Edinburgh, and that that is contrary to the terms of the foundation. I do not know whether that is precisely what the reporter had in view, but certainly, as the matter stands, it bears something of that appearance; and it rather appears to me that the simple way of getting the better of that difficulty is to omit the mention of Leith altogether, and let the matter stand as it is with that exception. In regard to the seventh head, the Magistrates do not seem to object to the appointment of a medical officer, but they think that his salary should not be fixed, but should be left to be varied according to the discretion of the trustees themselves. The object of the reporter in making this suggestion, I do not suppose to have been that the salary should be in all time coming 100 guineas a-year, because that would be a very unfavourable suggestion for the medical officer a hundred years hence; but if his salary is stated to be not less than 100 guineas, I think that would probably obviate all objection. There is a similar objection stated in regard to the salary of the lady visitor, who, it is suggested, should be appointed; and so far as the salary is concerned, that objection may be obviated in the same way. But then the Magistrates are of opinion that there should be no lady visitor, or, at all events, that they should be left to their own discretion to employ such an officer or not as they think fit. I believe your Lordships are all of opinion that the suggestions of the reporter in this respect ought to be adhered to, as a very useful and valuable suggestion. In the ninth article, which relates to the scales of allowance, the reporter proposes that in future, instead of the two scales of £20 and £10 now in use, there should be four scales, £25, £20, £15, and £10, it being in the power of the Governors to put those elected on whatever scale they think fit, on consideration of the ascertained circumstances of the applicant and the state of the pension roll. The Governors object to this proposal, and they are strongly of opinion that for the permanent administration of the charity there should be only two scales, the one scale being fixed at £15 instead of £10 as at present, and the other at £25 instead of £20 as at present. Now it rather appears to me, and I believe your Lordships are all agreed about that, that the suggestion of the reporter is too complicated, and that the more practical course is that selected by the Governors, that there should be two scales only, but raised, as they suggest, to £15 and £25 respectively. In regard to the 10th head of the recommendations, a considerable practical difficulty again suggests itself—viz., how it is to be ascertained what the person's income is from all sources. It would require a great deal of investigation, and it does not appear to us that the difficulty of making those inquiries, and the duty of making those inquiries, is one that can very well be laid upon the trustees of this fund. Upon the whole, we are inclined to think it is not desirable to introduce this condition, But it is quite right that, if a pensioner ceases to be a proper object of the charity, the charity should be withdrawn; and I do not think it is necessary to enact that as a part of any new scheme, because I presume that in this, as in all other charities, if a pensioner or recipient of bounty of this kind ceases to require relief, that relief must be withdrawn. The 11th article is a rule dependent on the adoption of the four scales of allowance, and therefore it will require to be modified in that respect. There does not seem to be objection to it in any other way. The 12th article also will require to be altered in conformity with the resolution to have only two scales. The 13th article is a little startling. The law is always very jealous of any interference with the freedom of marriage, and even people in the condition of pensioners on this fund cannot be deprived of the right of marrying if they see fit, notwithstanding that their age—not to be under fifty—seems rather to be a disqualification for entering into that happy taste. But it is not desirable, at all events, that the rule should be expressed as forfeiting the right to this fund upon marriage, because that is expressly enacting a penalty upon marriage. It certainly is a very fair subject for the consideration of the trustees of the charity that a person who is a pensioner upon their bounty has got married. It may indicate a change of circumstances altogether, and at all events it is a matter requiring investigation and consideration; and therefore, in place of enacting a forfeiture of this kind, we should be disposed rather to recommend that where marriage occurs in the case of one of the beneficiaries, his claim as a beneficiary of the charity shall be reconsidered by the trustees. The 14th article is, perhaps, a little imperfect, as is suggested by the Magistrates in their paper of objections. I presume that what the reporter meant was "supported by Parochial Boards in lunatic asylums;" and if that is the meaning of it, it seems quite right; but a person might be confined in a lunatic asylum and yet not be supported by the Parochial Authorities, and that might make a different case for consideration altogether. But with that addition—"supported by Parochial Boards in lunatic asylums"—the recommendation is quite right. Articles 15 and 16 seem to be quite unobjectionable. Article 17 is a little ambiguous. It may mean that private rights of patronage can only be exercised within twelve months after the death of the presentee, or it may mean that they can only be exercised after the lapse of twelve months.

Professor Macpherson.—I may mention that it is a condition in the grant of private patronage in every case in which it has been purchased.

The Lord President.—Is it so expressed?

Professor Macpherson.—It is, in every case.

The Lord President.—Still, it is not a very happy expression; but that absolves the reporter, at all events, from being the author of the words. What is meant, I understand, is that the right of patronage shall not be exercised till after the lapse of twelve months.

Professor Macpherson.—Yes.

The Lord President.—Then it may be expressed in this way:—"Private rights of patronage can only be exercised after the lapse of twelve months from the death of the last presentee." But, then, I do not know whether that might be held to apply to the presentations to the Alexander Mortification. If there were any chance of that, it would be necessary to except the Alexander Mortification from the operation of that rule; but perhaps it would hardly be supposed to apply to it.

Professor Macpherson.—It was not made a condition by the Magistrates of accepting the Alexander Fund; it was a condition of the right of patronage in the other cases.

The Lord President.—It might perhaps be right to add that the rule is not to apply to the Alexander Fund. The other suggestions of the reporter are not objected to by the Magistrates, and seem to be very suitable and well framed.

That, I think, exhausts the whole matter it is necessary to dispose of at present. But there is another question of general importance that has suggested itself to the minds of the Court in consultation, and which they wish to intimate to the parties, with a view to receiving any suggestions or any argument upon the subject that they may see fit to address to them. The trustees or governors of this charity are a very numerous body, and they would be still more numerous, as regards the Alexander Fund, by the addition of the ministers of Edinburgh in the future. The Court cannot help feeling that a charity of this kind would be more conveniently managed, and perhaps more beneficially managed, by a smaller number; and it would be quite within the power of the Court, in framing this scheme, to appoint that the administration of this charity should be in a committee of the whole body, to be chosen by the whole body. But as this is a topic that has not been hitherto discussed at all, and upon which we have not had the benefit of hearing the views of the Magistrates, we should still desire to do so. There are obvious considerations of convenience and advantage in favour of such a proposal, but there may be counter-considerations of equal or greater importance which have not occurred to the minds of the Court, and therefore we should be very sorry prematurely to pronounce any opinion upon the matter. But it will be understood that upon two matters we desire to hear further agreement and suggestion from the Magistrates—(1) With regard to that sum of £4000 which I have already mentioned, and (2) with regard to the propriety of providing that the administration of the charity shall be vested in a committee of the whole trustees, instead of being administered by the entire body. The other matter to which I have referred, connected with the framing of the scheme, will be very easily given effect to; and as regards the Alexander Fund it will be necessary, in order to ascertain what is the present capital sum upon the principles that I have endeavoured to explain, to make a further remit to Professor Macpherson and the accountant who shall be employed in the matter, to give us the requisite materials for carrying those principles into effect.

Lords Deas, Ardmillan, and Mure concurred.

Mr M'Laren.—Before your Lordships fix by interlocutor the mode or principle on which effect is to be given to your Lordships' judgment with regard to the question of accounting in the matter of the Alexander Mortification, a remark has occurred to me in reference to the mode of making allowance for the pecuniary legacies which have come into the Hospital funds since the year 1700. It is obvious that the inequality which these legacies would produce in the present proportions may be redressed in two ways,—either by taking the value of the legacies as at 1700, and thereby augmenting the capital sum at the credit of the Hospital as at that date, or those legacies having been simply invested in the ordinary way, and the income applied since that time—by deducting the amount of those legacies from the present value of the estate, and thereby diminishing the aggregate fund which is to be divisible between the Trinity Hospital and the Alexander Mortification.

The Lord President.—Deducting the amount as at present?

Mr M'Laren.—Yes. Suppose £20,000 had been left in legacies to the Hospital since 1700. You might just deduct £20,000 from the capital fund as at the present day, and divide the difference proportionally. Perhaps your Lordships will leave that point open for consideration; I would not like to say, without further inquiry, which view we would prefer.

The Lord President.—I should not like to foreclose any point upon which you desire to be heard. Perhaps we can deal with the matter in such a way as to give general instructions to the accountant. Your position is a very peculiar one now, because, according to the view of the Court, you are now divided, and you are in the position of representing both the general fund and the Alexander Fund, which seem to me to have conflicting interests.

Lord Deas.—Which fund are you speaking for now?

Mr M'Laren.—I want instructions simply as to the correct way of performing an arithmetical operation. It is quite right, of course, that the Magistrates should not any longer represent distinctively the interests of the Alexander Mortification, and perhaps some other body may be found to do so. I suppose Professor Macpherson will continue, under the remit, to look after the interests of the mortification.

The Lord President.—Yes; I think the interests of the Alexander Fund are very safe in his hands, without any separate appearance. I think that probably the proper way to proceed, as regards the Alexander Fund, would be to remit to the reporter substantially to give us the elements of that sum in proportion which we want, and he might also report any other mode of doing it that occurs to himself, or that might be suggested by the parties.

Mr M'Laren.—That will be quite satisfactory to us.

The Lord President.—I mean, any other mode than that mode which I suggested in the course of my observations. For example, suppose you were to say that the reporter is to value the heritable property of the Hospital, as at the year 1700, as worth 22 years' purchase, and suppose we were to say further, that he was to take into account the subsequent donations, drawing them back in value to the year 1700, at such rate of interest as he may suggest,—and also to give the alternate view,—and then to say that he should report any other mode of stating the proportions that occurs to him or that may be suggested.

Mr M'Laren.—There is also a question how far the Alexander Mortification would be entitled to participate in the heritable property specifically left to Trinity Hospital, —the original Trinity Hospital estate,—or whether it should only participate in the increase of any general funds which were afterwards invested. I believe the great part of the increase of this trust, as a whole, arises from the old Trinity lands having become available for building sites, and become more valuable. I think it would be a question for argument, whether the Alexander Mortification would be entitled to participate in that increase.

Lord Ardmillan.—The investments having been before the date of the mortification?

The Lord President.—Do you mean the original property of Trinity Hospital?

Mr M'Laren.—Yes. If your Lordships take that, as capitalised in 1700, at 22 years' purchase, the effect is to give to the Alexander Mortification a share of the benefit of all the increase in the Trinity Hospital property, over its capitalised value of 22 years' purchase in 1700,—in short, the conversion of agricultural land into building land, through causes no ways affected by the Alexander Fund.

The Lord President.—Yes, and for that and a great many other reasons that might be suggested, the mode of fixing the Alexander Fund is a rough one, but then you must keep in view that it is adopted for the purpose of saving you from a strict accounting. At the best, you know, anything of this kind must be very rough.

Mr M'Laren.—Of course it is impossible to have anything like an exact actual accounting, but according to the mode in which it is done, a very large alteration in the value of the special trust may be affected. But if your Lordships reserve this as open to us, that is all I desire.

The Lord President.—I think we can keep it open.

CHAPTER XXV.

THE ALEXANDER MORTIFICATION.

THE Alexander Mortification has of late years played so prominent a part in connection with the administration of the Trinity Hospital charity, that it seems requisite that special reference should be made to it. This is all the more desirable, inasmuch as the proceedings in the Court of Session have been fully recorded in the last chapter, and it seems reasonable that the present Governors and the friends of Trinity Hospital should be made acquainted with the grounds upon which the Town Council of the day considered it to be their duty, on the advice of the learned counsel whom they consulted, to carry this case to the House of Lords.

Mr James Alexander, who died in 1696, mortified or settled a sum of money in connection with Trinity Hospital, and the circumstances under which he gifted the money will appear evident in the statement which follows :—

1. The first and main point advocated in the appeal, was, whether the Alexander Fund had been improperly mixed with the funds of Trinity Hospital from 1700, and was therefore entitled to a proportionate share

of the increased value of all the lands purchased after that date by the Town Council. The result of this would be that, as already stated, according to Professor Macpherson, the Alexander Fund, which was a special fund, with a preference for the kin of the founder, or those who bore the same name, would be entitled to be credited with a capital sum of £30,537, 19s. 10d. as at 1873, whereas the original sum of the mortification amounted only as at 1700 to £2270, 0s. 8d. It should also be borne in mind that the interest of that sum had been duly applied every year. The result of the proposal was, therefore, prejudicial to the other beneficiaries of the Hospital, who had previously raised an action in the Law Courts to establish their rights which had been successful in the House of Lords in 1864.

The appellants denied that the Alexander Fund was mixed up with the Trinity Hospital funds in the way stated by the Court of Session, and was not therefore entitled to the increase.

The appellants considered it to be their duty to bring under the review of the House of Lords the whole findings of the Court of Session, in regard to the cases; but they specially refer to the cardinal finding of the Court below, wherein the Court held that in the year 1700, the said funds (*i.e.* the Alexander Fund) amounted in all to £2270, and that the said funds to that amount have been immixed, as aforesaid, with the funds and property of the Trinity Hospital, from an early period down to the present time, and must be held to have participated proportionally with the said funds and property in the increase of value of the aggregate funds and property, between the year 1700 and the year 1873.

If this finding is reversed, the subsequent findings in that interlocutor, and the findings in the subsequent interlocutor of 13th March 1878, relative to the amount of the Alexander Fund, and on the principles on which it is to be ascertained, must necessarily also be reversed.

The grounds upon which this finding was made by the Court, are stated in the opinion of the Lord President, already quoted.

Before examining the Lord President's views, it is desirable that the appellants' case should be stated.

The Print then goes on to narrate the origin of the charity, and its reconstruction after the Reformation, with the regulating charters of the charity. It states the object of the charity, and refers to the beidmen and the sick poor, who were lodged and maintained within the walls of the Hospital, and the boarding out of several who could not be allowed to live within the building.

It alludes to the fact that, since 1567, and almost exclusively since 1587, the institution had been under the sole management and control of the Magistrates and Town Council of the City of Edinburgh.

It then goes on to state that, in addition to its original property, it had received more than 140 separate mortifications or endowments, of the value of 200 merks or upwards, most of which were for the benefit of the poor of the Hospital generally, but some of which continued preferences in the first instance.

The origin of the Alexander Mortification is then referred to. It would appear that Mr James Alexander, son of the deceased Mr John Alexander, parson of Hoddam, granted two deeds of mortification. The first was dated 23d October 1695, and the second was an eik to that deed, dated also 23d October 1695. Both deeds were put on record on 25th February 1697. By the principal deed of mortification, the said James Alexander, on the narrative that certain debts were due to him by the Earl of Annandale and Sir James Johnstone of Westerhall, disponed to and in favour of the Trinity Hospital, and the poor thereof after specified, "and to John Miller, present thesaurer thereof, and succeeding thesaurers of the same, for the use and behove, and to the effect after specified," the sum of 40,000 merks Scots.

The yearly profit and interest of this sum Mr Alexander appointed to be employed "towards the accommodating and entertaining of twelve indigent persons,—viz., eight men and four women, or failzing the said number of men qualified, and applying in manner after mentioned, als many women in their place as will make up the full number; or failzing the said number of women, als many men qualified, and applying in manner after mentioned, as will make up the full number . . . . who have been of good reputation, and have not fallen into decay through their own vice or prodigalitie, to be received into the said Hospitall, being for the time unmarried, and not under fiftie years of age at their entre, and to remaine and continue unmarried in the said Hospitall during their lyfetime, and to be accomodate and entertained therein at the rate and expense of the other persons who are or shall be received in, and entertained upon the former mortificatione belonging to the said Hospitall."

The special qualifications of the beneficiaries are thus declared:—"That the patrons underwritten of this present mortification shall be obbleidged to receive into the benefite thereof such persons, men or women, qualified in manner foresaid. *First*, those of my own kindred, friends or relatives upon father or mother side; *secondlie*, those of my own sirname of Alexander, who shall apply for the benefite thereof, within the space of three score days next after any vacancies shall occur, and that whether they be burgesses of Edinburgh or not; and failzing thereof, such indigent persones qualified in manner foresaid, as the said patrons underwritten shall think fitt."

Then there follows a dispositive clause of certain specific securities or debts, being the debts due by the Earl of Annandale and Sir James Johnstone, estimated as amounting in all to 40,000 merks, "in favour of the said Hospitall, and indigent persones foresaid, and of the said John Miller, merchant in Edinburgh, present thesaurer of the said

Hospitall, and his successors in the said office of the samen, and patrons after specified as feoffees of trust and administrators for the use and behove of the said Hospitall and indigent persones foresaid."

With reference to the investment of the sum mortified, it was provided "That how often and whensoever the somes of money above mortified and disponed, or any part thereof, shall be uplifted by the said John Miller, thesaurer, and his successors in office, thesaurers of the said Hospitall, and patrons foresaid, they shall be bund and obblidged, likeas by their acceptation hereof they for themselves, and in name of their successors, bind and oblidge them and their successors in the said offices, als oft of new agane, to secure, wair, bestow, and employ the same upon sufficiente and well holdine land, or other good and sufficient securitie, for annual rent, payable to the said thesaurer of the said Hospitall and patrons thereof and their successors, in name and behalf and for the use and behove of the said Hospitall and indigent persones foresaid."

The patrons nominated by the deed were "The Right Honourable the Lord Provost and Bailzies and Councell of Edinburgh and their successors in office for the communitie thereof, and ministers of the said burgh * present and to come;" and the power of presentation to the benefit of the mortification was conferred upon the patrons.

By the eik added by Mr Alexander of the same date, he mortified another sum under the same conditions; but as the additional amount was never received from his debtors, it is unnecessary to make any further allusion to it.

* At the date when this benefaction was made, the two ministers of Trinity College Church were members of the Governing Body, who had charge of the affairs of the Hospital. This state of matters continued down to 1729-30, when on the 12th day of March, Lord Islay, in his Decree Arbitral, decreed as follows:—"And finds, decerns, and declares, that the Council, ordinary and extraordinary, have the sole power and right of governing the Trinity Hospital, and cannot delegate the same to any other person or persons whatsoever." If then, the twelve

Mr Alexander, the truster, died in 1696.

The amount of the funds so bequeathed remained as a debt on the original security of the Annandale estates until Lammas 1744, when it was paid up. The sum then realised was £1725, 7s. 8½d. The debt of Sir William Johnstone of Westerhall was not paid up until 1753, when it amounted, exclusive of interest, to £544, 13s. 0d. The two sums were therefore £2270, 1s. 8½d.

No part of this money could have been mixed up with or applied to the purchase of the estate of Dean. The entry of that purchase, according to Professor Macpherson's Report is to the following effect:—

"1739.—Part of the estate of Dean was purchased, and extensive permanent improvements immediately executed, the whole at a cost of (sterling) . . . . . £4634, 13 11½."

This was the only purchase of importance made by the Governors of the Hospital after the year 1700. The lands of Coatfield and Quarryholes had been acquired antecedent to this. The estate of Dean is now likely to become a very valuable one, one of the most eligible in the near future for feuing purposes. The lands originally purchased were at first called simply part of Dean estate. Subsequently, however, a portion of it having been enclosed, it received the name of "Dean Parks," and the remainder was called "Blinkbonny."

It would appear, however, that the entry already referred to from Professor Macpherson's Report was not quite accurate. The purchase of the lands was made in 1734, and the whole improvements were com-

beneficiaries provided for in Mr Alexander's will were to be maintained within the Hospital under the conditions provided for in his settlement, this of itself was a sufficient reason for the non-interference of the clergy. A mere desire, or whim of an individual donor, could not alter the constitution of an old-established institution when the law was against the same, under the charters of foundation and otherwise. This view appears to the writer not to have been so strongly put before the Courts of Law as it might have been.

pleted and the charges therefor approved of by a Committee of the Governors, and paid for in 1738. The purchase was authorised to be made for behoof of Trinity Hospital. The following were the special funds which contributed to the purchase, viz. :—The Mortifications of

Charles Scherare,
Sir James M'Lurge, of Vogrie,
Lady Grizel Sempill,
William Brown, Dalgowrie,
George Watson,
John Wightman, of Mauldsly,
John Hog, of Cambo,
Robert Murray, and
John Young.

No part of the funds of the Alexander Mortification could, therefore, be used for the purpose; inasmuch as they were at that date still invested in the original securities handed over by the representatives of the truster, viz., the Annandale and Westerhall bonds. Notwithstanding of the above facts, the Court of Session held that the Alexander Fund was entitled to receive a proportionate share of the increase of the value of the lands of Dean which had been purchased out of Trinity Hospital Funds and not out of the Alexander Funds.

The statement of the Corporation goes on to show how the Alexander Funds were re-invested, after the original bonds were realised. At the time permanent securities were not available. This is frequently the case in everyone's experience, and never more so than at the present time. If there was any intermixing of the Alexander Funds with the Trinity Hospital revenues, it could only have dated from the year when these became available to the trustees for re-investment. The investments made at the time are all detailed in Professor

Macpherson's Report and relative appendices, to which it would be better to refer for details.

Part of the money seems to have been lent to the Corporation itself. This the Town Council defended, as it was done at the time *in optima fide*, and as being quite usual at the time. They further justified themselves in doing so, because the Imperial Parliament had recently sanctioned the very principle which the Court of Session and Professor Macpherson condemned.

The Court, following the judgment of the Lord President, having decided that the Alexander Funds had got immixed with those of Trinity Hospital, and that a count of reckoning of the same should take place from 1700, based upon the increased value of the Dean Parks estate, the Magistrates and Town Council, as advised by those whom they had consulted, considered it to be a wholly illegal proposition. They contended that, in any circumstances, such a claim, if at all legal, could not go further back than 1744 and 1753, when the respective amounts of the two bonds were paid over to them.

The Town Council further considered that the Remit from the House of Lords to the Court below did not contain any warrant for the extended and costly enquiry which the latter had thought fit to direct. The enquiry had embraced nearly three centuries of trust administration, involving accountability for a period of one hundred and seventy-eight years. Such a principle was opposed to the practice of the Court of Chancery, and to those principles which are applicable to the jurisdiction of the Scottish as well as the English Courts in relation to charities.

The statement for the Town Council pointed out that the Remit to the Court of Session was an enquiry of a more limited nature :—viz., to ascertain "of WHAT the PROPERTY of the said Hospital consists, and in what manner the MONEY received from the said RAILWAY COMPANY has been invested by the said defenders, and when such investments were made, and what sums have been received for interest thereon, and by whom and how such sums have been applied." There was thus no order for an enquiry into past administration. It appeared to be a somewhat strange way of describing an enquiry into the history and financial administration of a charity for three hundred years, to call such a statement "of what the property of the charity now consists." Several cases in the English Courts were quoted by the learned counsel on behalf of the Corporation's contentions.

Another point raised in the case was the proportion of the sexes benefited. This is a matter, however, of detail; and seems to be of little importance.

A more important matter, however, was that the number of twelve beneficiaries had not always been maintained in the house. The Town Council's reply to this assertion was (1.) That the Alexander Fund did not yield six per cent. as contemplated by the donor, and (2.) that the cost of the maintenance of the inmates gradually increased far beyond the amount he had contemplated.

There are other questions of minor consideration set forth, to which it does not seem requisite to allude.

The remaining question of consequence was that "the investments were not taken in the names of those directed." This refers to the fact that the ministers of Edinburgh never having accepted the trust, or acted as trustees, were not named as trustees in the investment of the funds, which were taken in the name of the Hospital treasurer. The learned counsel on this point state that—Inasmuch as the Hospital treasurer held these funds in trust for the charity, and as the amount of the capital fund was always clearly defined, or easily ascertainable, there is no force in this objection.

But the matter was also put in an alternative form, viz. :—"The patronage had not been exercised by the persons on whom it was bestowed." Against this, it was pleaded that the inaction of the ministers of Edinburgh could not be made a ground of charge against the Town Council, who undertook and discharged their trust. It was a mere matter of assumption, for which there was no evidence, that the ministers had the same means as any other trustees for ascertaining the terms of Mr Alexander's will.

In regard to whether the ministers of Edinburgh should in future be assumed, and which it was decided by the Court of Session in the affirmative,—a reference was made to the case of Dundee (*Baird and Others v. The Magistrates of Dundee*), where the decision of the House of Lords was as follows:—"And this House doth declare, that having regard to the *length of time* during which the Provost, Bailies, and Council of the town of Dundee have had the administration, as the trustees of the property arising from Johnstone's legacy, they, the Provost, Bailies, and Town Council, ought to be taken and declared to be the lawfully constituted trustees of the charity provided by the said legacy."

The Town Council drew attention to the fact of the admitted usage in favour of the Corporation's administration, and to the absence of any claim on the part of the ministers to participate in the disposal of the Alexander Mortification. They suggested that it was probable that it was arranged, at the time, when the bequest accrued, that the ministers should leave the care of this small endowment to the Magistrates and Council. It may be kept in view that Mr Alexander left his money to the Trinity Hospital Charity, and evidently intended that it should be managed as part of that foundation. It would be very inconvenient to the ministers of Edinburgh to be summoned to every meeting of the Town Council, at which any business connected with the Trinity Hospital was to be done. Not only would this be so, but if the trust were strictly carried out, the ministers would be kept waiting while the general business of the Trinity charity was being discussed, and would be called in only to vote in the matter of the nomination of the twelve pensioners amongst whom the proceeds of Alexander's legacy were to be divided. Such an arrangement would most probably be distasteful both to the Town Council and to the ministers.

Moreover the ministers of Edinburgh were a numerous body, not fewer than thirteen in number, assuming that the words in the interlocutor "The ministers of the said city, present and to come," refer only to the ministers of the old city churches; while, if these words are meant to include the whole ministers of the Established Church in Edinburgh, their number would be upwards of thirty. It would be extremely inconvenient to have so large a number of trustees, who besides, would be continually changing by new appointments, deaths, or removals.

It was further argued that a corporation is not bound to accept a bequest or endowment on any terms. The terms of a bequest might be such as to cause a corporation either to decline it, or to accept it only on condition of some change in non-essential matters. Three cases in the English Courts, in support of this contention, were referred to by counsel.

It was stated, on behalf of the Town Council, that it was very unlikely that their predecessors would have accepted the Alexander bequest under the condition of admitting another class of corporators into the administration of the charity; and the usage which has followed is, in their apprehension, evidence of an arrangement amounting to a qualified acceptance on their part, an acceptance on the condition that they should have the sole administration of the legacy. The objections to a divided administration of the Trinity Hospital fund are as strong still as they were at the time the bequest accrued.

The following were the reasons appended to the statement prepared by the learned counsel :—

First.—Because the finding that the Alexander Fund amounting to £2270, or thereby, has been immixed with the funds and property of the Trinity Hospital from an early period down to the present time, and must be held to have participated proportionally with the said funds and property in the increase of values of the aggregate funds and property between the year 1700 and the year 1873, is without foundation in fact.

Second.—Because the lands of Dean and Blinkbonny were purchased and paid for prior to 1739, out of moneys of Trinity Hospital, and not out of moneys of the Alexander Fund, which was at that date wholly invested in the original bonds over the Annandale and Westerhall estates, and consequently the Alexander Fund is not entitled to any share in the increase in the value of the lands of Dean and Blinkbonny.

Third.—Because the moneys belonging to the Alexander Fund were not at any time invested in the purchase of land; but, on the contrary, were paid up by the original debtors, and invested, along with certain other funds of the Trinity Hospital, in securities or investments which can be traced; and, therefore, the Alexander Fund is not entitled to any increase in value of any of the lands now held by the Hospital, and purchased out of the Hospital funds, but is entitled only to a proportionate share of the investments actually made with the moneys of the Alexander Fund.

Fourth.—Because the ministers of Edinburgh are not now entitled, after the long contrary usage, to claim a right to be joined as trustees in the administration of the Alexander Fund. And it is not expedient that they should be so found.

The written pleadings in the case bear the names of

Edward E. Kay, Q.C. (now Lord Justice Sir E. E. Kay).

John M'Laren (afterwards Lord Advocate, and now Lord M'Laren).

Æneas J. G. Mackay (Ex-Professor of History, and now Sheriff of Fifeshire).

CHAPTER XXVI.

THE THIRD HOUSE OF LORDS' CASE.

HEN the case of the Alexander Benefaction came to be discussed before the House of Lords, on the 21st day of July 1879, there were present

Lord Hatherley, as Lord Chancellor,
Lord Blackburn, and
Lord Gordon.

The learned counsel having been heard, it fell to Lord Blackburn to deliver the leading opinion. It was to the following effect:—

LORD BLACKBURN.—My Lords,—The Town Council of Edinburgh were the administrators of Trinity Hospital, and as such held considerable funds before the year 1696. In that year Mr James Alexander died, having previously made a mortification to the Lord Provost and Town Council of Edinburgh and their successors in office, and the ministers of the said Burgh present and to come. The ministers at that time did not take any steps to assert their right to join in administering this mortification. The Council got possession of the funds, and from the time they did so down to the making of the interlocutors appealed against, administered those funds as if they had been mortified to them as administrators of the funds of Trinity Hospital.

In a suit for the proper administration of the funds of Trinity Hospital, the Court of Session had to decide a great many questions. Two and two only of their decisions are now by this Appeal brought before this House:—1. The Court of Session decided that the funds of the Alexander Mortification ought to have been from the beginning administered by the Council and the ministers and not by the Council alone, and that notwithstanding the length of time during which a contrary practice had prevailed, they could not sanction it in future; and that the funds of that mortification must be in future administered, in terms of the mortifier's trust, by the Council and the ministers.

This was the first decision appealed against. I think none of your Lordships who heard the argument doubted that the Court of Session could not have decided otherwise; and the counsel for the appellants were not able to urge anything substantial against this decision.

But then, having determined that the Alexander Fund was to be administered separately in future, there arose a question what was the fund which was to be so administered. I do not think that I can state the point more briefly than is done by the Lord President. He says:—"The funds left by Mr Alexander were invested in particular securities, and those securities were not called up or changed until about the middle of the last century, and we have distinct evidence of what the amount of the fund was at that time. Now, if we proceeded upon the principle of a strict accounting against the Magistrates here as trustees, of course the way of bringing out the balance would be to charge them with this capital, as at the date when we find it in their hands, and then charge them with the income as it accrued, and let them discharge themselves the best way they could. But it rather appears to me that, in a case of this kind, and looking to the nature of the trust and the way in which it was necessarily administered, that would be too strict a principle of accounting; and while I think it is our undoubted duty to separate this Alexander Fund, and secure that it shall be administered as a separate trust in all time coming, we may deal with bygones in a way more favourable for the administrators of Trinity Hospital. The income of the fund has apparently been spent, and it has not been spent, so far as we can see, upon purposes alien to the intentions and wishes of the founder. His wishes and intentions have only been to a certain extent disregarded; that is to say, the fund has not been in the right hands of administration, and there has not been in the selection of the objects of the bounty that order of preference which he desired. But still the fair result of the evidence appears to be that, at all events for a very long period, the income of the Alexander Fund was bestowed upon poor and indigent persons of the kind generally here contemplated. It was employed, along with the income of the other funds of the Hospital, generally, for such purposes; and therefore I cannot see that there can be, especially against a shifting body of trustees like the Magistrates and Town Council of Edinburgh, any responsibility for the expenditure of that income. It is not alleged that they appropriated this fund to their own purposes as individuals, or that they appropriated it to the uses of the Corporation of the City of Edinburgh. If that had been so, it would have raised a question of a very different kind. But that does not appear to have been so, and therefore I incline to the opinion that, in so far as regards the past income of this fund, there is no room for any accounting at all.

"But then the next question comes to be:—How are we to ascertain what sum now in the hands of those trustees will adequately and fairly represent the capital of the Alexander Fund? Now that is a question of some difficulty, but at the same time I think it admits of a solution. We know that the Alexander Fund was invested upon two bonds, as it was originally settled by the donor himself—the one upon the Annandale estates for £1725, 17s. 8½d., and the other upon the Westerhall estates for £544, 13s. of sterling money; for I am speaking now of the amount as converted into sterling money and actually paid up in the course of last century. These two sums amount together to £2270. Now the mortification was in the year 1695, and it may certainly be assumed, without any great stretch, that that money came into the hands of the Hospital trustees by the beginning of the last century, say in the year 1700. Therefore they were possessed in 1700 of this capital sum as representing the Alexander Mortification. They were at the same time possessed of a very considerable estate belonging to the Hospital, and it is not at all difficult to ascertain what the amount of that estate was. In that way we discover what was the relative or comparative value of those two estates in the year 1700. But it is very apparent upon the face of the report before us, and the abundant information which we have on the subject, that this joint mixed estate, consisting to a large extent of the funds and estate of the Hospital proper, but also to a more limited extent of Alexander's Fund, has largely increased in amount and value between the year 1700 and the present day. Now it seems to me that this estate so jointly administered having greatly increased in value between these two dates, the Alexander Fund must be entitled to participate in that prosperity. Thus, supposing that in 1700 the estate of the Hospital proper amounted to £10,000 in value, and the Alexander Fund to £2000 in value, making together £12,000, but that at the present day the joint estate, as it appears in the hands of the administrators, amounts to £50,000 in value, then that £50,000 must be apportioned between the same funds in the same proportion that they bore to each other in the year 1700, that is as 10 to 2. I am taking the figures I have mentioned as entirely suppositious, not supposing they represent the entire value by any means. On the contrary the value as we see is very much greater. Now there may be some little difficulty in adjusting the precise way in which this result is to be brought about." He then proceeds to give various directions as to what was to be done in ascertaining the amount, which I need not further notice.

No other way was suggested at the Bar in which the fund, if the two were inextricably mixed up, could be apportioned except that of taking the proportion which the two funds bore to each other and dividing the mixed fund in that proportion, and I cannot myself see any other way. But it was argued that the two funds were not inextricably mixed up, and the point which the appellants' counsel made was fairly raised by the facts as to the purchase of the Dean estate. It appears that the Town Council in 1734 purchased this estate for £3675. In course of time that estate has become part of the Town of Edinburgh, and is now worth a very large sum of money, and this has been a very profitable investment. At dates subsequent to 1734, they invested funds in City Bonds, and the City having become insolvent and compounded with its creditors, this has been a losing investment.

The decision of the Court of Session is that the investments are to be taken as made for the mixed funds, and that on the figures supposed by the Lord President, the Alexander Fund is entitled to two-twelfths of the profit made by the profitable investment in the Dean estate, and is to bear two-twelfths of the loss on the unprofitable investments in City Bonds. And the result of that will be that in administering the Alexander Fund the administrators will have the management of a very considerably larger sum than what the testator Alexander had and mortified in 1695. The contention of the appellants is, that the investment in the Dean estate is to be considered as made exclusively for the benefit of Trinity Hospital, and that the Alexander Fund will have no share in the profitable investment, but will have to bear a share of the loss on the subsequent investments, so that the fund now to be administered as the Alexander Fund will be less than what the mortifier left in 1695. This is a result which does not at the first view seem so fair and just as that produced by the decision of the Court of Session.

In order to understand the grounds on which their argument is based, it is necessary to examine what the facts were. The testator Alexander left in 1696 the funds available for his mortification invested in two bonds. The administrators of Trinity Hospital, by usurpation, became possessed of the control of both those bonds before 1734, and they in fact received the interest on those bonds and mixed the interest thus received with the revenue which they received from the property of Trinity Hospital, and from that mixed revenue defrayed the expenses which they incurred for the whole charity, without making any distinction whatever as to whether those expenses were incurred for objects proper under the terms of the Alexander Mortification, or for purposes proper under the Trinity Hospital charity only. This is clearly proved by the account for the year 1722, which was in process, though not printed, and which was produced at the Bar during the argument. No doubt this was wrong; but, as pointed out by the Lord President in the passage I have read, these purposes were not alien to each other, and, though wrong, this was not a wrong like what it would have been if they had appropriated it to their own purposes. But though they treated the funds as one, the two bonds remained in specie just as Alexander left them, not called up.

When the Council bought the Dean estate in 1739, they gave directions to their Treasurer to pay for it, and for that purpose to uplift some securities, including the bond over Westraw for £544, 13s. 0d. which was one of the bonds left by Alexander. Nothing could more clearly prove that in making the investment the Council were (as far as intention went) intending to make an investment for the behoof of the whole mixed fund, which they, improperly it is true, treated as one fund. But the Treasurer did not follow these instructions. In his account, after showing what the whole disbursements in paying for the Dean estate and improvements on it had been, and that there remained a balance of £465, 18s. 5d. unpaid, he adds this:—"Tho' the Accomptant was authorized by the Council to uplift £544, 13s. 0d. st. contd. in Sir James Johnstone's heritable bond to the hospital to replace the above charge, which, as it was well secured, and the interest duly paid, he judged it more for the interest of the hospital to uplift only the sum due by Mr John and Mr Charles Cockburn, their bond being £200 stg., and the meantime to advance the rest himself, £200, 0s. 0d. Balance due to him on acct. of the inclosing, £265, 18s. 5d." Consequently the two bonds remained in specie not called up for some years later.

The argument founded on this was that as the bonds remained in specie and earmarked as it were, and as it appeared that the estate of Dean was in fact paid for out of funds originally belonging to Trinity Hospital and uplifted for that

2 Y

purpose, it followed as a matter of law that, whatever the Council intended, the funds must be followed, and that the Dean estate belonged exclusively to Trinity Hospital. According to this reasoning, if the Treasurer had obeyed his instructions, the Alexander Fund would have been entitled to share in the Dean estate in the proportion which £544, 13s. 0d. bore to the whole cost. As he did not, they are to have no share in it.

This makes the question depend entirely on an accident, and is not a satisfactory result; still if the law was settled that it was so, we must follow it. But I do not think there is any case, either in England, or Scotland, in which such a question has been raised. No doubt when the question has been whether those who represented the trust could claim property on the ground that it was procured by trust funds which they had a right to follow, the identity of the fund is all-important. But such a case as the present as to an investment has never, that I can find, been raised.

In *Pennell* v. *Duffell* (4 De Gex, Macnaghten and Gordon, 372) it might have been raised, but those entitled to the different estates which then were proved to be jointly entitled to the fund very sensibly settled the proportions in which they were entitled without going to law about it.

Being therefore, as I think it is, a new question, it must be settled on principles of justice. Speaking for myself alone, I should have had great difficulty in deciding this case if it had come before me as sitting in the Court of Session. I doubt whether I should have had acuteness enough to discover the mode in which the Court of Session have solved the difficulty. But they have solved it in a way perfectly consistent with justice and good sense, and not inconsistent with any technical rule of law, and no other solution has been suggested which would be so satisfactory. I certainly, therefore, am not prepared to advise your Lordships to reverse the judgment below, especially seeing that I am not prepared to advise your Lordships to adopt any other rule.

I move, therefore, that the interlocutors below should be affirmed and the Appeal dismissed, with costs.

The judgment of the Appellate Court was as follows:—"Interlocutors appealed from, affirmed; and Appeal dismissed, with costs."

At this point terminates the historical part of the Trinity College and Trinity Hospital. It must be referred to another volume to deal with the new scheme of administration which was adopted, based on the interlocutor of the Court of Session of date February 3, 1880. The second Volume will also comprise the voluminous Report of Professor Macpherson, with the valuable information therein conveyed; as well as the various answers and replies of the Town Council in regard to the said Report, so long as it was a matter of discussion between the Lords of Council and Session on the one hand and the Lord Provost, Magistrates, and Town Council, as the administrators of the Trinity Hospital charity, on the other.

INDEX.

COLSTON AND COMPANY, LIMITED, PRINTERS, EDINBURGH.

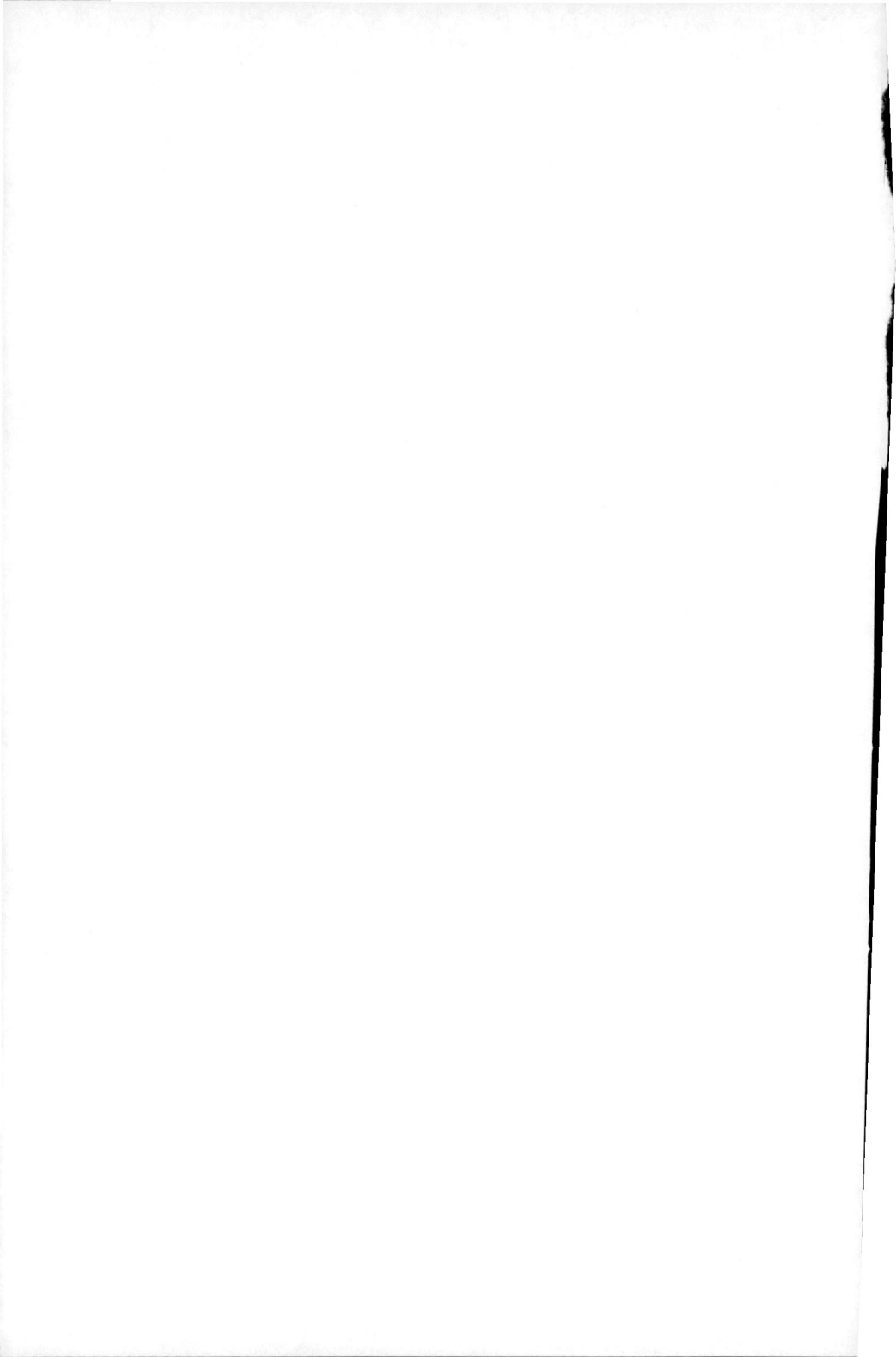

www.ingramcontent.com/pod-product-compliance
Lightning Source LLC
Chambersburg PA
CBHW032302280326
41932CB00009B/666

* 9 7 8 3 3 3 7 0 2 0 6 9 9 *